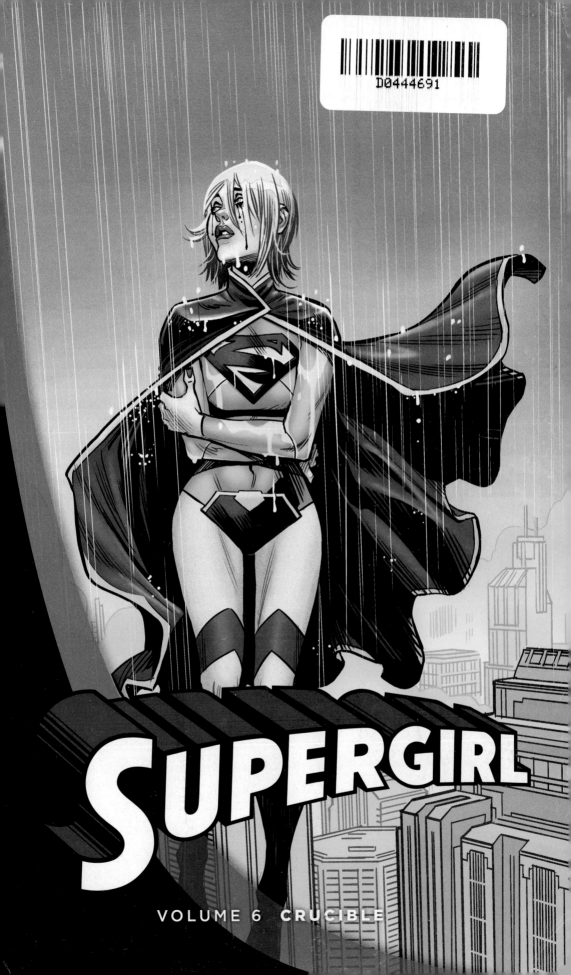

SUPERGIRL

VOLUME 6 CRUCIBLE

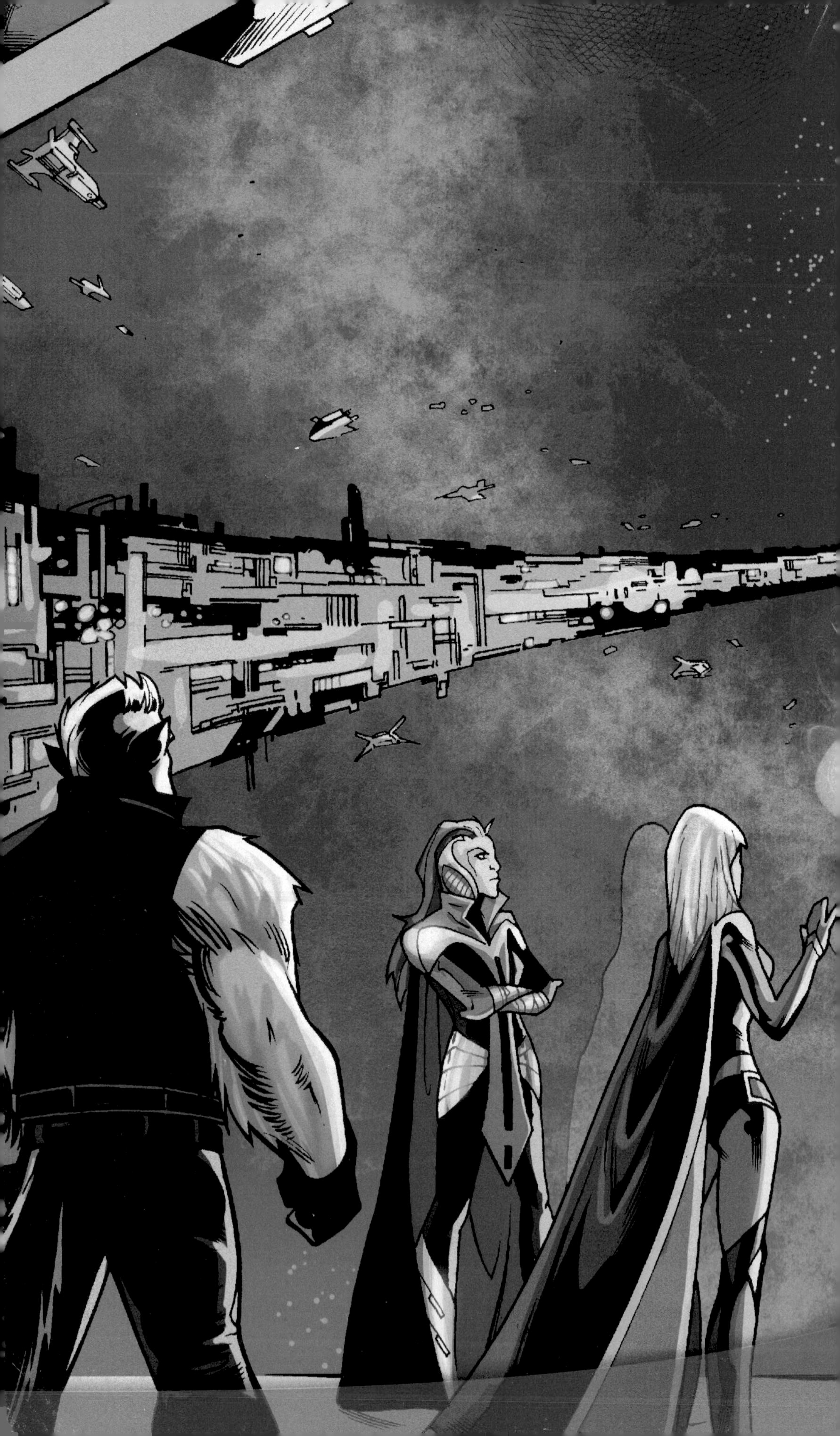

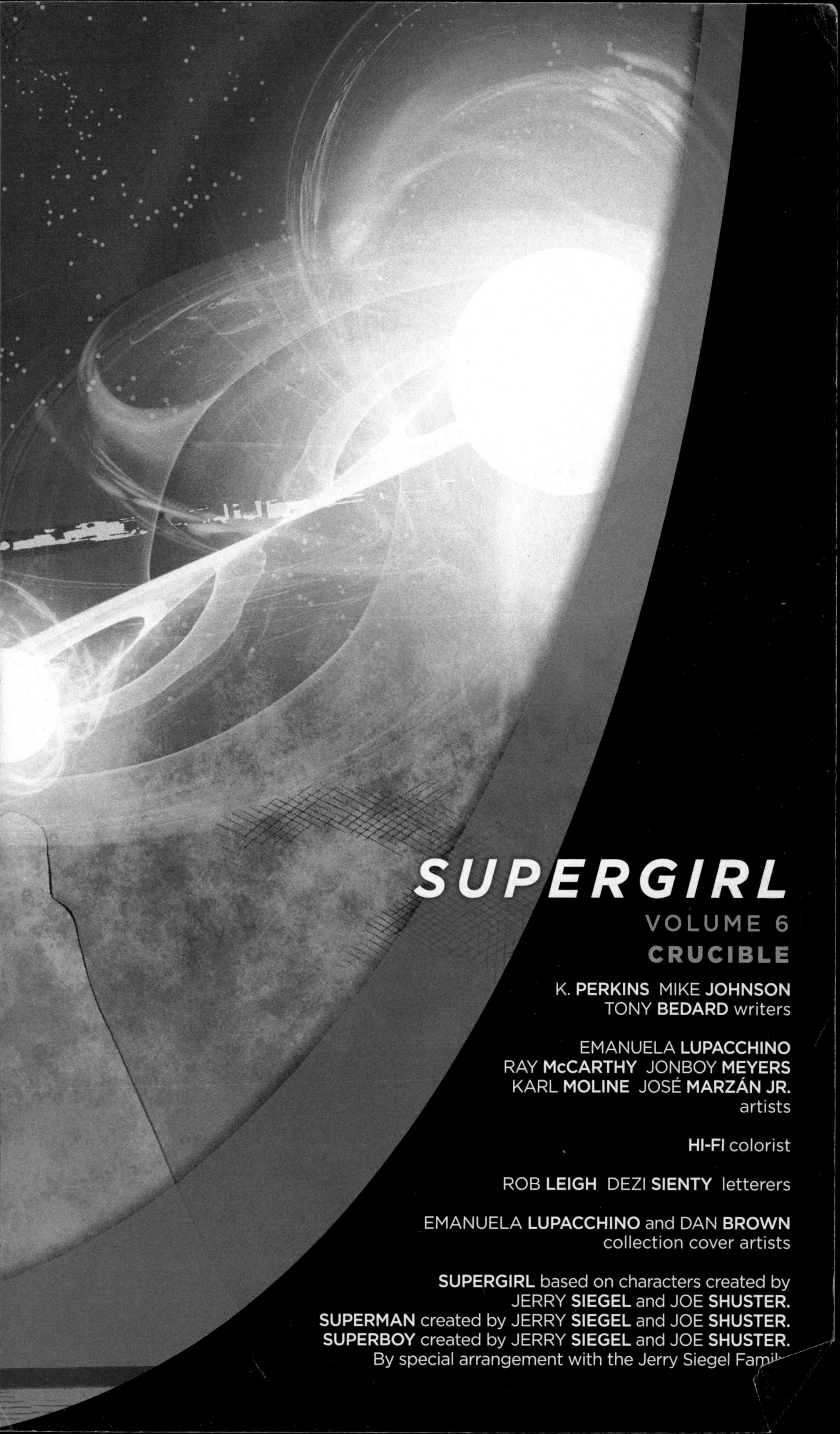

SUPERGIRL

VOLUME 6

CRUCIBLE

K. **PERKINS** MIKE **JOHNSON**
TONY **BEDARD** writers

EMANUELA **LUPACCHINO**
RAY **McCARTHY** JONBOY **MEYERS**
KARL **MOLINE** JOSÉ **MARZÁN JR.**
artists

HI-FI colorist

ROB **LEIGH** DEZI **SIENTY** letterers

EMANUELA **LUPACCHINO** and DAN **BROWN**
collection cover artists

SUPERGIRL based on characters created by
JERRY **SIEGEL** and JOE **SHUSTER.**
SUPERMAN created by JERRY **SIEGEL** and JOE **SHUSTER.**
SUPERBOY created by JERRY **SIEGEL** and JOE **SHUSTER.**
By special arrangement with the Jerry Siegel Fami

RICKEY PURDIN   EDDIE BERGANZA Editors – Original Series
JEREMY BENT Assistant Editor – Original Series   LIZ ERICKSON Editor
ROBBIN BROSTERMAN Design Director – Books ROBBIE BIEDERMAN Publication Design

BOB HARRAS Senior VP – Editor-in-Chief, DC Comics

DIANE NELSON President DAN DIDIO and JIM LEE Co-Publishers GEOFF JOHNS Chief Creative Officer
AMIT DESAI Senior VP – Marketing and Franchise Management
AMY GENKINS Senior VP – Business and Legal Affairs NAIRI GARDINER Senior VP – Finance
JEFF BOISON VP – Publishing Planning MARK CHIARELLO VP – Art Direction and Design
JOHN CUNNINGHAM VP – Marketing TERRI CUNNINGHAM VP – Editorial Administration
LARRY GANEM VP – Talent Relations and Services ALISON GILL Senior VP – Manufacturing and Operations
HANK KANALZ Senior VP – Vertigo and Integrated Publishing JAY KOGAN VP – Business and Legal Affairs, Publishing
JACK MAHAN VP – Business Affairs, Talent NICK NAPOLITANO VP – Manufacturing Administration SUE POHJA VP – Book Sales
FRED RUIZ VP – Manufacturing Operations COURTNEY SIMMONS Senior VP – Publicity BOB WAYNE Senior VP – Sales

SUPERGIRL VOLUME 6: CRUCIBLE

DC Comics, 4000 Warner Blvd., Burbank, CA 91522
A Warner Bros. Entertainment Company. Printed by RR Donnelley, Owensville, MO. 6/12/15.
ISBN: 978-1-4012-5541-1

Library of Congress Cataloging-in-Publication Data

Bedard, Tony.
Supergirl. Volume 6 / Tony Bedard, writer ; Emanuela Lupacchino, artist.
pages cm. — (The New 52!)
Kara must deal with the fall-out of the green Kryptonite skies over a dead Earth, and the horrors still to come! This volume features a
SUPERMAN: DOOMED tie-in and FUTURES END: SUPERGIRL #1! Collects SUPERGIRL #34-40, and FUTURES END: SUPERGIRL #1.
ISBN 978-1-4012-5541-1 (paperback)
1. Graphic novels. I. Lupacchino, Emanuela, illustrator. II. Title.
PN6728.S89N46 2015

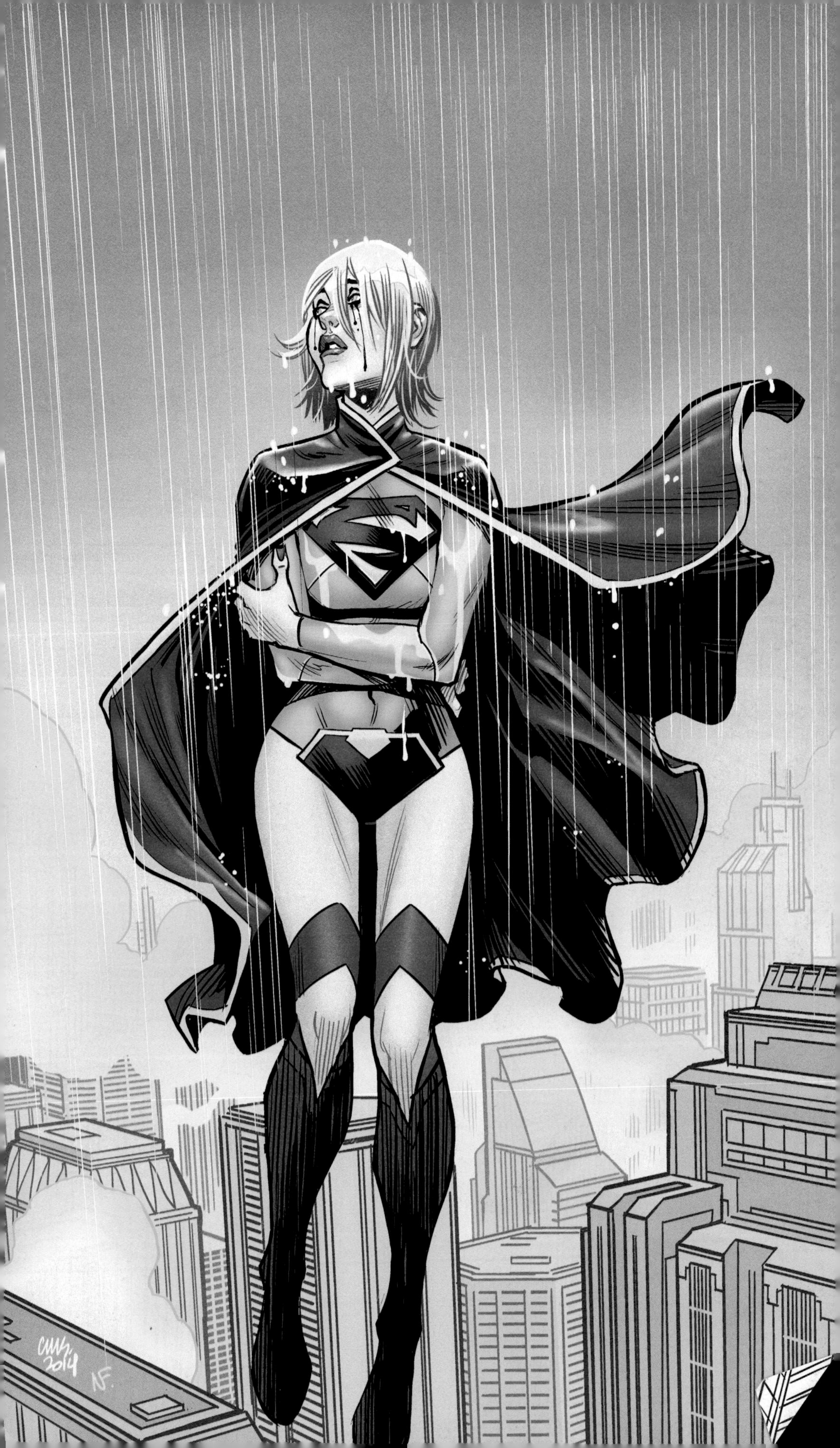

THE GIRL WHO FELL TO EARTH

TONY BEDARD writer KARL MOLINE penciller JOSÉ MARZÁN JR. inker HI-FI colorist ROB LEIGH letterer
cover art by CAMERON STEWART with NATHAN FAIRBAIRN

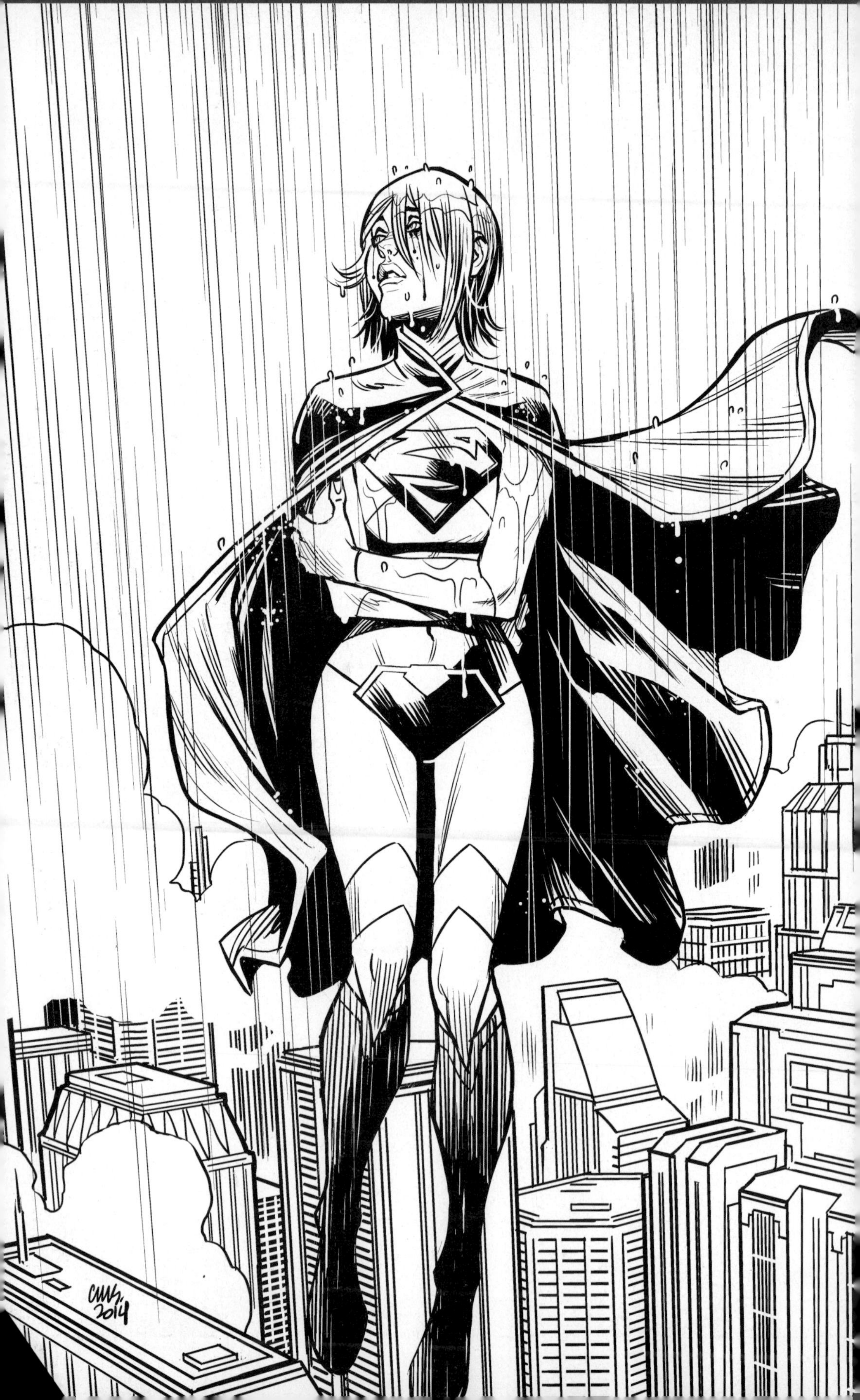
CMS 2014

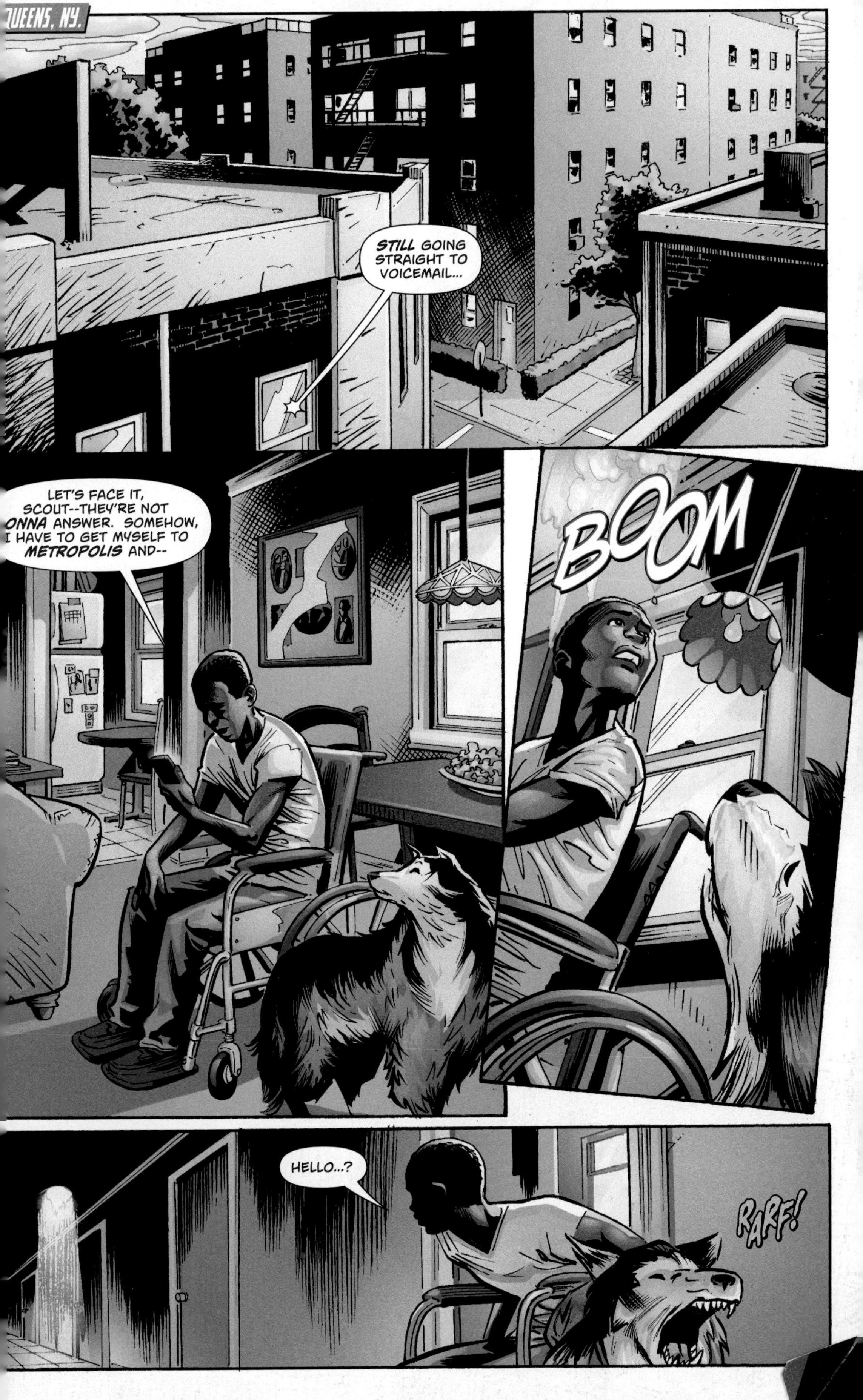
QUEENS, NY.
STILL GOING STRAIGHT TO VOICEMAIL...
LET'S FACE IT, SCOUT--THEY'RE NOT ONNA ANSWER. SOMEHOW, I HAVE TO GET MYSELF TO METROPOLIS AND--
BOOM
HELLO...?
RARF!

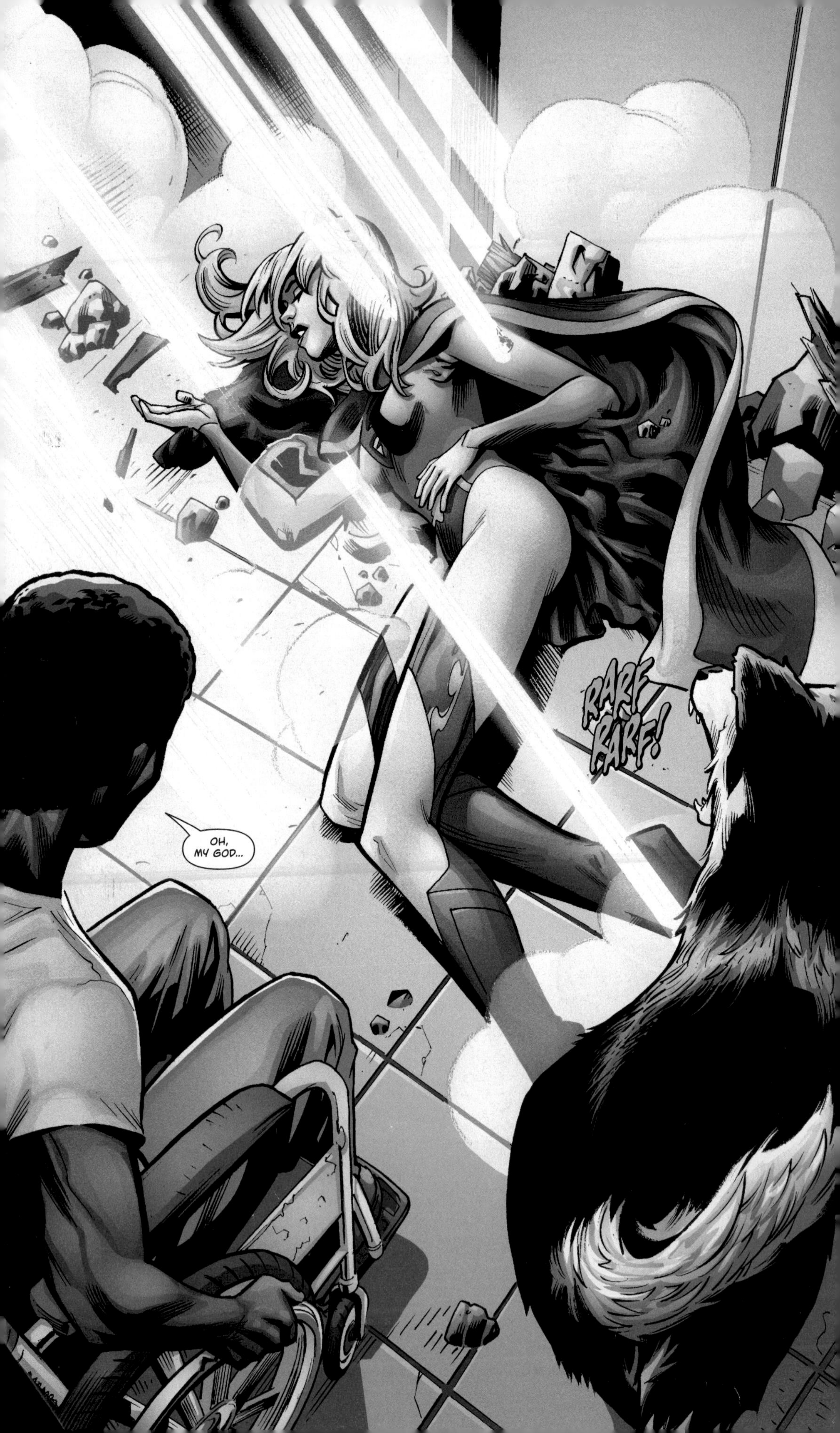
RARF RARF!
OH, MY GOD...

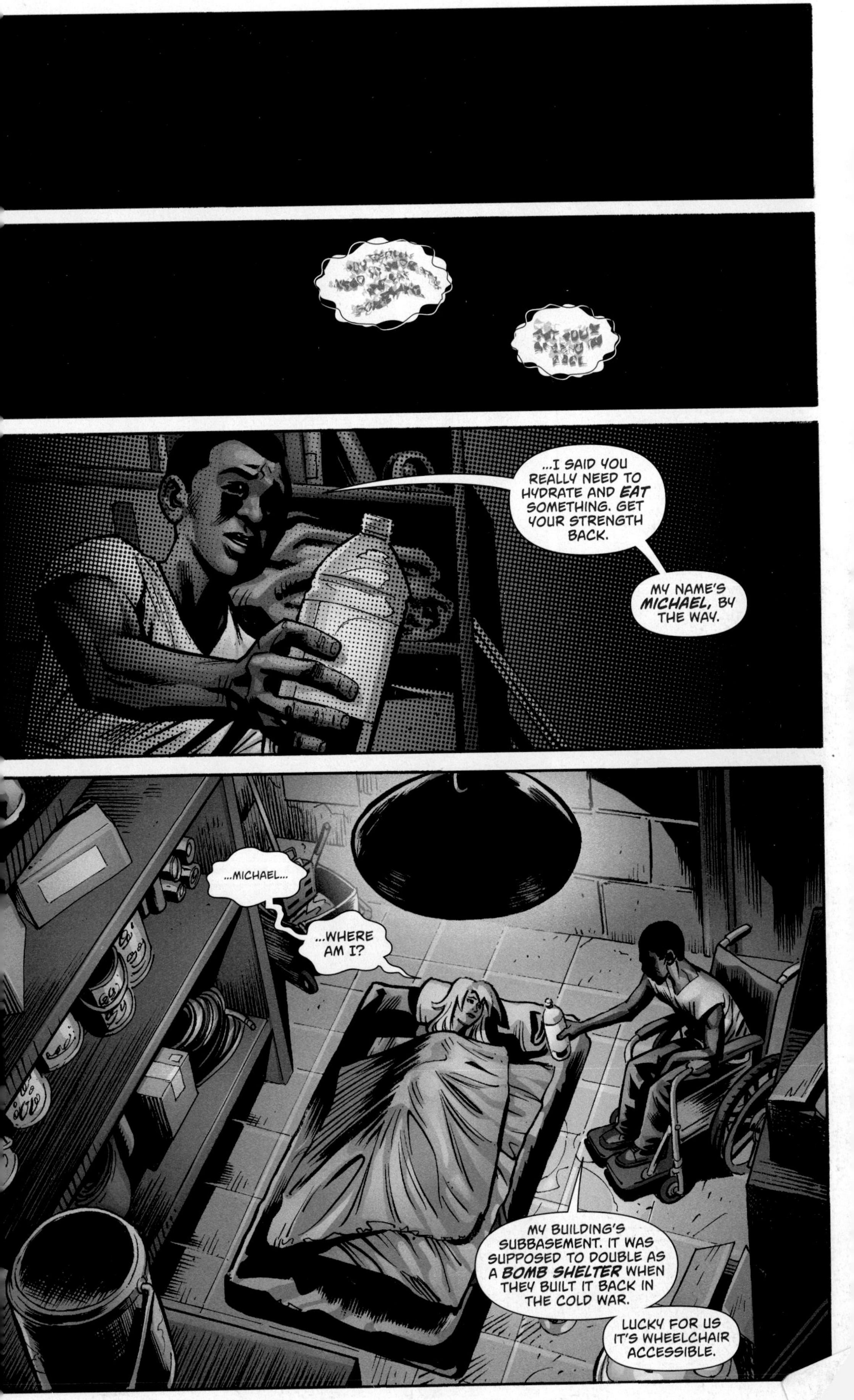
...I SAID YOU REALLY NEED TO HYDRATE AND EAT SOMETHING. GET YOUR STRENGTH BACK.
MY NAME'S MICHAEL, BY THE WAY.
...MICHAEL...
...WHERE AM I?
MY BUILDING'S SUBBASEMENT. IT WAS SUPPOSED TO DOUBLE AS A BOMB SHELTER WHEN THEY BUILT IT BACK IN THE COLD WAR.
LUCKY FOR US IT'S WHEELCHAIR ACCESSIBLE.

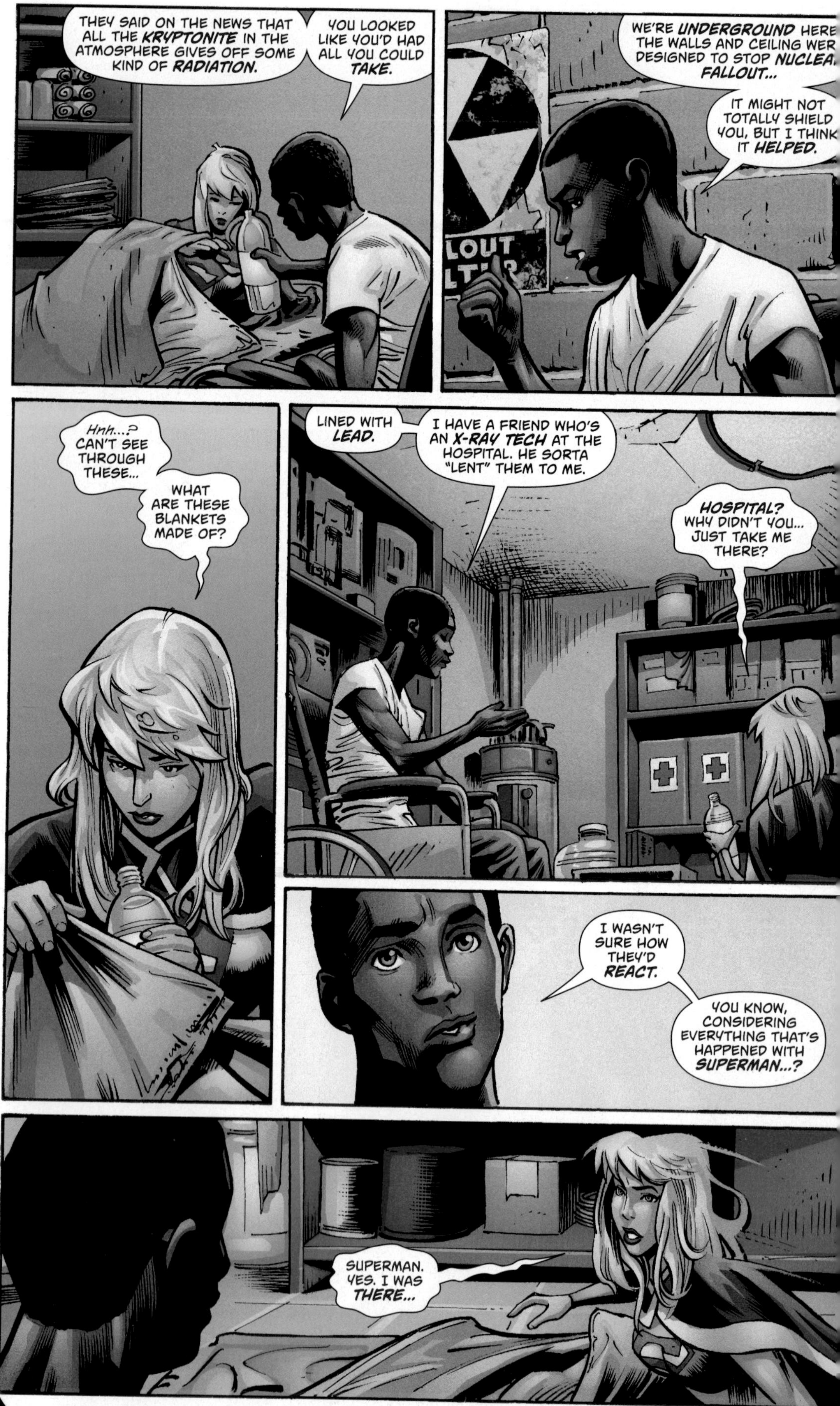

THEY SAID ON THE NEWS THAT ALL THE KRYPTONITE IN THE ATMOSPHERE GIVES OFF SOME KIND OF RADIATION.
YOU LOOKED LIKE YOU'D HAD ALL YOU COULD TAKE.
WE'RE UNDERGROUND HERE. THE WALLS AND CEILING WERE DESIGNED TO STOP NUCLEAR FALLOUT...
IT MIGHT NOT TOTALLY SHIELD YOU, BUT I THINK IT HELPED.
Hnh...? CAN'T SEE THROUGH THESE...
WHAT ARE THESE BLANKETS MADE OF?
LINED WITH LEAD.
I HAVE A FRIEND WHO'S AN X-RAY TECH AT THE HOSPITAL. HE SORTA "LENT" THEM TO ME.
HOSPITAL? WHY DIDN'T YOU... JUST TAKE ME THERE?
I WASN'T SURE HOW THEY'D REACT.
YOU KNOW, CONSIDERING EVERYTHING THAT'S HAPPENED WITH SUPERMAN...?
SUPERMAN. YES. I WAS THERE...

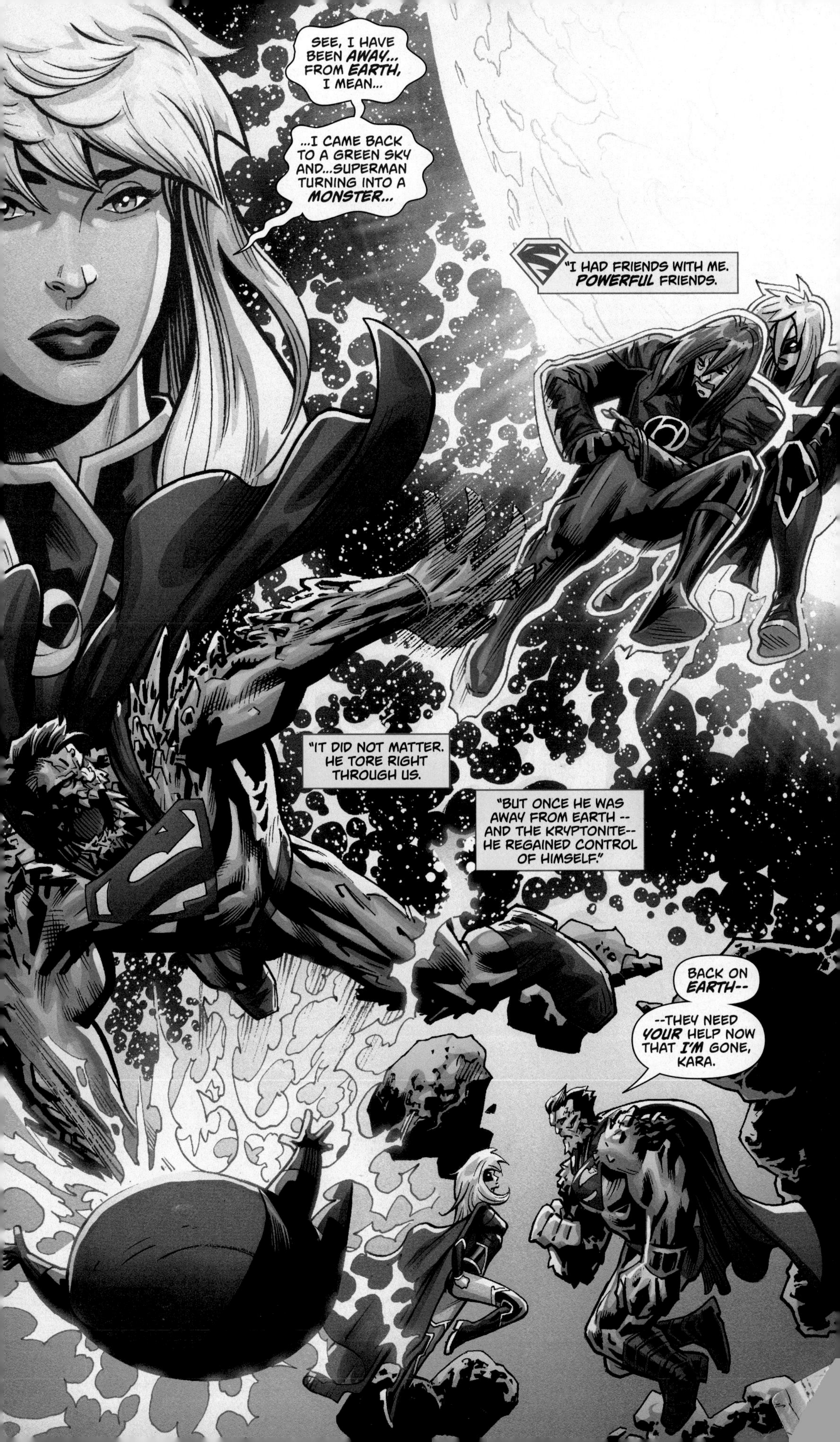
SEE, I HAVE BEEN AWAY... FROM EARTH, I MEAN...
...I CAME BACK TO A GREEN SKY AND...SUPERMAN TURNING INTO A MONSTER...
"I HAD FRIENDS WITH ME. POWERFUL FRIENDS.
"IT DID NOT MATTER. HE TORE RIGHT THROUGH US.
"BUT ONCE HE WAS AWAY FROM EARTH -- AND THE KRYPTONITE-- HE REGAINED CONTROL OF HIMSELF."
BACK ON EARTH--
--THEY NEED YOUR HELP NOW THAT I'M GONE, KARA.

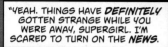

"YEAH. THINGS HAVE *DEFINITELY* GOTTEN STRANGE WHILE YOU WERE AWAY, SUPERGIRL. I'M SCARED TO TURN ON THE *NEWS.*"

"FIRST THAT SMALLVILLE STORY. THEN SUPERMAN FOUGHT SOMETHING THEY CALLED *DOOMSDAY,* AND AT FIRST THEY SAID SUPERMAN *WON.*"

"NEXT THING I HEARD, SUPERMAN WENT *CRAZY.* HE STARTED FIGHTING HIS OWN *FRIENDS.*"

THE ARMY MUST'VE GOTTEN DESPERATE, BECAUSE THEY DROPPED A *KRYPTONITE BOMB* ON HIM.

IF THEY WERE TRYING TO CHASE HIM AWAY, I GUESS IT *WORKED.*

I JUST NEVER REALIZED HOW *PARANOID* OUR MILITARY WAS OF, Y'KNOW... PEOPLE LIKE *YOU.*

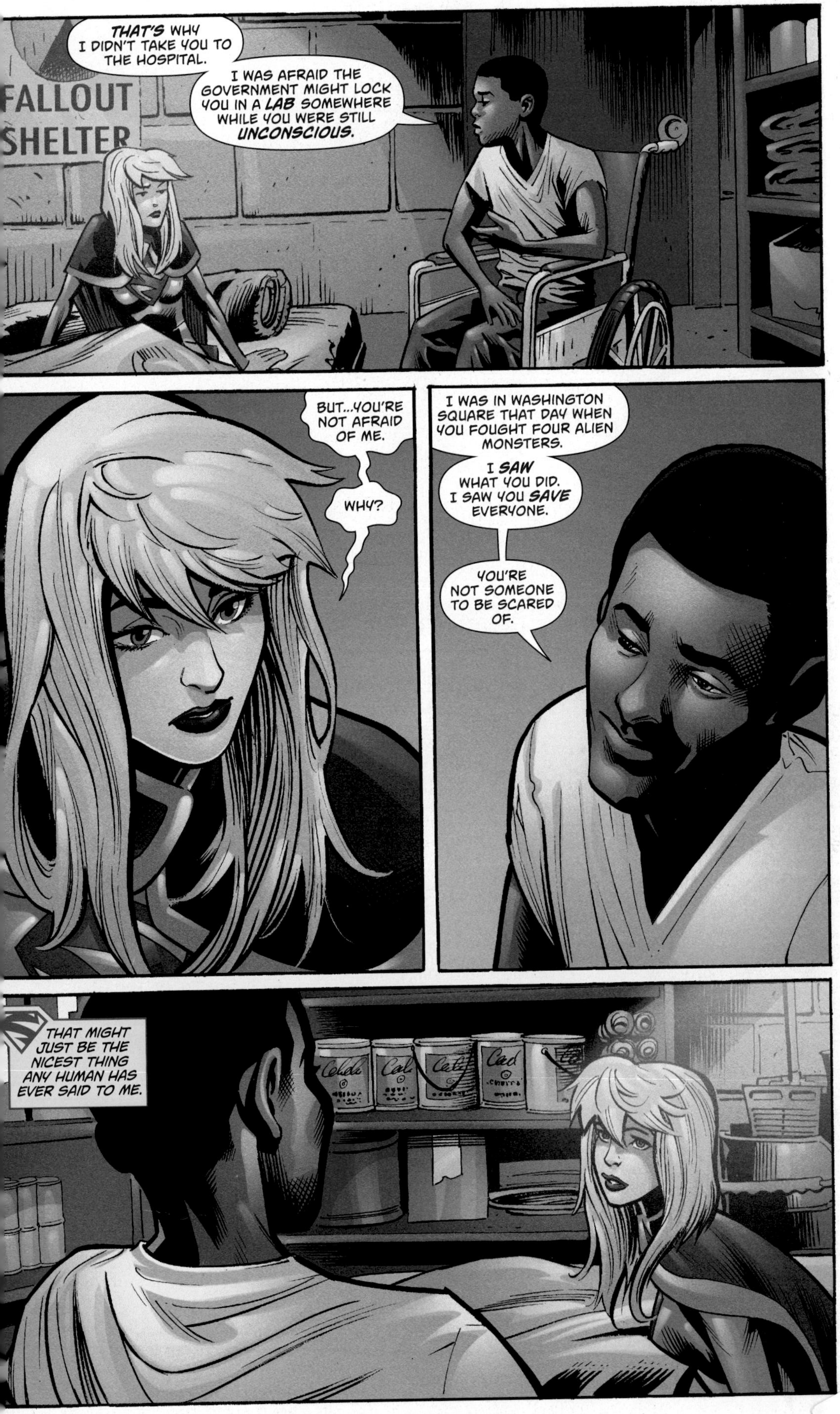
FALLOUT SHELTER
THAT'S WHY I DIDN'T TAKE YOU TO THE HOSPITAL.
I WAS AFRAID THE GOVERNMENT MIGHT LOCK YOU IN A LAB SOMEWHERE WHILE YOU WERE STILL UNCONSCIOUS.
BUT...YOU'RE NOT AFRAID OF ME.
WHY?
I WAS IN WASHINGTON SQUARE THAT DAY WHEN YOU FOUGHT FOUR ALIEN MONSTERS.
I SAW WHAT YOU DID. I SAW YOU SAVE EVERYONE.
YOU'RE NOT SOMEONE TO BE SCARED OF.
THAT MIGHT JUST BE THE NICEST THING ANY HUMAN HAS EVER SAID TO ME.

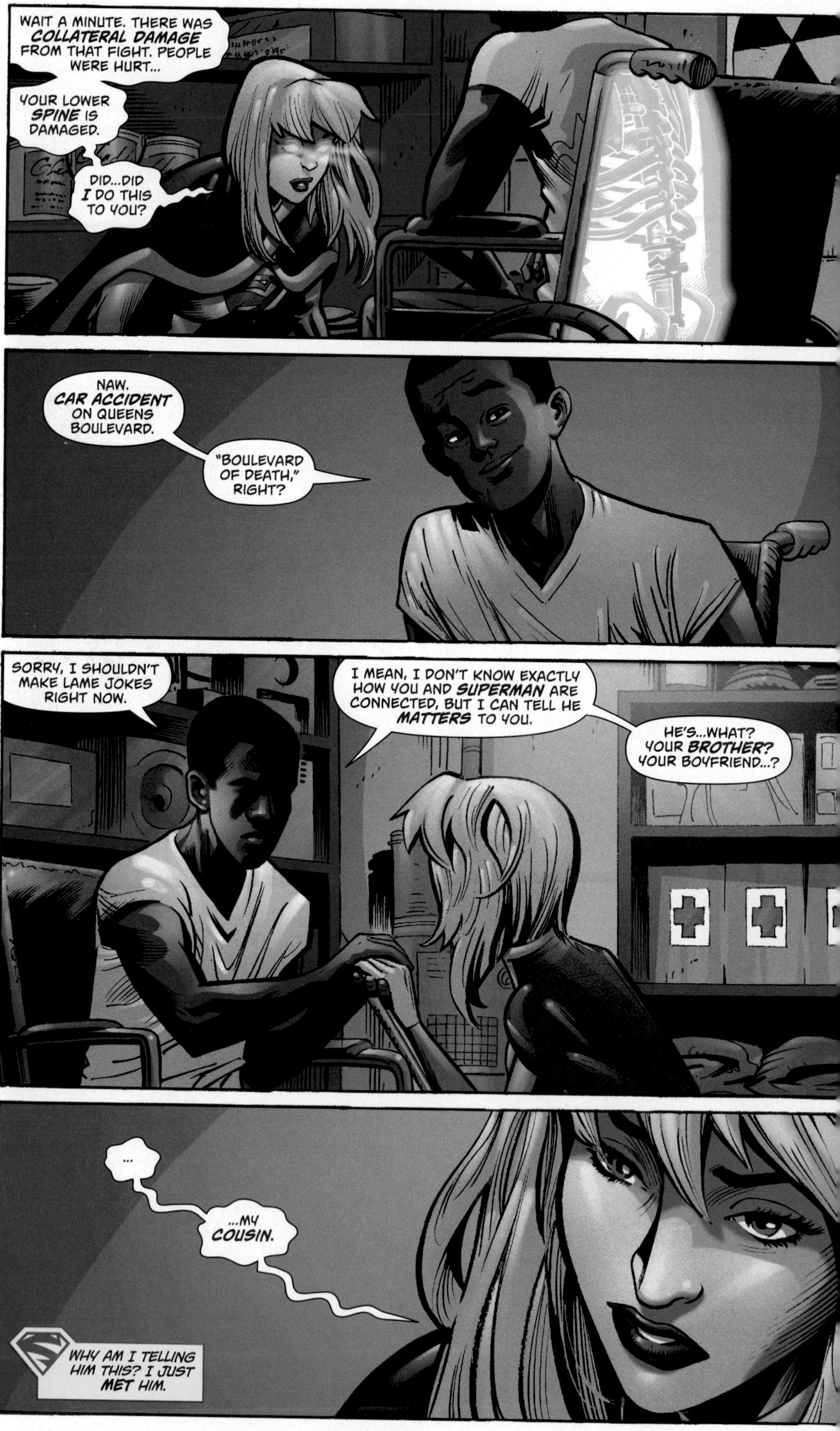
WAIT A MINUTE. THERE WAS COLLATERAL DAMAGE FROM THAT FIGHT. PEOPLE WERE HURT...
YOUR LOWER SPINE IS DAMAGED.
DID...DID I DO THIS TO YOU?
NAW. CAR ACCIDENT ON QUEENS BOULEVARD.
"BOULEVARD OF DEATH," RIGHT?
SORRY, I SHOULDN'T MAKE LAME JOKES RIGHT NOW.
I MEAN, I DON'T KNOW EXACTLY HOW YOU AND SUPERMAN ARE CONNECTED, BUT I CAN TELL HE MATTERS TO YOU.
HE'S...WHAT? YOUR BROTHER? YOUR BOYFRIEND...?
...
...MY COUSIN.
WHY AM I TELLING HIM THIS? I JUST MET HIM.

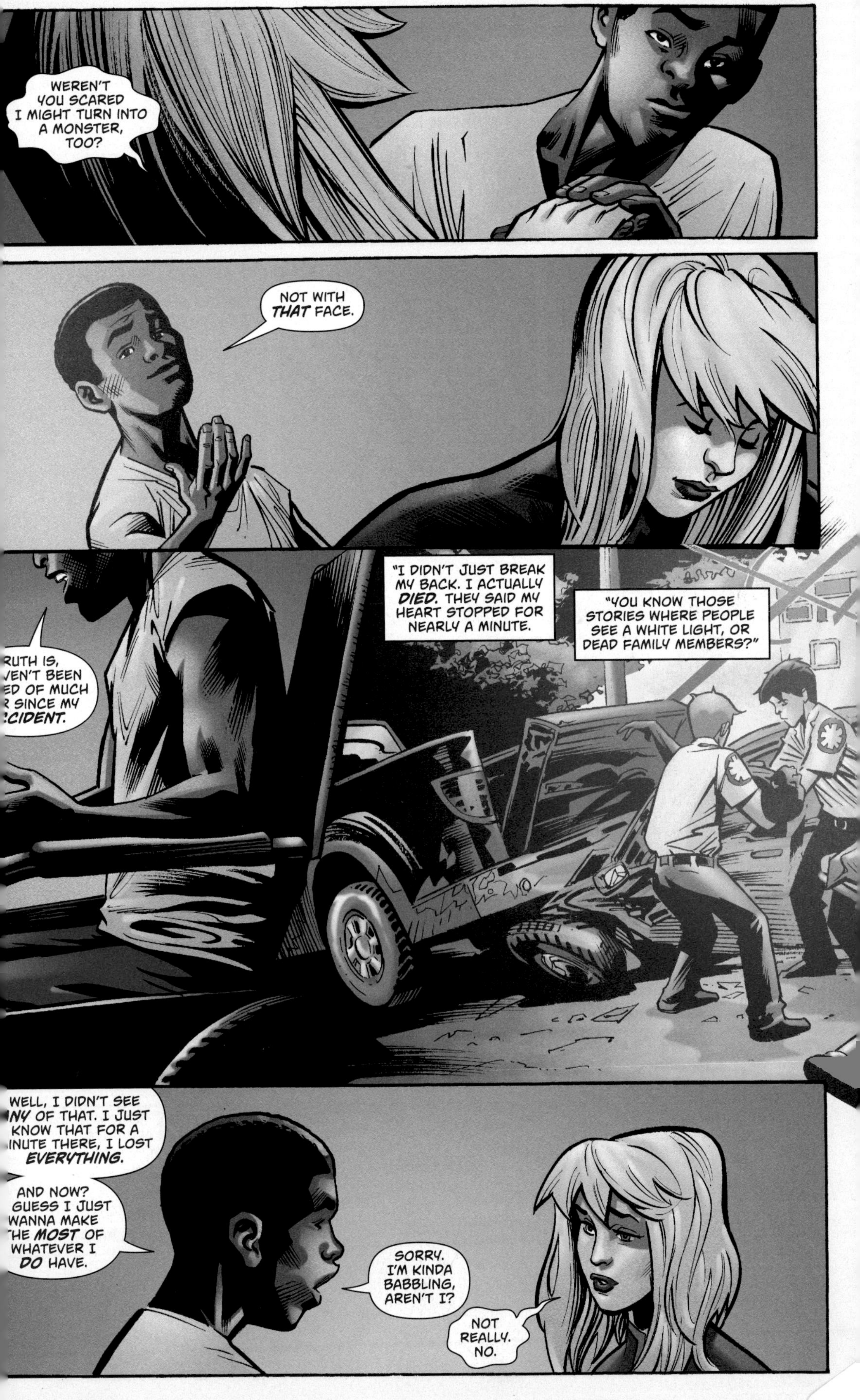
WEREN'T YOU SCARED I MIGHT TURN INTO A MONSTER, TOO?
NOT WITH THAT FACE.
RUTH IS, VEN'T BEEN ED OF MUCH R SINCE MY CIDENT.
"I DIDN'T JUST BREAK MY BACK. I ACTUALLY DIED. THEY SAID MY HEART STOPPED FOR NEARLY A MINUTE.
"YOU KNOW THOSE STORIES WHERE PEOPLE SEE A WHITE LIGHT, OR DEAD FAMILY MEMBERS?"
WELL, I DIDN'T SEE NY OF THAT. I JUST KNOW THAT FOR A INUTE THERE, I LOST EVERYTHING.
AND NOW? GUESS I JUST WANNA MAKE THE MOST OF WHATEVER I DO HAVE.
SORRY. I'M KINDA BABBLING, AREN'T I?
NOT REALLY. NO.

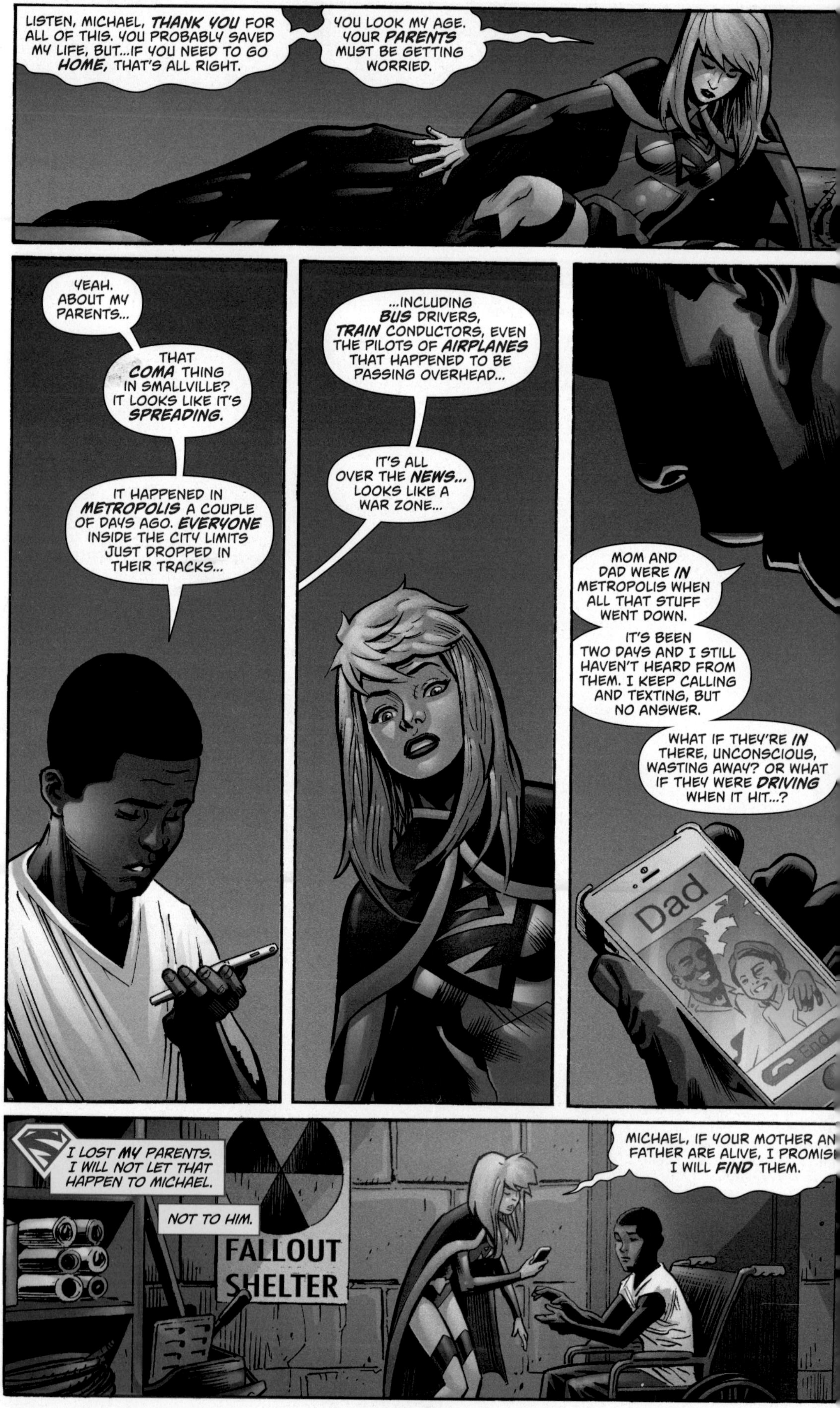
LISTEN, MICHAEL, THANK YOU FOR ALL OF THIS. YOU PROBABLY SAVED MY LIFE, BUT...IF YOU NEED TO GO HOME, THAT'S ALL RIGHT.
YOU LOOK MY AGE. YOUR PARENTS MUST BE GETTING WORRIED.
YEAH. ABOUT MY PARENTS...
THAT COMA THING IN SMALLVILLE? IT LOOKS LIKE IT'S SPREADING.
IT HAPPENED IN METROPOLIS A COUPLE OF DAYS AGO. EVERYONE INSIDE THE CITY LIMITS JUST DROPPED IN THEIR TRACKS...
...INCLUDING BUS DRIVERS, TRAIN CONDUCTORS, EVEN THE PILOTS OF AIRPLANES THAT HAPPENED TO BE PASSING OVERHEAD...
IT'S ALL OVER THE NEWS... LOOKS LIKE A WAR ZONE...
MOM AND DAD WERE IN METROPOLIS WHEN ALL THAT STUFF WENT DOWN.
IT'S BEEN TWO DAYS AND I STILL HAVEN'T HEARD FROM THEM. I KEEP CALLING AND TEXTING, BUT NO ANSWER.
WHAT IF THEY'RE IN THERE, UNCONSCIOUS, WASTING AWAY? OR WHAT IF THEY WERE DRIVING WHEN IT HIT...?
Dad
End
I LOST MY PARENTS. I WILL NOT LET THAT HAPPEN TO MICHAEL.
NOT TO HIM.
FALLOUT SHELTER
MICHAEL, IF YOUR MOTHER AN FATHER ARE ALIVE, I PROMIS I WILL FIND THEM.

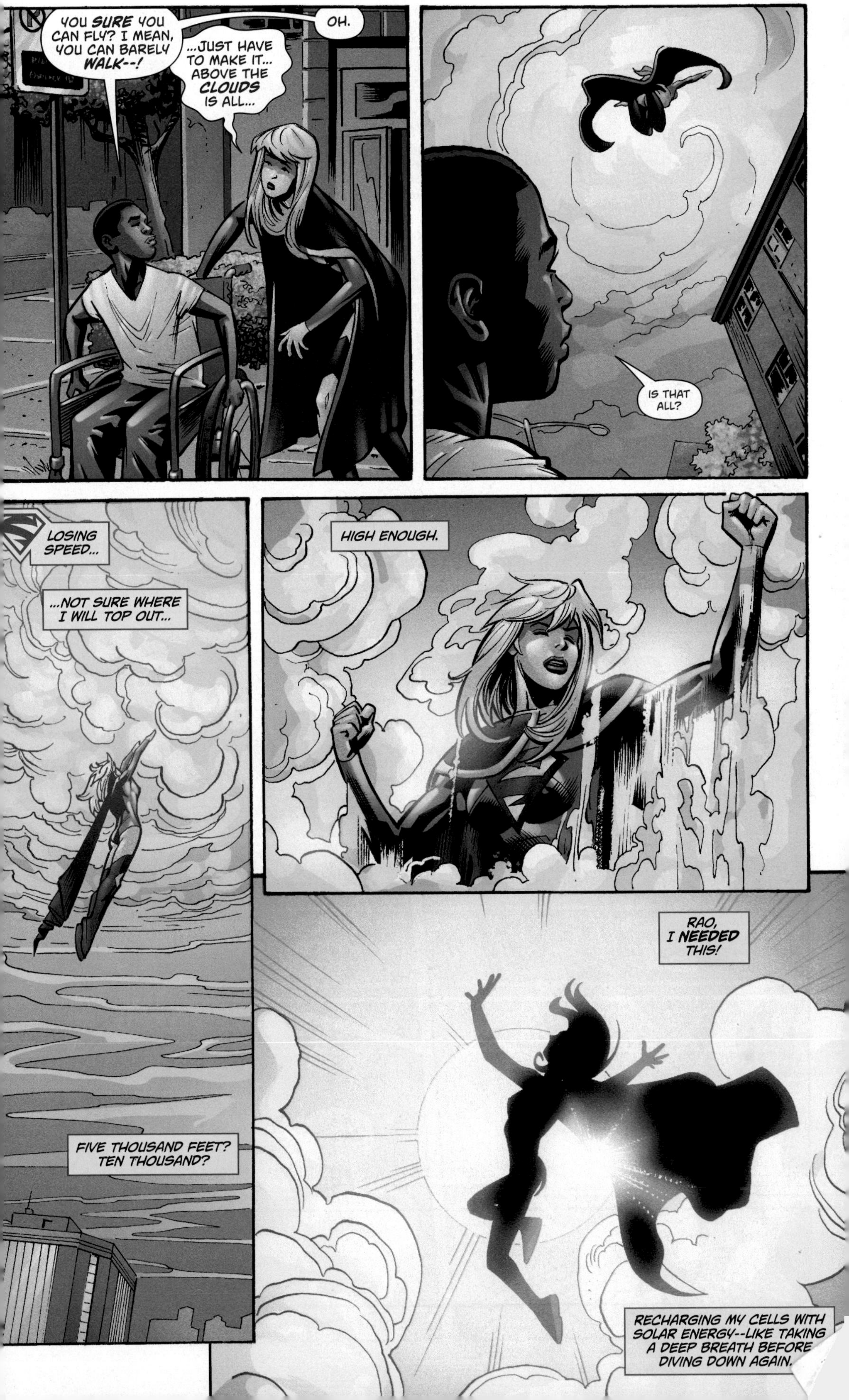
YOU SURE YOU CAN FLY? I MEAN, YOU CAN BARELY WALK--!
...JUST HAVE TO MAKE IT... ABOVE THE CLOUDS IS ALL...
OH.
IS THAT ALL?
LOSING SPEED...
...NOT SURE WHERE I WILL TOP OUT...
FIVE THOUSAND FEET? TEN THOUSAND?
HIGH ENOUGH.
RAO, I NEEDED THIS!
RECHARGING MY CELLS WITH SOLAR ENERGY--LIKE TAKING A DEEP BREATH BEFORE DIVING DOWN AGAIN.

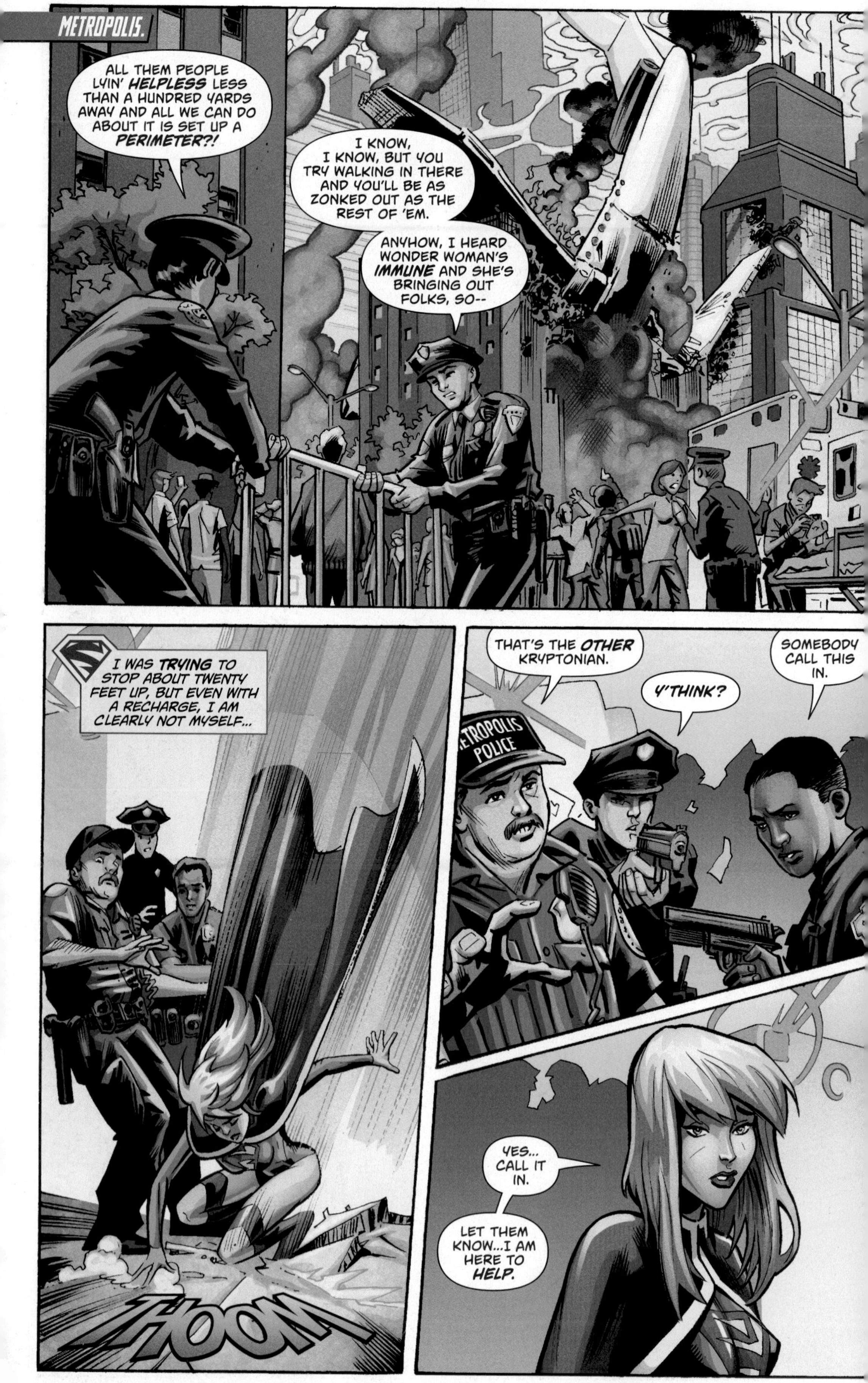
METROPOLIS.
ALL THEM PEOPLE LYIN' HELPLESS LESS THAN A HUNDRED YARDS AWAY AND ALL WE CAN DO ABOUT IT IS SET UP A PERIMETER?!
I KNOW, I KNOW, BUT YOU TRY WALKING IN THERE AND YOU'LL BE AS ZONKED OUT AS THE REST OF 'EM.
ANYHOW, I HEARD WONDER WOMAN'S IMMUNE AND SHE'S BRINGING OUT FOLKS, SO--
I WAS TRYING TO STOP ABOUT TWENTY FEET UP, BUT EVEN WITH A RECHARGE, I AM CLEARLY NOT MYSELF...
THOOM
THAT'S THE OTHER KRYPTONIAN.
Y'THINK?
SOMEBODY CALL THIS IN.
METROPOLIS POLICE
YES... CALL IT IN.
LET THEM KNOW...I AM HERE TO HELP.

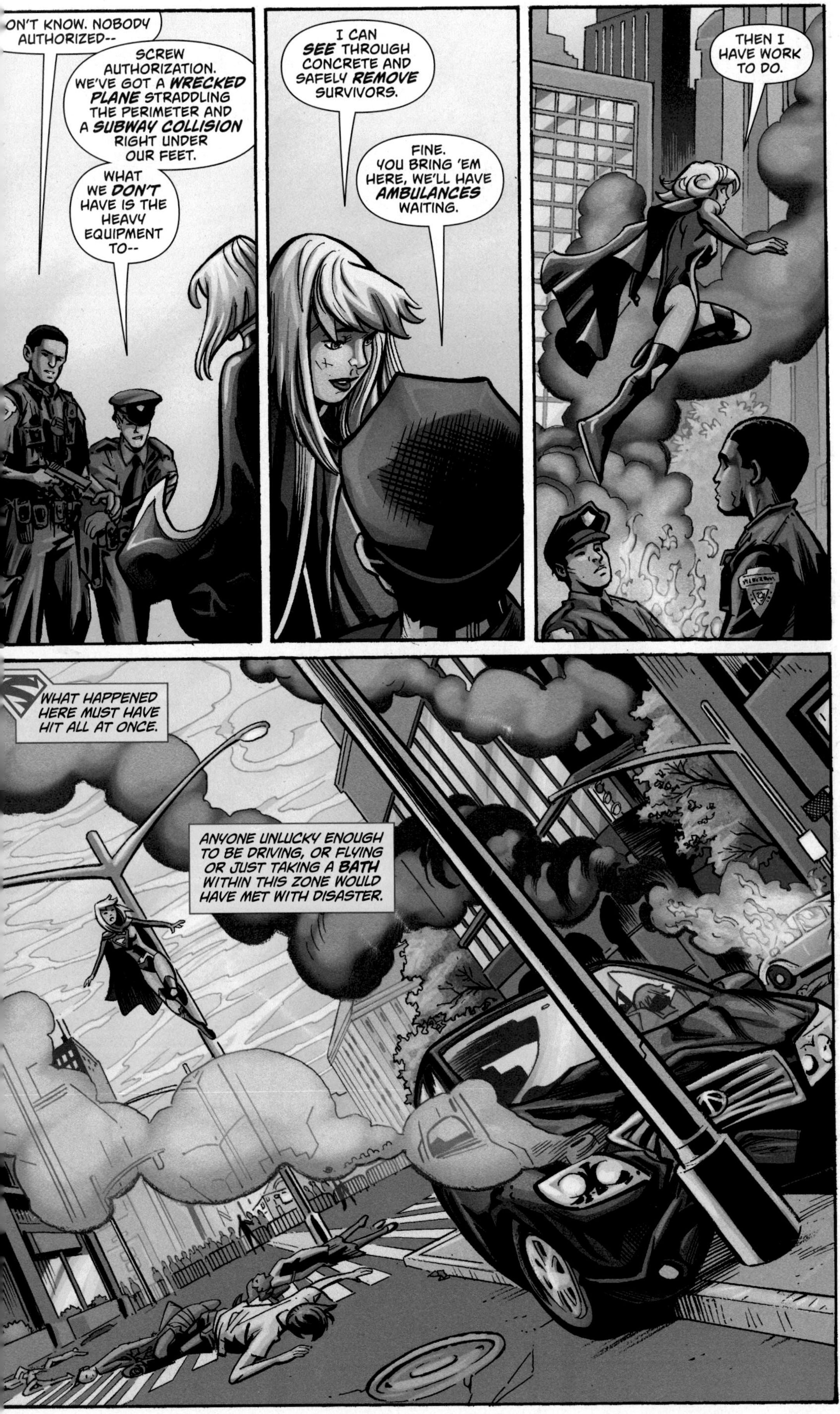
ON'T KNOW. NOBODY AUTHORIZED--
SCREW AUTHORIZATION. WE'VE GOT A WRECKED PLANE STRADDLING THE PERIMETER AND A SUBWAY COLLISION RIGHT UNDER OUR FEET.
WHAT WE DON'T HAVE IS THE HEAVY EQUIPMENT TO--
I CAN SEE THROUGH CONCRETE AND SAFELY REMOVE SURVIVORS.
FINE. YOU BRING 'EM HERE, WE'LL HAVE AMBULANCES WAITING.
THEN I HAVE WORK TO DO.
WHAT HAPPENED HERE MUST HAVE HIT ALL AT ONCE.
ANYONE UNLUCKY ENOUGH TO BE DRIVING, OR FLYING OR JUST TAKING A BATH WITHIN THIS ZONE WOULD HAVE MET WITH DISASTER.

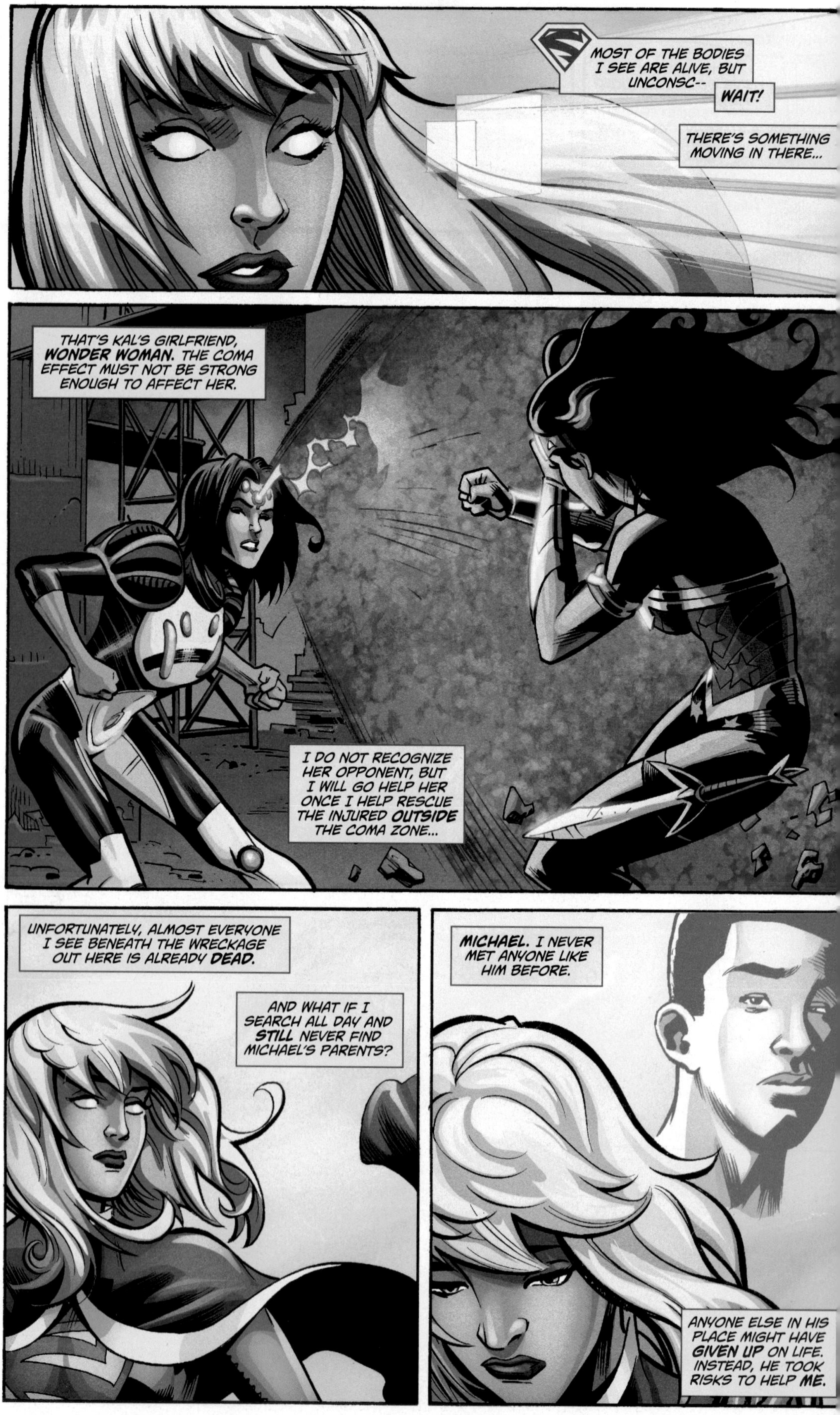

MOST OF THE BODIES I SEE ARE ALIVE, BUT UNCONSC--
WAIT!
THERE'S SOMETHING MOVING IN THERE...
THAT'S KAL'S GIRLFRIEND, WONDER WOMAN. THE COMA EFFECT MUST NOT BE STRONG ENOUGH TO AFFECT HER.
I DO NOT RECOGNIZE HER OPPONENT, BUT I WILL GO HELP HER ONCE I HELP RESCUE THE INJURED OUTSIDE THE COMA ZONE...
UNFORTUNATELY, ALMOST EVERYONE I SEE BENEATH THE WRECKAGE OUT HERE IS ALREADY DEAD.
AND WHAT IF I SEARCH ALL DAY AND STILL NEVER FIND MICHAEL'S PARENTS?
MICHAEL. I NEVER MET ANYONE LIKE HIM BEFORE.
ANYONE ELSE IN HIS PLACE MIGHT HAVE GIVEN UP ON LIFE. INSTEAD, HE TOOK RISKS TO HELP ME.

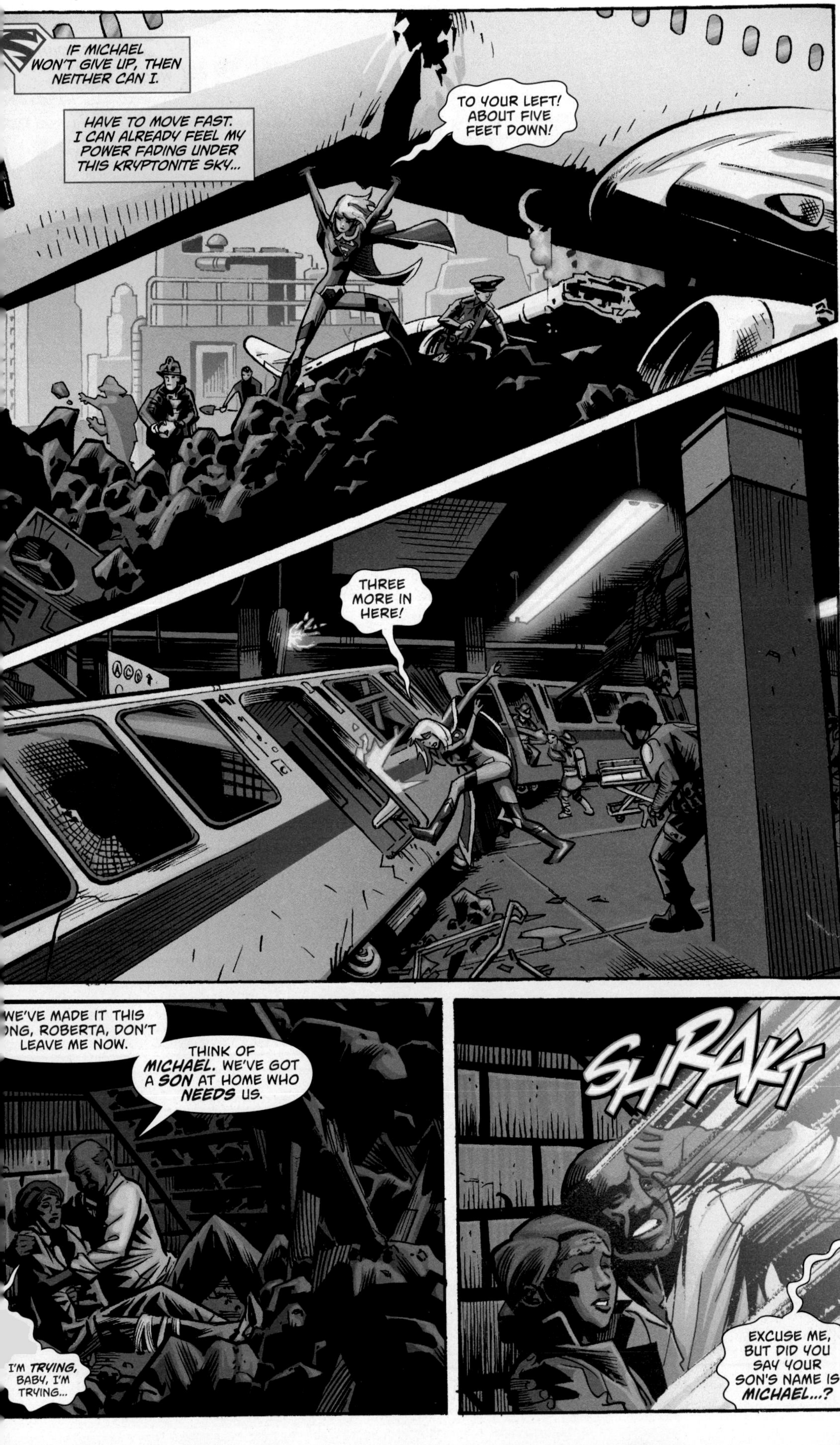

IF MICHAEL WON'T GIVE UP, THEN NEITHER CAN I.
HAVE TO MOVE FAST. I CAN ALREADY FEEL MY POWER FADING UNDER THIS KRYPTONITE SKY...
TO YOUR LEFT! ABOUT FIVE FEET DOWN!
THREE MORE IN HERE!
WE'VE MADE IT THIS ONG, ROBERTA, DON'T LEAVE ME NOW.
THINK OF MICHAEL. WE'VE GOT A SON AT HOME WHO NEEDS US.
I'M TRYING, BABY, I'M TRYING...
SHRAKT
EXCUSE ME, BUT DID YOU SAY YOUR SON'S NAME IS MICHAEL...?

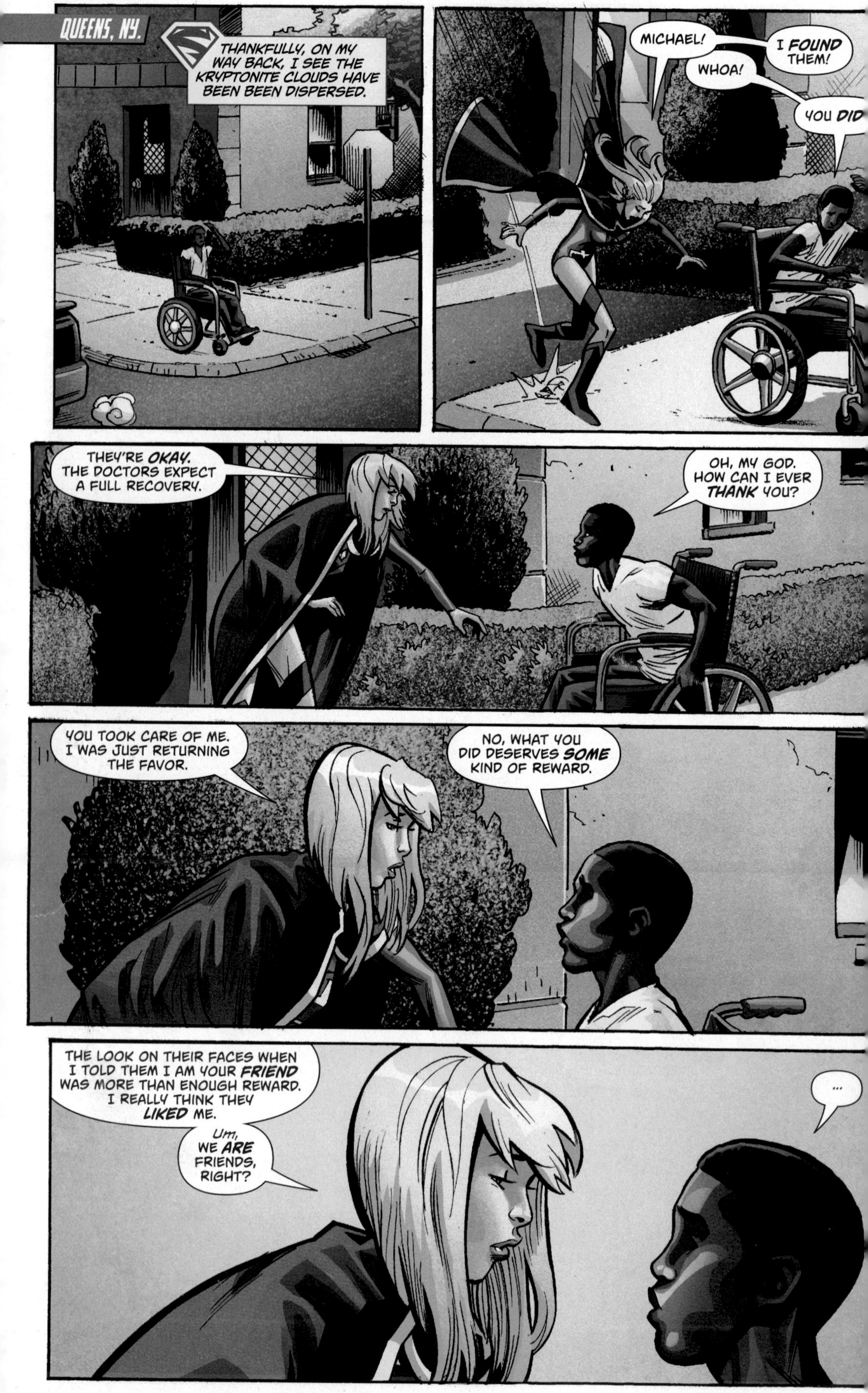
QUEENS, NY.
THANKFULLY, ON MY WAY BACK, I SEE THE KRYPTONITE CLOUDS HAVE BEEN BEEN DISPERSED.
MICHAEL!
I FOUND THEM!
WHOA!
YOU DID
THEY'RE OKAY. THE DOCTORS EXPECT A FULL RECOVERY.
OH, MY GOD. HOW CAN I EVER THANK YOU?
YOU TOOK CARE OF ME. I WAS JUST RETURNING THE FAVOR.
NO, WHAT YOU DID DESERVES SOME KIND OF REWARD.
THE LOOK ON THEIR FACES WHEN I TOLD THEM I AM YOUR FRIEND WAS MORE THAN ENOUGH REWARD. I REALLY THINK THEY LIKED ME.
Um, WE ARE FRIENDS, RIGHT?
...

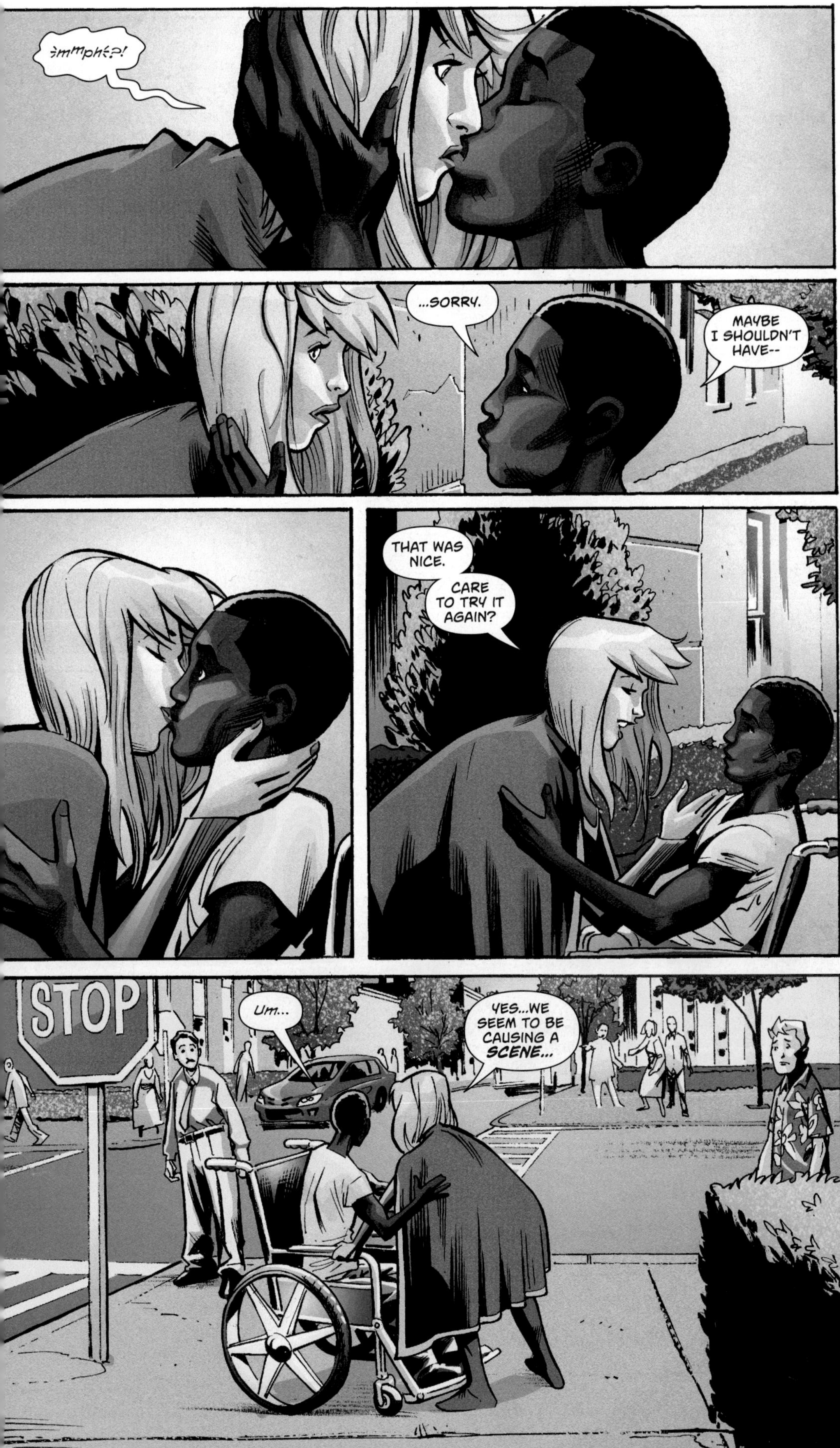
mmph?!
...SORRY.
MAYBE I SHOULDN'T HAVE--
THAT WAS NICE.
CARE TO TRY IT AGAIN?
STOP
Um...
YES...WE SEEM TO BE CAUSING A SCENE...

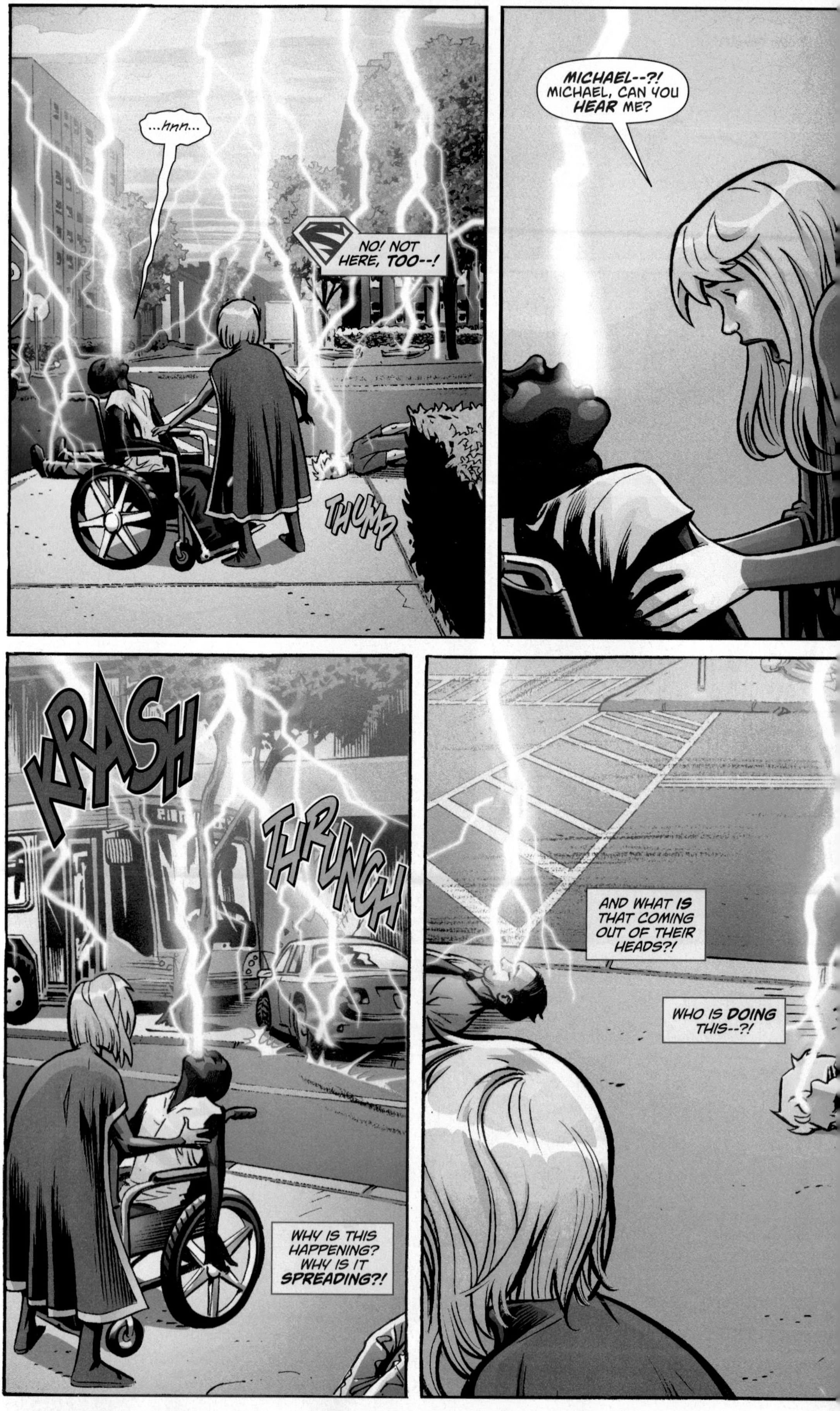
...hnn...
NO! NOT HERE, TOO--!
THUMP
MICHAEL--?! MICHAEL, CAN YOU HEAR ME?
KRASH
THRUNCH
WHY IS THIS HAPPENING? WHY IS IT SPREADING?!
AND WHAT IS THAT COMING OUT OF THEIR HEADS?!
WHO IS DOING THIS--?!

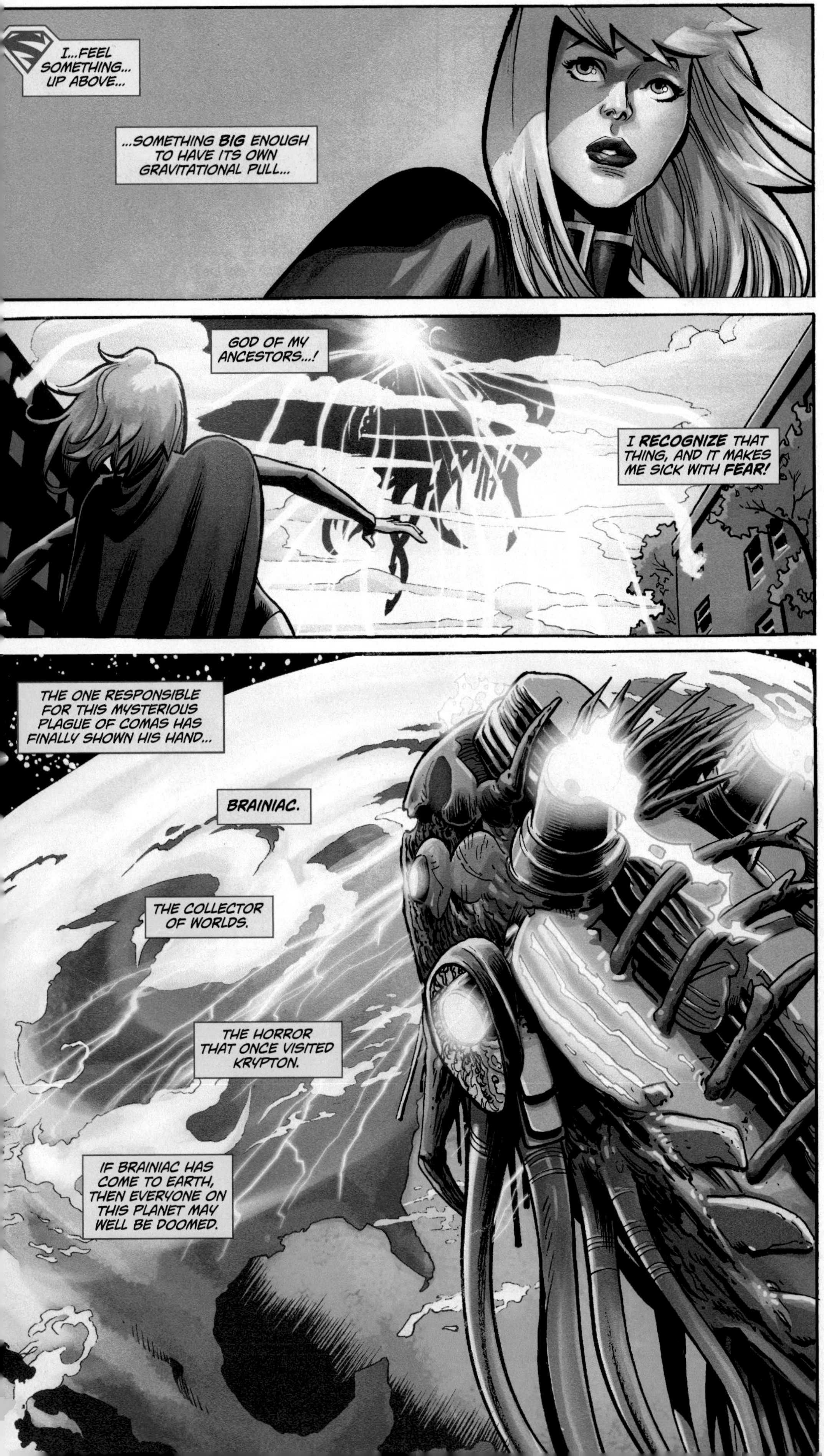
I...FEEL SOMETHING... UP ABOVE...
...SOMETHING BIG ENOUGH TO HAVE ITS OWN GRAVITATIONAL PULL...
GOD OF MY ANCESTORS...!
I RECOGNIZE THAT THING, AND IT MAKES ME SICK WITH FEAR!
THE ONE RESPONSIBLE FOR THIS MYSTERIOUS PLAGUE OF COMAS HAS FINALLY SHOWN HIS HAND...
BRAINIAC.
THE COLLECTOR OF WORLDS.
THE HORROR THAT ONCE VISITED KRYPTON.
IF BRAINIAC HAS COME TO EARTH, THEN EVERYONE ON THIS PLANET MAY WELL BE DOOMED.

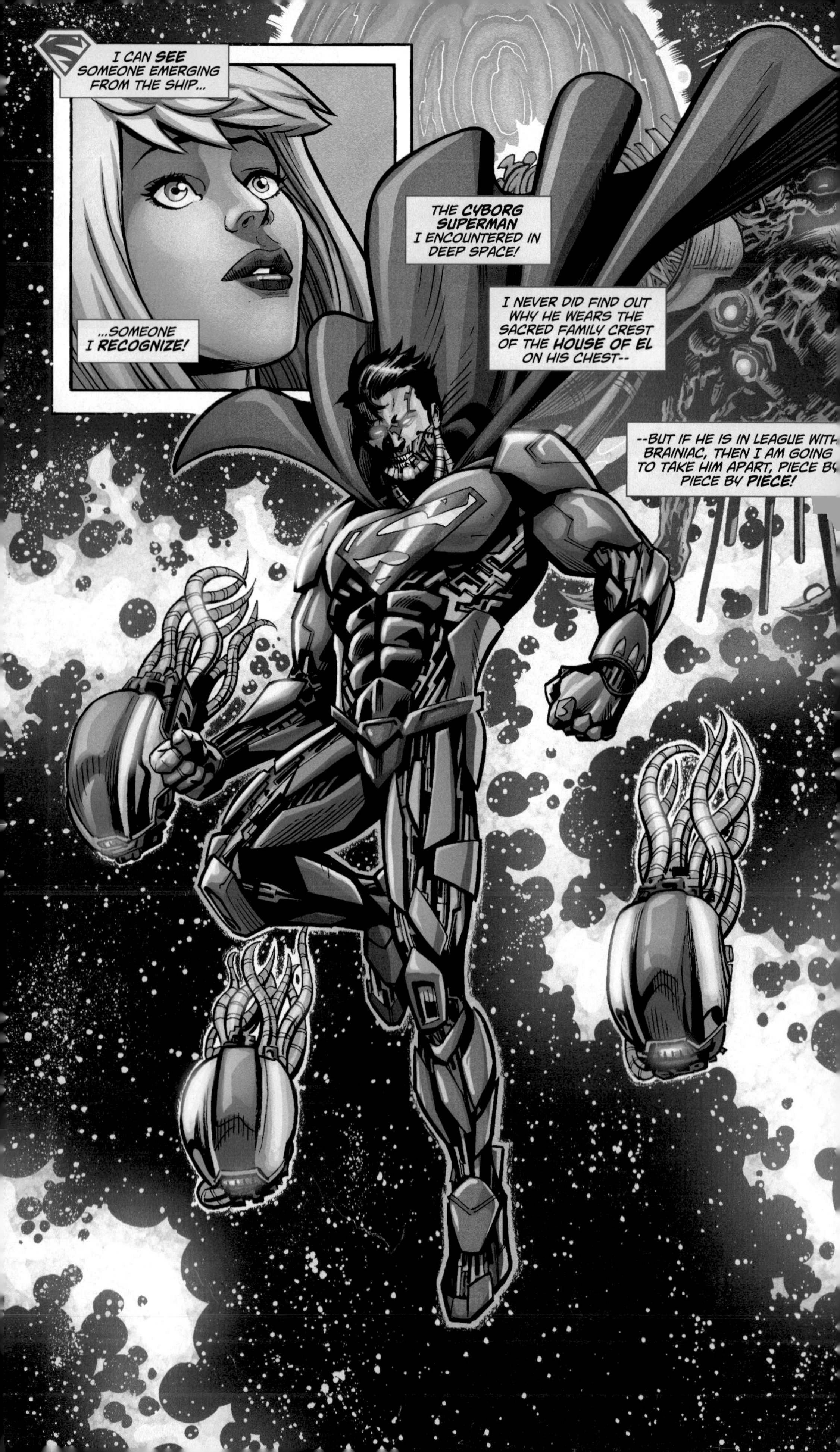
I CAN **SEE** SOMEONE EMERGING FROM THE SHIP...
...SOMEONE I **RECOGNIZE!**
THE **CYBORG SUPERMAN** I ENCOUNTERED IN DEEP SPACE!
I NEVER DID FIND OUT WHY HE WEARS THE SACRED FAMILY CREST OF THE **HOUSE OF EL** ON HIS CHEST--
--BUT IF HE IS IN LEAGUE WITH BRAINIAC, THEN I AM GOING TO TAKE HIM APART, PIECE BY PIECE BY **PIECE!**

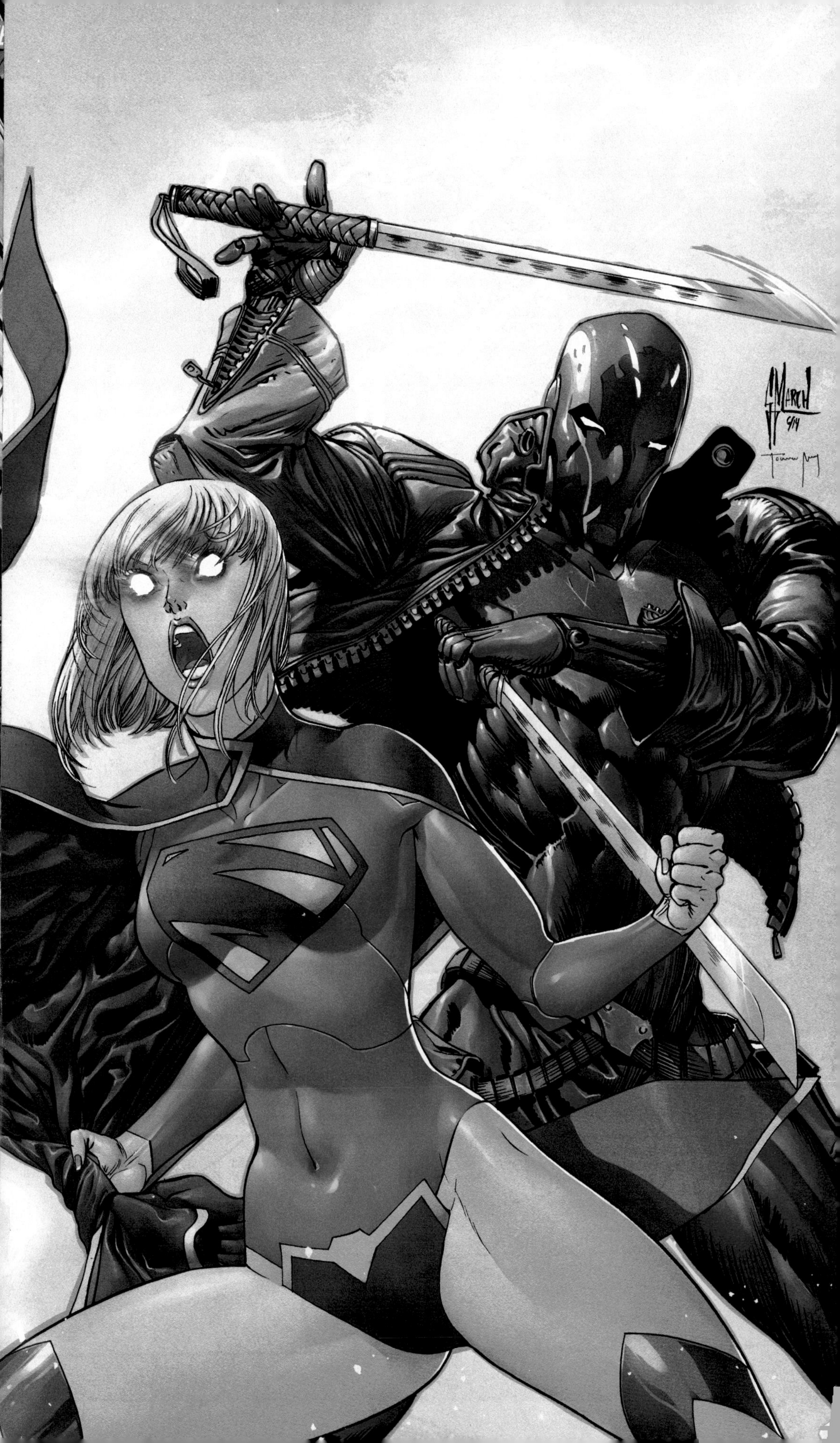
MARCH
6/14

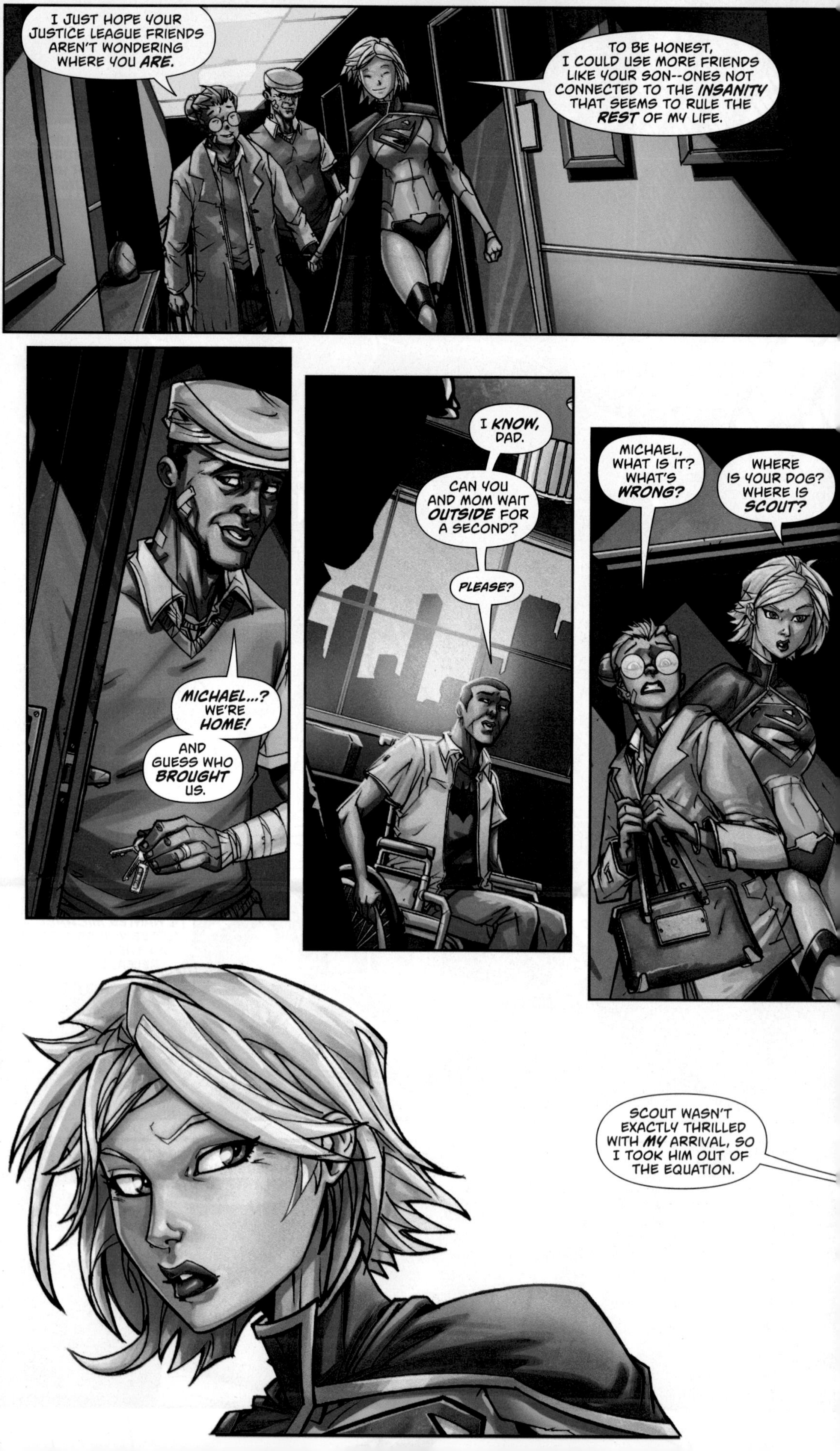
I JUST HOPE YOUR JUSTICE LEAGUE FRIENDS AREN'T WONDERING WHERE YOU *ARE.*
TO BE HONEST, I COULD USE MORE FRIENDS LIKE YOUR SON--ONES NOT CONNECTED TO THE *INSANITY* THAT SEEMS TO RULE THE *REST* OF MY LIFE.
MICHAEL...? WE'RE *HOME!*
AND GUESS WHO *BROUGHT* US.
I *KNOW,* DAD.
CAN YOU AND MOM WAIT *OUTSIDE* FOR A SECOND?
PLEASE?
MICHAEL, WHAT IS IT? WHAT'S *WRONG?*
WHERE IS YOUR DOG? WHERE IS *SCOUT?*
SCOUT WASN'T EXACTLY THRILLED WITH *MY* ARRIVAL, SO I TOOK HIM OUT OF THE EQUATION.

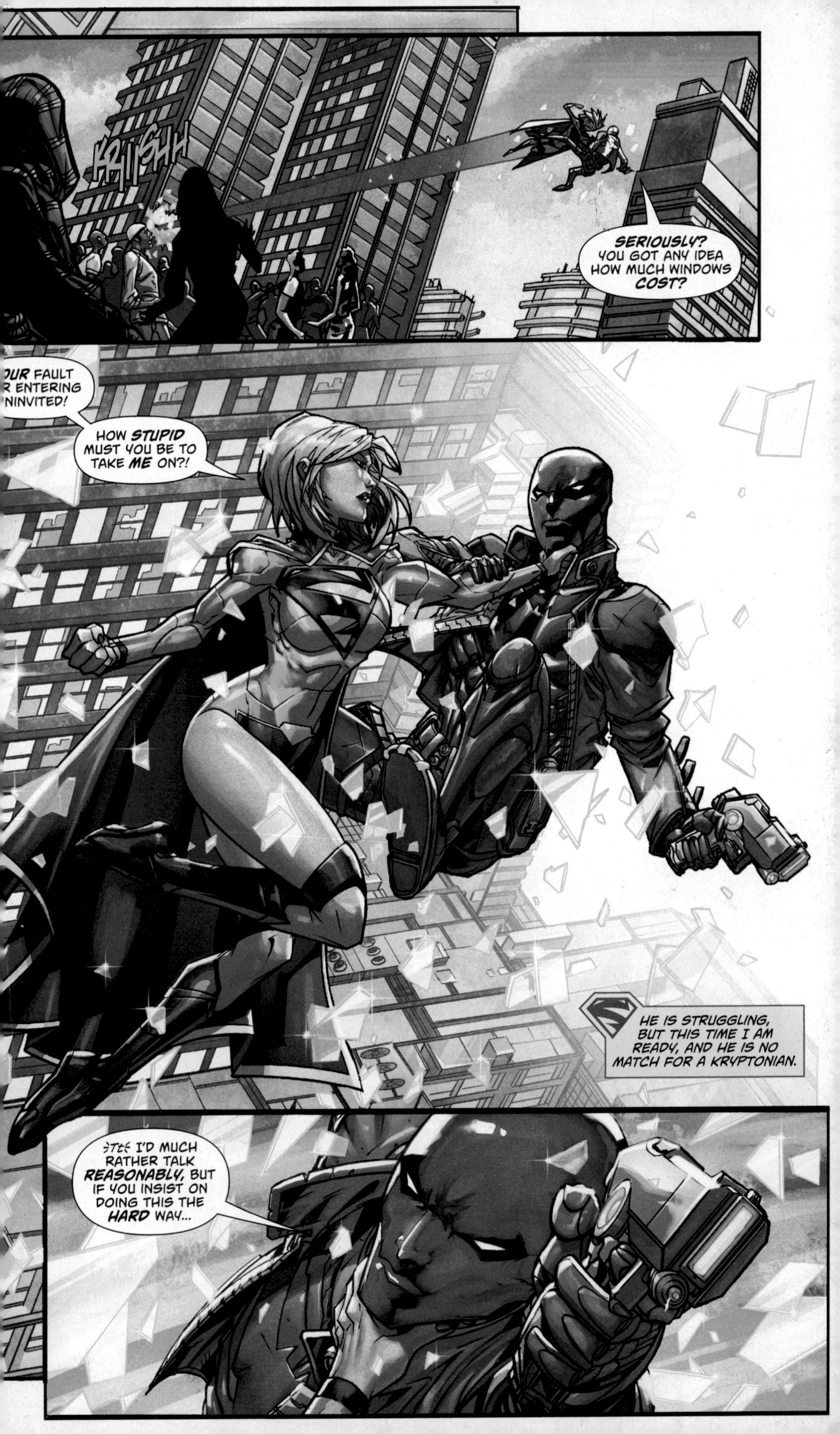
SERIOUSLY? YOU GOT ANY IDEA HOW MUCH WINDOWS COST?
OUR FAULT R ENTERING NINVITED!
HOW STUPID MUST YOU BE TO TAKE ME ON?!
HE IS STRUGGLING, BUT THIS TIME I AM READY, AND HE IS NO MATCH FOR A KRYPTONIAN.
I'D MUCH RATHER TALK REASONABLY, BUT IF YOU INSIST ON DOING THIS THE HARD WAY...

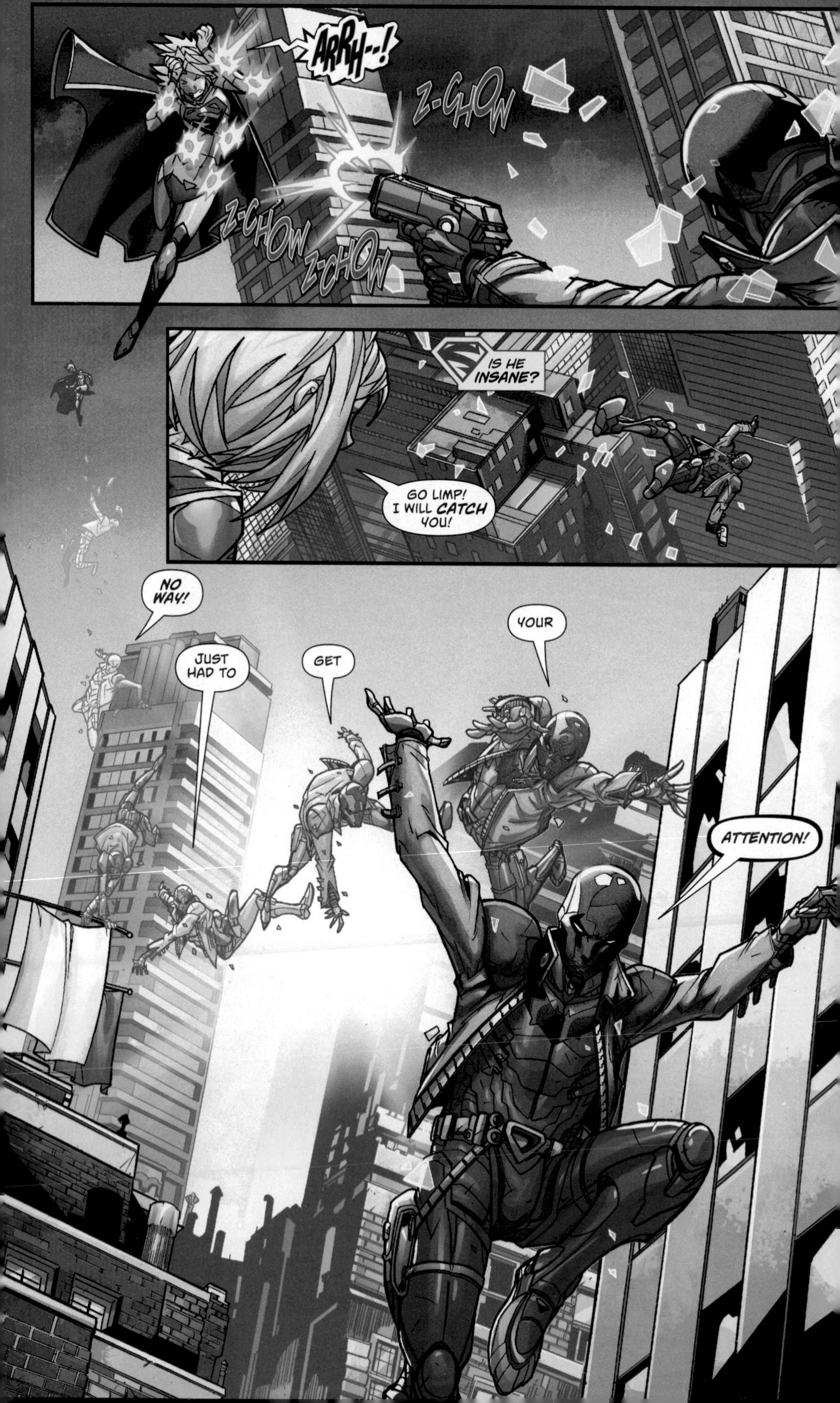
ARRH--!
Z-CHOW
Z-CHOW
Z-CHOW
IS HE INSANE?
GO LIMP! I WILL CATCH YOU!
NO WAY!
JUST HAD TO
GET
YOUR
ATTENTION!

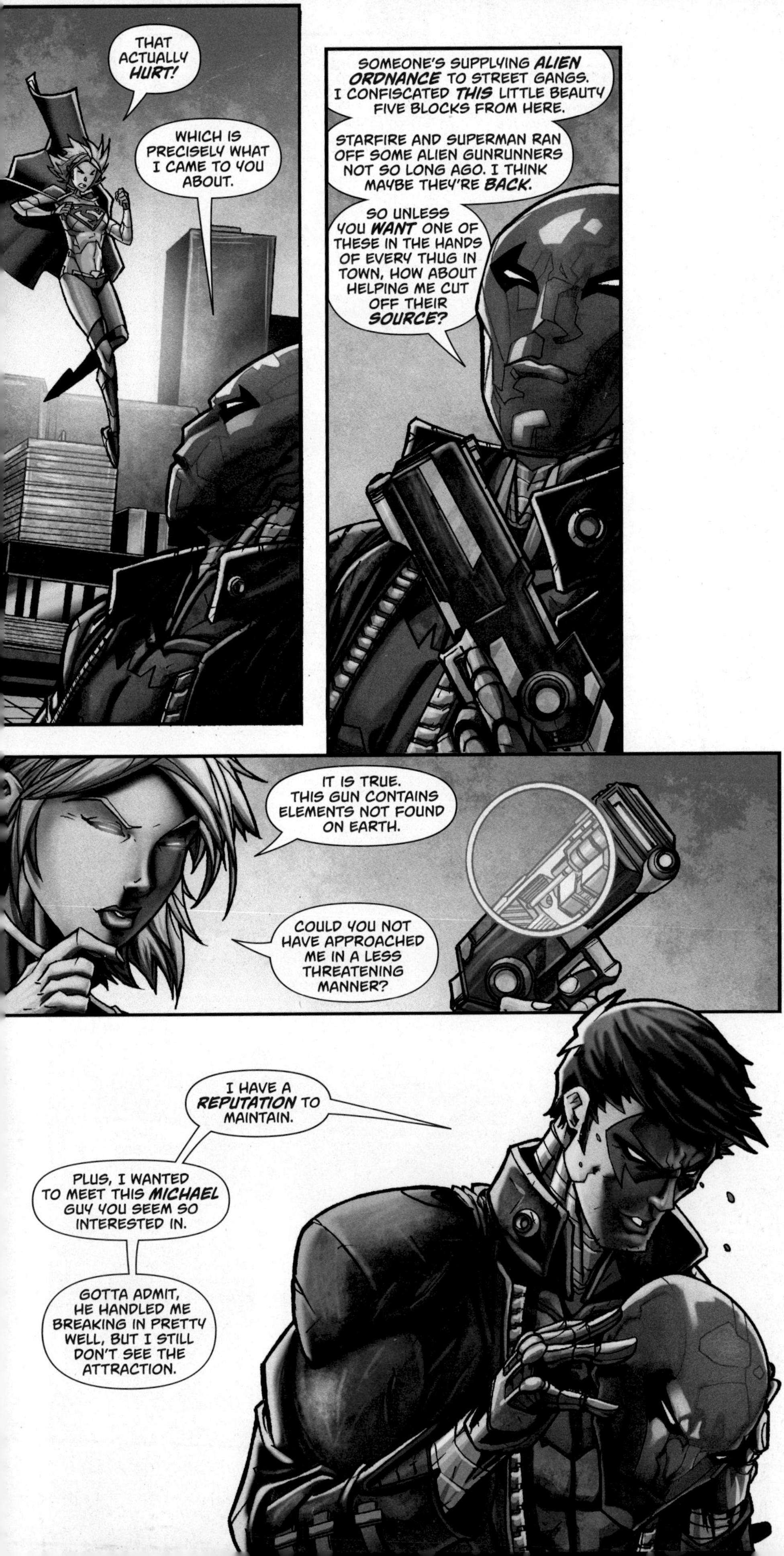
THAT ACTUALLY HURT!
WHICH IS PRECISELY WHAT I CAME TO YOU ABOUT.
SOMEONE'S SUPPLYING ALIEN ORDNANCE TO STREET GANGS. I CONFISCATED THIS LITTLE BEAUTY FIVE BLOCKS FROM HERE.
STARFIRE AND SUPERMAN RAN OFF SOME ALIEN GUNRUNNERS NOT SO LONG AGO. I THINK MAYBE THEY'RE BACK.
SO UNLESS YOU WANT ONE OF THESE IN THE HANDS OF EVERY THUG IN TOWN, HOW ABOUT HELPING ME CUT OFF THEIR SOURCE?
IT IS TRUE. THIS GUN CONTAINS ELEMENTS NOT FOUND ON EARTH.
COULD YOU NOT HAVE APPROACHED ME IN A LESS THREATENING MANNER?
I HAVE A REPUTATION TO MAINTAIN.
PLUS, I WANTED TO MEET THIS MICHAEL GUY YOU SEEM SO INTERESTED IN.
GOTTA ADMIT, HE HANDLED ME BREAKING IN PRETTY WELL, BUT I STILL DON'T SEE THE ATTRACTION.

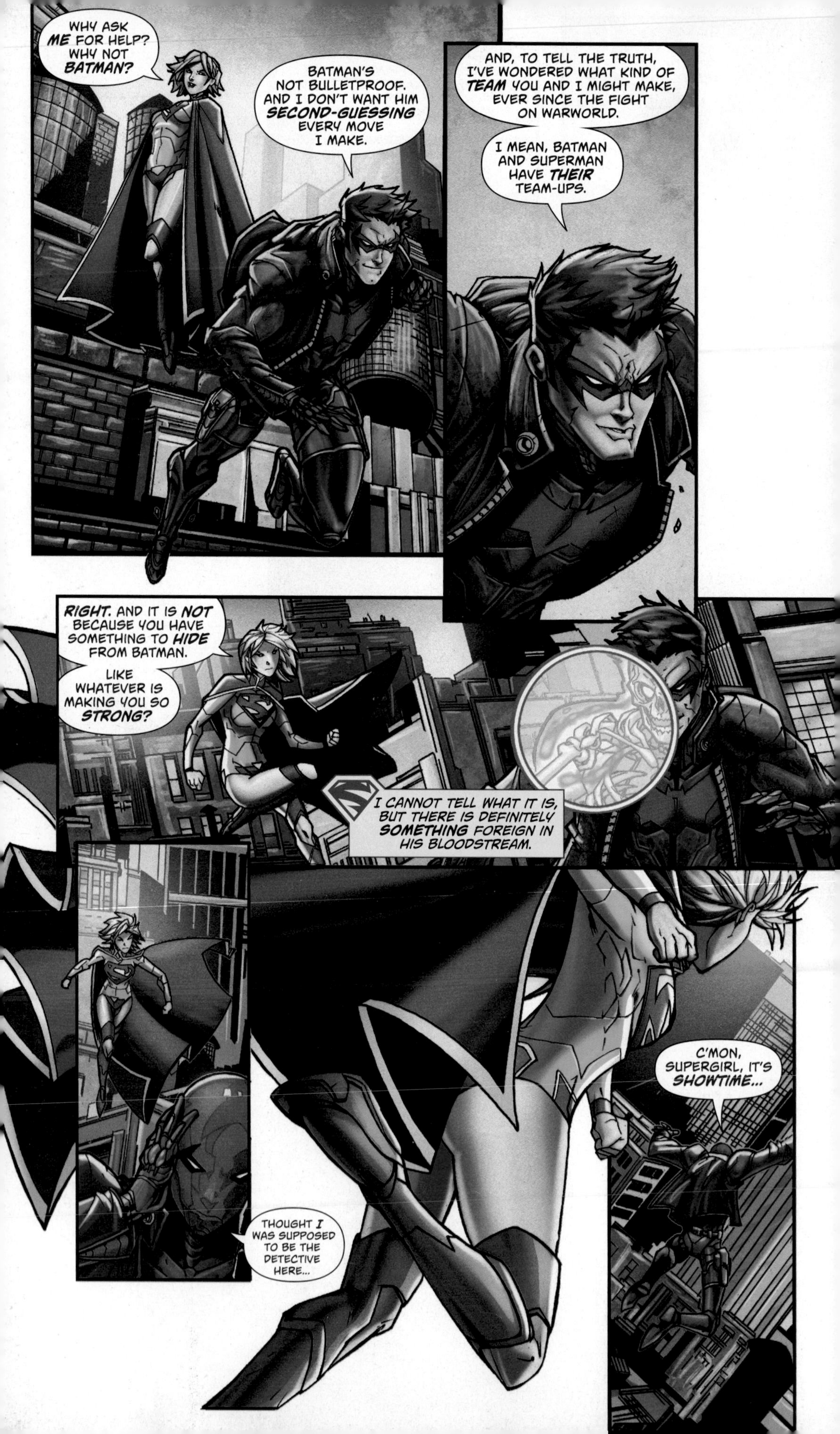
WHY ASK ME FOR HELP? WHY NOT BATMAN?
BATMAN'S NOT BULLETPROOF. AND I DON'T WANT HIM SECOND-GUESSING EVERY MOVE I MAKE.
AND, TO TELL THE TRUTH, I'VE WONDERED WHAT KIND OF TEAM YOU AND I MIGHT MAKE, EVER SINCE THE FIGHT ON WARWORLD.
I MEAN, BATMAN AND SUPERMAN HAVE THEIR TEAM-UPS.
RIGHT. AND IT IS NOT BECAUSE YOU HAVE SOMETHING TO HIDE FROM BATMAN.
LIKE WHATEVER IS MAKING YOU SO STRONG?
I CANNOT TELL WHAT IT IS, BUT THERE IS DEFINITELY SOMETHING FOREIGN IN HIS BLOODSTREAM.
THOUGHT I WAS SUPPOSED TO BE THE DETECTIVE HERE...
C'MON, SUPERGIRL, IT'S SHOWTIME...

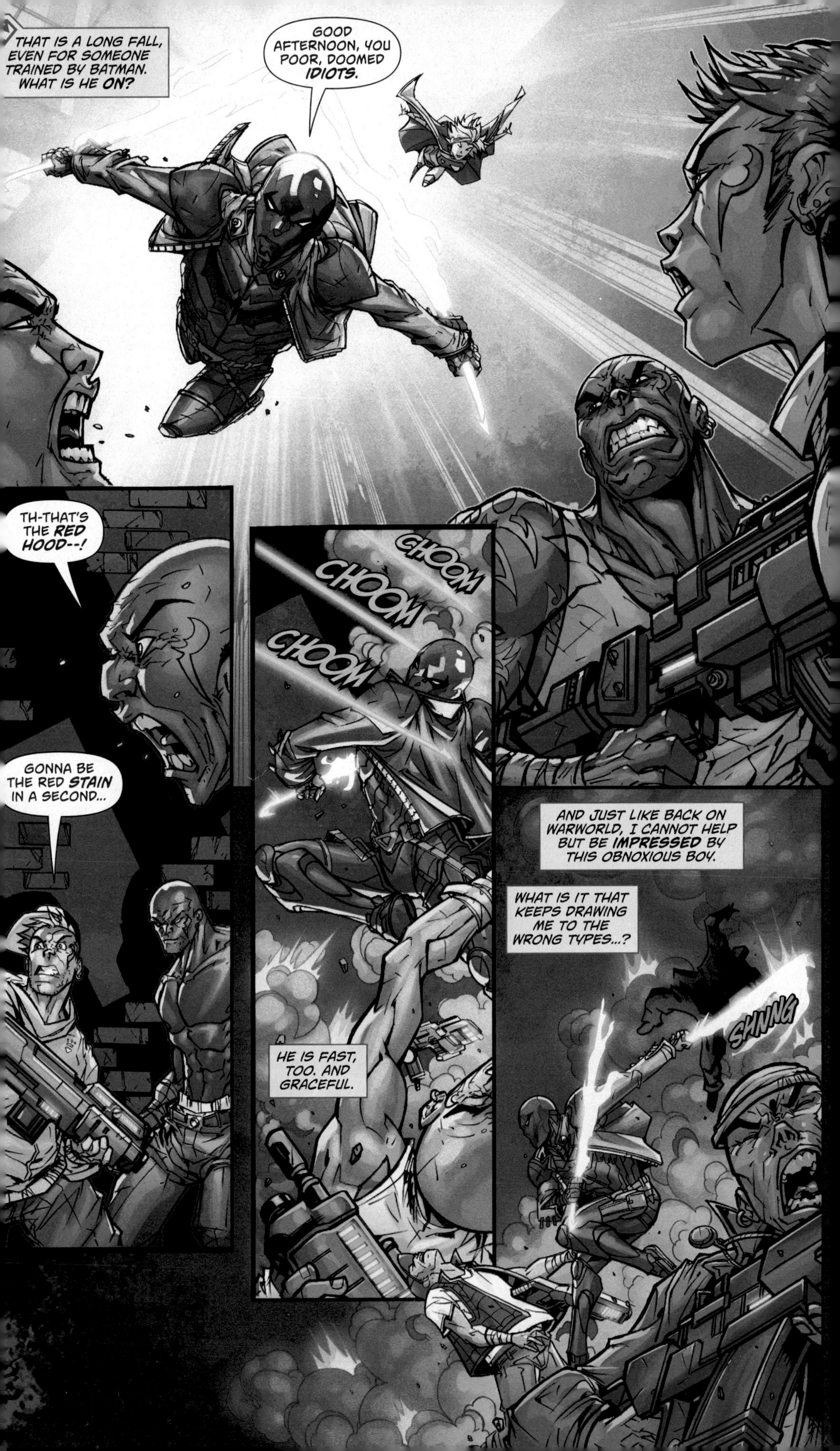
THAT IS A LONG FALL, EVEN FOR SOMEONE TRAINED BY BATMAN. WHAT IS HE ON?
GOOD AFTERNOON, YOU POOR, DOOMED IDIOTS.
TH-THAT'S THE RED HOOD--!
GONNA BE THE RED STAIN IN A SECOND...
CHOOM
CHOOM
CHOOM
HE IS FAST, TOO. AND GRACEFUL.
AND JUST LIKE BACK ON WARWORLD, I CANNOT HELP BUT BE IMPRESSED BY THIS OBNOXIOUS BOY.
WHAT IS IT THAT KEEPS DRAWING ME TO THE WRONG TYPES...?
SHING

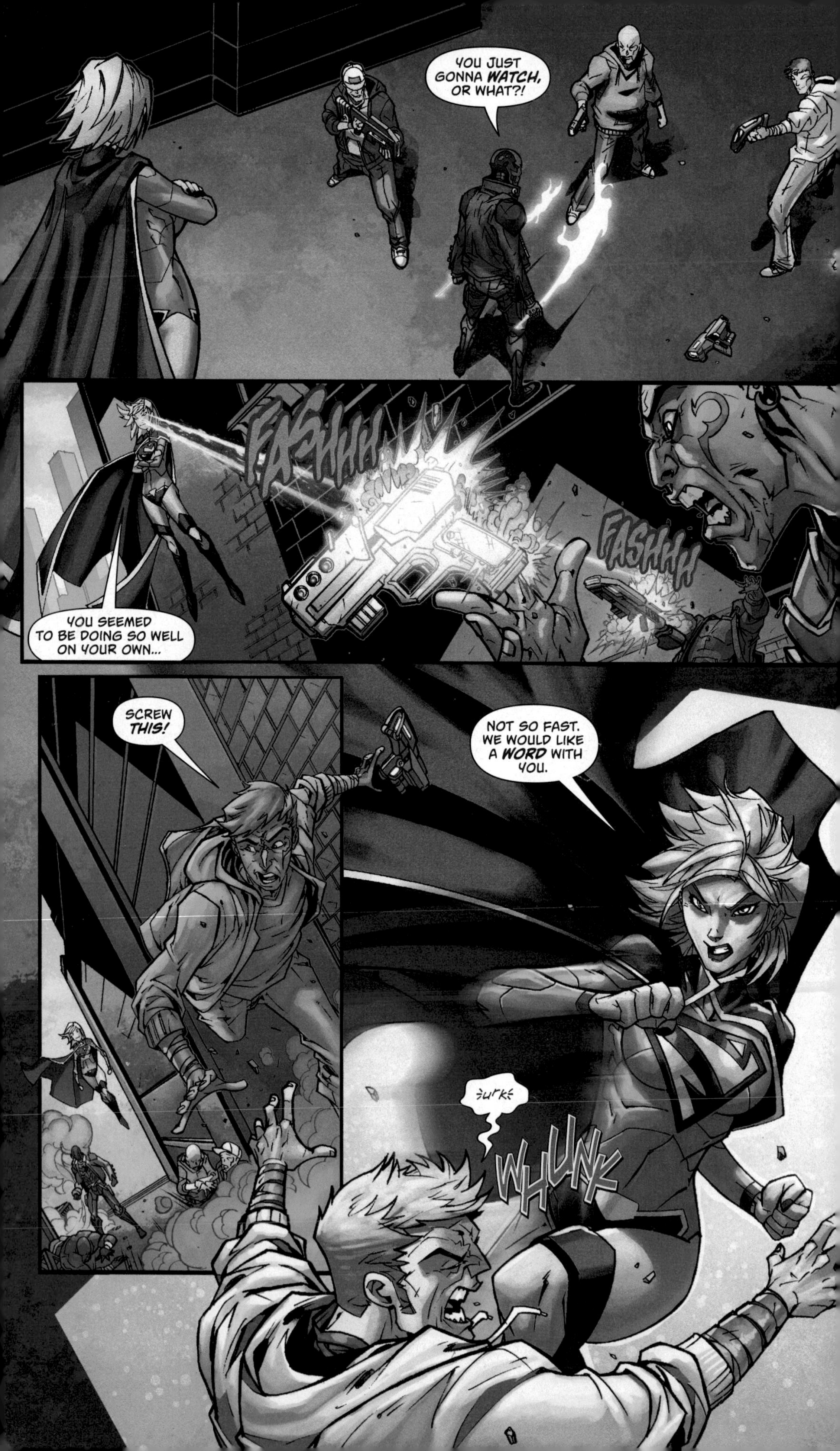

YOU JUST GONNA WATCH, OR WHAT?!
FASHHH
YOU SEEMED TO BE DOING SO WELL ON YOUR OWN...
FASHHH
SCREW THIS!
NOT SO FAST. WE WOULD LIKE A WORD WITH YOU.
urk
WHUNK

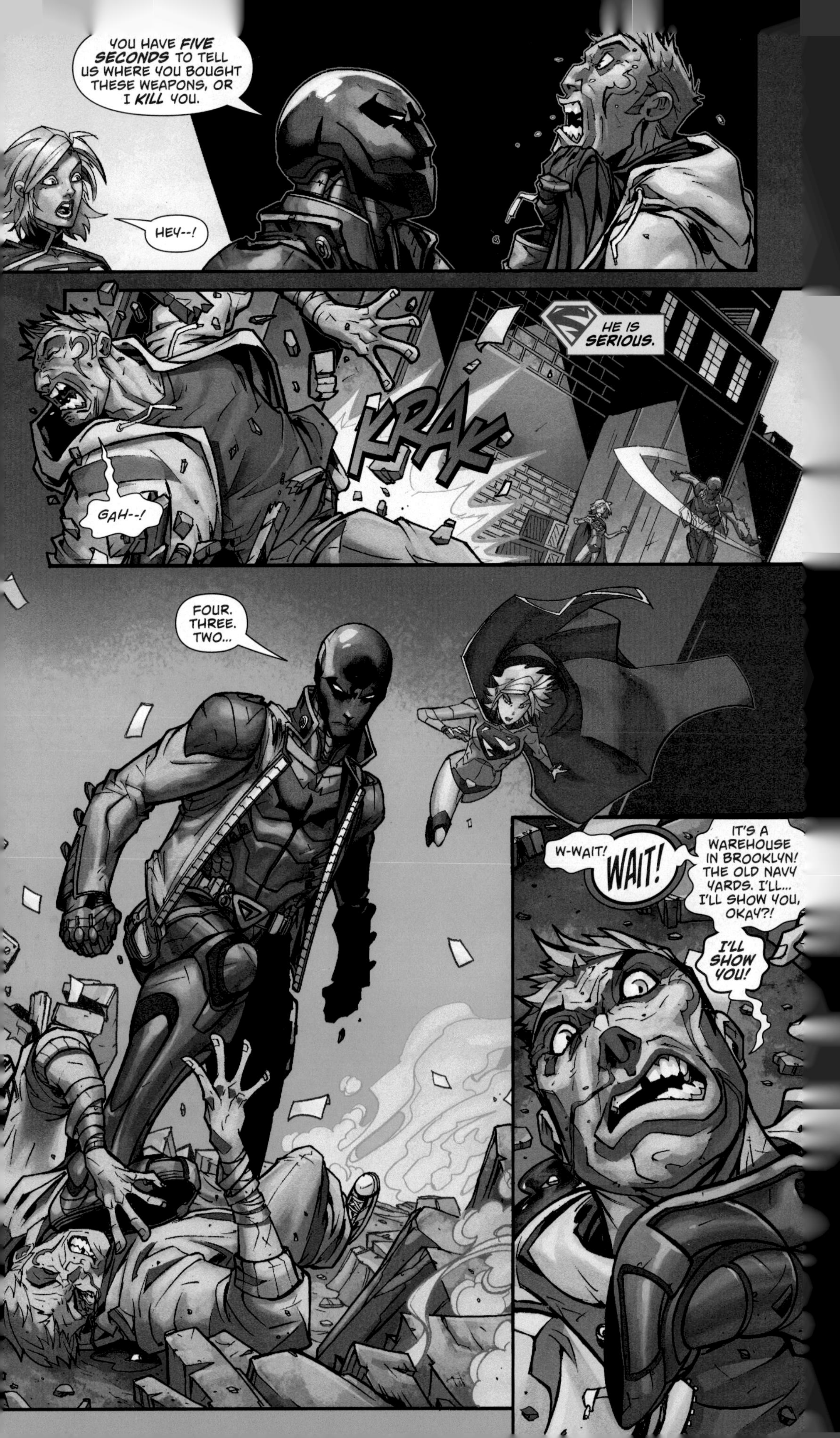
YOU HAVE FIVE SECONDS TO TELL US WHERE YOU BOUGHT THESE WEAPONS, OR I KILL YOU.
HEY--!
HE IS SERIOUS.
KRAK
GAH--!
FOUR. THREE. TWO...
W-WAIT!
WAIT!
IT'S A WAREHOUSE IN BROOKLYN! THE OLD NAVY YARDS. I'LL... I'LL SHOW YOU, OKAY?!
I'LL SHOW YOU!

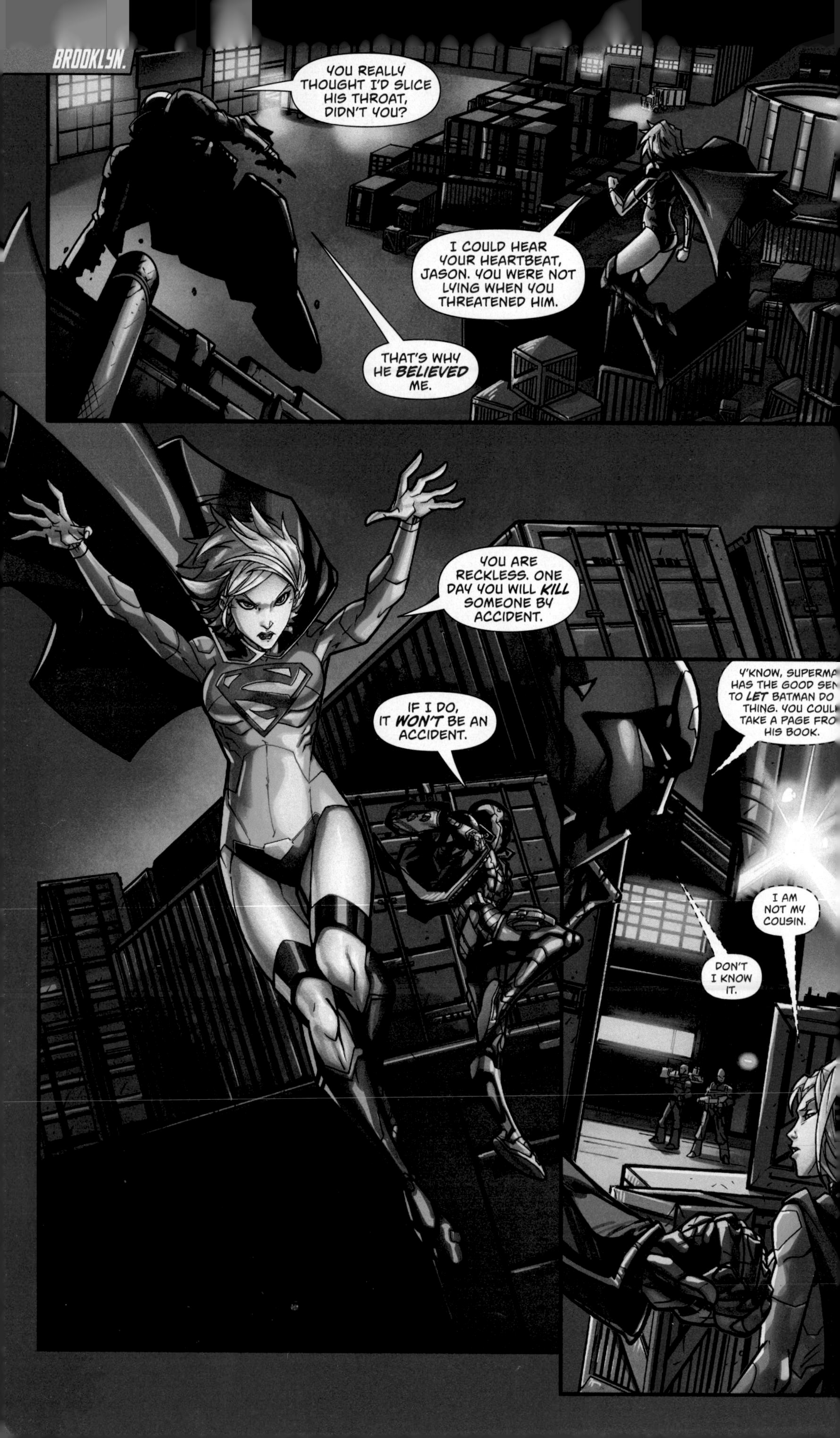
BROOKLYN.
YOU REALLY THOUGHT I'D SLICE HIS THROAT, DIDN'T YOU?
I COULD HEAR YOUR HEARTBEAT, JASON. YOU WERE NOT LYING WHEN YOU THREATENED HIM.
THAT'S WHY HE BELIEVED ME.
YOU ARE RECKLESS. ONE DAY YOU WILL KILL SOMEONE BY ACCIDENT.
IF I DO, IT WON'T BE AN ACCIDENT.
I AM NOT MY COUSIN.
DON'T I KNOW IT.

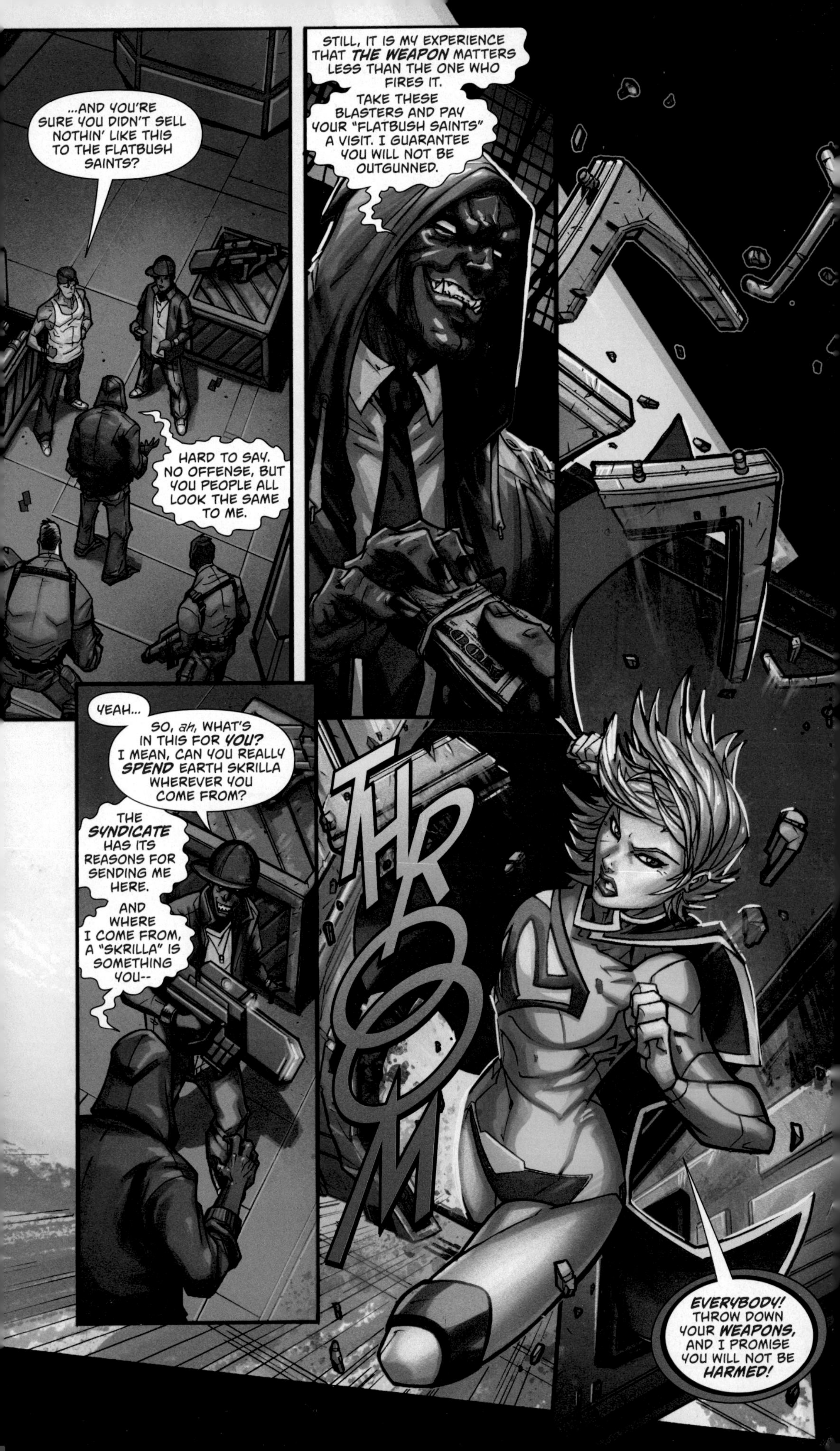
...AND YOU'RE SURE YOU DIDN'T SELL NOTHIN' LIKE THIS TO THE FLATBUSH SAINTS?
HARD TO SAY. NO OFFENSE, BUT YOU PEOPLE ALL LOOK THE SAME TO ME.
STILL, IT IS MY EXPERIENCE THAT THE WEAPON MATTERS LESS THAN THE ONE WHO FIRES IT.
TAKE THESE BLASTERS AND PAY YOUR "FLATBUSH SAINTS" A VISIT. I GUARANTEE YOU WILL NOT BE OUTGUNNED.
YEAH...
SO, ah, WHAT'S IN THIS FOR YOU? I MEAN, CAN YOU REALLY SPEND EARTH SKRILLA WHEREVER YOU COME FROM?
THE SYNDICATE HAS ITS REASONS FOR SENDING ME HERE.
AND WHERE I COME FROM, A "SKRILLA" IS SOMETHING YOU--
THROOM
EVERYBODY! THROW DOWN YOUR WEAPONS, AND I PROMISE YOU WILL NOT BE HARMED!

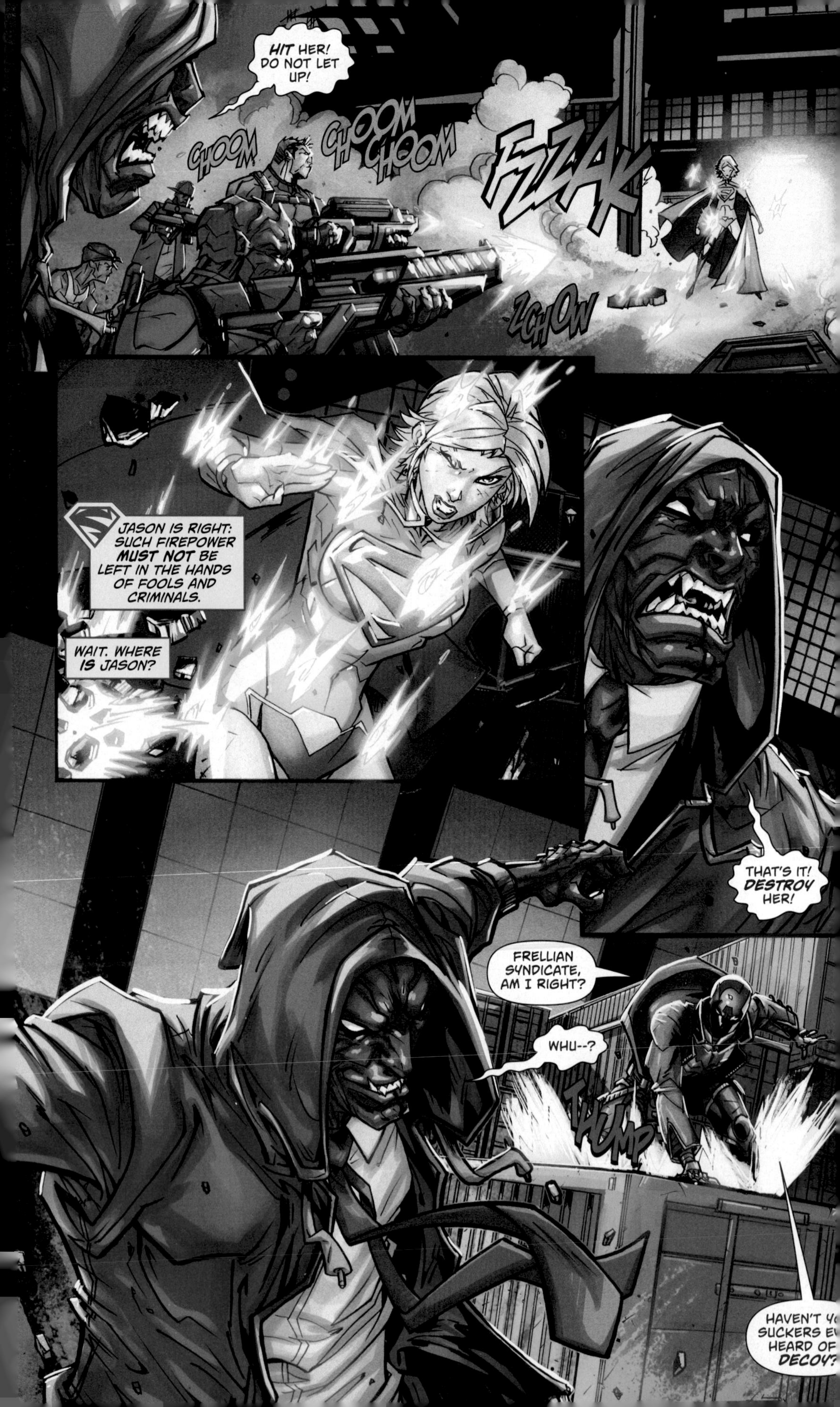
HIT HER! DO NOT LET UP!
CHOOM
CHOOM CHOOM CHOOM
FZZAK
ZCHOW
JASON IS RIGHT: SUCH FIREPOWER MUST NOT BE LEFT IN THE HANDS OF FOOLS AND CRIMINALS.
WAIT. WHERE IS JASON?
THAT'S IT! DESTROY HER!
FRELLIAN SYNDICATE, AM I RIGHT?
WHU--?
THUMP
HAVEN'T YO SUCKERS EV HEARD OF DECOY?

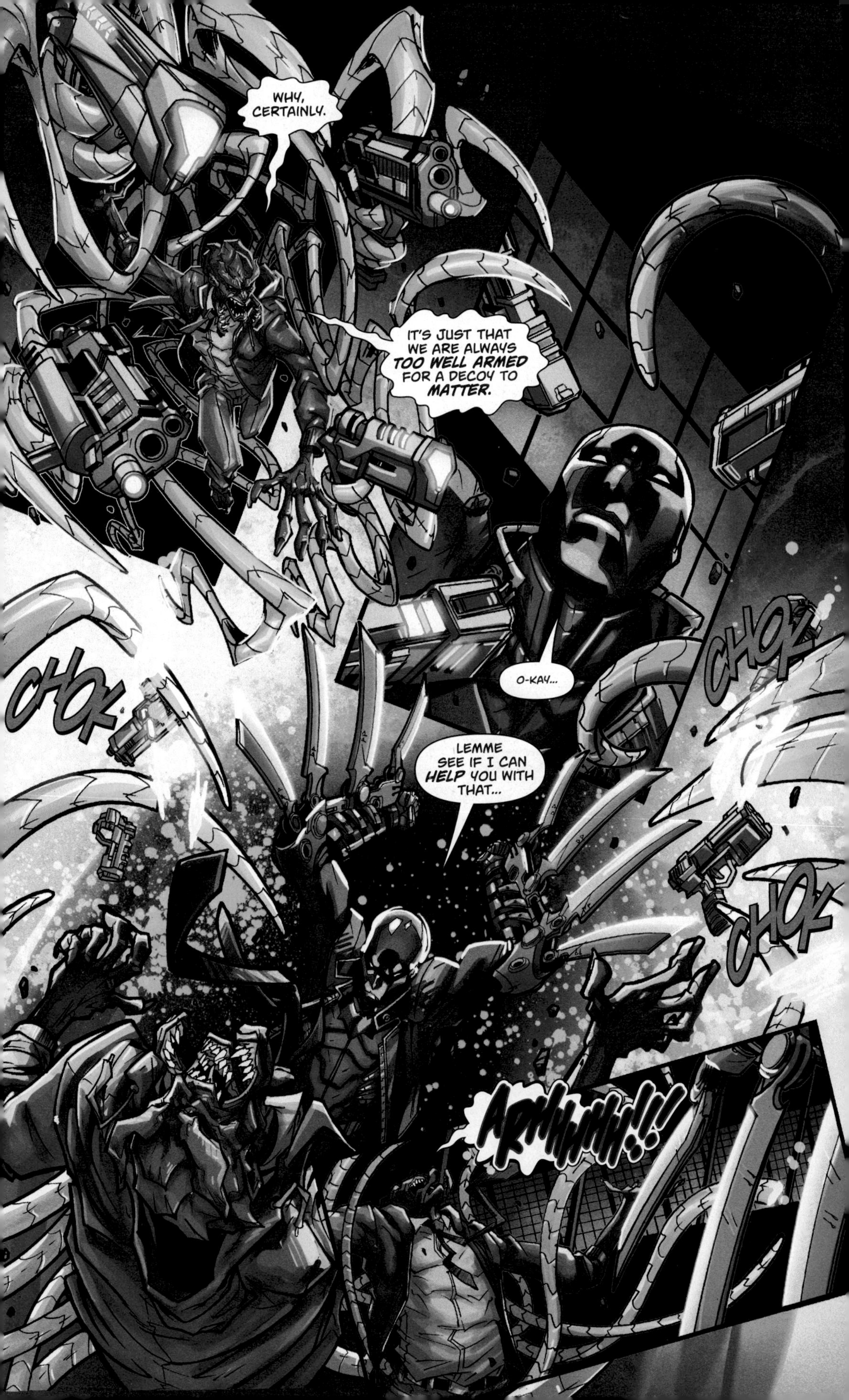
WHY, CERTAINLY.
IT'S JUST THAT WE ARE ALWAYS TOO WELL ARMED FOR A DECOY TO MATTER.
O-KAY...
LEMME SEE IF I CAN HELP YOU WITH THAT...
CHOK
CHOK
CHOK
ARHHHHH!!!

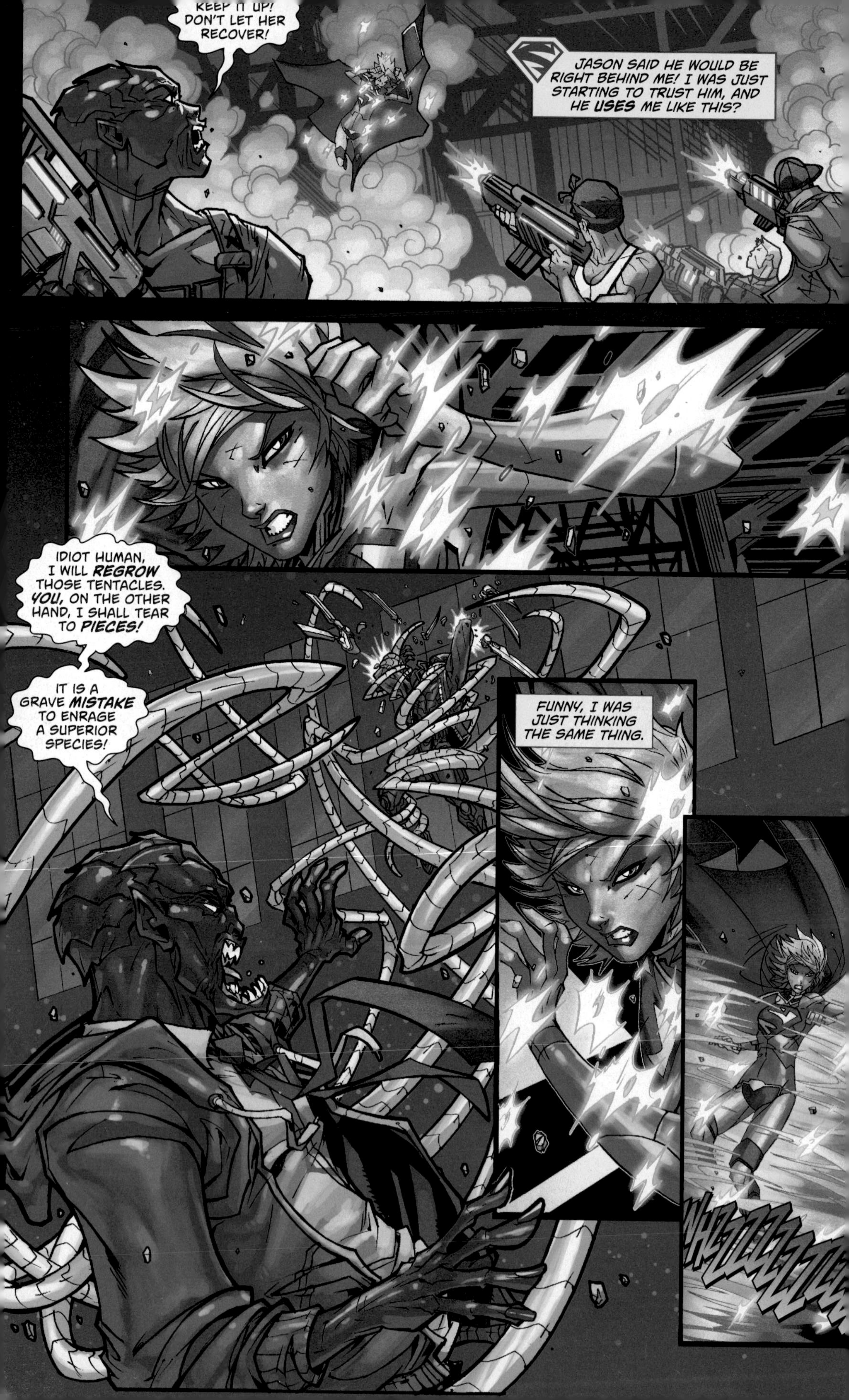
KEEP IT UP! DON'T LET HER RECOVER!
JASON SAID HE WOULD BE RIGHT BEHIND ME! I WAS JUST STARTING TO TRUST HIM, AND HE USES ME LIKE THIS?
IDIOT HUMAN, I WILL REGROW THOSE TENTACLES. YOU, ON THE OTHER HAND, I SHALL TEAR TO PIECES!
IT IS A GRAVE MISTAKE TO ENRAGE A SUPERIOR SPECIES!
FUNNY, I WAS JUST THINKING THE SAME THING.
WHZZZZZZZ

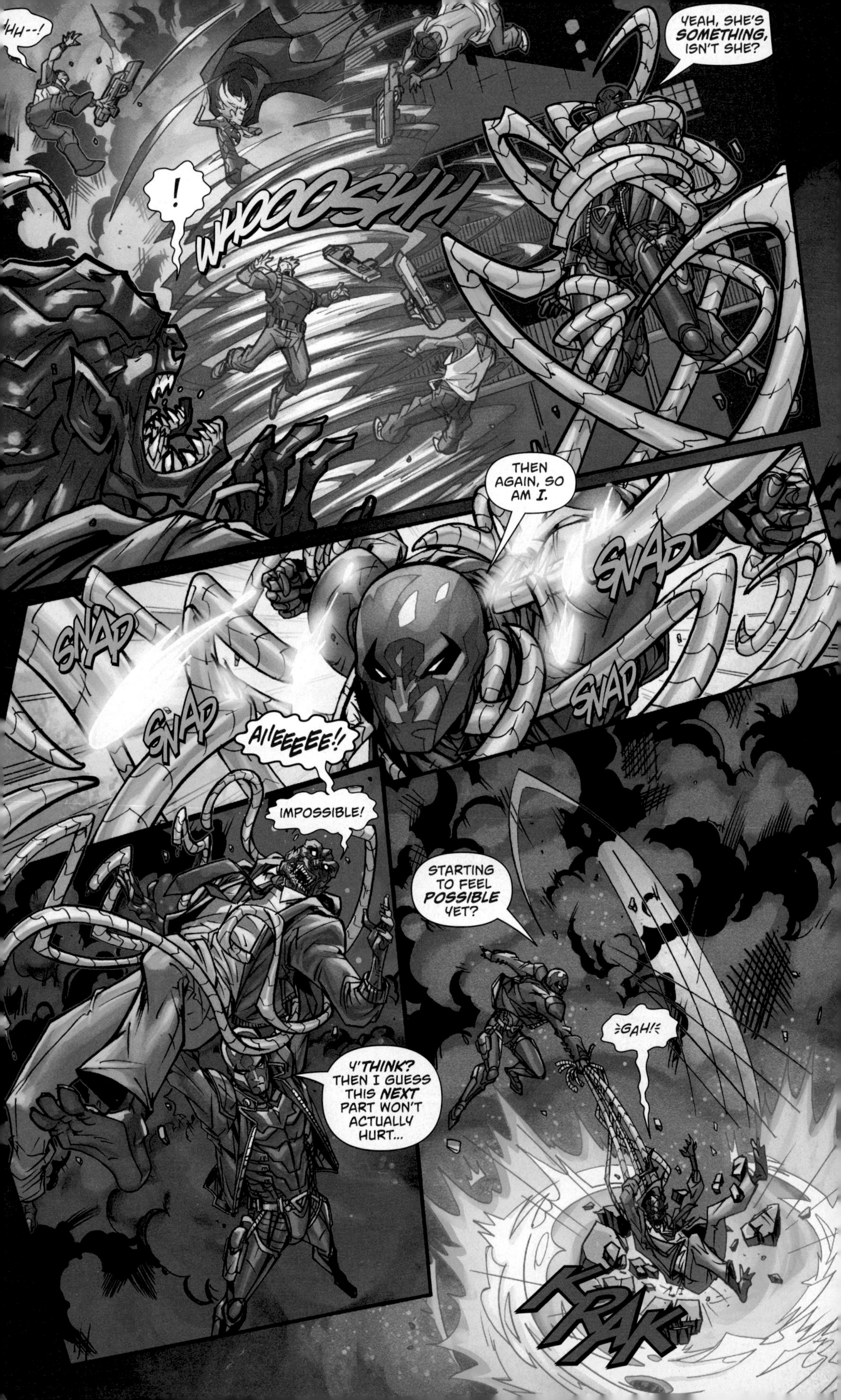

HH--!
YEAH, SHE'S SOMETHING, ISN'T SHE?
!
WHOOOSHH
THEN AGAIN, SO AM I.
SNAP
SNAP
SNAP
SNAP
AIIEEEEE!!
IMPOSSIBLE!
Y'THINK? THEN I GUESS THIS NEXT PART WON'T ACTUALLY HURT...
STARTING TO FEEL POSSIBLE YET?
GAH!
KRAK

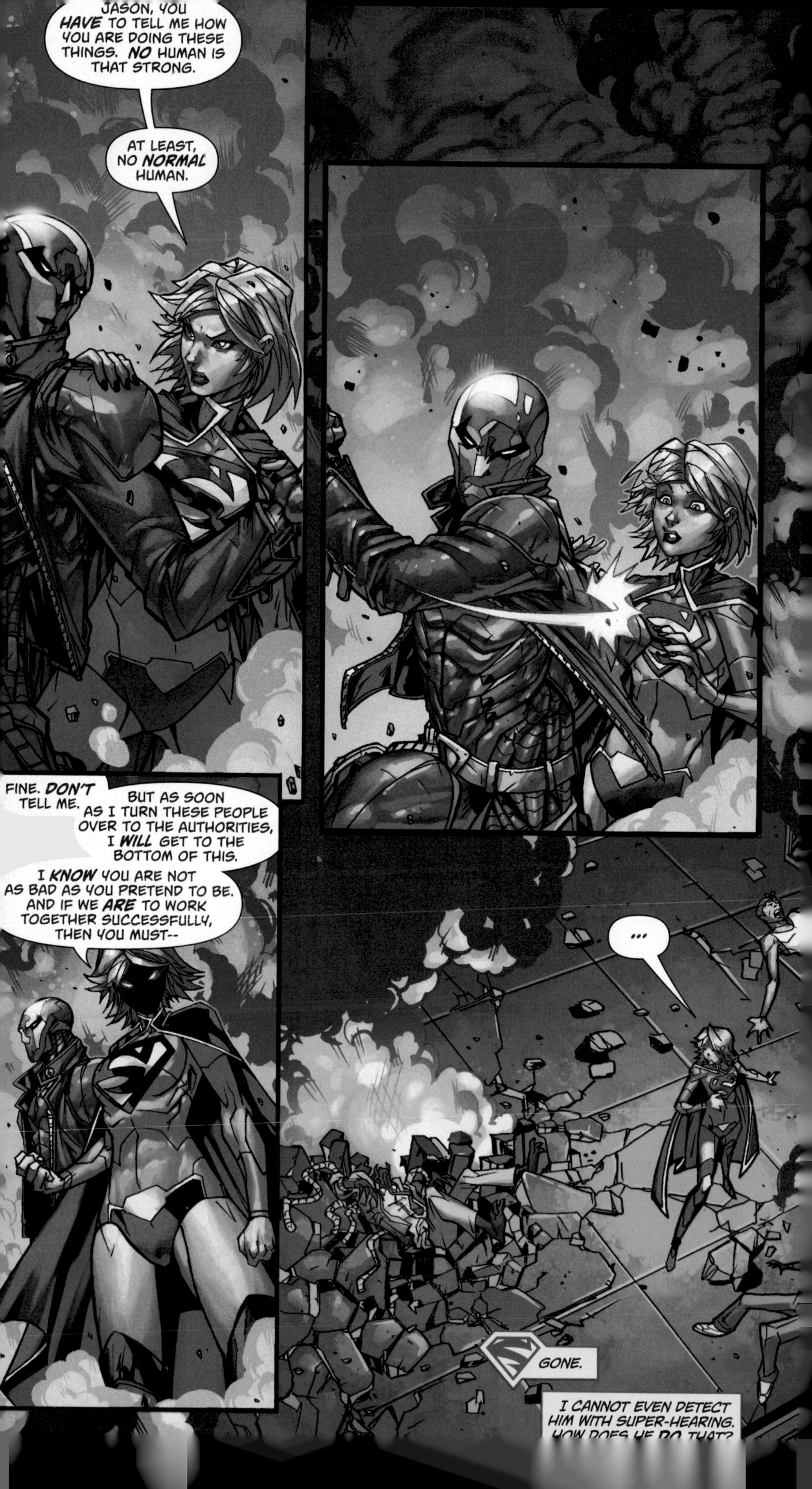
JASON, YOU HAVE TO TELL ME HOW YOU ARE DOING THESE THINGS. NO HUMAN IS THAT STRONG.
AT LEAST, NO NORMAL HUMAN.
FINE. DON'T TELL ME.
BUT AS SOON AS I TURN THESE PEOPLE OVER TO THE AUTHORITIES, I WILL GET TO THE BOTTOM OF THIS.
I KNOW YOU ARE NOT AS BAD AS YOU PRETEND TO BE. AND IF WE ARE TO WORK TOGETHER SUCCESSFULLY, THEN YOU MUST--
...
GONE.
I CANNOT EVEN DETECT HIM WITH SUPER-HEARING.

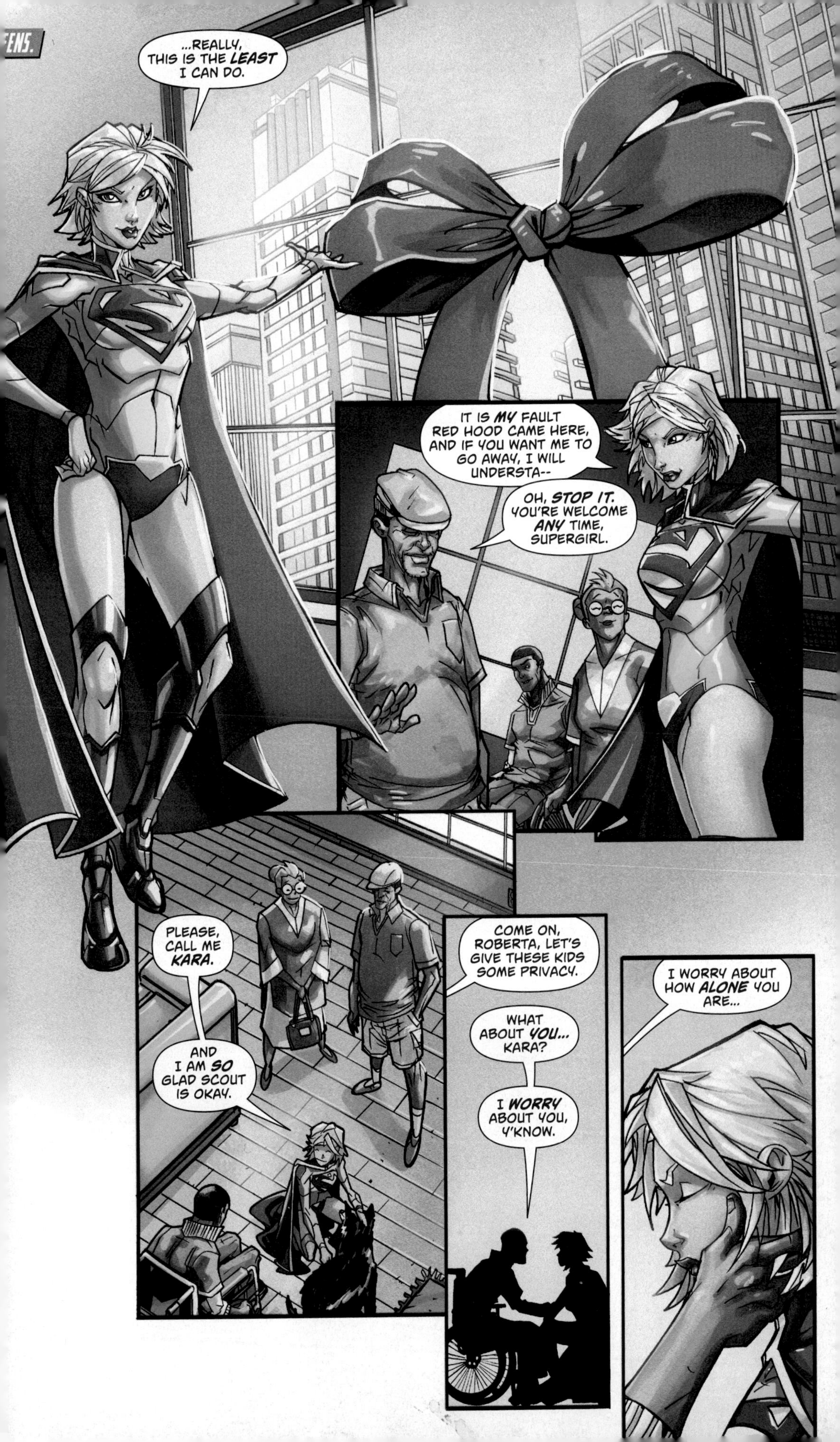

ENS.
...REALLY, THIS IS THE LEAST I CAN DO.
IT IS MY FAULT RED HOOD CAME HERE, AND IF YOU WANT ME TO GO AWAY, I WILL UNDERSTA--
OH, STOP IT. YOU'RE WELCOME ANY TIME, SUPERGIRL.
PLEASE, CALL ME KARA.
AND I AM SO GLAD SCOUT IS OKAY.
COME ON, ROBERTA, LET'S GIVE THESE KIDS SOME PRIVACY.
WHAT ABOUT YOU... KARA?
I WORRY ABOUT YOU, Y'KNOW.
I WORRY ABOUT HOW ALONE YOU ARE...

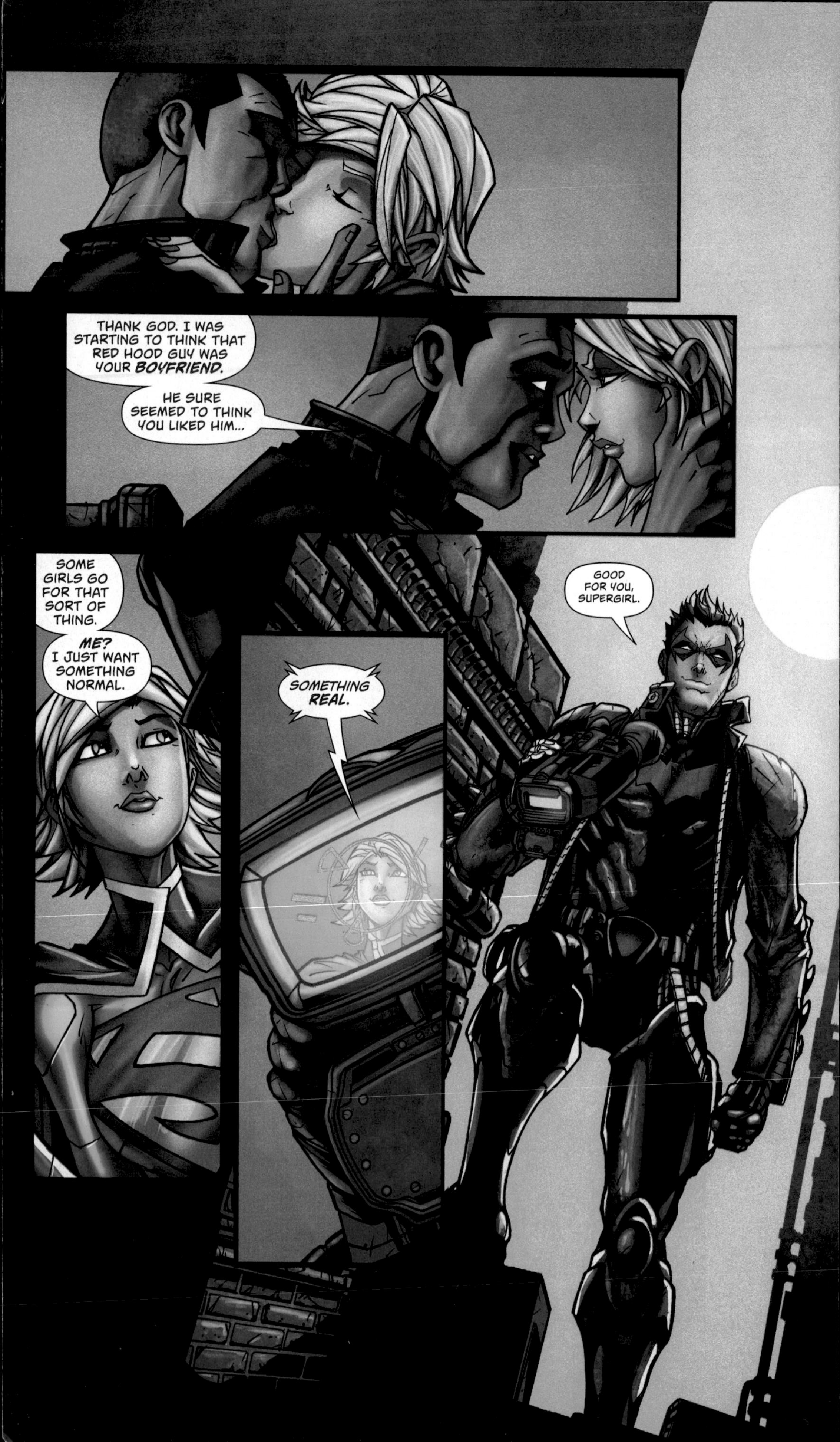

THANK GOD. I WAS STARTING TO THINK THAT RED HOOD GUY WAS YOUR BOYFRIEND.
HE SURE SEEMED TO THINK YOU LIKED HIM...
SOME GIRLS GO FOR THAT SORT OF THING.
ME? I JUST WANT SOMETHING NORMAL.
SOMETHING REAL.
GOOD FOR YOU, SUPERGIRL.

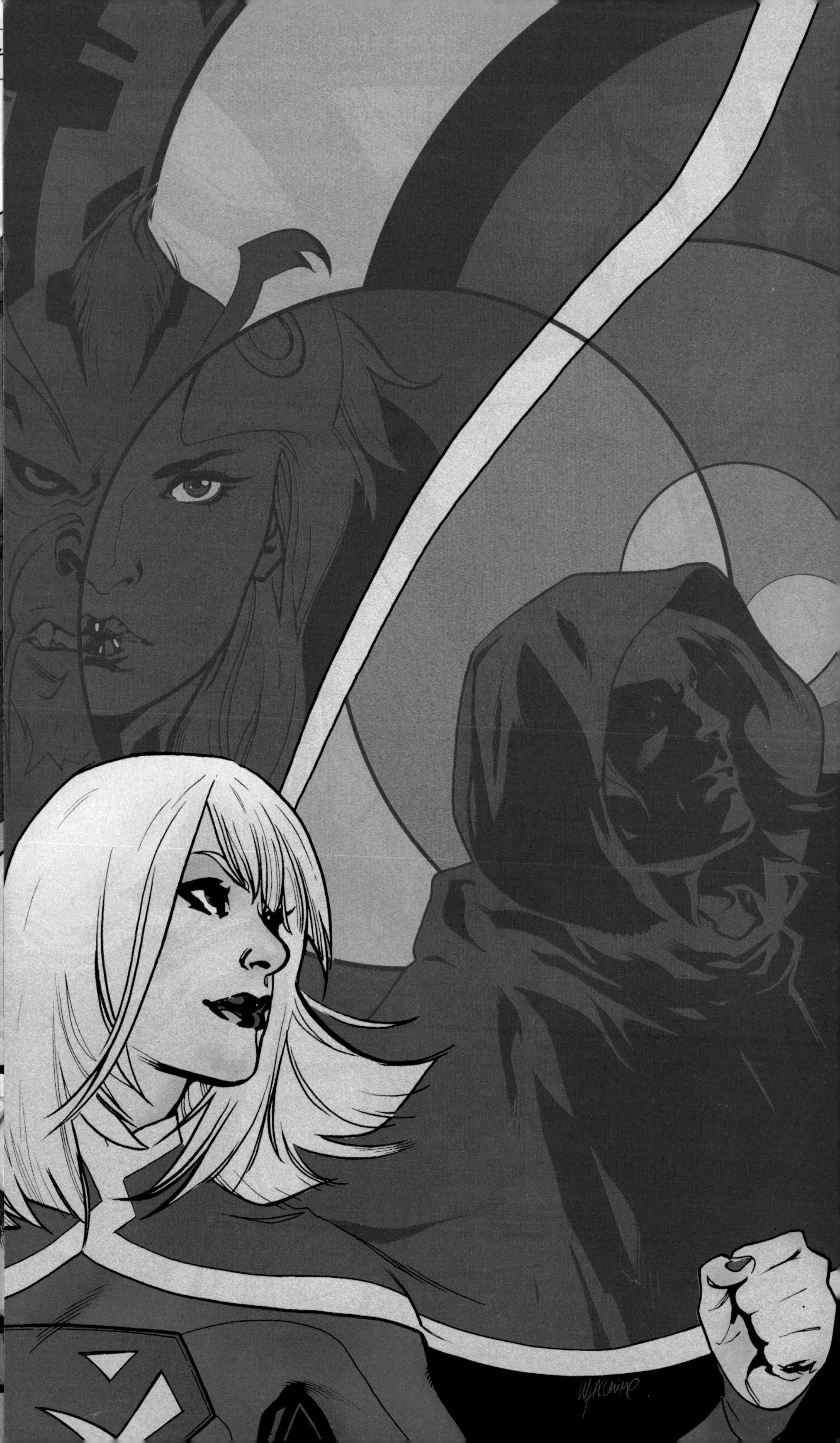

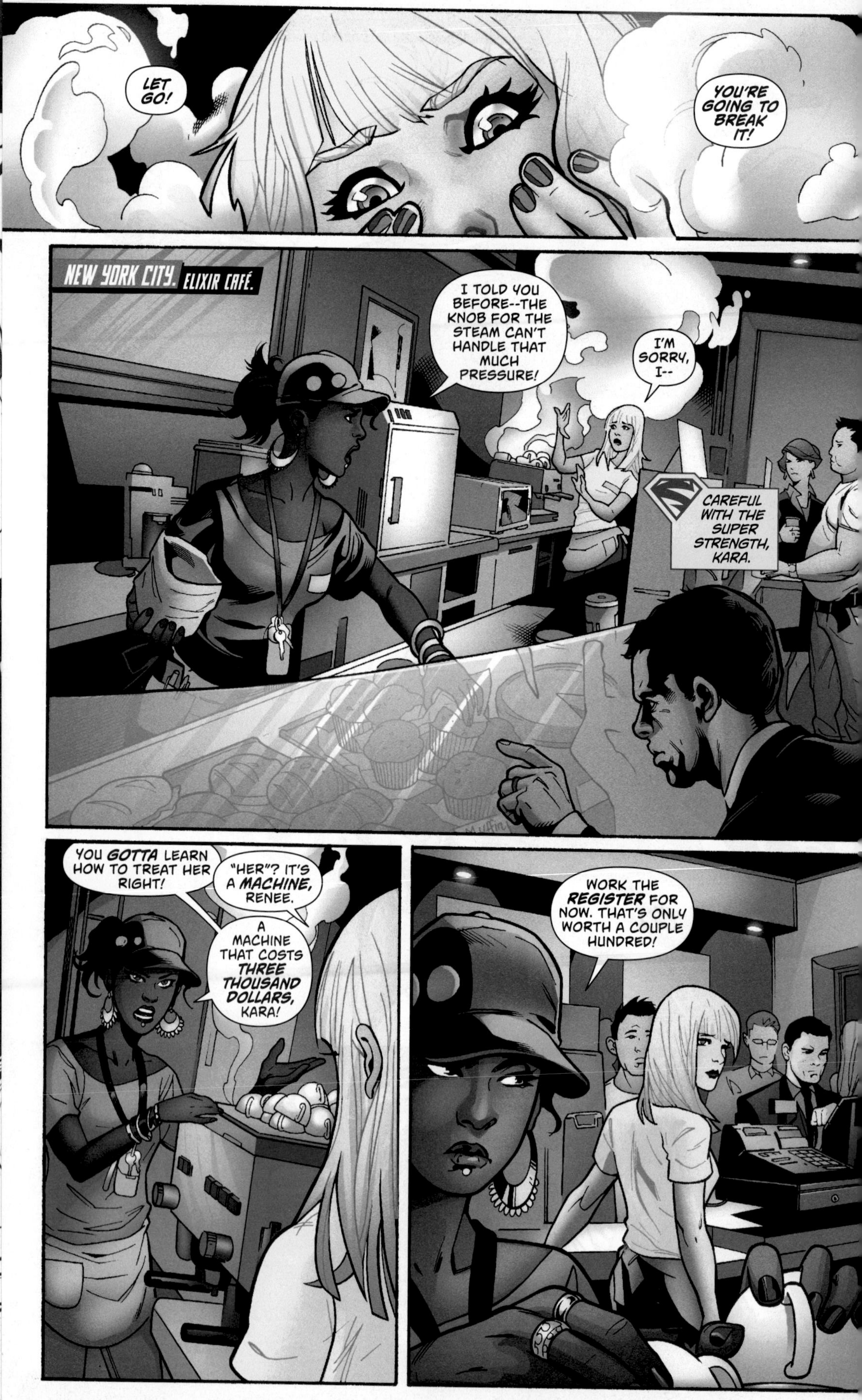
LET GO!
YOU'RE GOING TO BREAK IT!
NEW YORK CITY. ELIXIR CAFÉ.
I TOLD YOU BEFORE--THE KNOB FOR THE STEAM CAN'T HANDLE THAT MUCH PRESSURE!
I'M SORRY, I--
CAREFUL WITH THE SUPER STRENGTH, KARA.
YOU GOTTA LEARN HOW TO TREAT HER RIGHT!
"HER"? IT'S A MACHINE, RENEE.
A MACHINE THAT COSTS THREE THOUSAND DOLLARS, KARA!
WORK THE REGISTER FOR NOW. THAT'S ONLY WORTH A COUPLE HUNDRED!

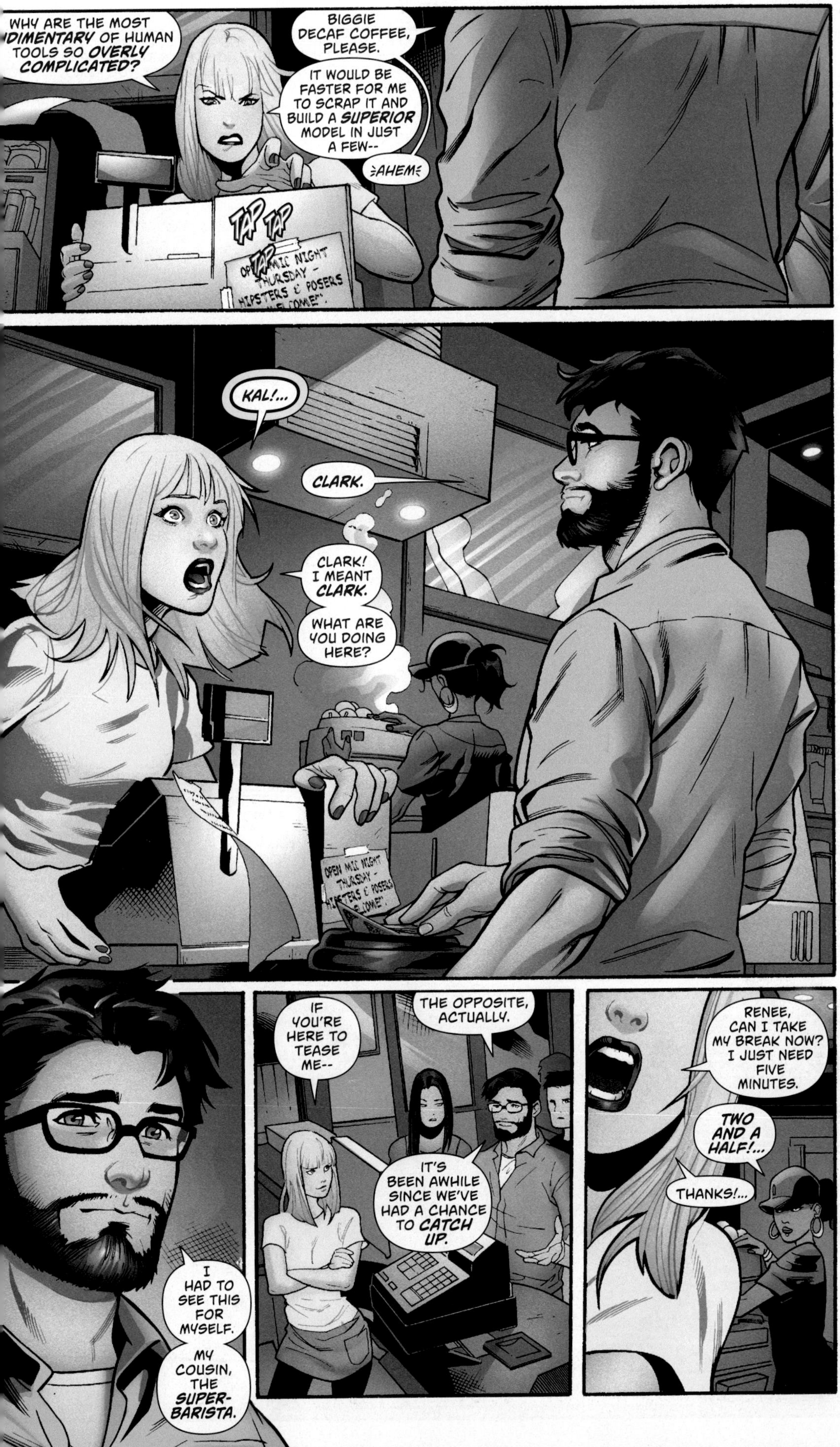
WHY ARE THE MOST RUDIMENTARY OF HUMAN TOOLS SO OVERLY COMPLICATED?
BIGGIE DECAF COFFEE, PLEASE.
IT WOULD BE FASTER FOR ME TO SCRAP IT AND BUILD A SUPERIOR MODEL IN JUST A FEW--
AHEM
TAP TAP TAP
OPEN MIC NIGHT THURSDAY - HIPSTERS & POSERS WELCOME!
KAL!...
CLARK.
CLARK! I MEANT CLARK.
WHAT ARE YOU DOING HERE?
OPEN MIC NIGHT THURSDAY - HIPSTERS & POSERS WELCOME!
I HAD TO SEE THIS FOR MYSELF.
MY COUSIN, THE SUPER-BARISTA.
IF YOU'RE HERE TO TEASE ME--
THE OPPOSITE, ACTUALLY.
IT'S BEEN AWHILE SINCE WE'VE HAD A CHANCE TO CATCH UP.
RENEE, CAN I TAKE MY BREAK NOW? I JUST NEED FIVE MINUTES.
TWO AND A HALF!...
THANKS!...

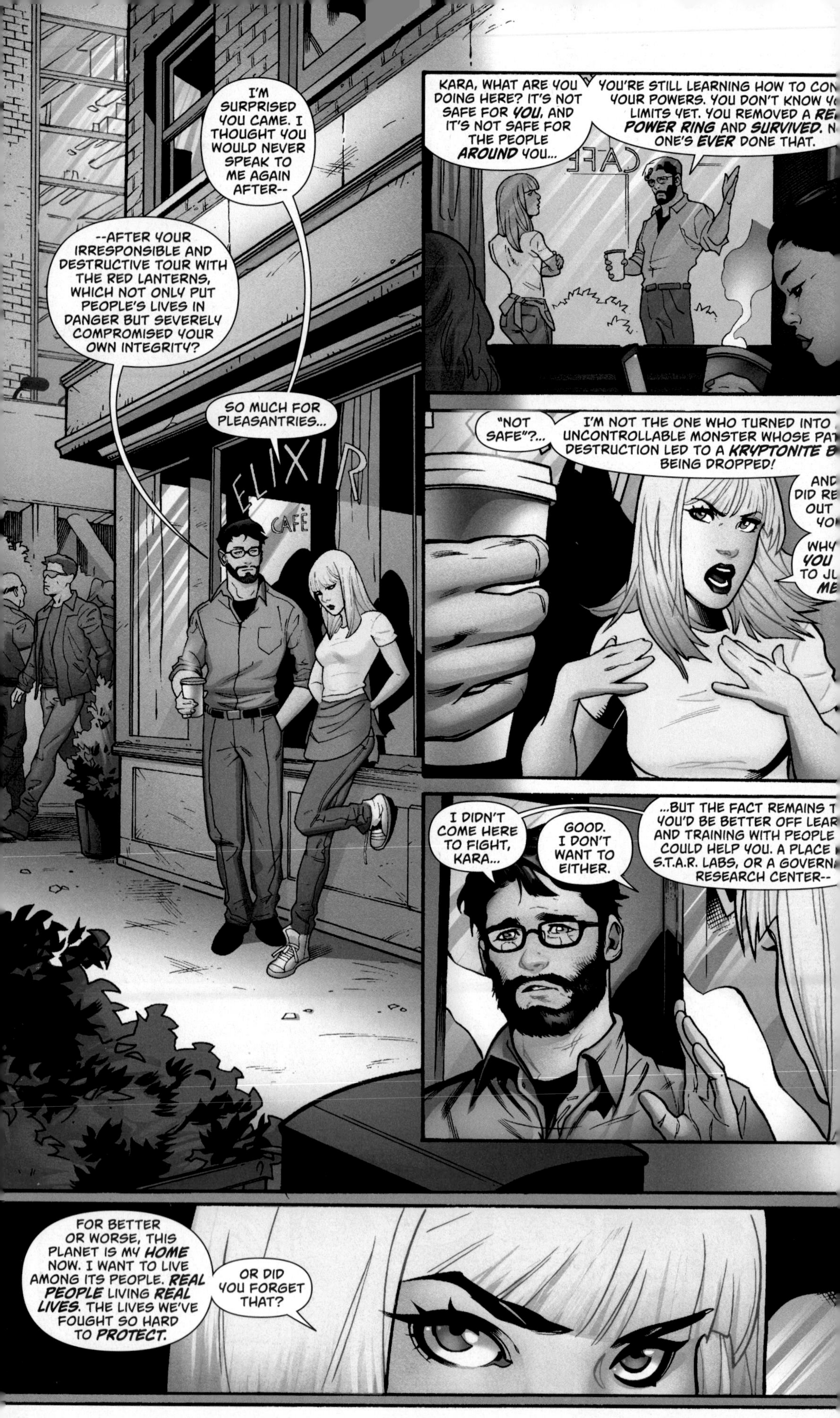

I'M SURPRISED YOU CAME. I THOUGHT YOU WOULD NEVER SPEAK TO ME AGAIN AFTER--
--AFTER YOUR IRRESPONSIBLE AND DESTRUCTIVE TOUR WITH THE RED LANTERNS, WHICH NOT ONLY PUT PEOPLE'S LIVES IN DANGER BUT SEVERELY COMPROMISED YOUR OWN INTEGRITY?
SO MUCH FOR PLEASANTRIES...
ELIXIR
CAFÉ
KARA, WHAT ARE YOU DOING HERE? IT'S NOT SAFE FOR *YOU*, AND IT'S NOT SAFE FOR THE PEOPLE *AROUND* YOU...
YOU'RE STILL LEARNING HOW TO CON YOUR POWERS. YOU DON'T KNOW YO LIMITS YET. YOU REMOVED A *RE POWER RING* AND *SURVIVED*. N ONE'S *EVER* DONE THAT.
"NOT SAFE"?...
I'M NOT THE ONE WHO TURNED INTO UNCONTROLLABLE MONSTER WHOSE PAT DESTRUCTION LED TO A *KRYPTONITE* B BEING DROPPED!
I DIDN'T COME HERE TO FIGHT, KARA...
GOOD. I DON'T WANT TO EITHER.
...BUT THE FACT REMAINS T YOU'D BE BETTER OFF LEAR AND TRAINING WITH PEOPLE COULD HELP YOU. A PLACE S.T.A.R. LABS, OR A GOVERN RESEARCH CENTER--
FOR BETTER OR WORSE, THIS PLANET IS MY *HOME* NOW. I WANT TO LIVE AMONG ITS PEOPLE. *REAL PEOPLE* LIVING *REAL LIVES*. THE LIVES WE'VE FOUGHT SO HARD TO *PROTECT*.
OR DID YOU FORGET THAT?

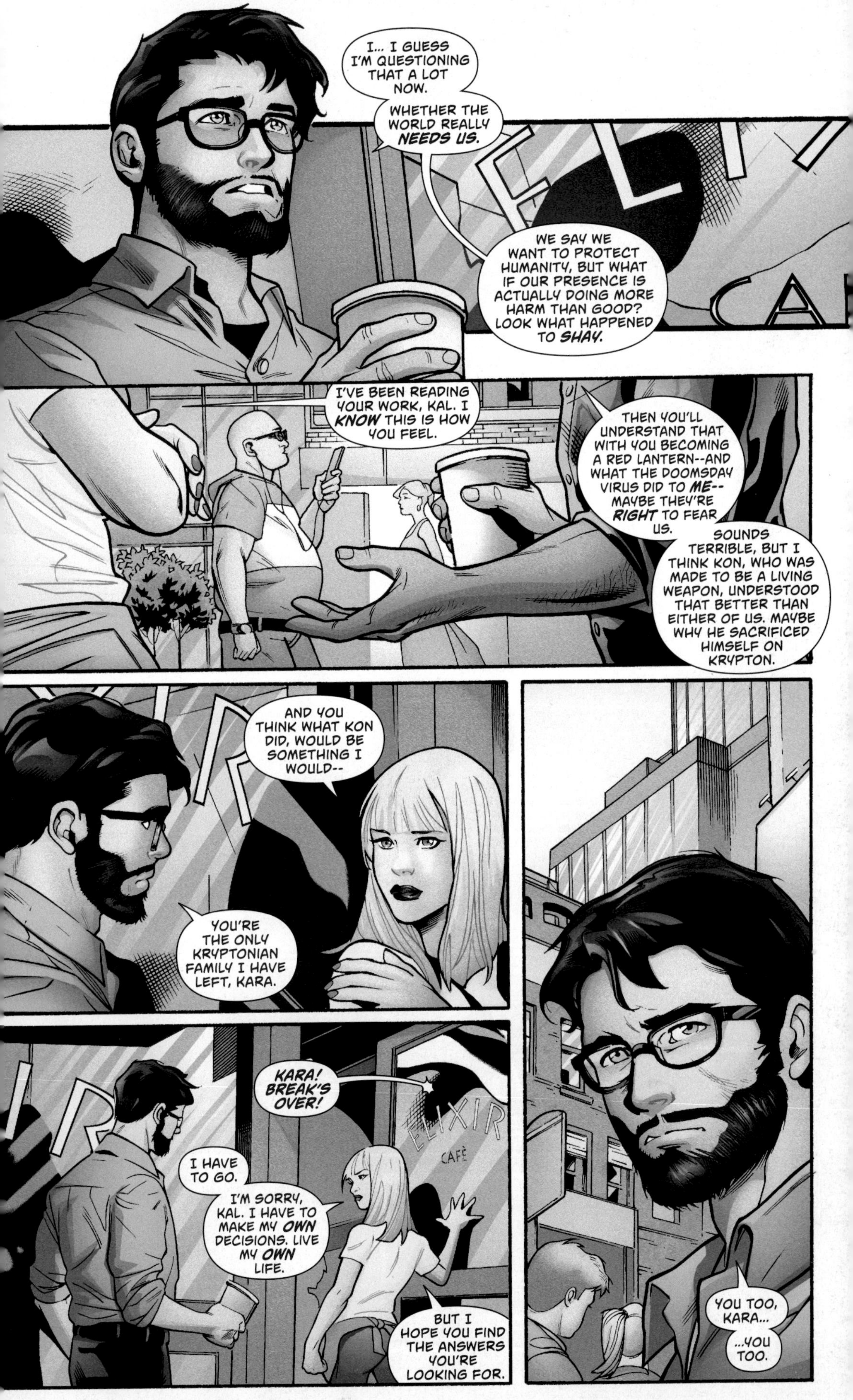

I... I GUESS I'M QUESTIONING THAT A LOT NOW.
WHETHER THE WORLD REALLY NEEDS US.
WE SAY WE WANT TO PROTECT HUMANITY, BUT WHAT IF OUR PRESENCE IS ACTUALLY DOING MORE HARM THAN GOOD? LOOK WHAT HAPPENED TO SHAY.
CA
I'VE BEEN READING YOUR WORK, KAL. I KNOW THIS IS HOW YOU FEEL.
THEN YOU'LL UNDERSTAND THAT WITH YOU BECOMING A RED LANTERN--AND WHAT THE DOOMSDAY VIRUS DID TO ME--MAYBE THEY'RE RIGHT TO FEAR US.
SOUNDS TERRIBLE, BUT I THINK KON, WHO WAS MADE TO BE A LIVING WEAPON, UNDERSTOOD THAT BETTER THAN EITHER OF US. MAYBE WHY HE SACRIFICED HIMSELF ON KRYPTON.
AND YOU THINK WHAT KON DID, WOULD BE SOMETHING I WOULD--
YOU'RE THE ONLY KRYPTONIAN FAMILY I HAVE LEFT, KARA.
KARA! BREAK'S OVER!
ELIXIR
CAFÈ
I HAVE TO GO.
I'M SORRY, KAL. I HAVE TO MAKE MY OWN DECISIONS. LIVE MY OWN LIFE.
BUT I HOPE YOU FIND THE ANSWERS YOU'RE LOOKING FOR.
YOU TOO, KARA...
...YOU TOO.

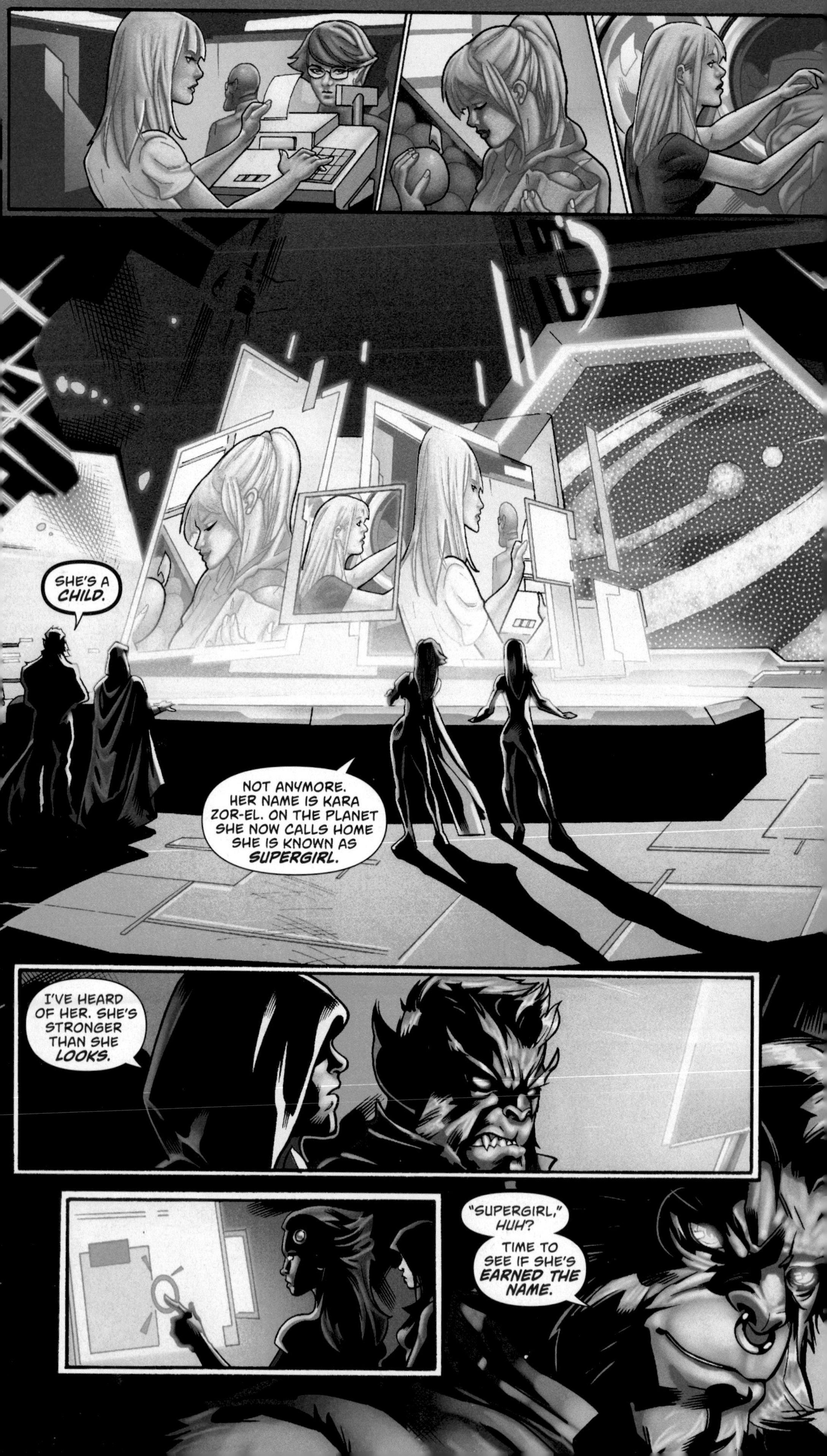
SHE'S A CHILD.
NOT ANYMORE. HER NAME IS KARA ZOR-EL. ON THE PLANET SHE NOW CALLS HOME SHE IS KNOWN AS SUPERGIRL.
I'VE HEARD OF HER. SHE'S STRONGER THAN SHE LOOKS.
"SUPERGIRL," HUH?
TIME TO SEE IF SHE'S EARNED THE NAME.

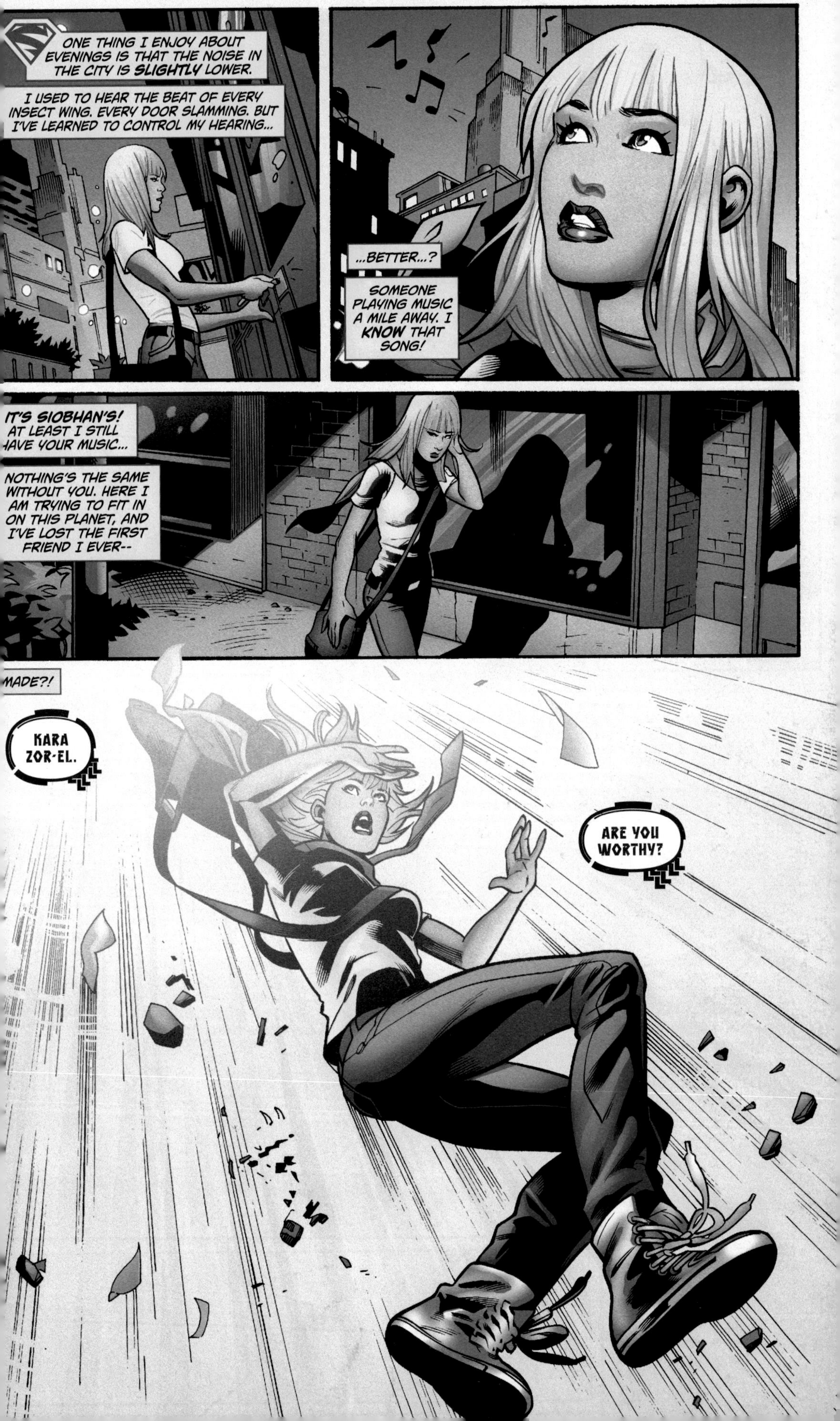
ONE THING I ENJOY ABOUT EVENINGS IS THAT THE NOISE IN THE CITY IS SLIGHTLY LOWER.
I USED TO HEAR THE BEAT OF EVERY INSECT WING. EVERY DOOR SLAMMING. BUT I'VE LEARNED TO CONTROL MY HEARING...
...BETTER...?
SOMEONE PLAYING MUSIC A MILE AWAY. I KNOW THAT SONG!
IT'S SIOBHAN'S! AT LEAST I STILL HAVE YOUR MUSIC...
NOTHING'S THE SAME WITHOUT YOU. HERE I AM TRYING TO FIT IN ON THIS PLANET, AND I'VE LOST THE FIRST FRIEND I EVER--
MADE?!
KARA ZOR-EL.
ARE YOU WORTHY?

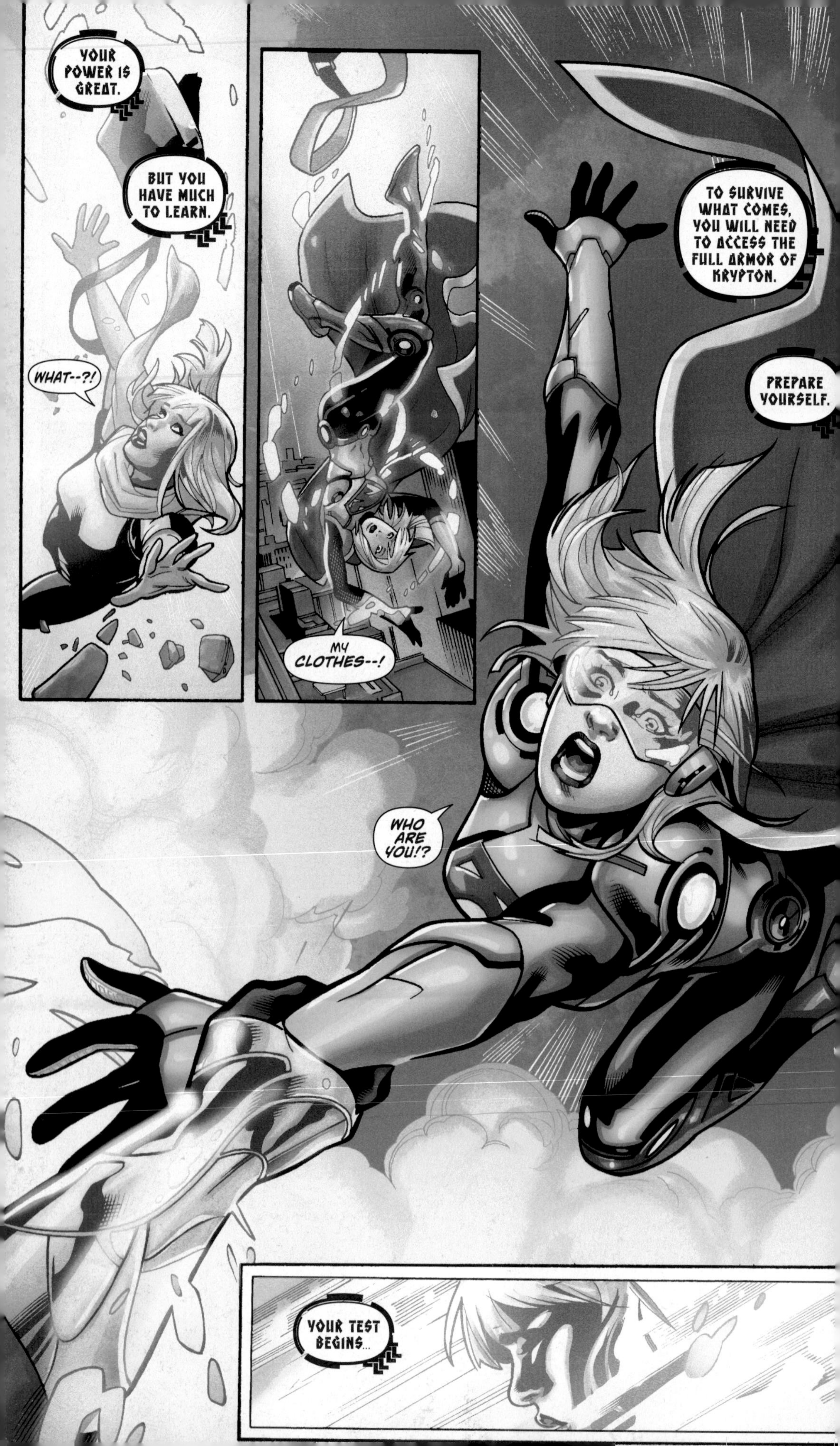
YOUR POWER IS GREAT.
BUT YOU HAVE MUCH TO LEARN.
WHAT--?!
MY CLOTHES--!
TO SURVIVE WHAT COMES, YOU WILL NEED TO ACCESS THE FULL ARMOR OF KRYPTON.
PREPARE YOURSELF.
WHO ARE YOU!?
YOUR TEST BEGINS...

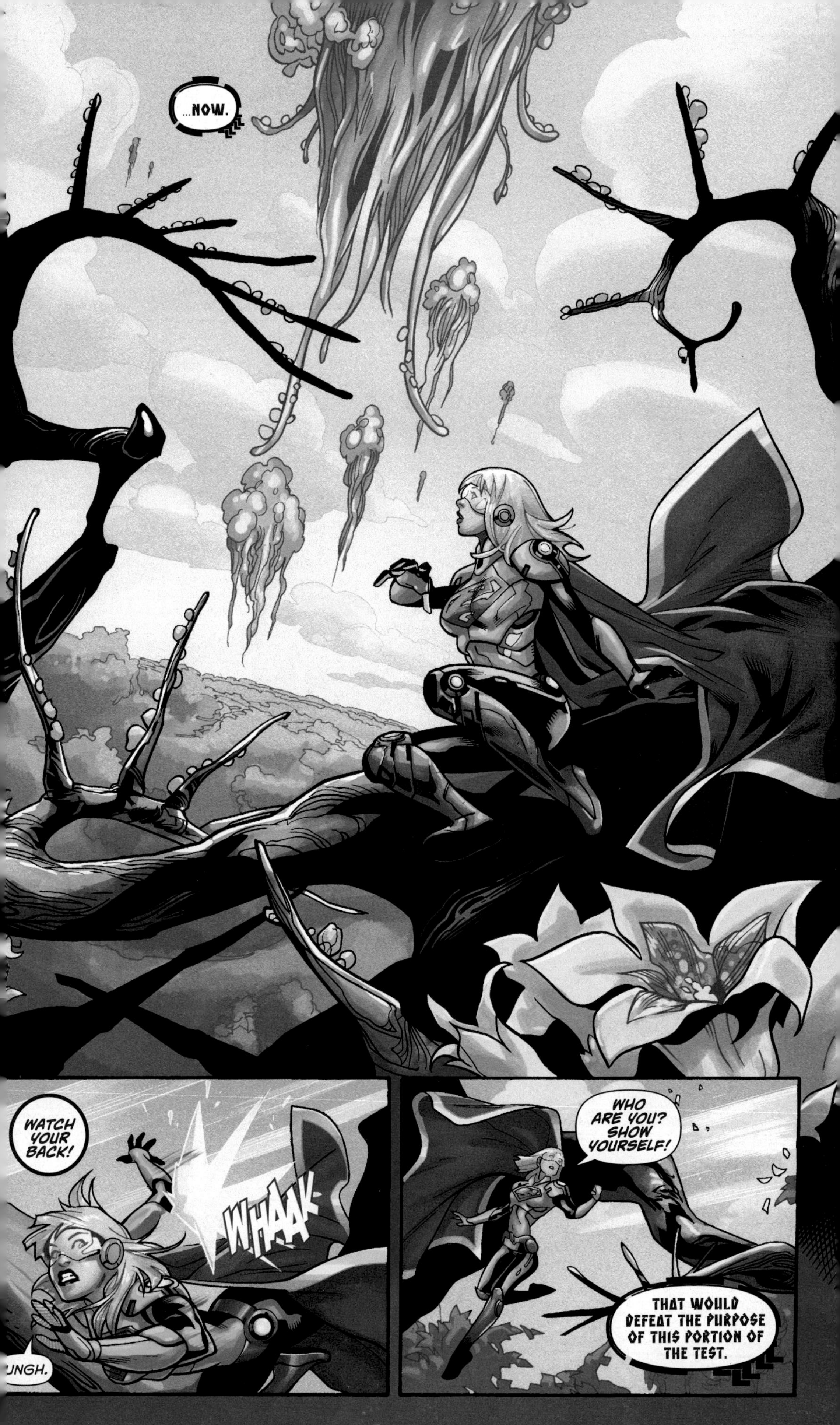
...NOW.
WATCH YOUR BACK!
WHAAK
UNGH.
WHO ARE YOU? SHOW YOURSELF!
THAT WOULD DEFEAT THE PURPOSE OF THIS PORTION OF THE TEST.

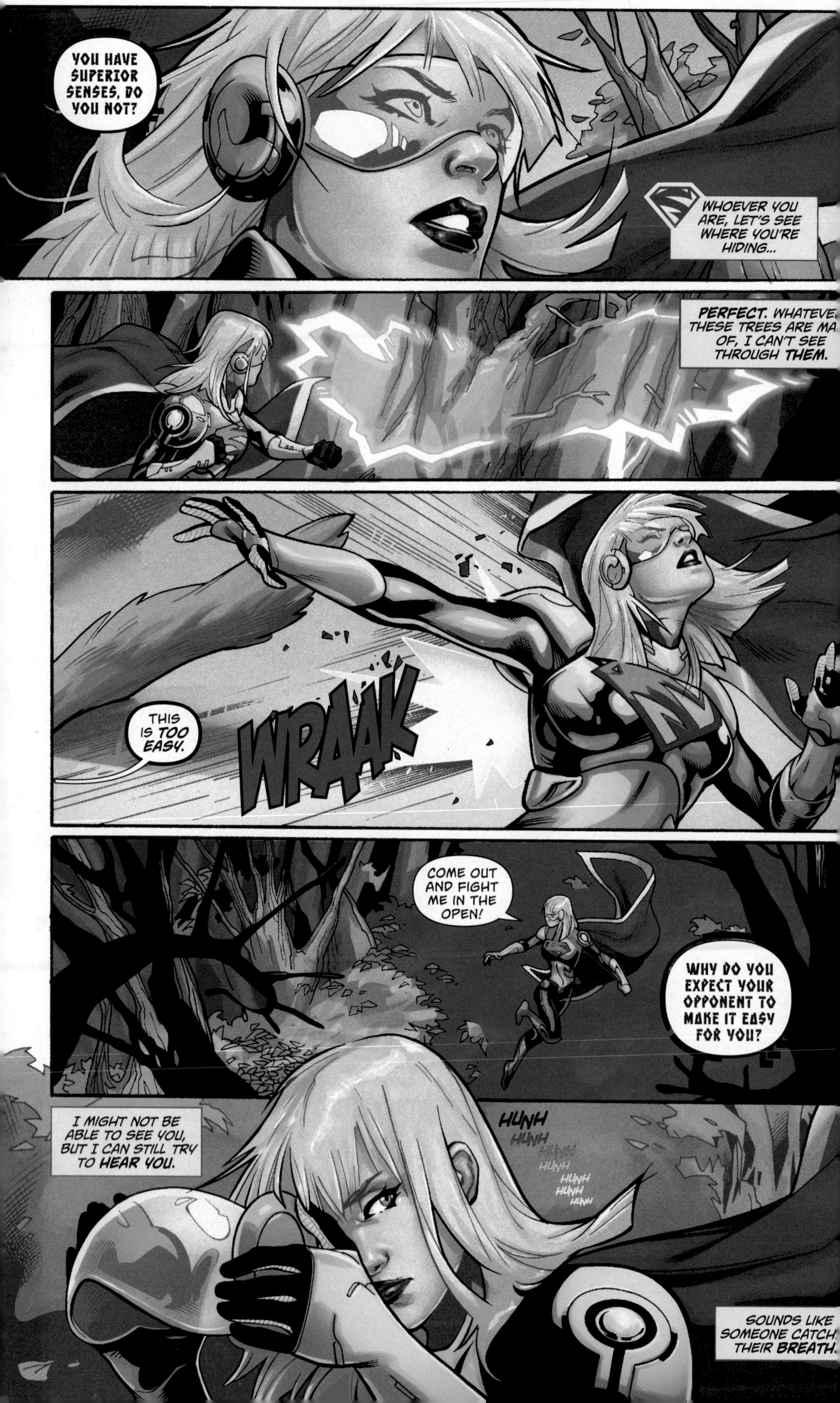
YOU HAVE SUPERIOR SENSES, DO YOU NOT?
WHOEVER YOU ARE, LET'S SEE WHERE YOU'RE HIDING...
PERFECT. WHATEVE THESE TREES ARE MA OF, I CAN'T SEE THROUGH THEM.
THIS IS TOO EASY.
WRAAK
COME OUT AND FIGHT ME IN THE OPEN!
WHY DO YOU EXPECT YOUR OPPONENT TO MAKE IT EASY FOR YOU?
I MIGHT NOT BE ABLE TO SEE YOU, BUT I CAN STILL TRY TO HEAR YOU.
HUNH HUNH HUNH HUNH HUNH HUNH HUNH
SOUNDS LIKE SOMEONE CATCH THEIR BREATH.

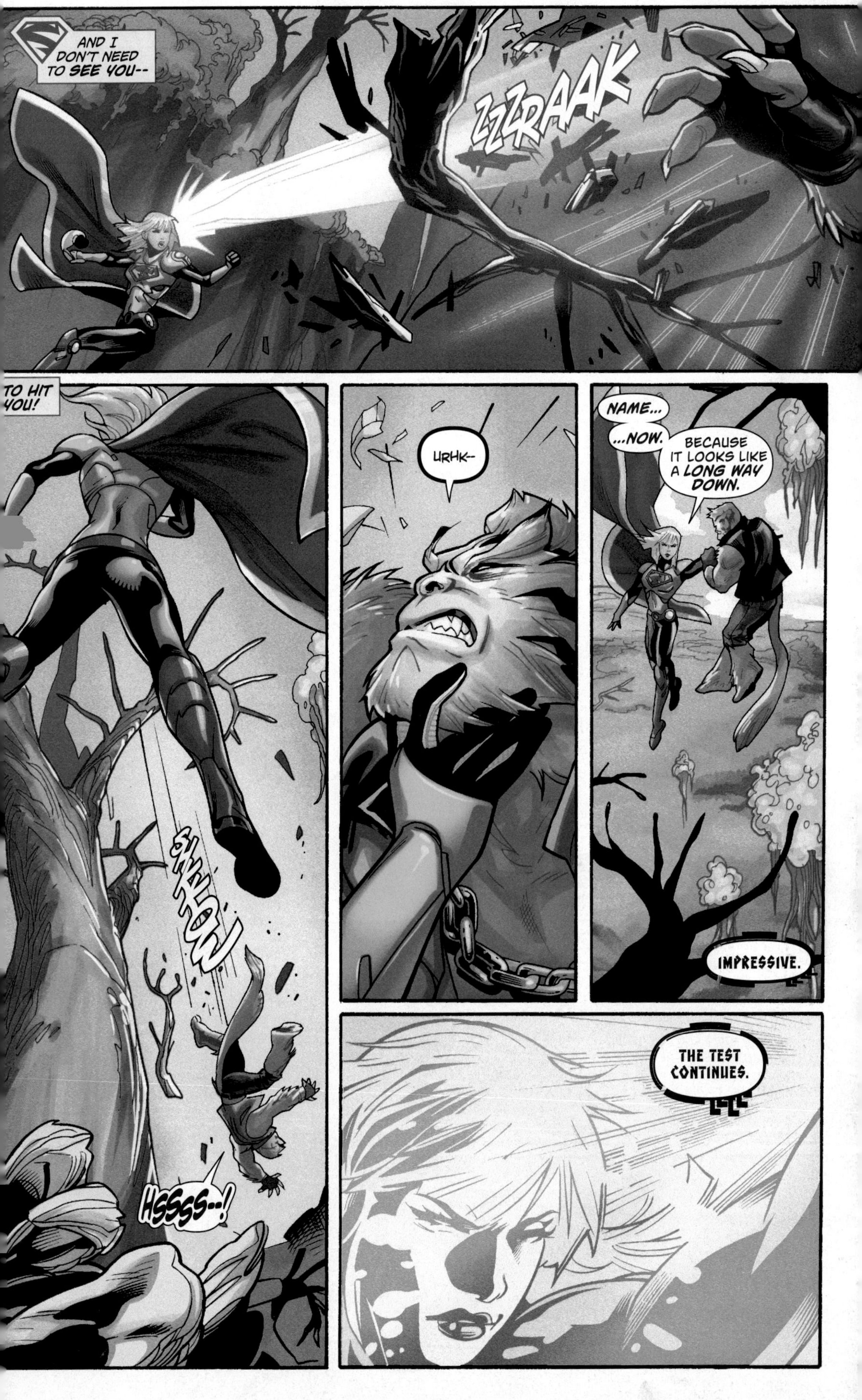
AND I DON'T NEED TO SEE YOU--
ZZZRAAK
TO HIT YOU!
SHKOW
HSSSS--!
URHK--
NAME...
...NOW.
BECAUSE IT LOOKS LIKE A LONG WAY DOWN.
IMPRESSIVE.
THE TEST CONTINUES.

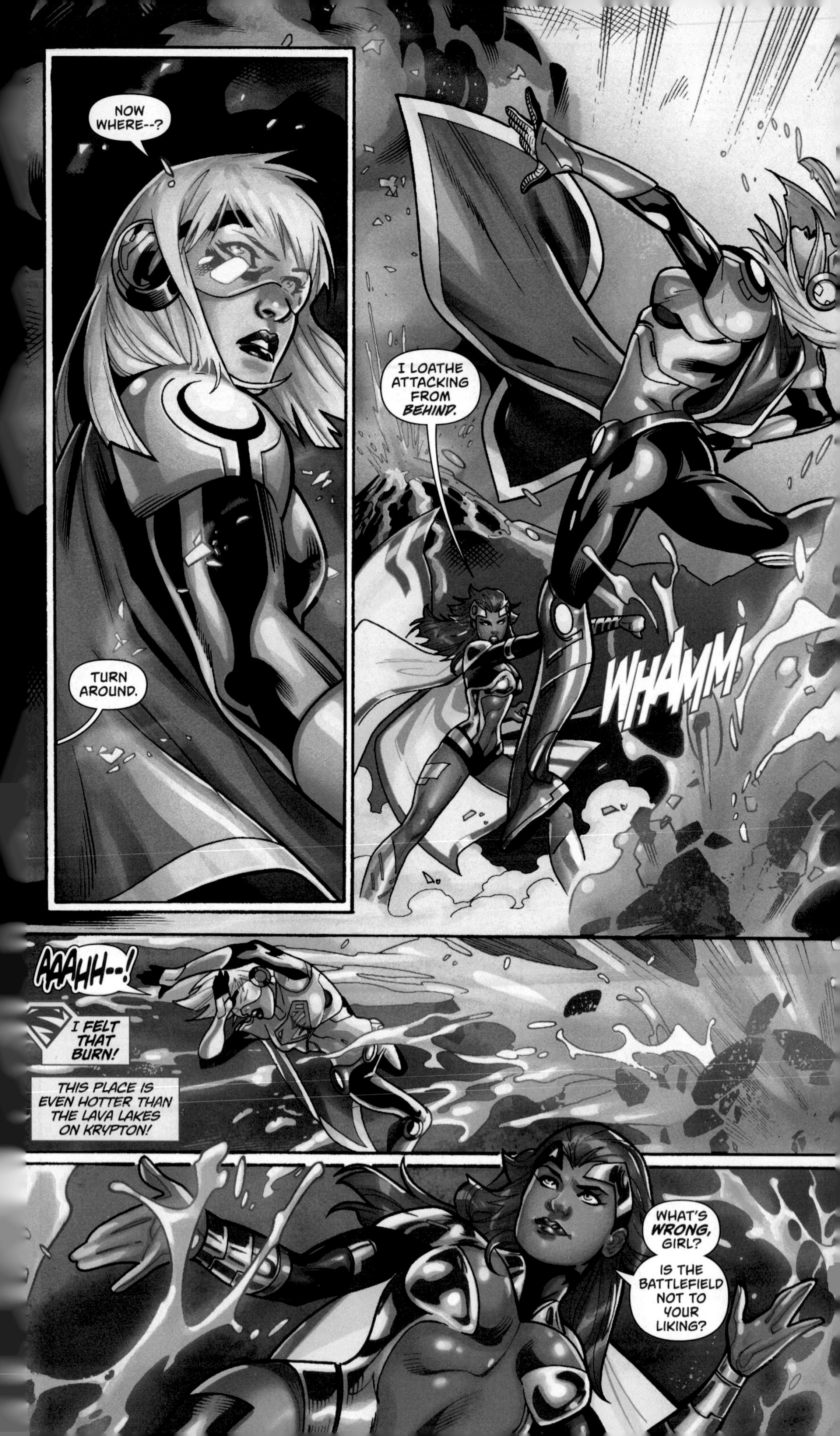
NOW WHERE--?
TURN AROUND.
I LOATHE ATTACKING FROM *BEHIND.*
WHAMM
AAAHH--!
I FELT THAT BURN!
THIS PLACE IS EVEN HOTTER THAN THE LAVA LAKES ON KRYPTON!
WHAT'S *WRONG,* GIRL?
IS THE BATTLEFIELD NOT TO YOUR LIKING?

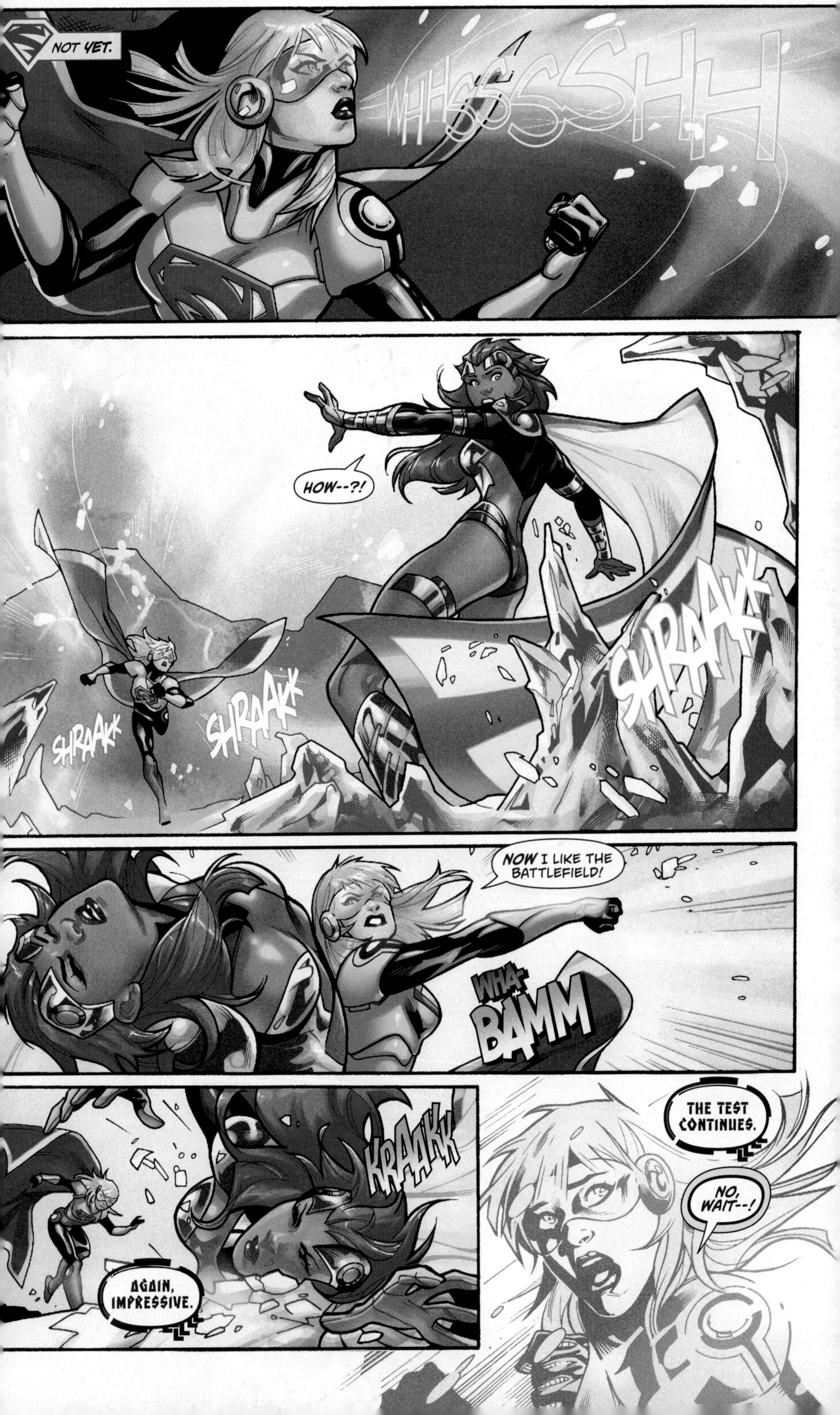
NOT YET.
WHHSSSSHH
HOW--?!
SHRAAKK
SHRAAKK
SHRAAKK
NOW I LIKE THE BATTLEFIELD!
WHA-BAMM
KRAAKK
AGAIN, IMPRESSIVE.
THE TEST CONTINUES.
NO, WAIT--!

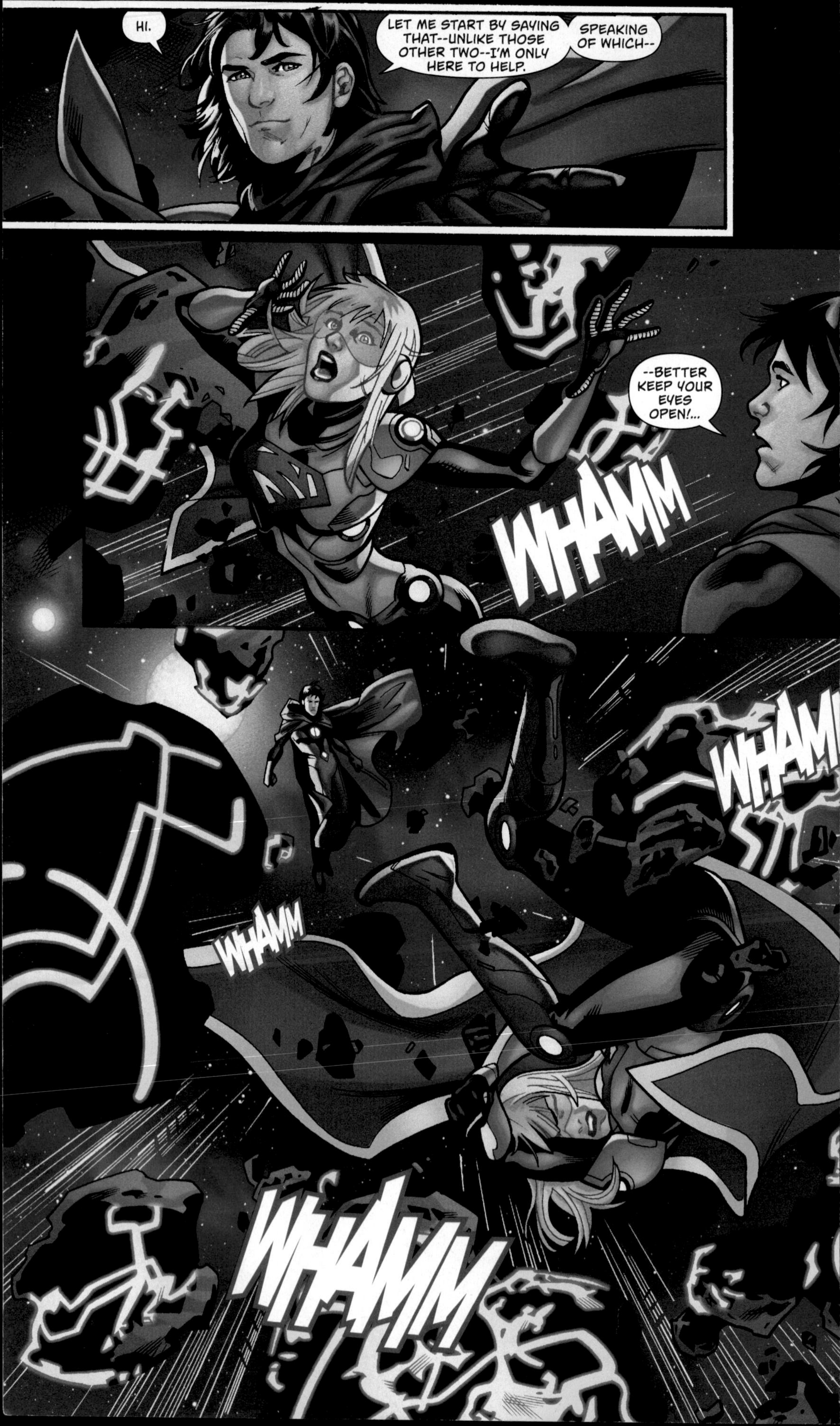

HI.
LET ME START BY SAYING THAT--UNLIKE THOSE OTHER TWO--I'M ONLY HERE TO HELP.
SPEAKING OF WHICH--
--BETTER KEEP YOUR EYES OPEN!...
WHAMM
WHAM
WHAMM
WHAMM

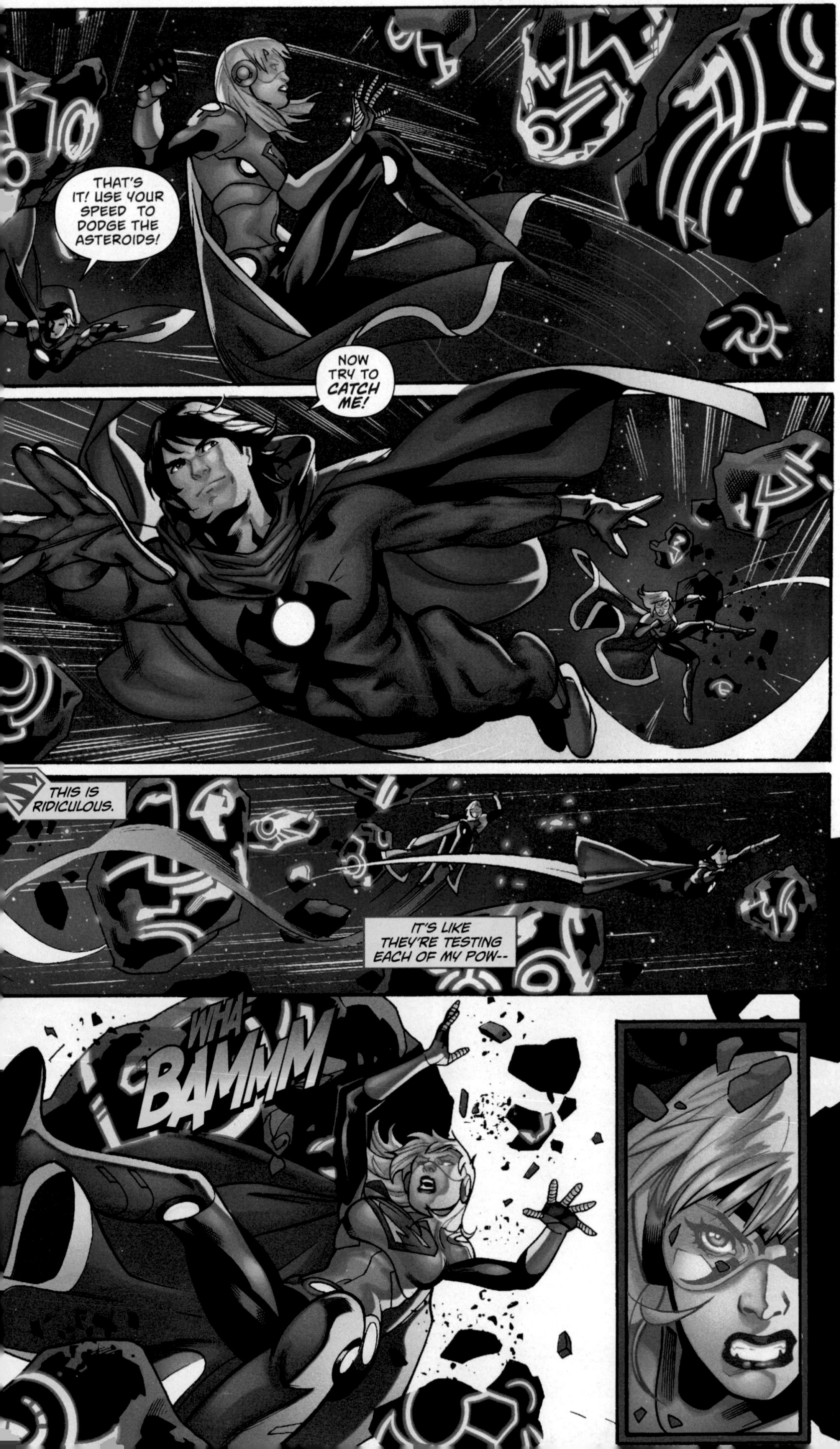
THAT'S IT! USE YOUR SPEED TO DODGE THE ASTEROIDS!
NOW TRY TO CATCH ME!
THIS IS RIDICULOUS.
IT'S LIKE THEY'RE TESTING EACH OF MY POW--
WHA-BAMMM

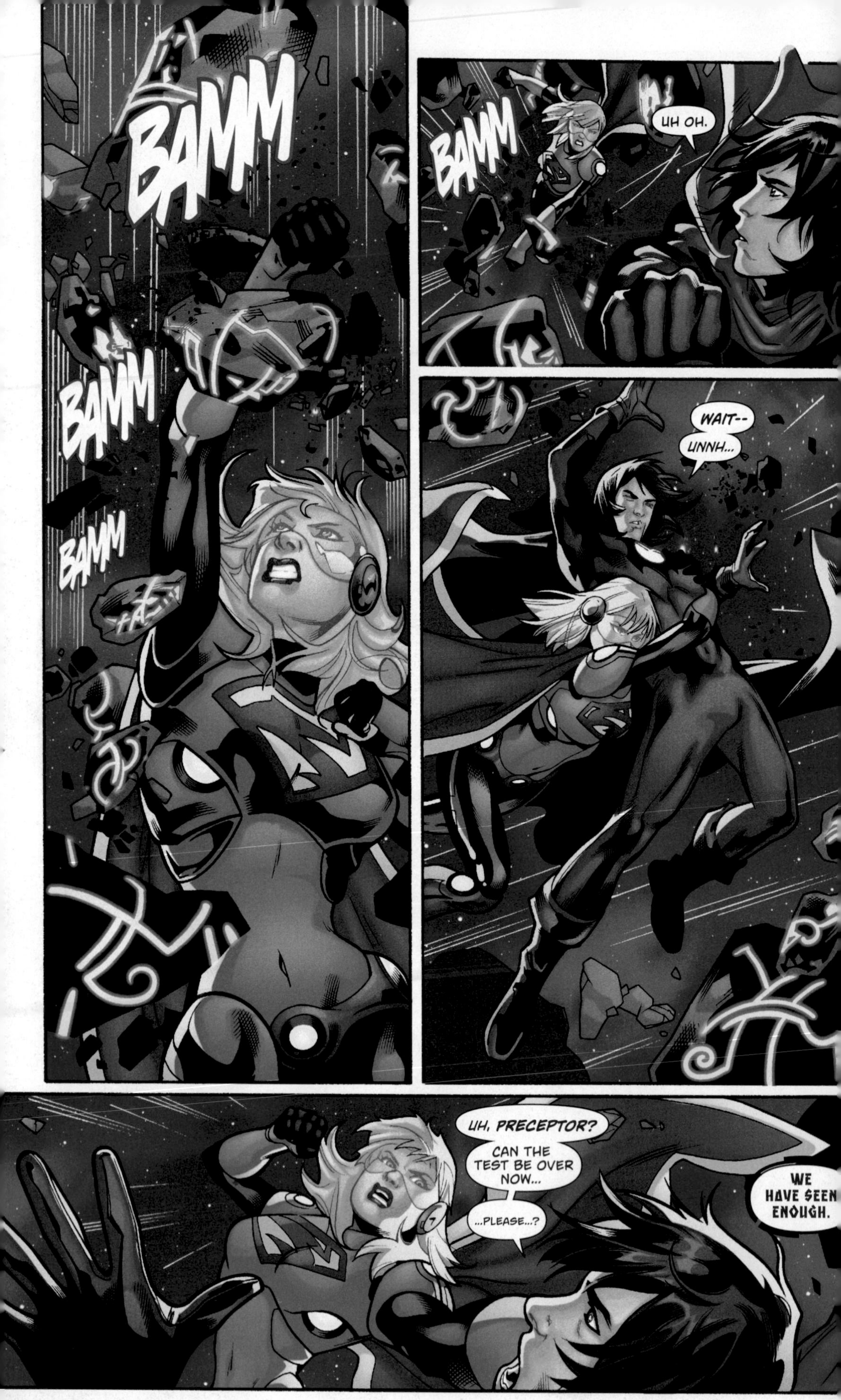
BAMM
BAMM
BAMM
BAMM
UH OH.
WAIT-- UNNH...
UH, PRECEPTOR?
CAN THE TEST BE OVER NOW...
...PLEASE...?
WE HAVE SEEN ENOUGH.

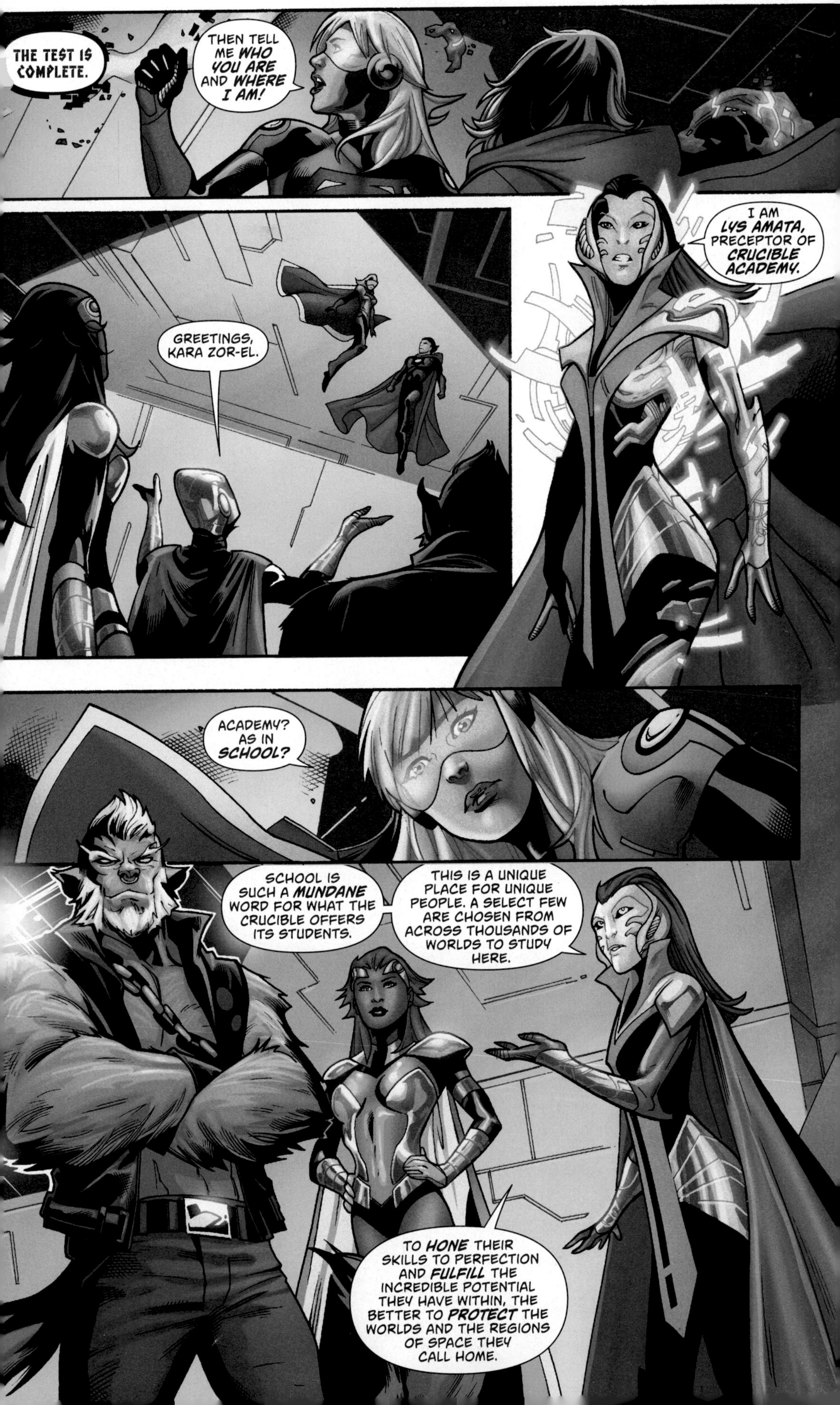
THE TEST IS COMPLETE.
THEN TELL ME WHO YOU ARE AND WHERE I AM!
I AM LYS AMATA, PRECEPTOR OF CRUCIBLE ACADEMY.
GREETINGS, KARA ZOR-EL.
ACADEMY? AS IN SCHOOL?
SCHOOL IS SUCH A MUNDANE WORD FOR WHAT THE CRUCIBLE OFFERS ITS STUDENTS.
THIS IS A UNIQUE PLACE FOR UNIQUE PEOPLE. A SELECT FEW ARE CHOSEN FROM ACROSS THOUSANDS OF WORLDS TO STUDY HERE.
TO HONE THEIR SKILLS TO PERFECTION AND FULFILL THE INCREDIBLE POTENTIAL THEY HAVE WITHIN, THE BETTER TO PROTECT THE WORLDS AND THE REGIONS OF SPACE THEY CALL HOME.

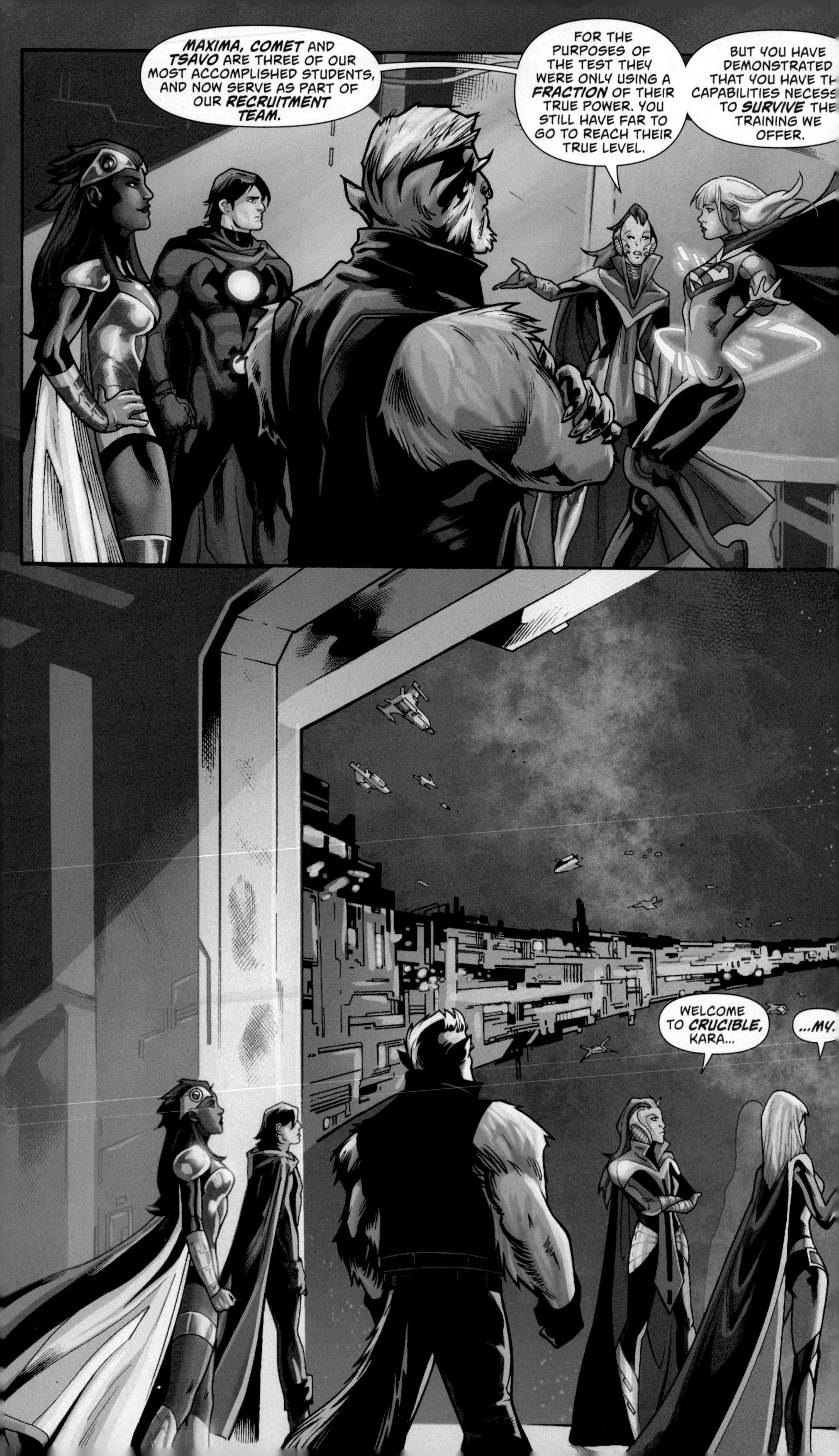
MAXIMA, COMET AND TSAVO ARE THREE OF OUR MOST ACCOMPLISHED STUDENTS, AND NOW SERVE AS PART OF OUR RECRUITMENT TEAM.
FOR THE PURPOSES OF THE TEST THEY WERE ONLY USING A FRACTION OF THEIR TRUE POWER. YOU STILL HAVE FAR TO GO TO REACH THEIR TRUE LEVEL.
BUT YOU HAVE DEMONSTRATED THAT YOU HAVE TH CAPABILITIES NECESS TO SURVIVE THE TRAINING WE OFFER.
WELCOME TO CRUCIBLE, KARA...
...MY.

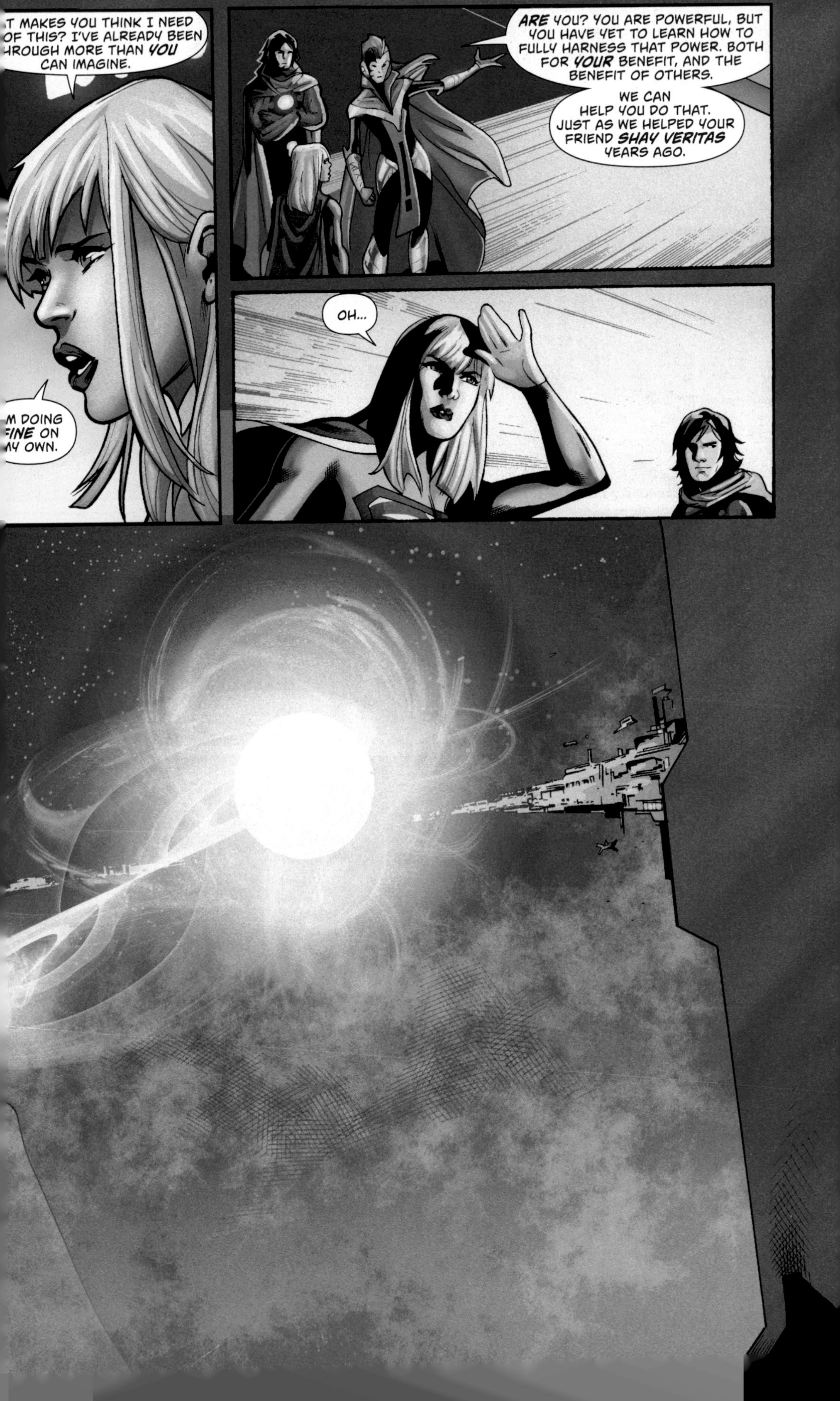

T MAKES YOU THINK I NEED OF THIS? I'VE ALREADY BEEN HROUGH MORE THAN YOU CAN IMAGINE.
M DOING FINE ON MY OWN.
ARE YOU? YOU ARE POWERFUL, BUT YOU HAVE YET TO LEARN HOW TO FULLY HARNESS THAT POWER. BOTH FOR YOUR BENEFIT, AND THE BENEFIT OF OTHERS.
WE CAN HELP YOU DO THAT. JUST AS WE HELPED YOUR FRIEND SHAY VERITAS YEARS AGO.
OH...

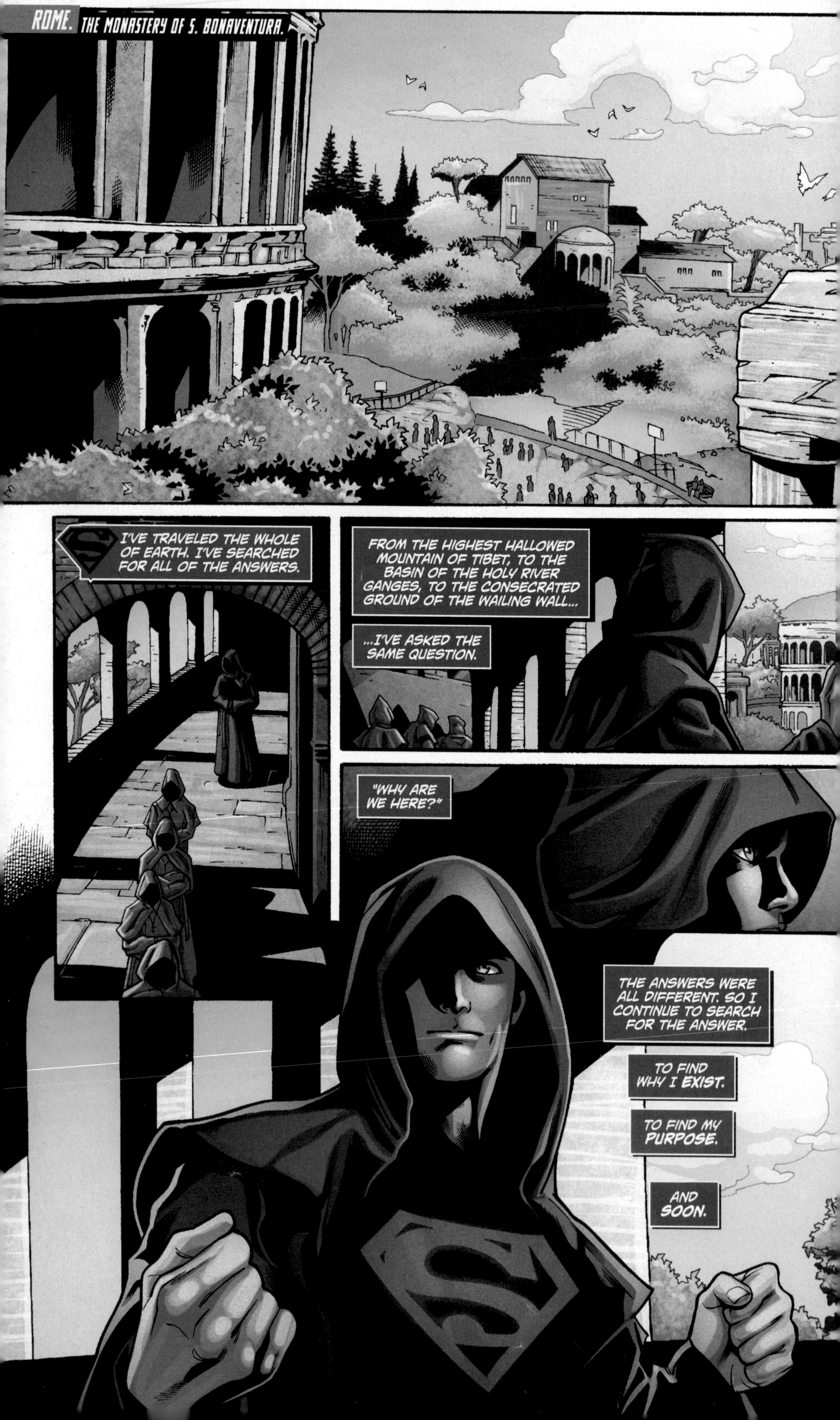
ROME. THE MONASTERY OF S. BONAVENTURA.
I'VE TRAVELED THE WHOLE OF EARTH. I'VE SEARCHED FOR ALL OF THE ANSWERS.
FROM THE HIGHEST HALLOWED MOUNTAIN OF TIBET, TO THE BASIN OF THE HOLY RIVER GANGES, TO THE CONSECRATED GROUND OF THE WAILING WALL...
...I'VE ASKED THE SAME QUESTION.
"WHY ARE WE HERE?"
THE ANSWERS WERE ALL DIFFERENT. SO I CONTINUE TO SEARCH FOR THE ANSWER.
TO FIND WHY I EXIST.
TO FIND MY PURPOSE.
AND SOON.

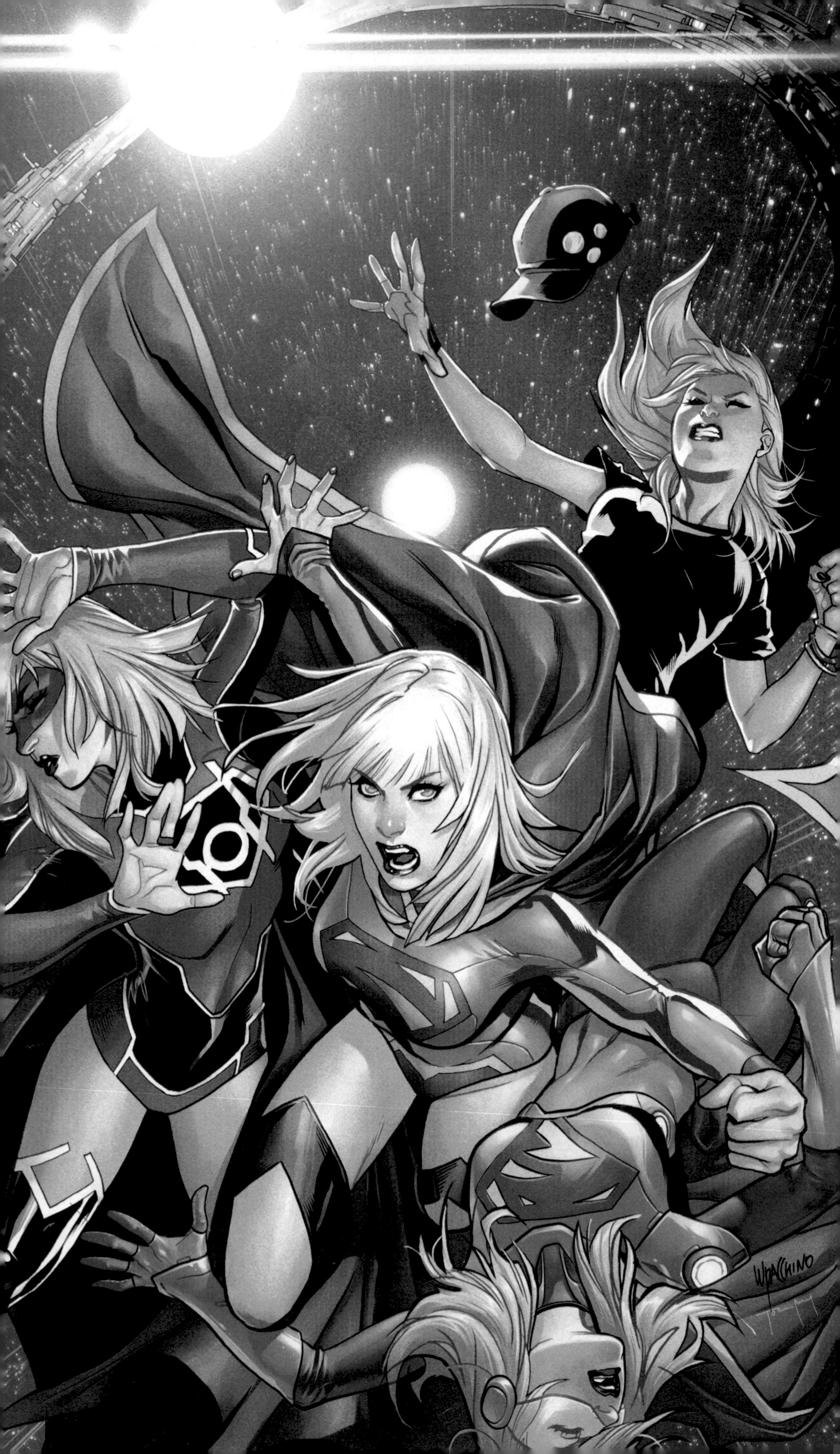

CRUCIBLE: PART 2

K. PERKINS MIKE JOHNSON writers **EMANUELA LUPACCHINO** penciller **RAY McCARTHY** inker **HI-FI** colorist **DEZI SIENTY** letterer
cover art by **EMANUELA LUPACCHINO** and **TOMEU MOREY**

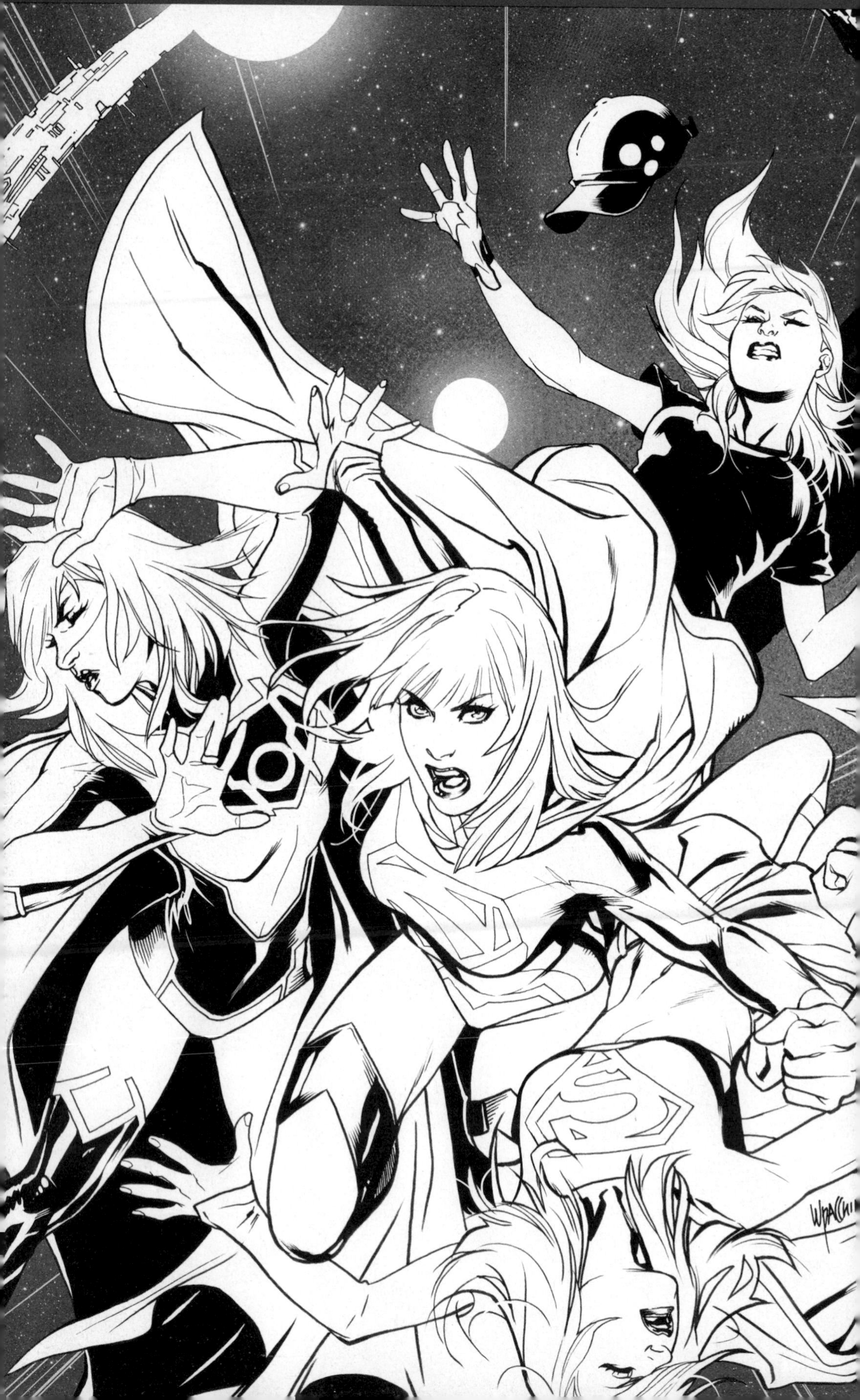

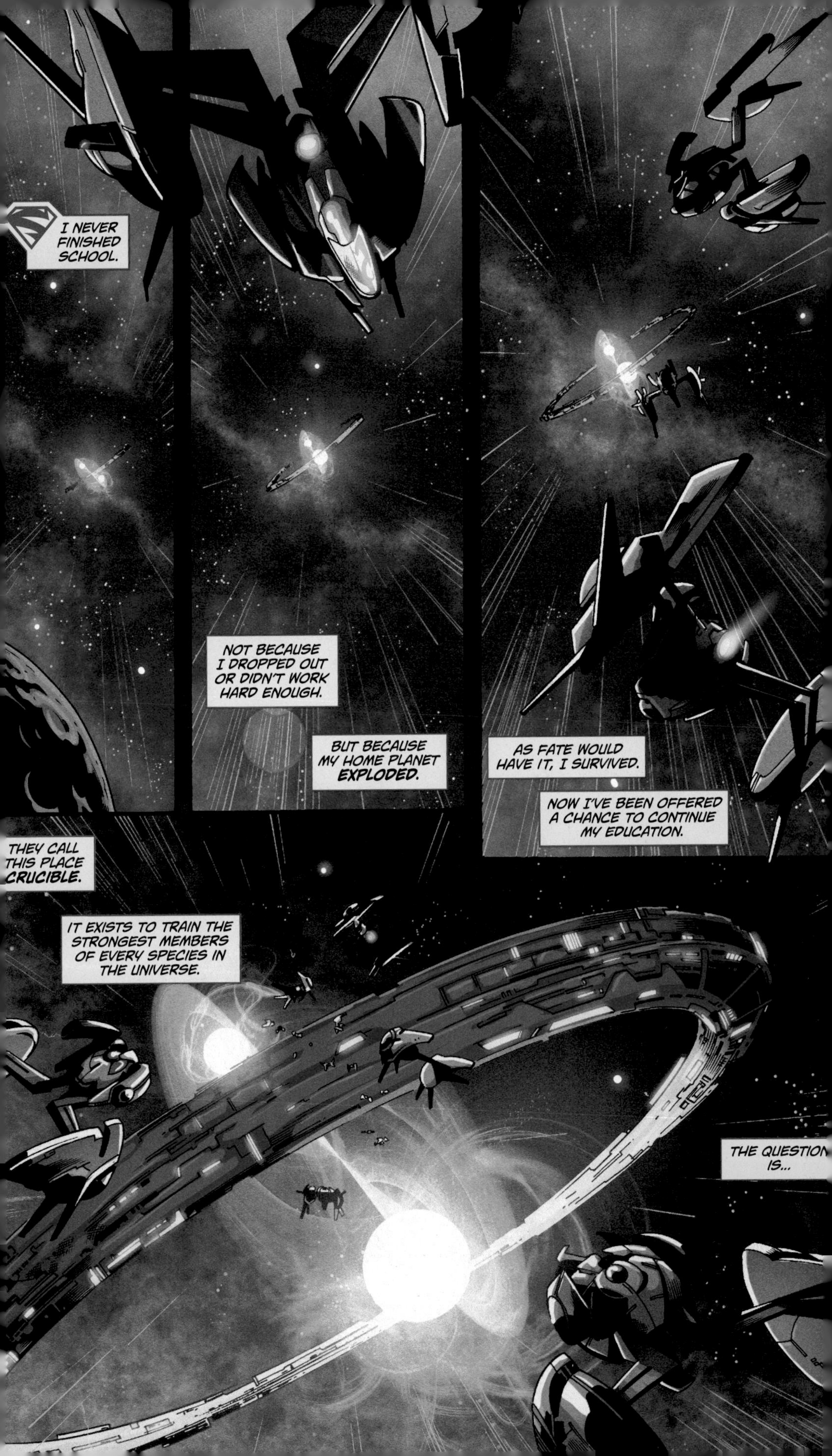

I NEVER FINISHED SCHOOL.
NOT BECAUSE I DROPPED OUT OR DIDN'T WORK HARD ENOUGH.
BUT BECAUSE MY HOME PLANET **EXPLODED.**
AS FATE WOULD HAVE IT, I SURVIVED.
NOW I'VE BEEN OFFERED A CHANCE TO CONTINUE MY EDUCATION.
THEY CALL THIS PLACE **CRUCIBLE.**
IT EXISTS TO TRAIN THE STRONGEST MEMBERS OF EVERY SPECIES IN THE UNIVERSE.
THE QUESTION IS...

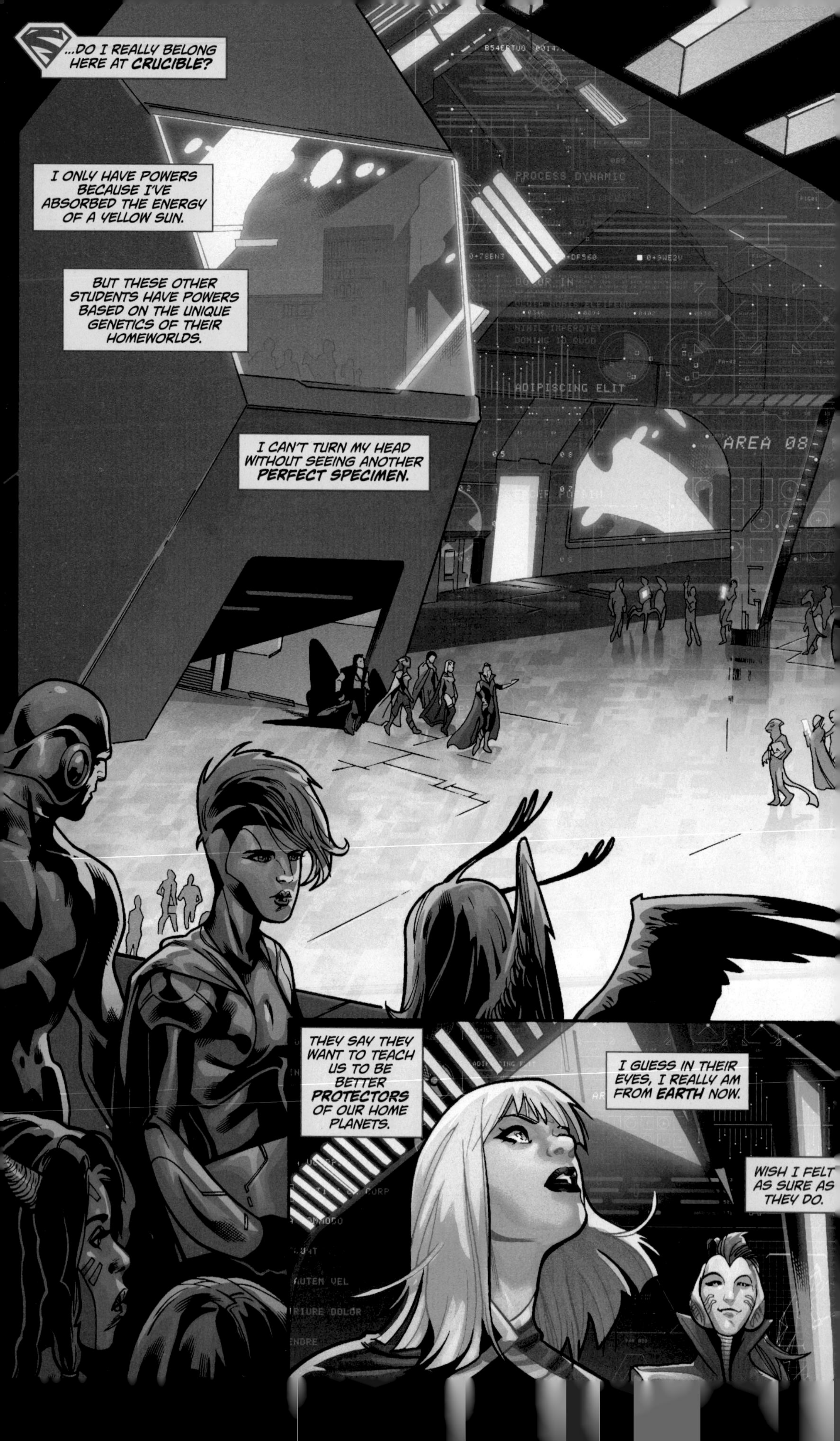
...DO I REALLY BELONG HERE AT CRUCIBLE?
I ONLY HAVE POWERS BECAUSE I'VE ABSORBED THE ENERGY OF A YELLOW SUN.
BUT THESE OTHER STUDENTS HAVE POWERS BASED ON THE UNIQUE GENETICS OF THEIR HOMEWORLDS.
I CAN'T TURN MY HEAD WITHOUT SEEING ANOTHER PERFECT SPECIMEN.
AREA 08
THEY SAY THEY WANT TO TEACH US TO BE BETTER PROTECTORS OF OUR HOME PLANETS.
I GUESS IN THEIR EYES, I REALLY AM FROM EARTH NOW.
WISH I FELT AS SURE AS THEY DO.

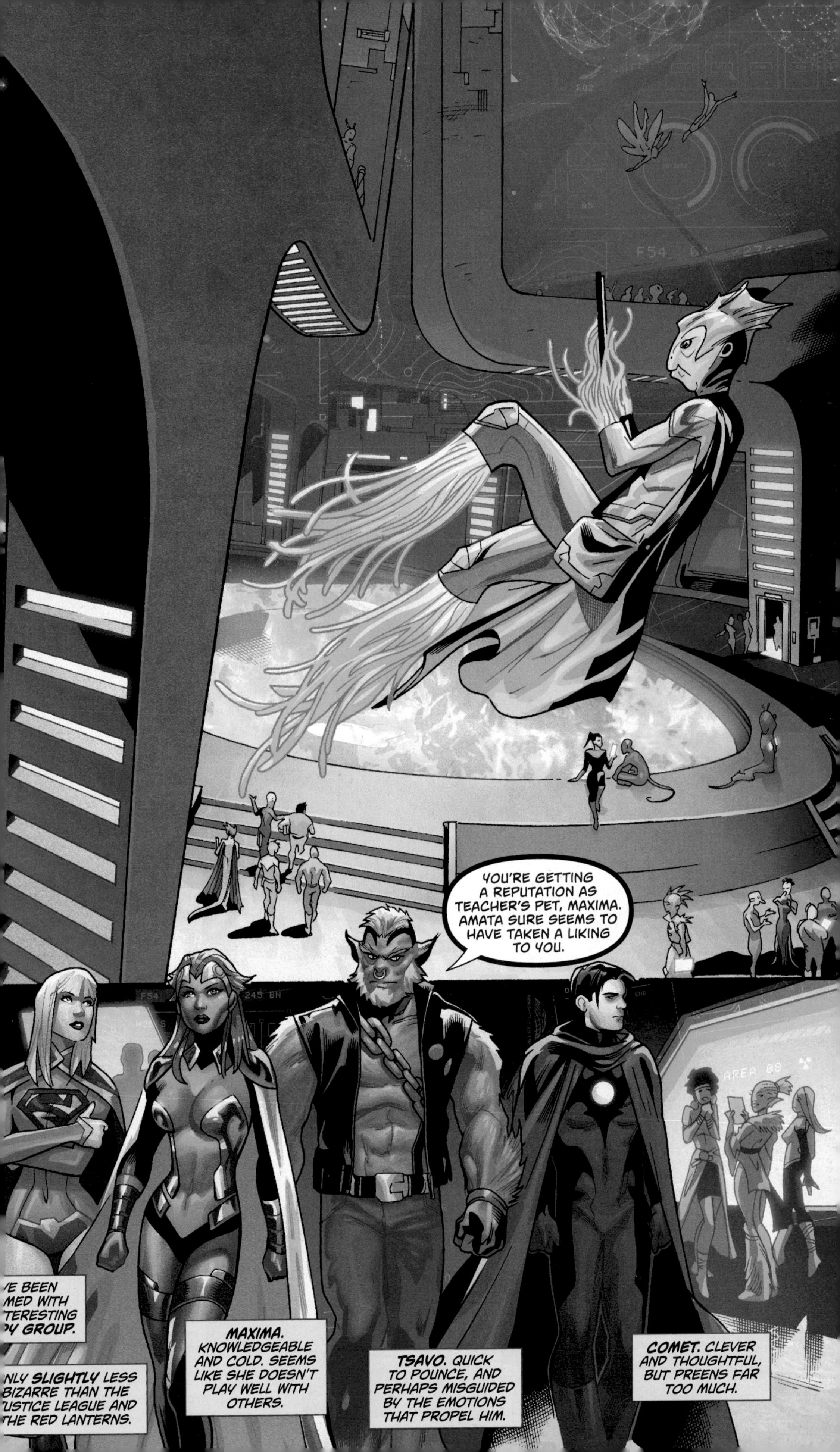
YOU'RE GETTING A REPUTATION AS TEACHER'S PET, MAXIMA. AMATA SURE SEEMS TO HAVE TAKEN A LIKING TO YOU.
'VE BEEN MED WITH TERESTING DY GROUP.
NLY SLIGHTLY LESS BIZARRE THAN THE USTICE LEAGUE AND THE RED LANTERNS.
MAXIMA. KNOWLEDGEABLE AND COLD. SEEMS LIKE SHE DOESN'T PLAY WELL WITH OTHERS.
TSAVO. QUICK TO POUNCE, AND PERHAPS MISGUIDED BY THE EMOTIONS THAT PROPEL HIM.
COMET. CLEVER AND THOUGHTFUL, BUT PREENS FAR TOO MUCH.

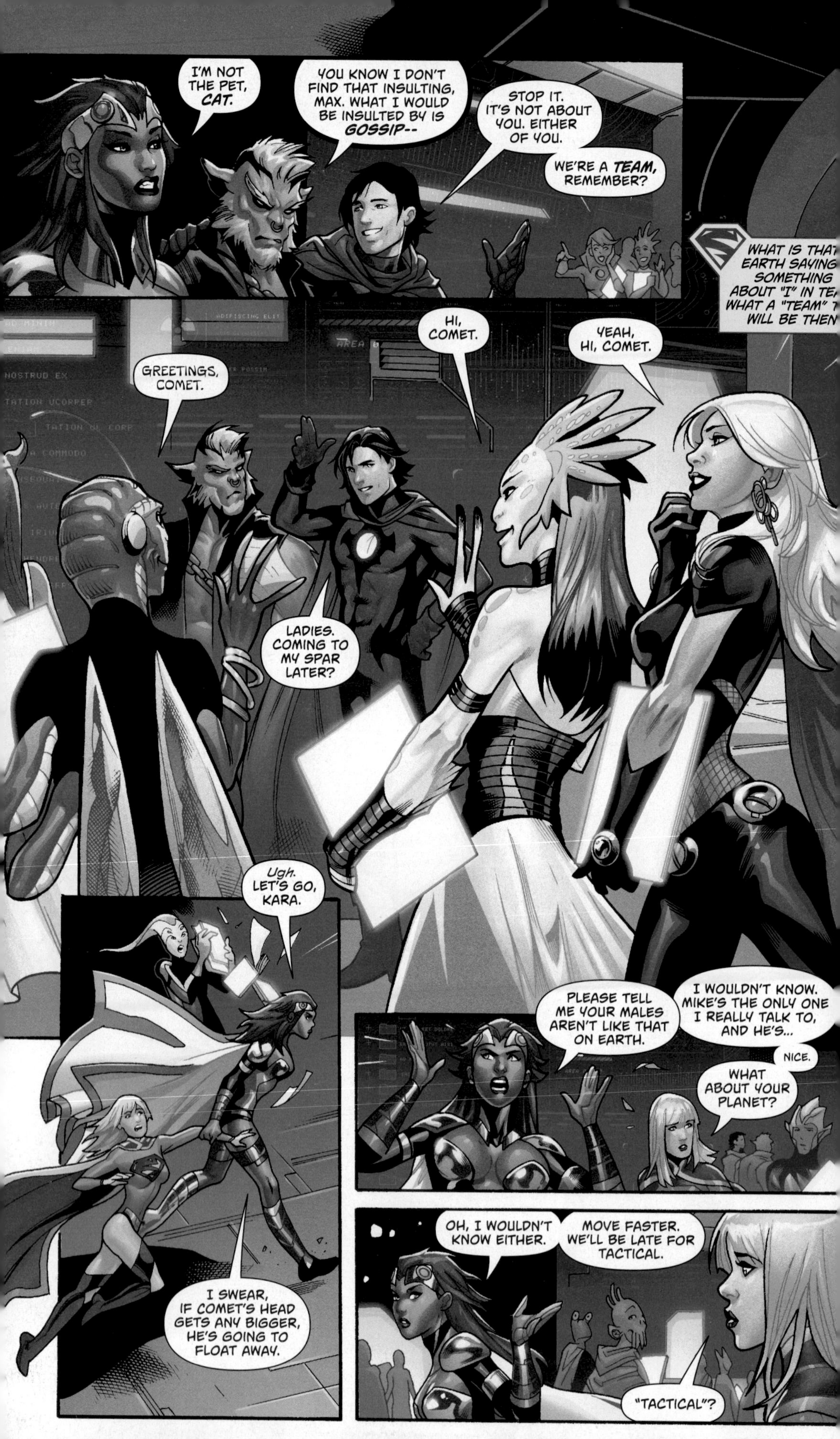

I'M NOT THE PET, *CAT.*
YOU KNOW I DON'T FIND THAT INSULTING, MAX. WHAT I WOULD BE INSULTED BY IS *GOSSIP--*
STOP IT. IT'S NOT ABOUT YOU. EITHER OF YOU.
WE'RE A *TEAM,* REMEMBER?
WHAT IS THAT EARTH SAYING SOMETHING ABOUT "I" IN TE WHAT A "TEAM" WILL BE THEN
GREETINGS, COMET.
HI, COMET.
YEAH, HI, COMET.
LADIES. COMING TO MY SPAR LATER?
Ugh. LET'S GO, KARA.
I SWEAR, IF COMET'S HEAD GETS ANY BIGGER, HE'S GOING TO FLOAT AWAY.
PLEASE TELL ME YOUR MALES AREN'T LIKE THAT ON EARTH.
I WOULDN'T KNOW. MIKE'S THE ONLY ONE I REALLY TALK TO, AND HE'S...
NICE.
WHAT ABOUT YOUR PLANET?
OH, I WOULDN'T KNOW EITHER.
MOVE FASTER. WE'LL BE LATE FOR TACTICAL.
"TACTICAL"?

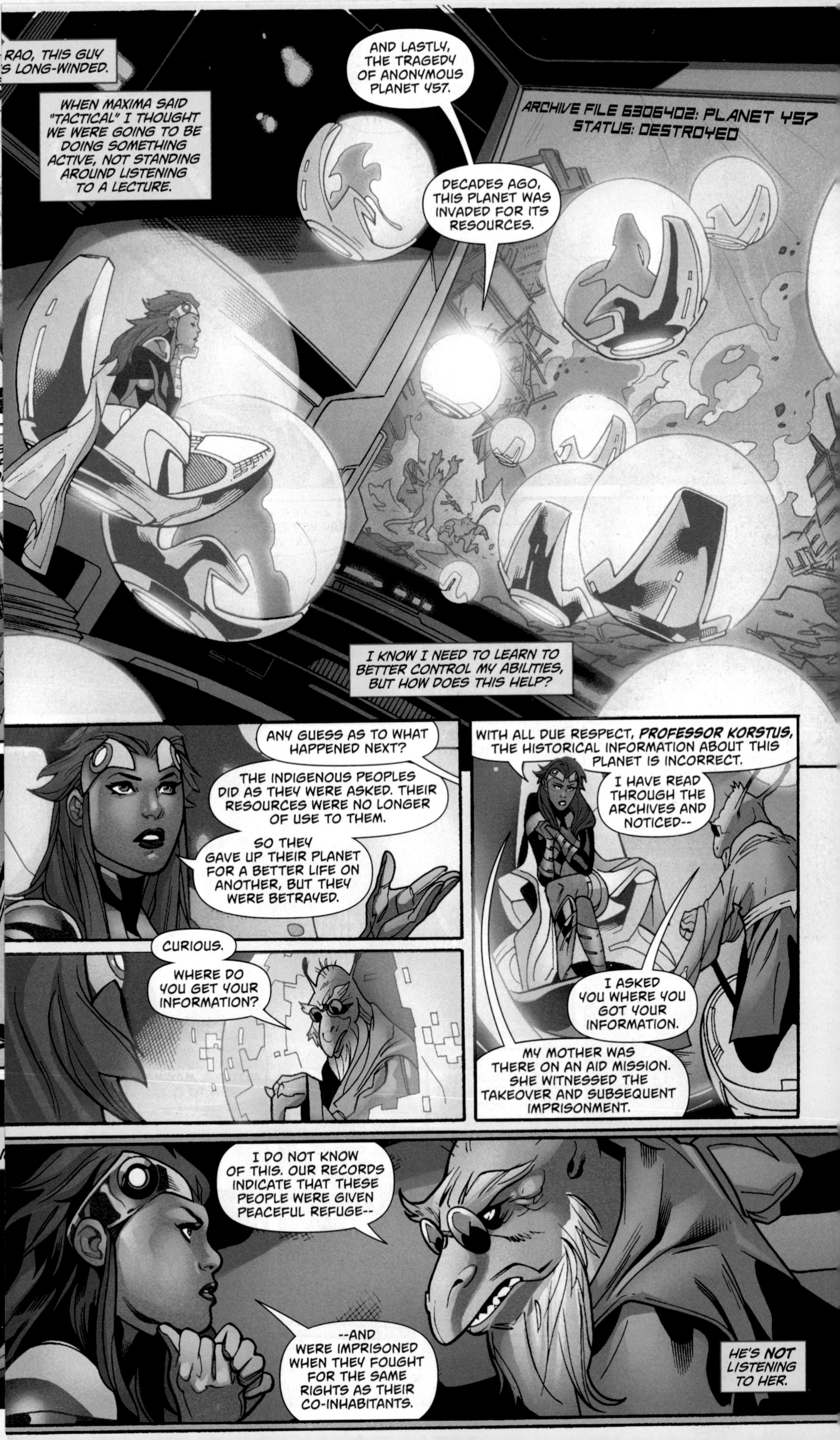
RAO, THIS GUY IS LONG-WINDED.
WHEN MAXIMA SAID "TACTICAL" I THOUGHT WE WERE GOING TO BE DOING SOMETHING ACTIVE, NOT STANDING AROUND LISTENING TO A LECTURE.
AND LASTLY, THE TRAGEDY OF ANONYMOUS PLANET Y57.
ARCHIVE FILE 6306402: PLANET Y57
STATUS: DESTROYED
DECADES AGO, THIS PLANET WAS INVADED FOR ITS RESOURCES.
I KNOW I NEED TO LEARN TO BETTER CONTROL MY ABILITIES, BUT HOW DOES THIS HELP?
ANY GUESS AS TO WHAT HAPPENED NEXT?
THE INDIGENOUS PEOPLES DID AS THEY WERE ASKED. THEIR RESOURCES WERE NO LONGER OF USE TO THEM.
SO THEY GAVE UP THEIR PLANET FOR A BETTER LIFE ON ANOTHER, BUT THEY WERE BETRAYED.
WITH ALL DUE RESPECT, PROFESSOR KORSTUS, THE HISTORICAL INFORMATION ABOUT THIS PLANET IS INCORRECT.
I HAVE READ THROUGH THE ARCHIVES AND NOTICED--
CURIOUS.
WHERE DO YOU GET YOUR INFORMATION?
I ASKED YOU WHERE YOU GOT YOUR INFORMATION.
MY MOTHER WAS THERE ON AN AID MISSION. SHE WITNESSED THE TAKEOVER AND SUBSEQUENT IMPRISONMENT.
I DO NOT KNOW OF THIS. OUR RECORDS INDICATE THAT THESE PEOPLE WERE GIVEN PEACEFUL REFUGE--
--AND WERE IMPRISONED WHEN THEY FOUGHT FOR THE SAME RIGHTS AS THEIR CO-INHABITANTS.
HE'S NOT LISTENING TO HER.

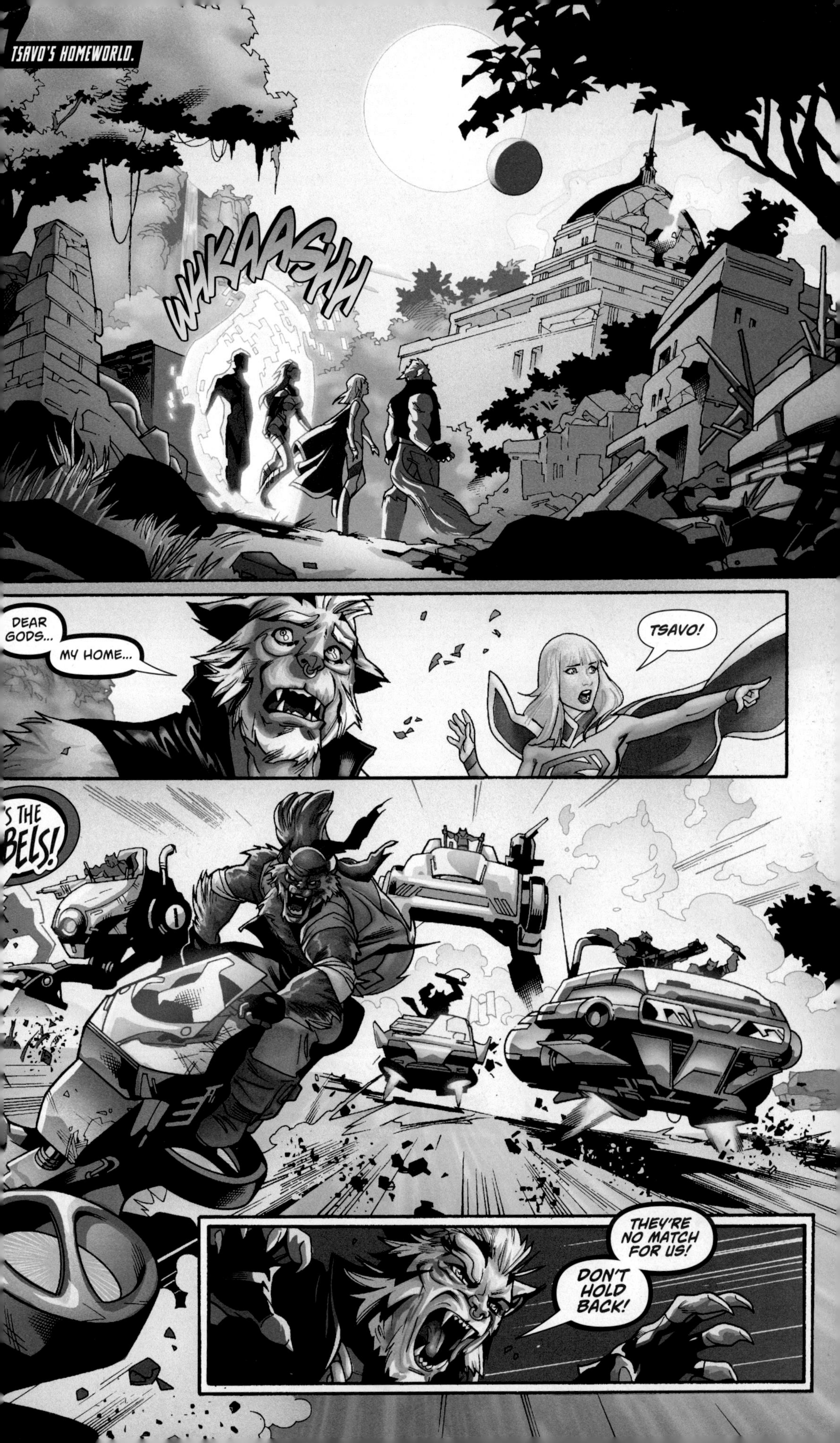
TSAVO'S HOMEWORLD.
WHKAASHH
DEAR GODS...
MY HOME...
TSAVO!
'S THE
BELS!
THEY'RE NO MATCH FOR US!
DON'T HOLD BACK!

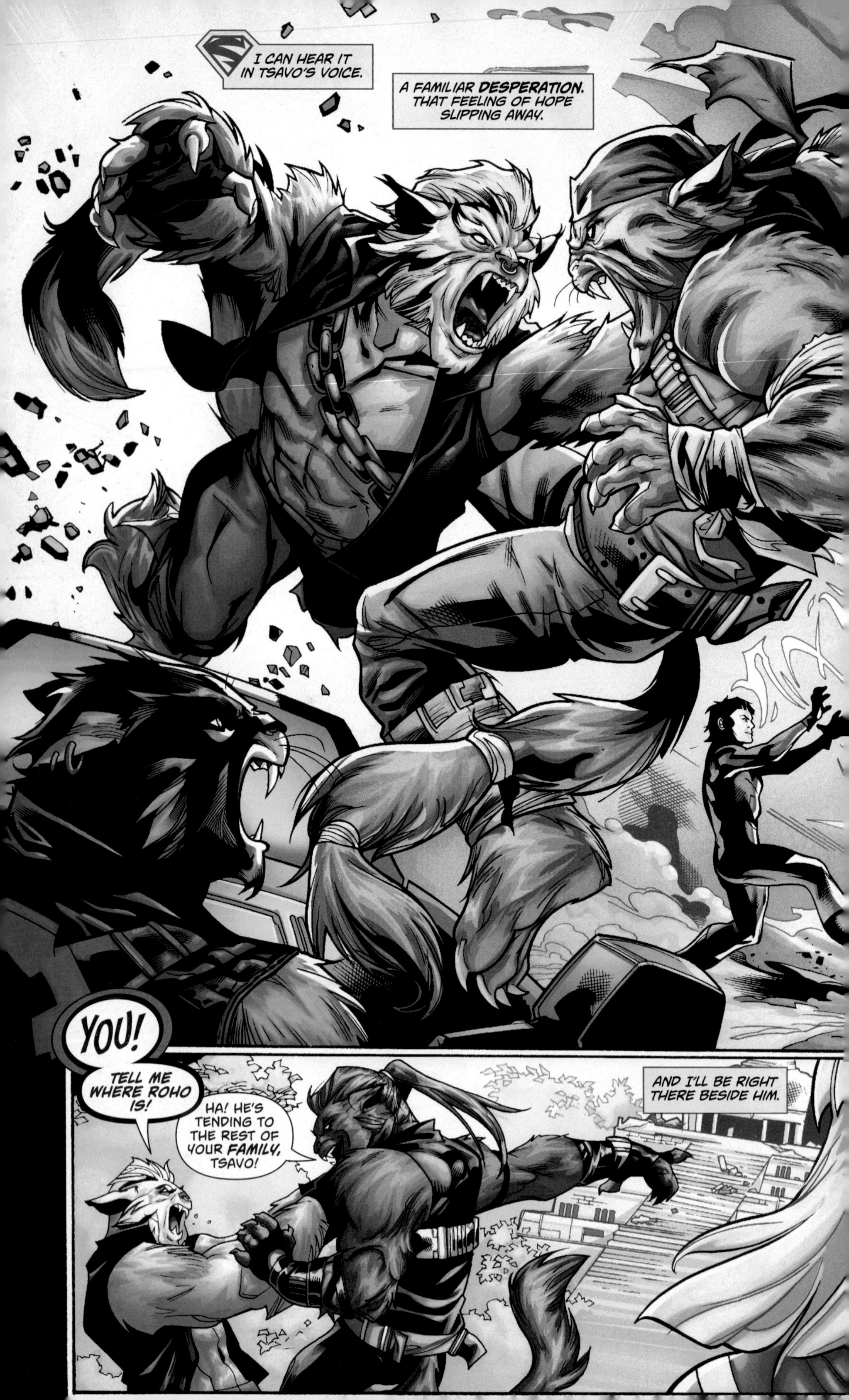
I CAN HEAR IT IN TSAVO'S VOICE.
A FAMILIAR DESPERATION. THAT FEELING OF HOPE SLIPPING AWAY.
YOU!
TELL ME WHERE ROHO IS!
HA! HE'S TENDING TO THE REST OF YOUR FAMILY, TSAVO!
AND I'LL BE RIGHT THERE BESIDE HIM.

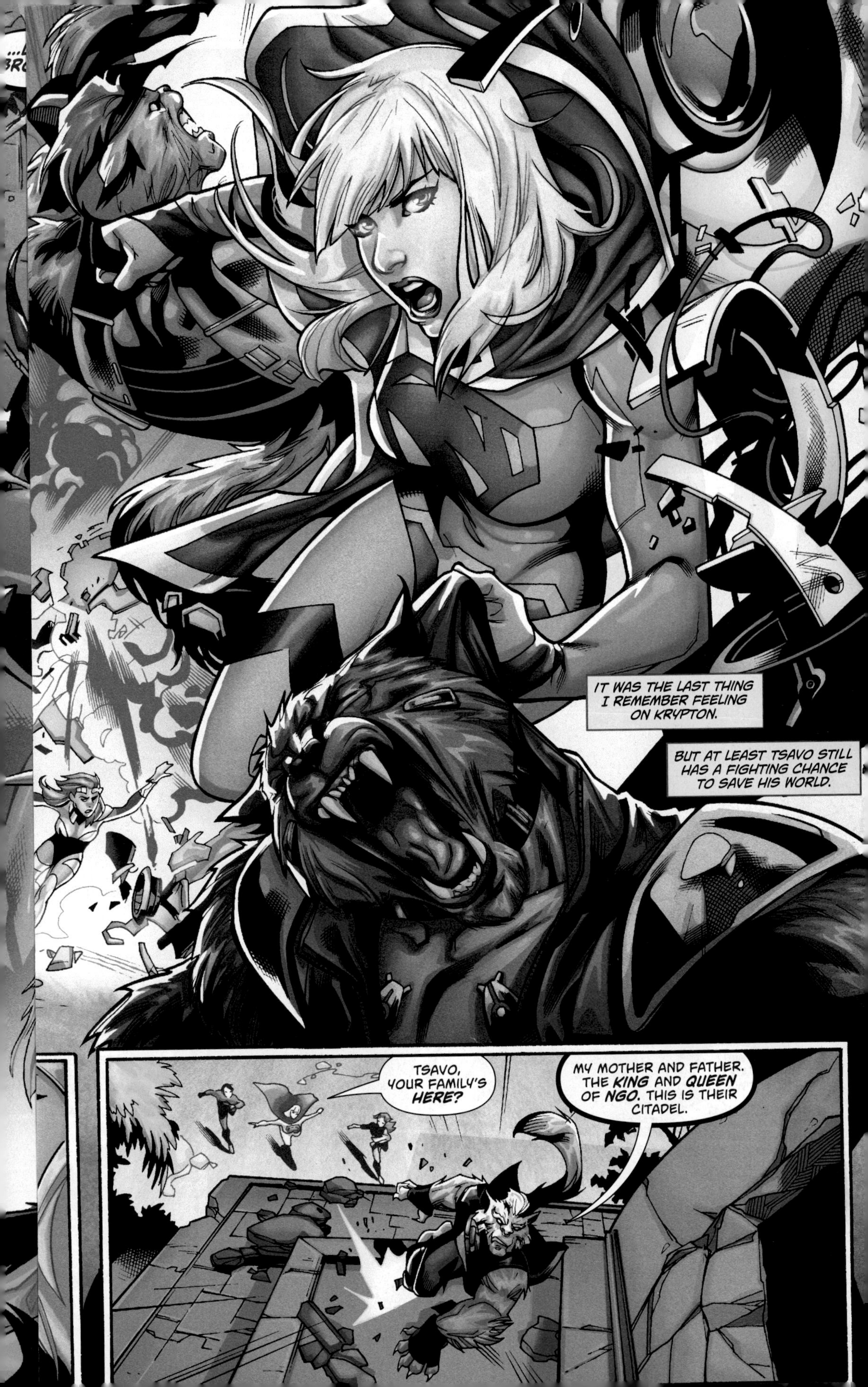
IT WAS THE LAST THING I REMEMBER FEELING ON KRYPTON.
BUT AT LEAST TSAVO STILL HAS A FIGHTING CHANCE TO SAVE HIS WORLD.
TSAVO, YOUR FAMILY'S HERE?
MY MOTHER AND FATHER. THE KING AND QUEEN OF NGO. THIS IS THEIR CITADEL.

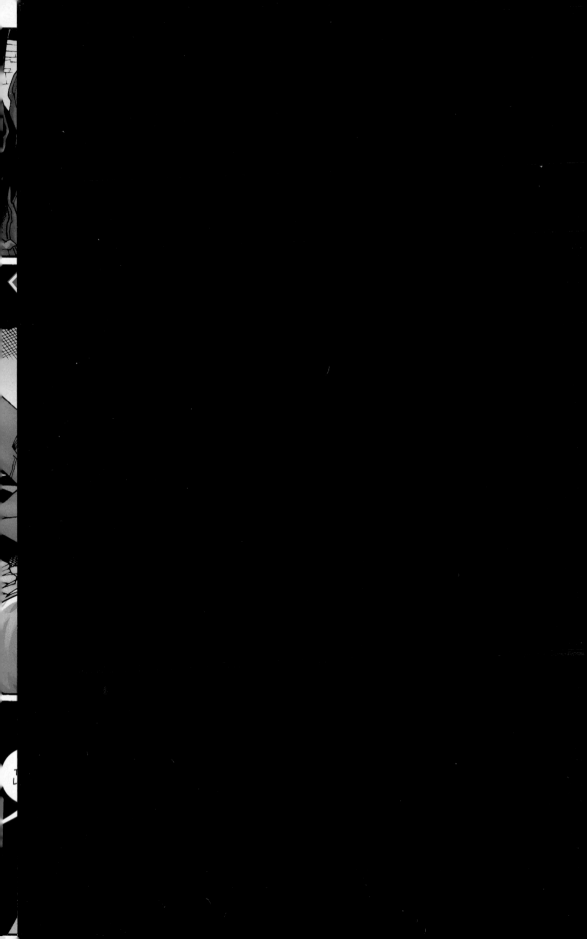

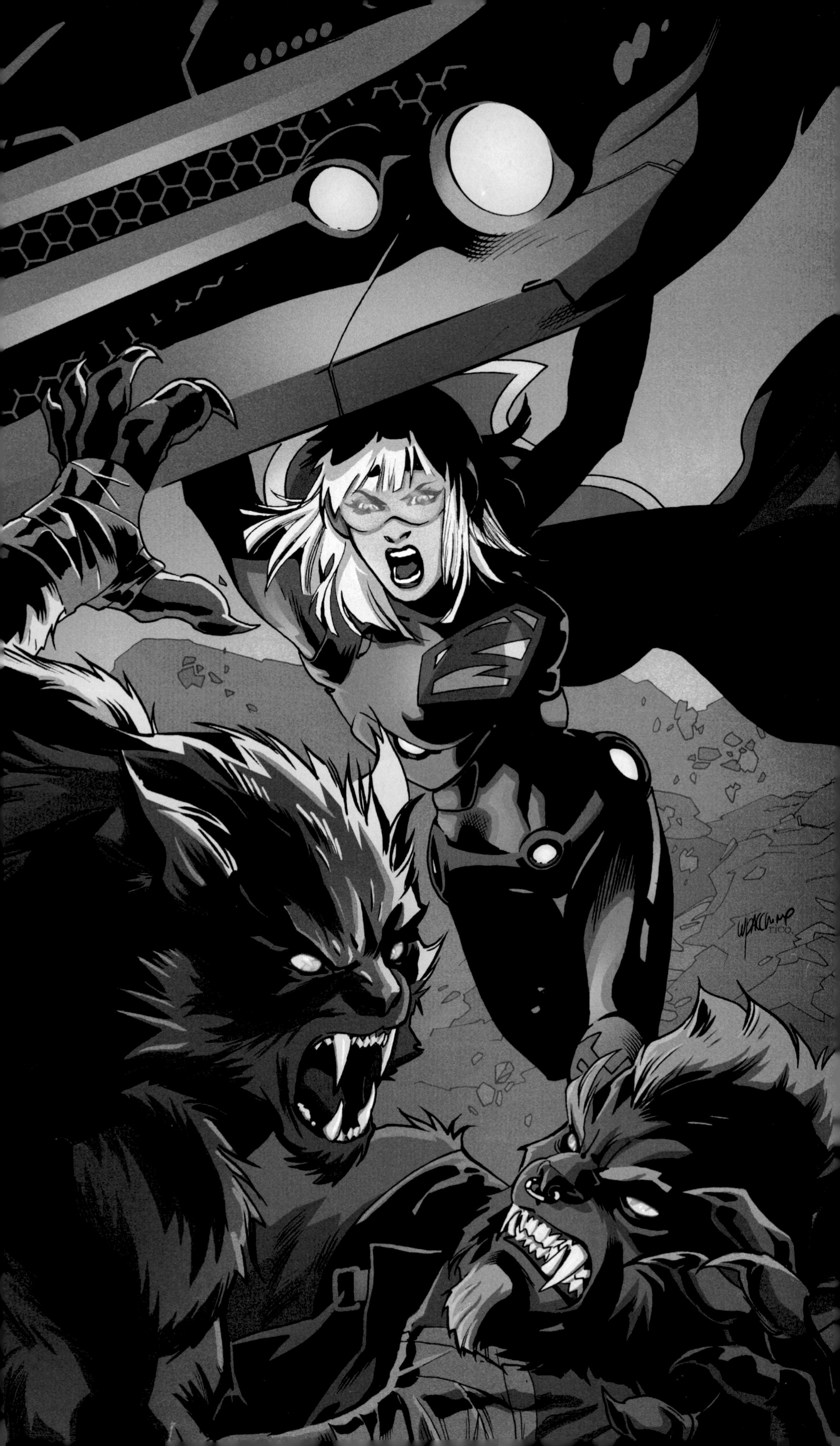

CRUCIBLE: PART 3

K. PERKINS MIKE JOHNSON writers EMANUELA LUPACCHINO penciller RAY McCARTHY inker HI-FI colorist ROB LEIGH letterer
cover art by EMANUELA LUPACCHINO and RICO RENZI

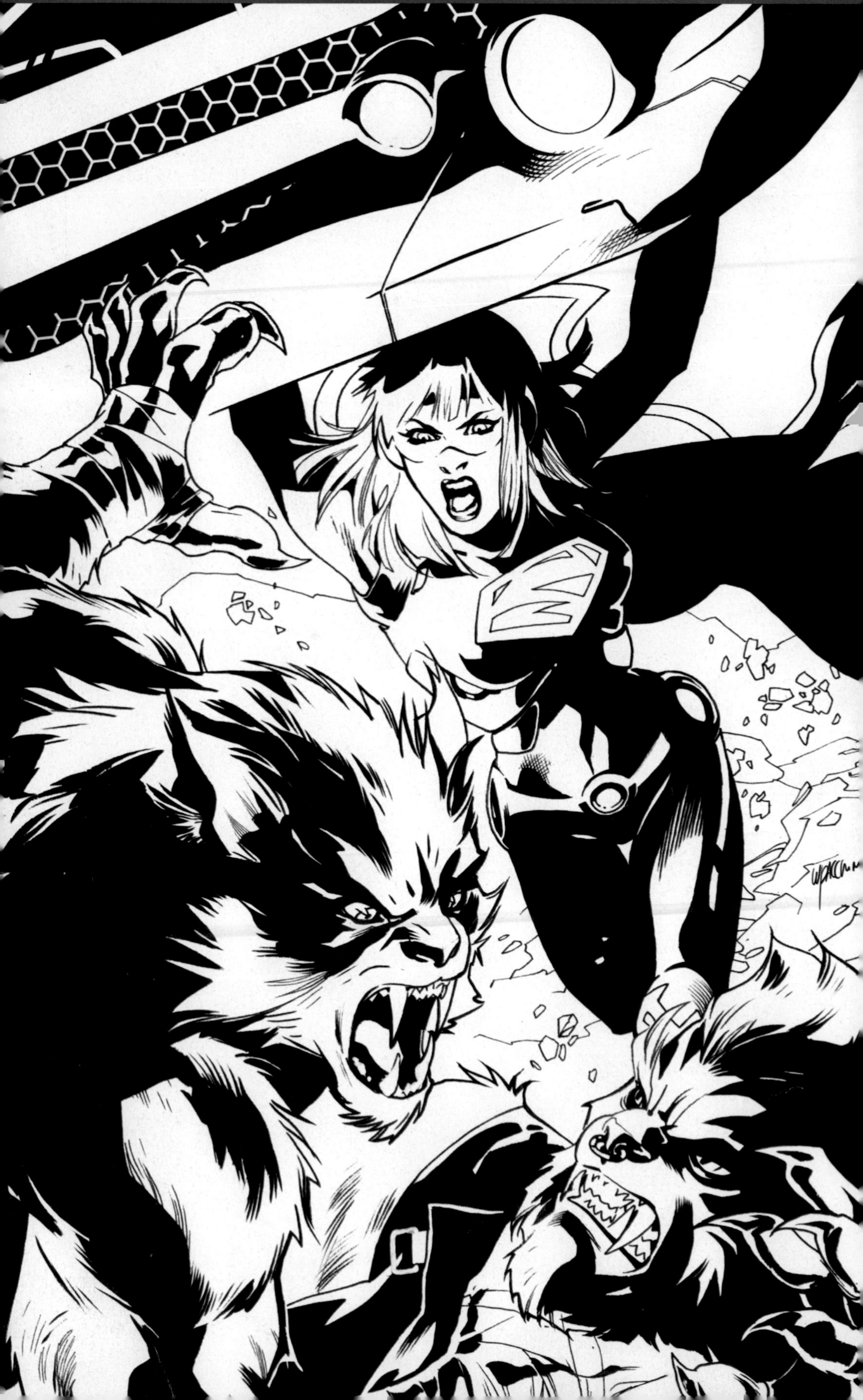

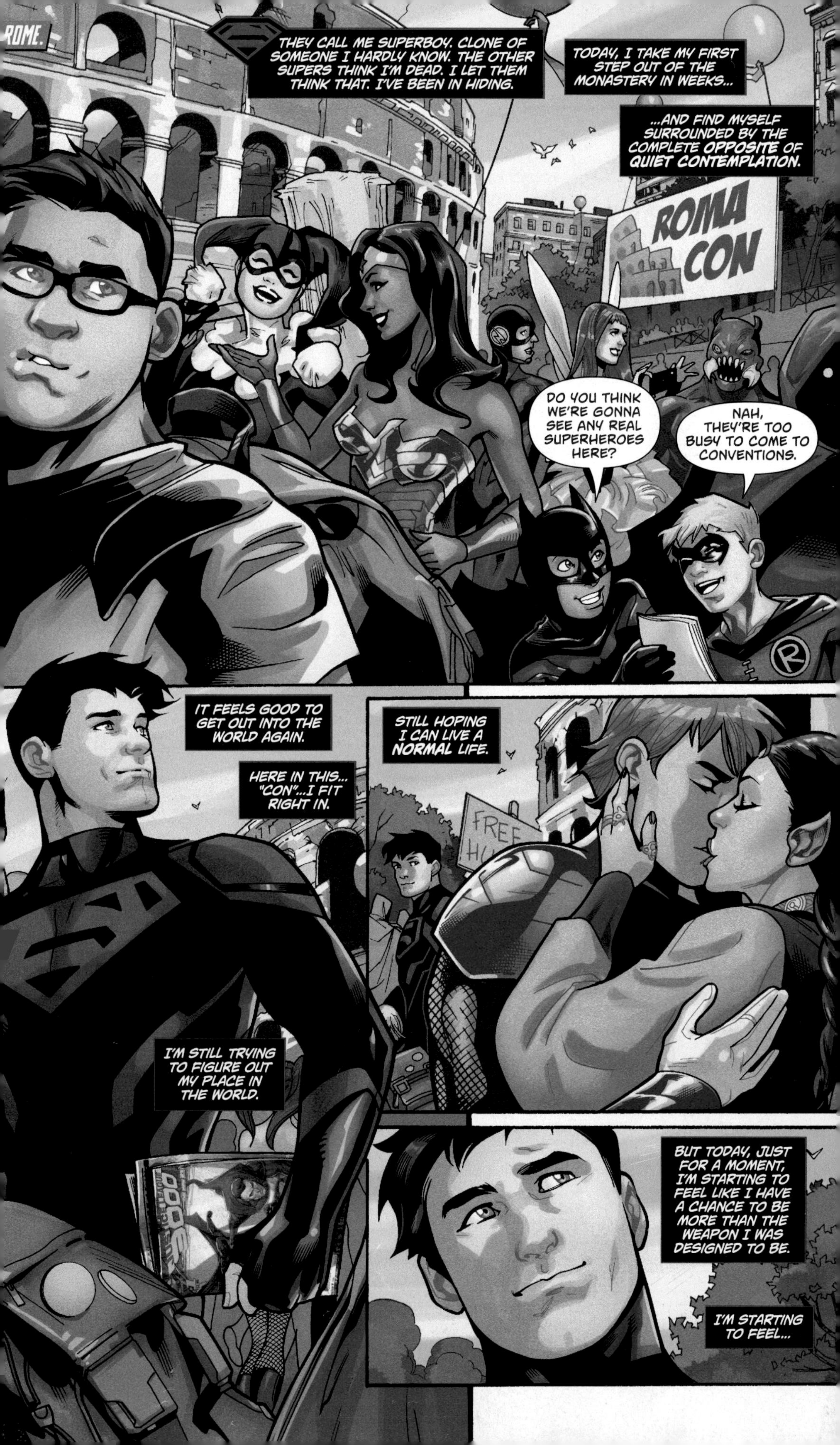
ROME.
THEY CALL ME SUPERBOY. CLONE OF SOMEONE I HARDLY KNOW. THE OTHER SUPERS THINK I'M DEAD. I LET THEM THINK THAT. I'VE BEEN IN HIDING.
TODAY, I TAKE MY FIRST STEP OUT OF THE MONASTERY IN WEEKS...
...AND FIND MYSELF SURROUNDED BY THE COMPLETE OPPOSITE OF QUIET CONTEMPLATION.
ROMA CON
DO YOU THINK WE'RE GONNA SEE ANY REAL SUPERHEROES HERE?
NAH, THEY'RE TOO BUSY TO COME TO CONVENTIONS.
IT FEELS GOOD TO GET OUT INTO THE WORLD AGAIN.
HERE IN THIS... "CON"...I FIT RIGHT IN.
I'M STILL TRYING TO FIGURE OUT MY PLACE IN THE WORLD.
STILL HOPING I CAN LIVE A NORMAL LIFE.
BUT TODAY, JUST FOR A MOMENT, I'M STARTING TO FEEL LIKE I HAVE A CHANCE TO BE MORE THAN THE WEAPON I WAS DESIGNED TO BE.
I'M STARTING TO FEEL...

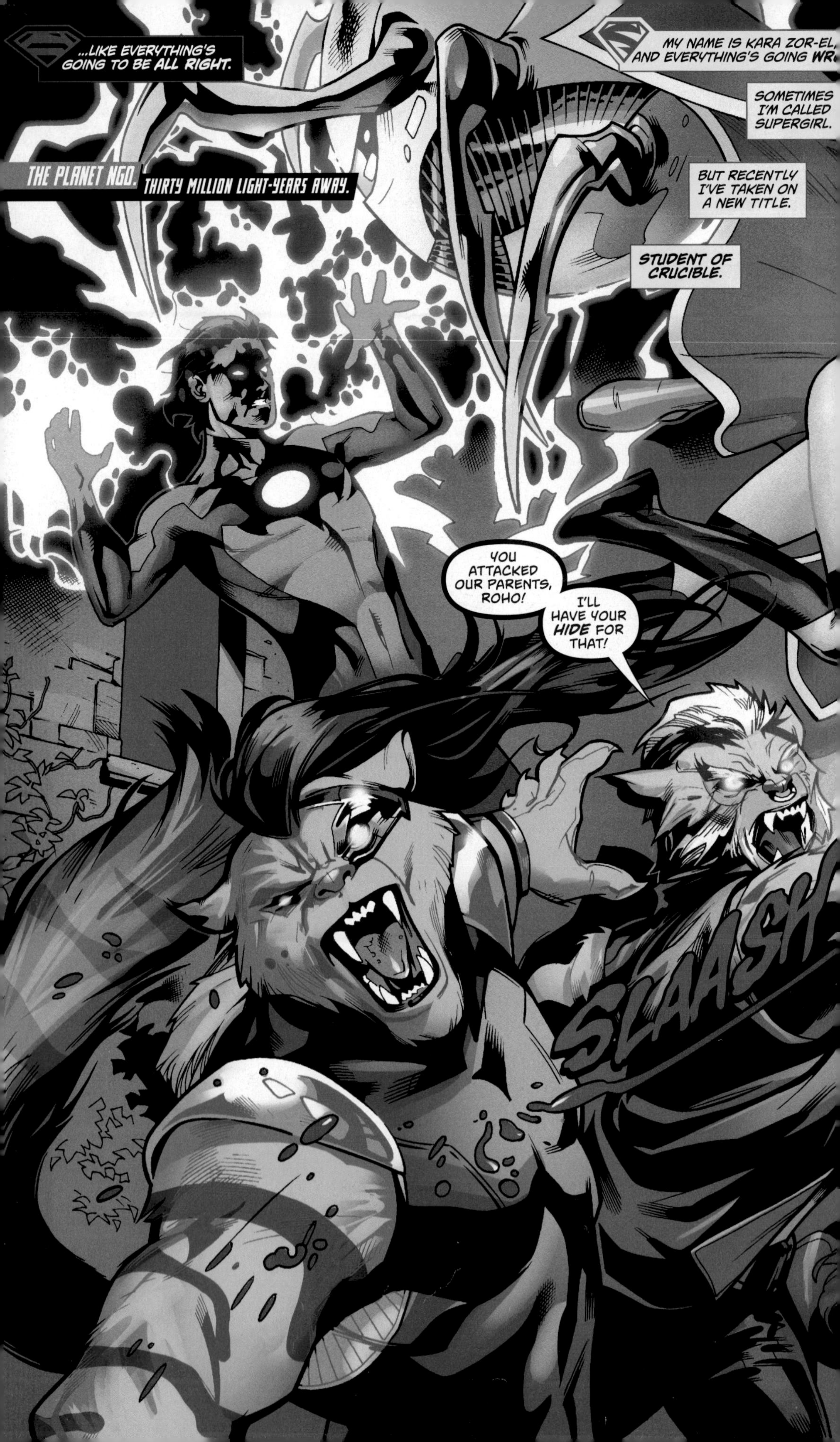
...LIKE EVERYTHING'S GOING TO BE ALL RIGHT.
MY NAME IS KARA ZOR-EL, AND EVERYTHING'S GOING WR
SOMETIMES I'M CALLED SUPERGIRL.
THE PLANET NGO.
THIRTY MILLION LIGHT-YEARS AWAY.
BUT RECENTLY I'VE TAKEN ON A NEW TITLE.
STUDENT OF CRUCIBLE.
YOU ATTACKED OUR PARENTS, ROHO!
I'LL HAVE YOUR HIDE FOR THAT!
SLAASH

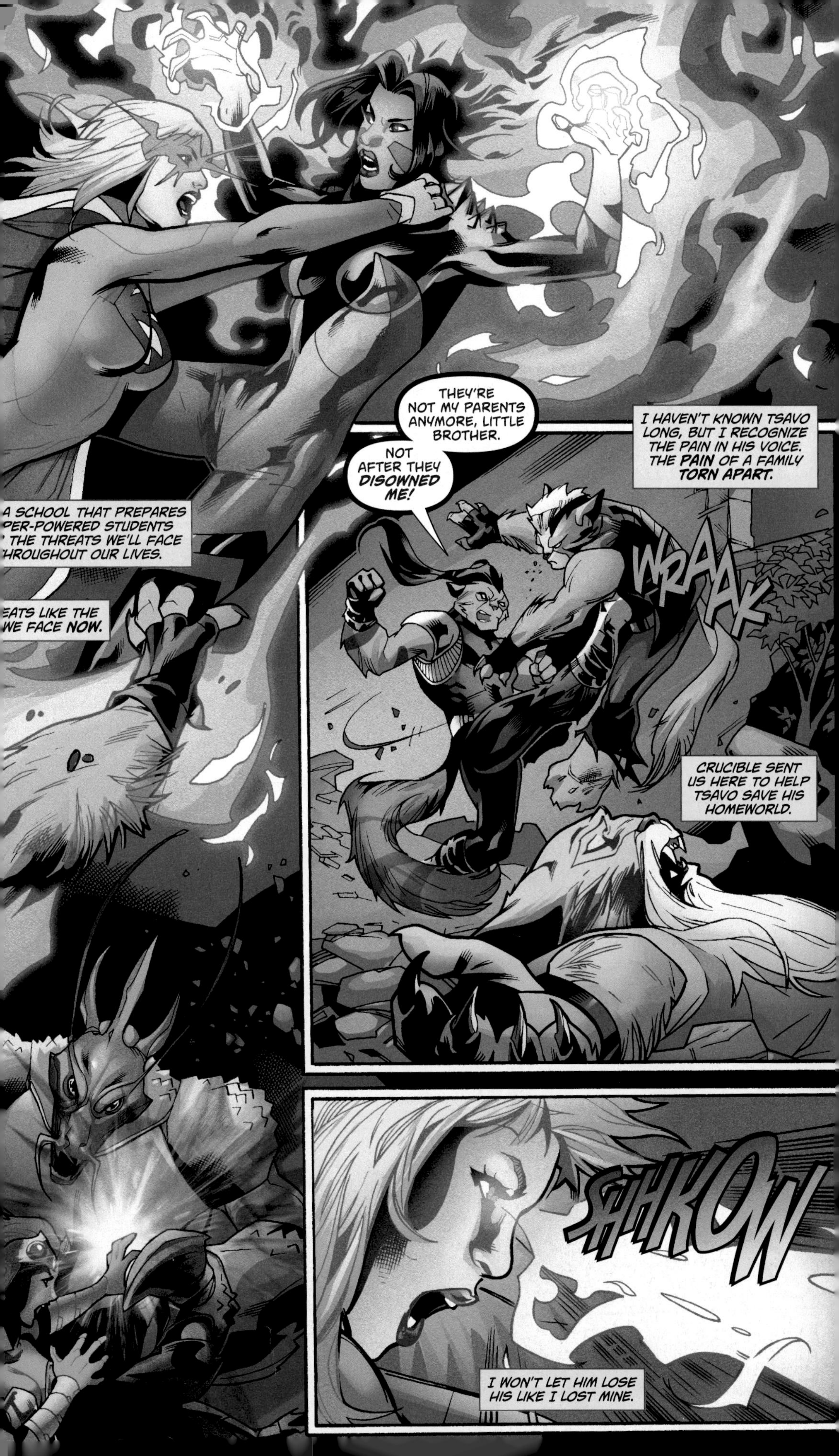

A SCHOOL THAT PREPARES
PER-POWERED STUDENTS
THE THREATS WE'LL FACE
HROUGHOUT OUR LIVES.
EATS LIKE THE
WE FACE NOW.
THEY'RE NOT MY PARENTS ANYMORE, LITTLE BROTHER.
NOT AFTER THEY DISOWNED ME!
I HAVEN'T KNOWN TSAVO LONG, BUT I RECOGNIZE THE PAIN IN HIS VOICE. THE PAIN OF A FAMILY TORN APART.
WRAAAK
CRUCIBLE SENT US HERE TO HELP TSAVO SAVE HIS HOMEWORLD.
SHHKOW
I WON'T LET HIM LOSE HIS LIKE I LOST MINE.

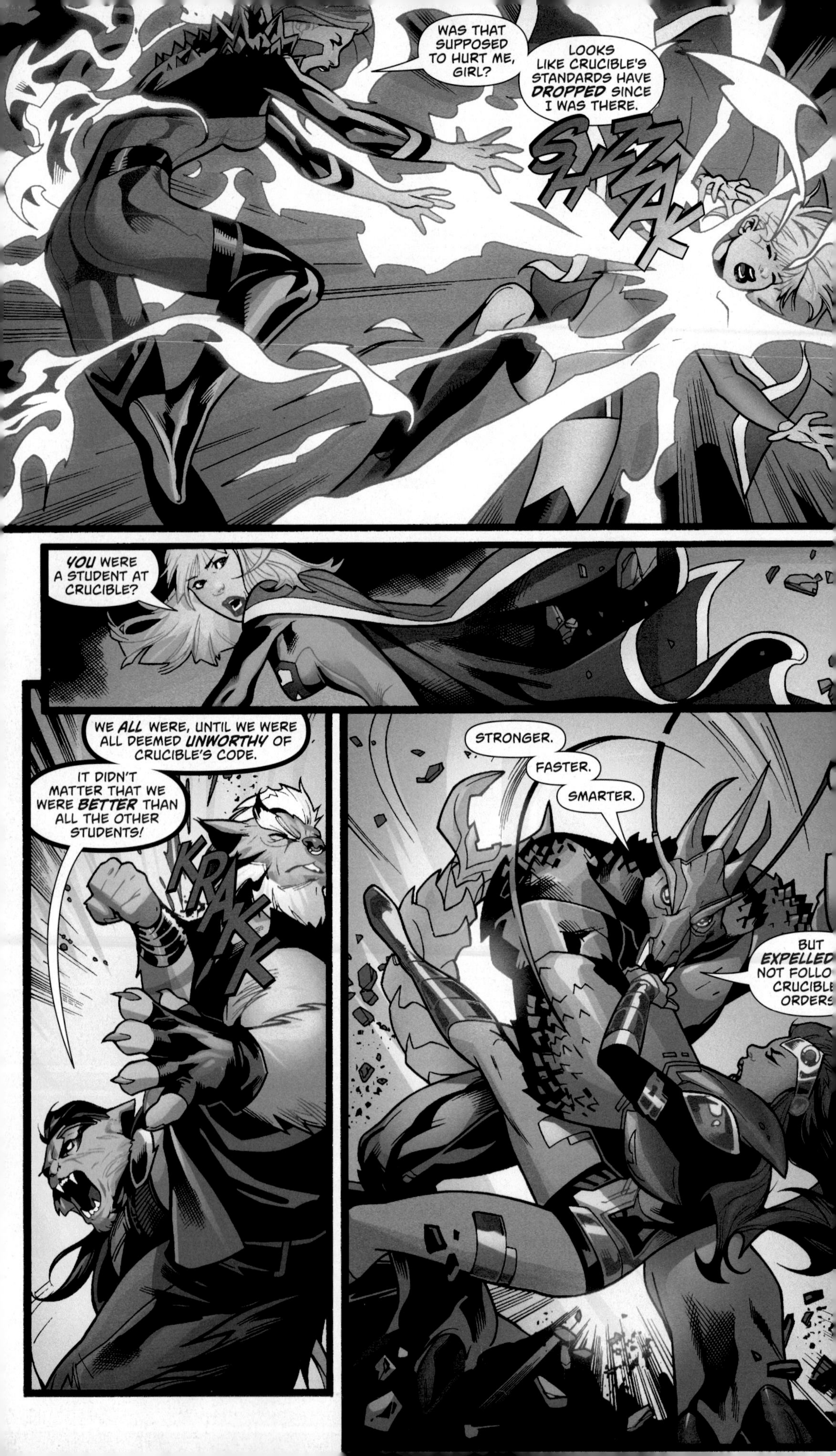

WAS THAT SUPPOSED TO HURT ME, GIRL?
LOOKS LIKE CRUCIBLE'S STANDARDS HAVE DROPPED SINCE I WAS THERE.
SHZZAK
YOU WERE A STUDENT AT CRUCIBLE?
WE ALL WERE, UNTIL WE WERE ALL DEEMED UNWORTHY OF CRUCIBLE'S CODE.
IT DIDN'T MATTER THAT WE WERE BETTER THAN ALL THE OTHER STUDENTS!
KRAKK
STRONGER.
FASTER.
SMARTER.

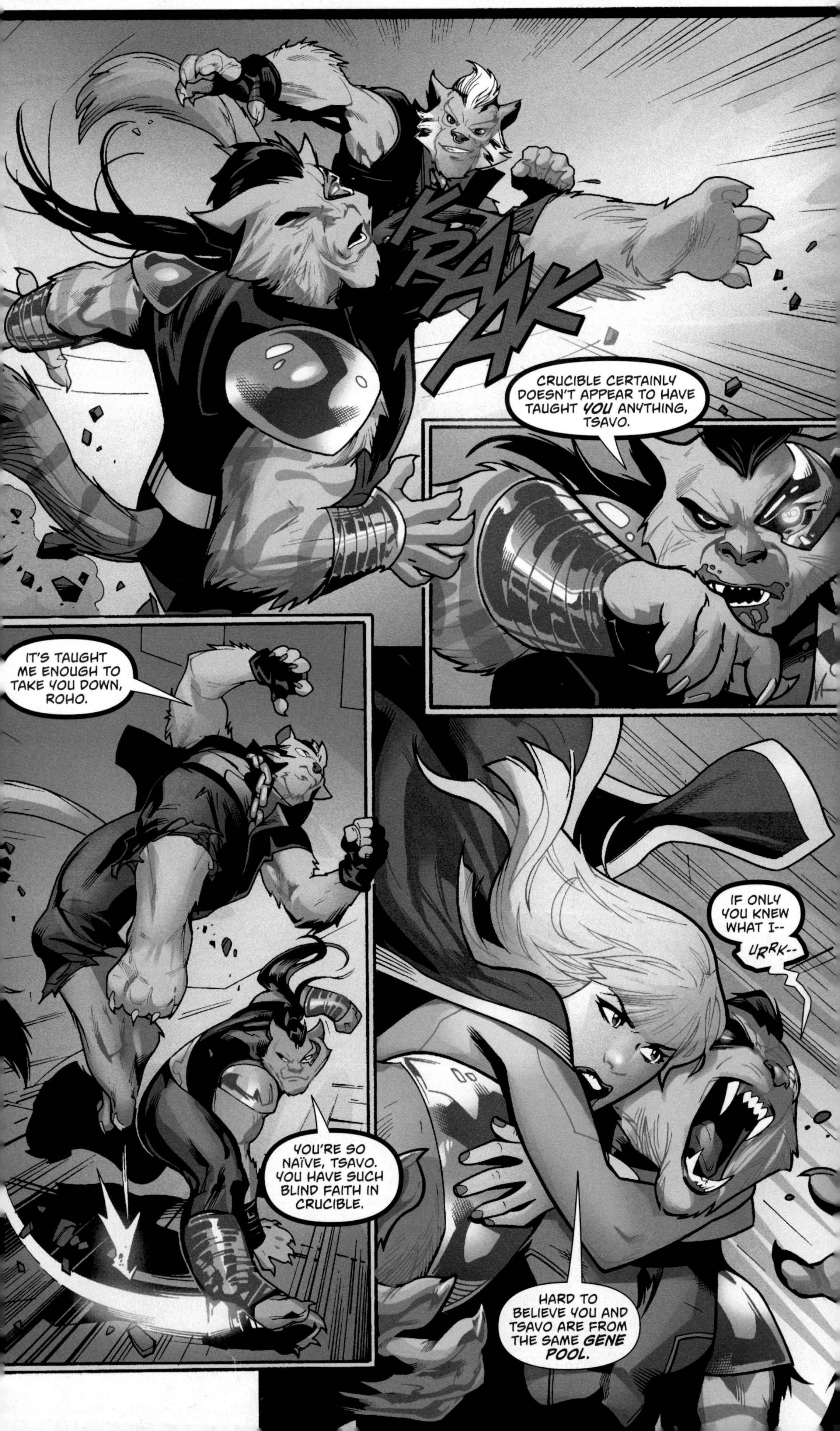
KRAK
CRUCIBLE CERTAINLY DOESN'T APPEAR TO HAVE TAUGHT *YOU* ANYTHING, TSAVO.
IT'S TAUGHT ME ENOUGH TO TAKE YOU DOWN, ROHO.
YOU'RE SO NAÏVE, TSAVO. YOU HAVE SUCH BLIND FAITH IN CRUCIBLE.
IF ONLY YOU KNEW WHAT I--
URRK--
HARD TO BELIEVE YOU AND TSAVO ARE FROM THE SAME *GENE POOL*.

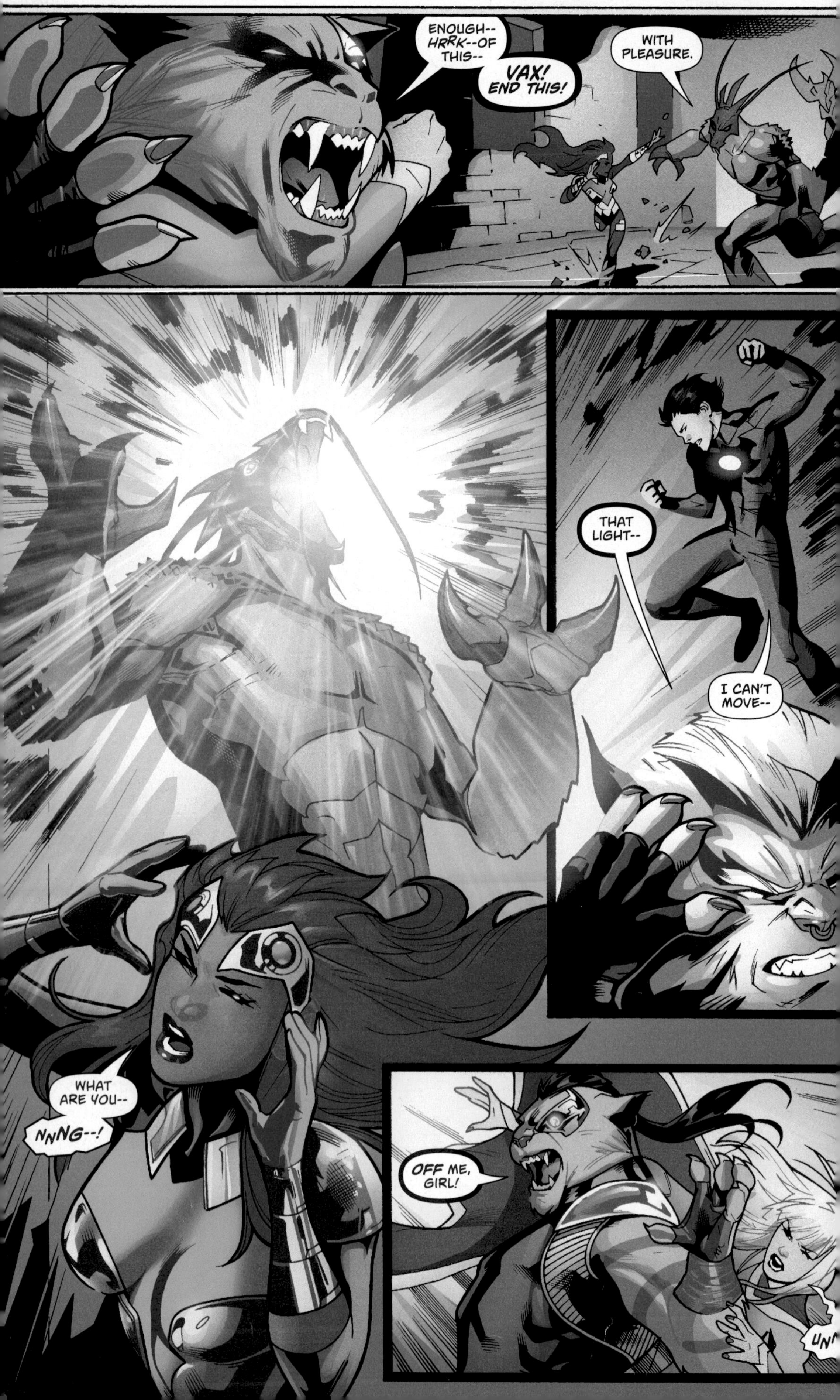
ENOUGH--HRRK--OF THIS--
VAX! END THIS!
WITH PLEASURE.
THAT LIGHT--
I CAN'T MOVE--
WHAT ARE YOU--
NNNG--!
OFF ME, GIRL!

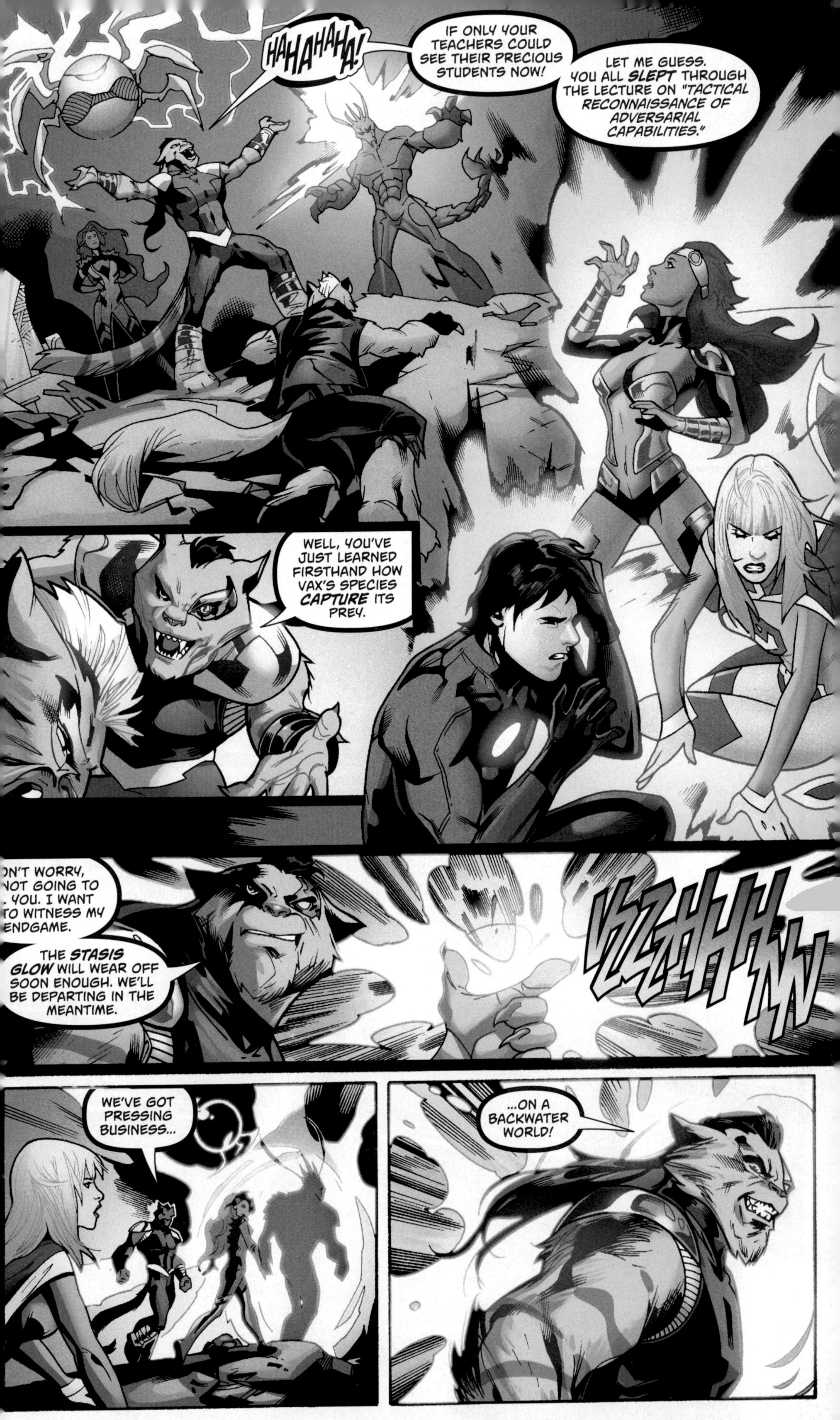
HAHAHAHA!
IF ONLY YOUR TEACHERS COULD SEE THEIR PRECIOUS STUDENTS NOW!
LET ME GUESS. YOU ALL SLEPT THROUGH THE LECTURE ON "TACTICAL RECONNAISSANCE OF ADVERSARIAL CAPABILITIES."
WELL, YOU'VE JUST LEARNED FIRSTHAND HOW VAX'S SPECIES CAPTURE ITS PREY.
ON'T WORRY, NOT GOING TO . YOU. I WANT TO WITNESS MY ENDGAME.
THE STASIS GLOW WILL WEAR OFF SOON ENOUGH. WE'LL BE DEPARTING IN THE MEANTIME.
VZZHHHNN
WE'VE GOT PRESSING BUSINESS...
...ON A BACKWATER WORLD!

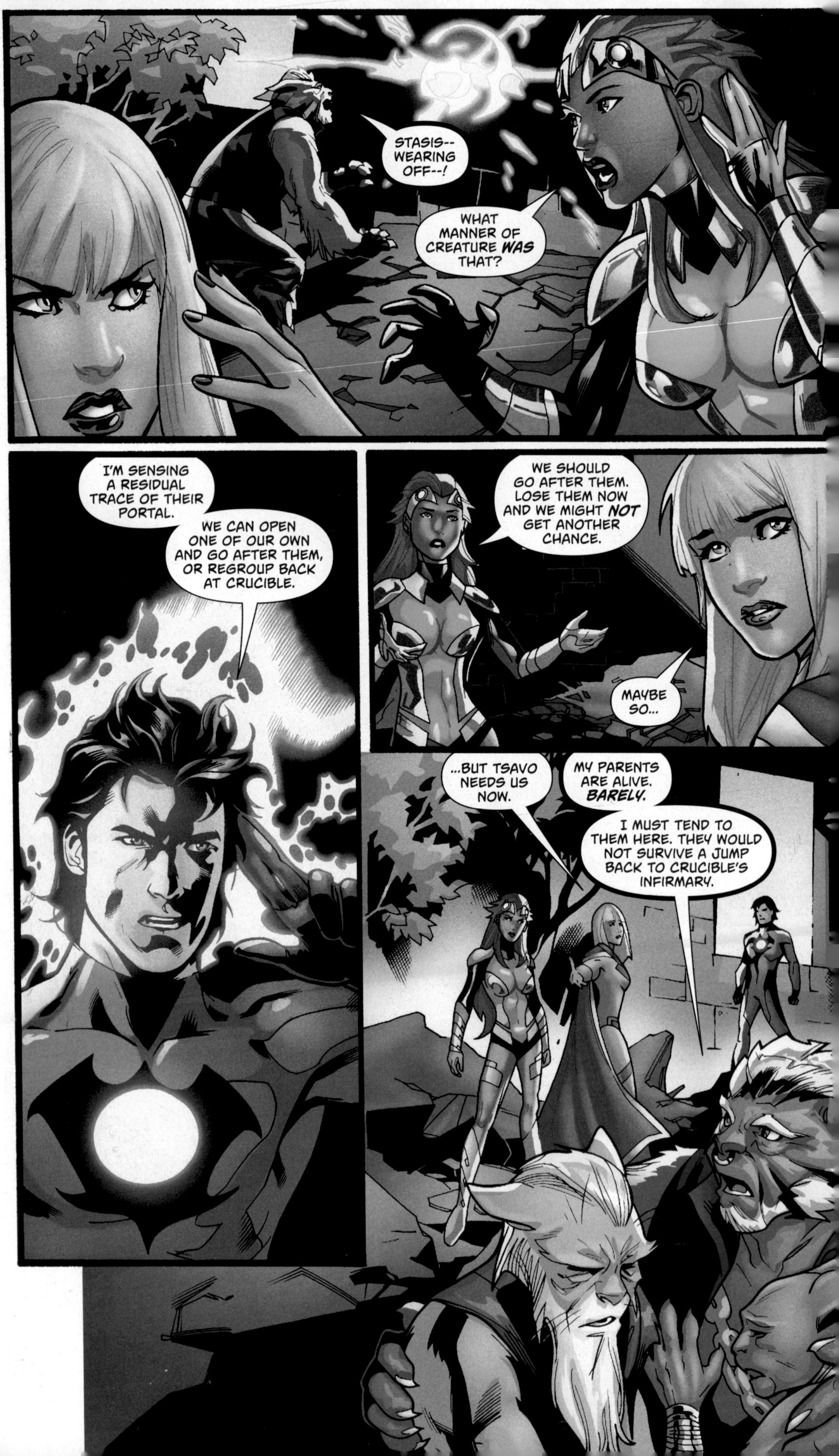
STASIS-- WEARING OFF--!
WHAT MANNER OF CREATURE *WAS* THAT?
I'M SENSING A RESIDUAL TRACE OF THEIR PORTAL.
WE CAN OPEN ONE OF OUR OWN AND GO AFTER THEM, OR REGROUP BACK AT CRUCIBLE.
WE SHOULD GO AFTER THEM. LOSE THEM NOW AND WE MIGHT *NOT* GET ANOTHER CHANCE.
MAYBE SO...
...BUT TSAVO NEEDS US NOW.
MY PARENTS ARE ALIVE. *BARELY.*
I MUST TEND TO THEM HERE. THEY WOULD NOT SURVIVE A JUMP BACK TO CRUCIBLE'S INFIRMARY.

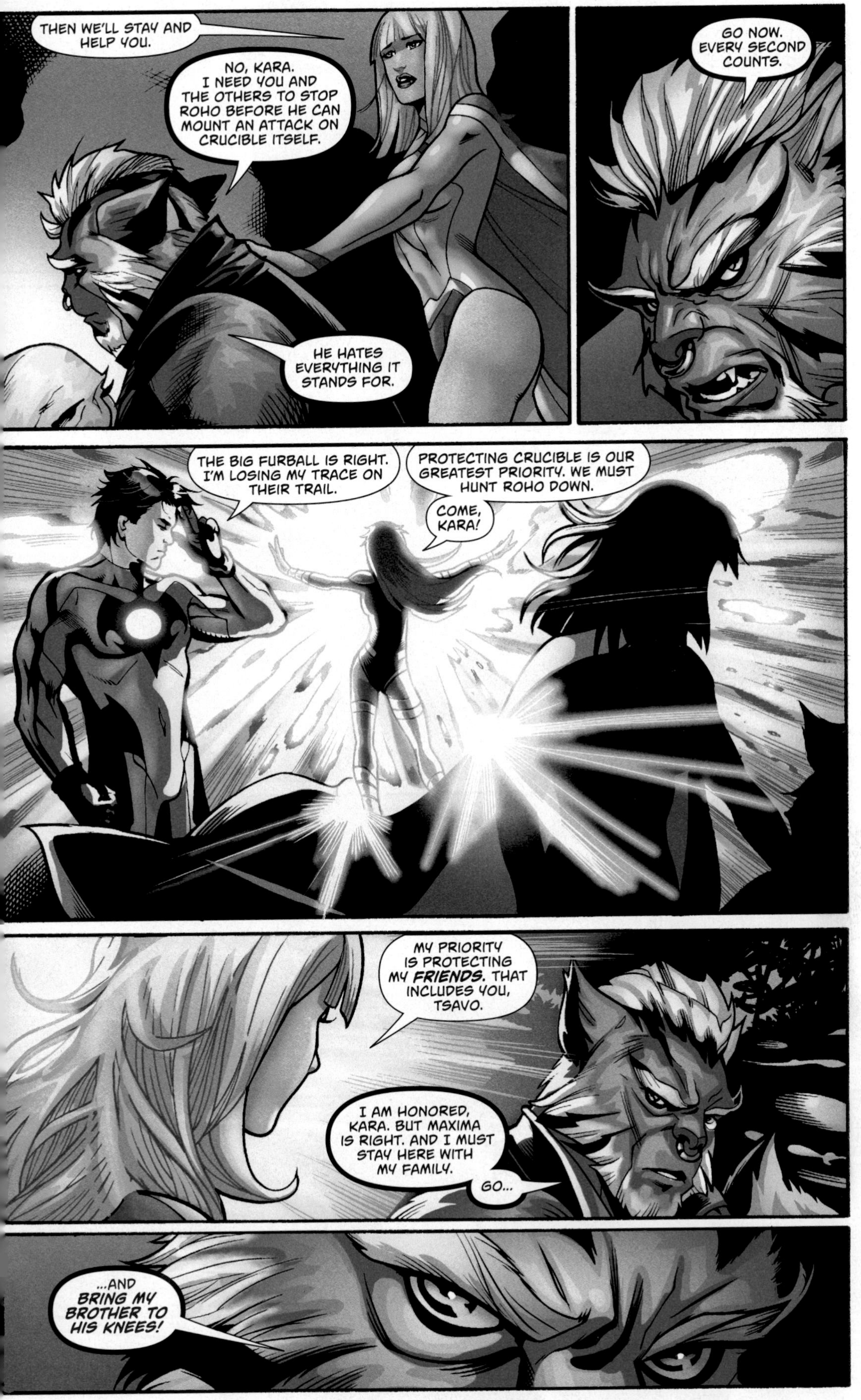
THEN WE'LL STAY AND HELP YOU.
NO, KARA. I NEED YOU AND THE OTHERS TO STOP ROHO BEFORE HE CAN MOUNT AN ATTACK ON CRUCIBLE ITSELF.
HE HATES EVERYTHING IT STANDS FOR.
GO NOW. EVERY SECOND COUNTS.
THE BIG FURBALL IS RIGHT. I'M LOSING MY TRACE ON THEIR TRAIL.
PROTECTING CRUCIBLE IS OUR GREATEST PRIORITY. WE MUST HUNT ROHO DOWN.
COME, KARA!
MY PRIORITY IS PROTECTING MY *FRIENDS*. THAT INCLUDES YOU, TSAVO.
I AM HONORED, KARA. BUT MAXIMA IS RIGHT. AND I MUST STAY HERE WITH MY FAMILY.
GO...
...AND *BRING MY BROTHER TO HIS KNEES!*

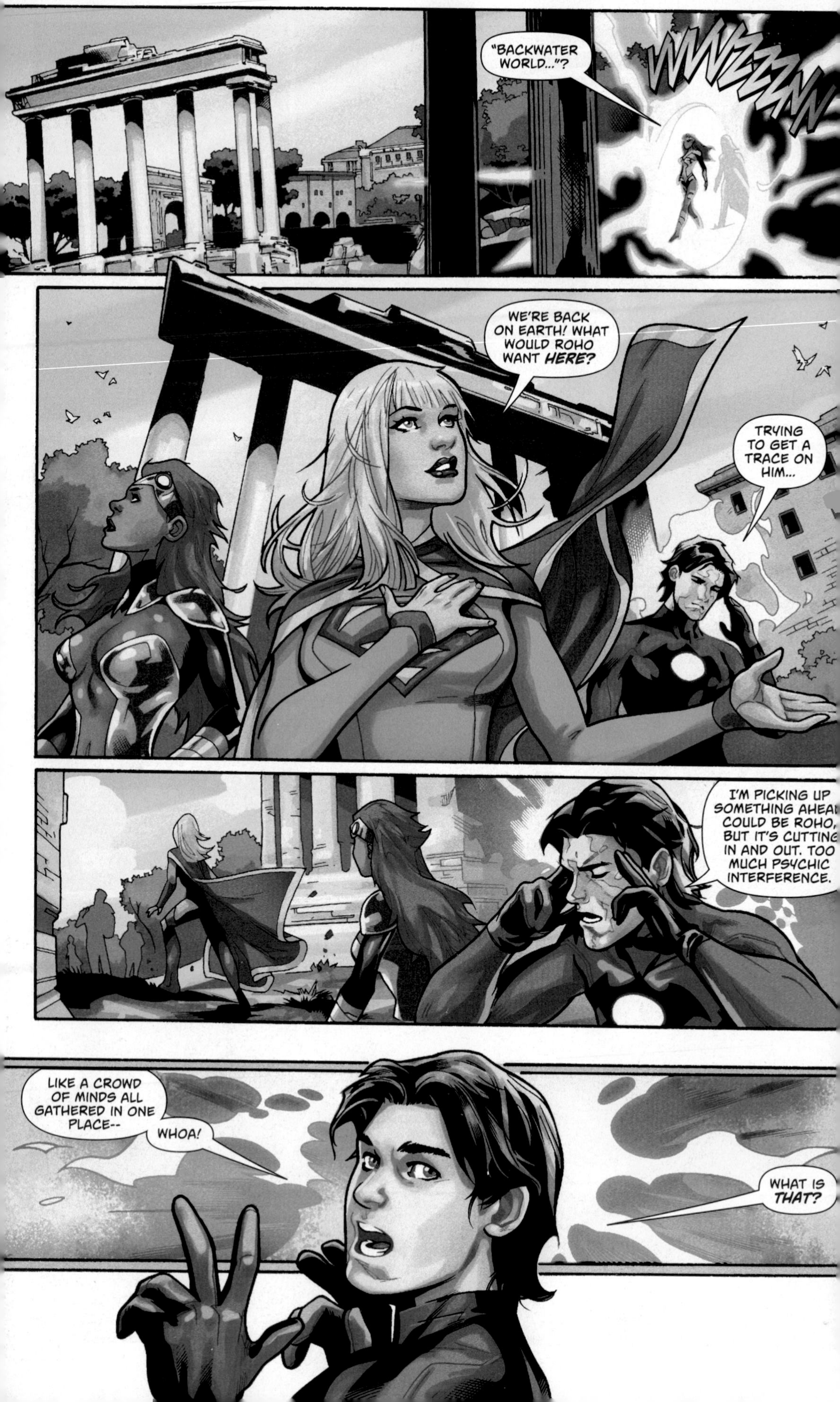
"BACKWATER WORLD..."?
VVVVZZZNN
WE'RE BACK ON EARTH! WHAT WOULD ROHO WANT *HERE?*
TRYING TO GET A TRACE ON HIM...
I'M PICKING UP SOMETHING AHEAD. COULD BE ROHO, BUT IT'S CUTTING IN AND OUT. TOO MUCH PSYCHIC INTERFERENCE.
LIKE A CROWD OF MINDS ALL GATHERED IN ONE PLACE--
WHOA!
WHAT IS *THAT?*

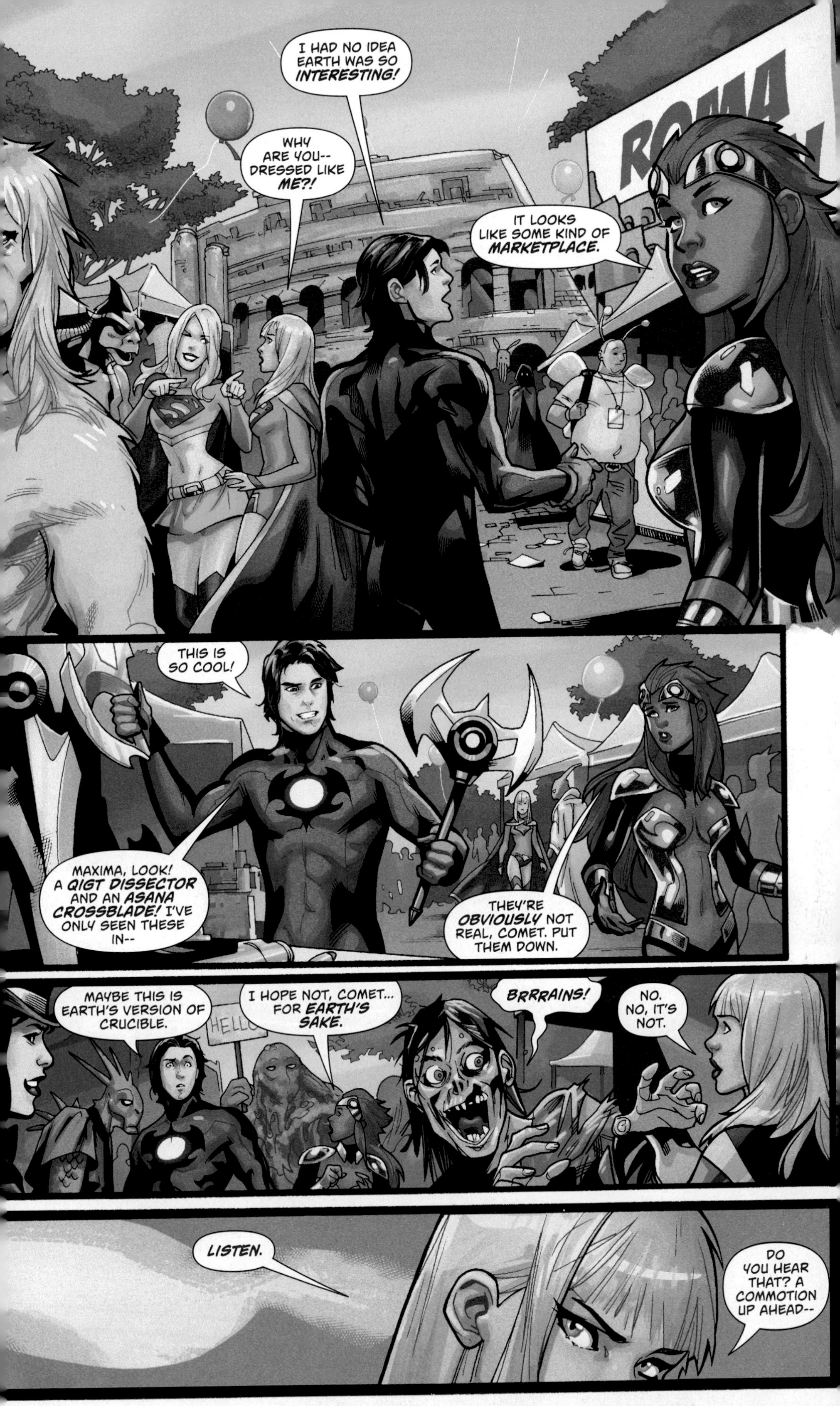

ROMA
I HAD NO IDEA EARTH WAS SO INTERESTING!
WHY ARE YOU-- DRESSED LIKE ME?!
IT LOOKS LIKE SOME KIND OF MARKETPLACE.
THIS IS SO COOL!
MAXIMA, LOOK! A QIGT DISSECTOR AND AN ASANA CROSSBLADE! I'VE ONLY SEEN THESE IN--
THEY'RE OBVIOUSLY NOT REAL, COMET. PUT THEM DOWN.
MAYBE THIS IS EARTH'S VERSION OF CRUCIBLE.
HELLO
I HOPE NOT, COMET... FOR EARTH'S SAKE.
BRRRAINS!
NO. NO, IT'S NOT.
LISTEN.
DO YOU HEAR THAT? A COMMOTION UP AHEAD--

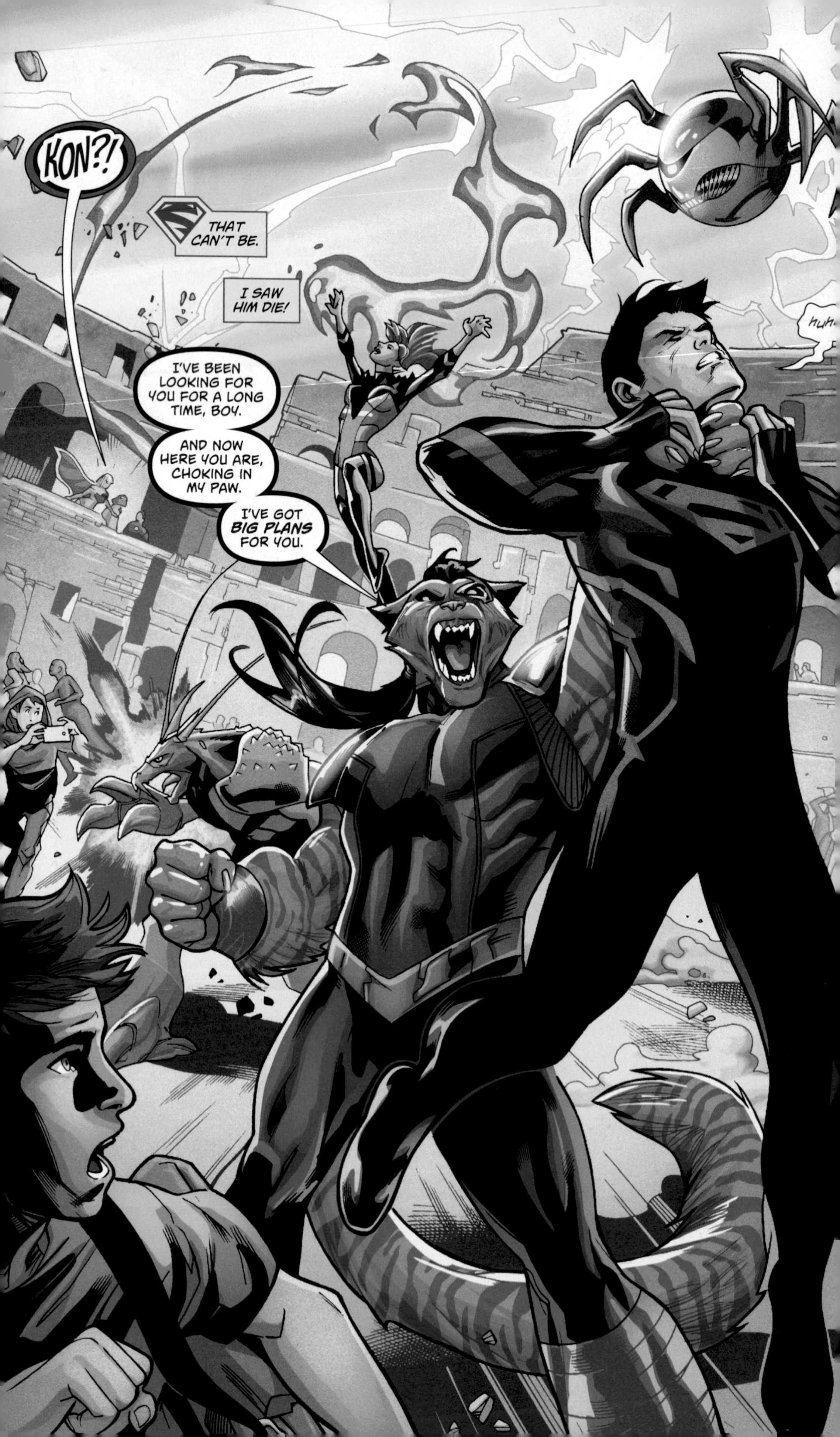
KON?!
THAT CAN'T BE.
I SAW HIM DIE!
huh
I'VE BEEN LOOKING FOR YOU FOR A LONG TIME, BOY.
AND NOW HERE YOU ARE, CHOKING IN MY PAW.
I'VE GOT BIG PLANS FOR YOU.

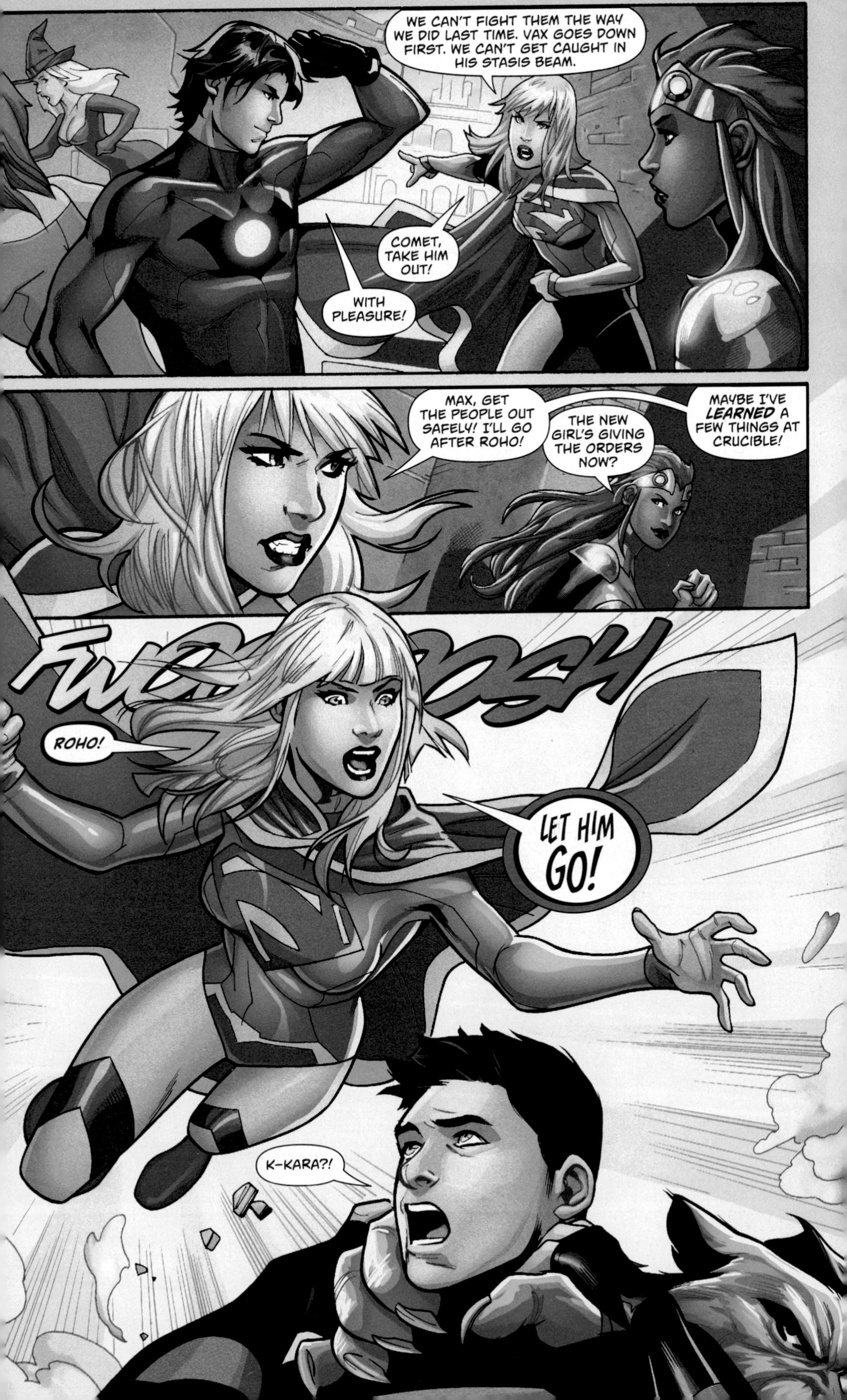
WE CAN'T FIGHT THEM THE WAY WE DID LAST TIME. VAX GOES DOWN FIRST. WE CAN'T GET CAUGHT IN HIS STASIS BEAM.
COMET, TAKE HIM OUT!
WITH PLEASURE!
MAX, GET THE PEOPLE OUT SAFELY! I'LL GO AFTER ROHO!
THE NEW GIRL'S GIVING THE ORDERS NOW?
MAYBE I'VE LEARNED A FEW THINGS AT CRUCIBLE!
ROHO!
LET HIM GO!
K-KARA?!

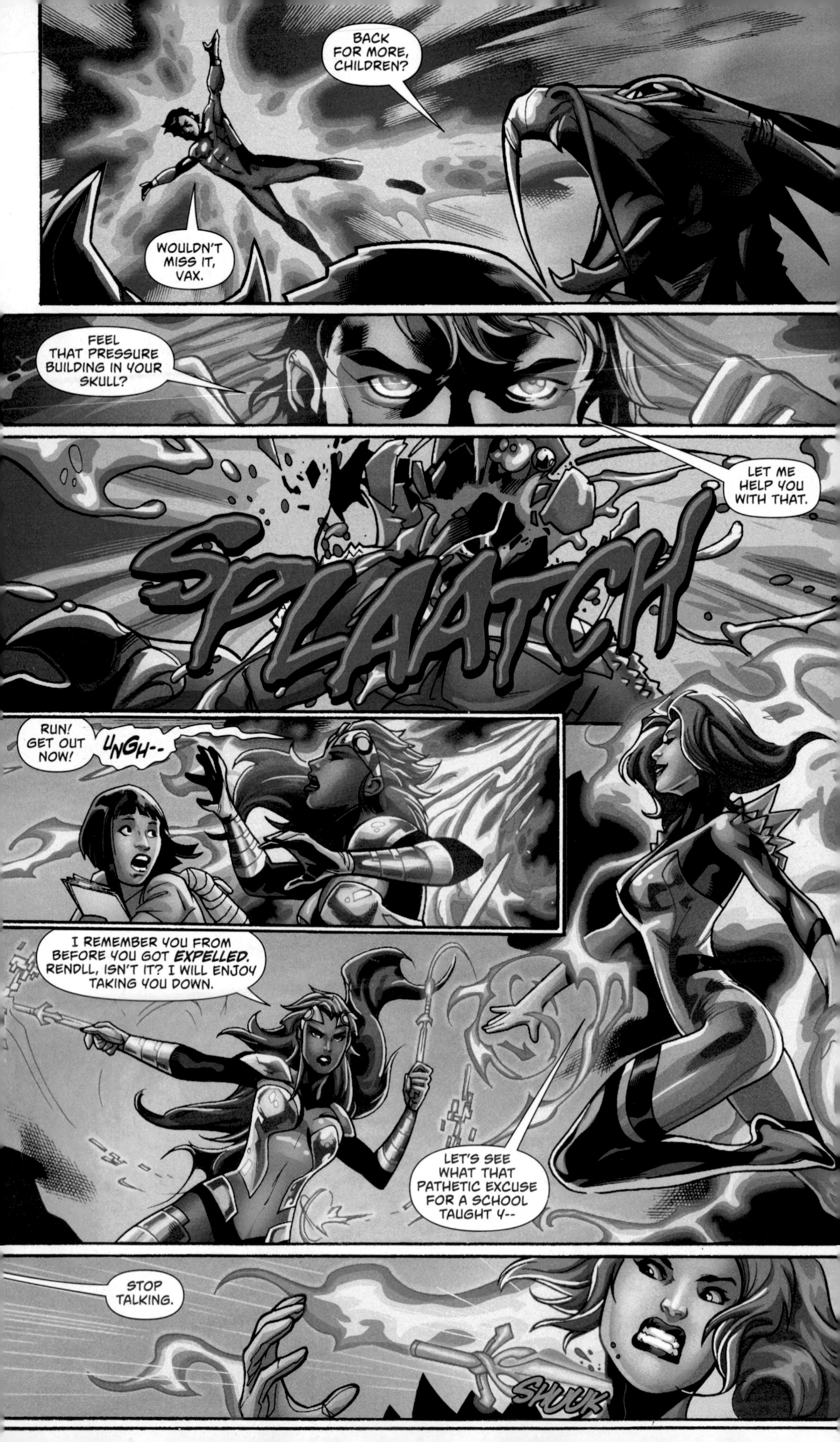
BACK FOR MORE, CHILDREN?
WOULDN'T MISS IT, VAX.
FEEL THAT PRESSURE BUILDING IN YOUR SKULL?
LET ME HELP YOU WITH THAT.
SPLAATCH
RUN! GET OUT NOW!
UNGH--
I REMEMBER YOU FROM BEFORE YOU GOT EXPELLED. RENDLL, ISN'T IT? I WILL ENJOY TAKING YOU DOWN.
LET'S SEE WHAT THAT PATHETIC EXCUSE FOR A SCHOOL TAUGHT Y--
STOP TALKING.
SHUUK

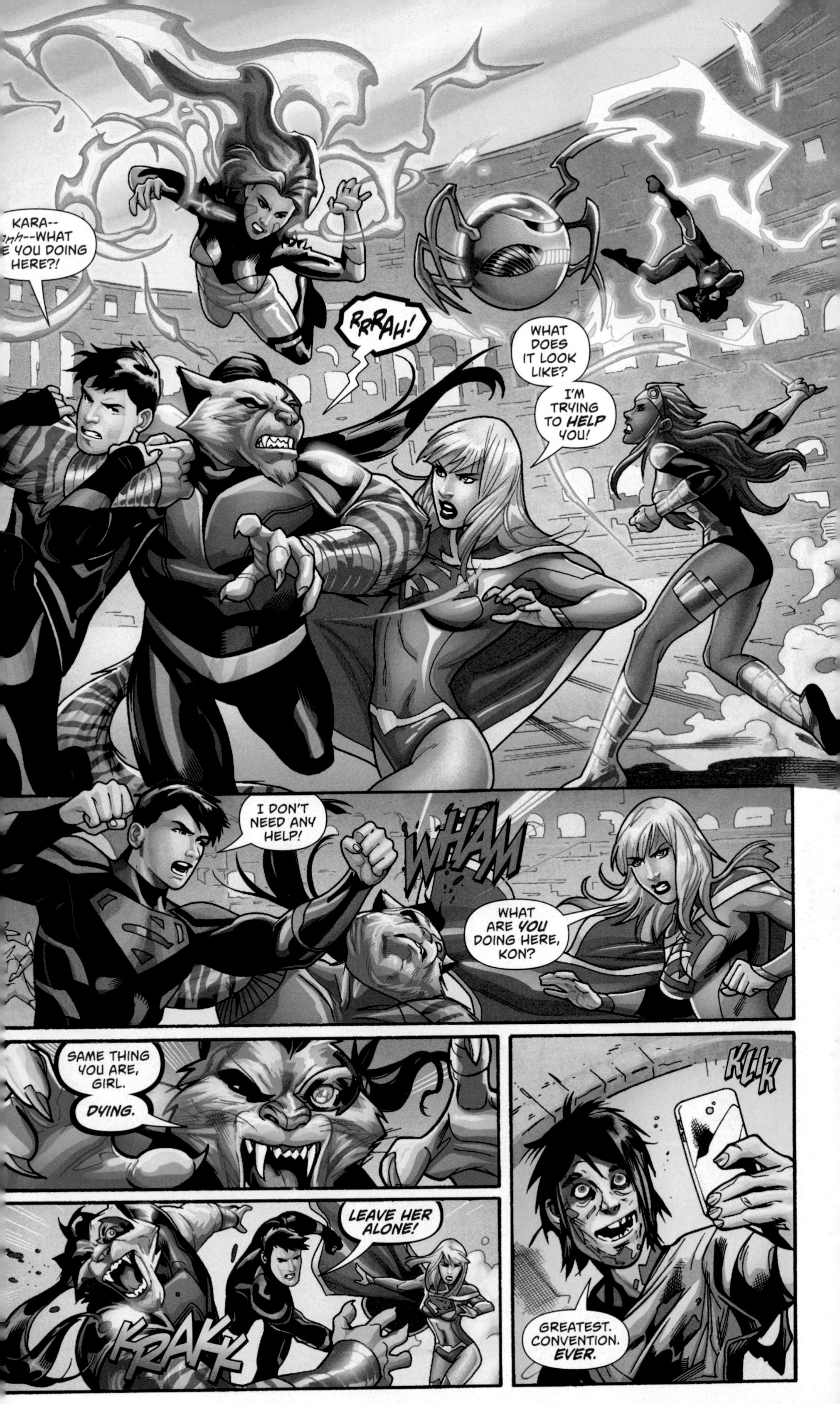

KARA-- nh--WHAT E YOU DOING HERE?!
RRRAH!
WHAT DOES IT LOOK LIKE?
I'M TRYING TO HELP YOU!
I DON'T NEED ANY HELP!
WHAM
WHAT ARE YOU DOING HERE, KON?
SAME THING YOU ARE, GIRL.
DYING.
LEAVE HER ALONE!
KRAKK
KLIK
GREATEST. CONVENTION. EVER.

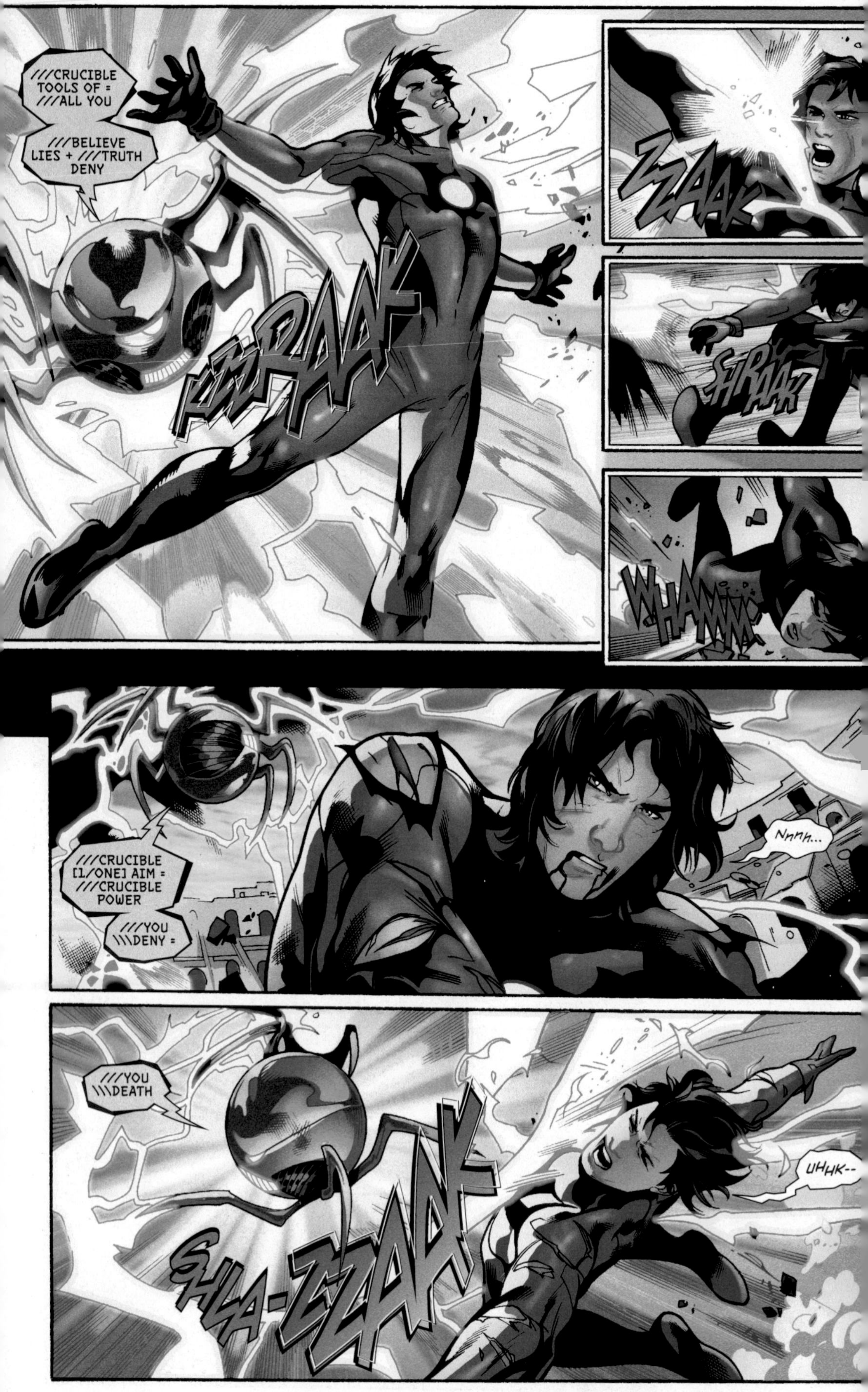
///CRUCIBLE TOOLS OF = ///ALL YOU
///BELIEVE LIES + ///TRUTH DENY
KRRAAK
ZZAAK
SHRAAK
WHAMM
///CRUCIBLE [1/ONE] AIM = ///CRUCIBLE POWER
///YOU \\\DENY =
Nnnn...
///YOU \\\DEATH
SHLA-ZZAAK
UHHK--

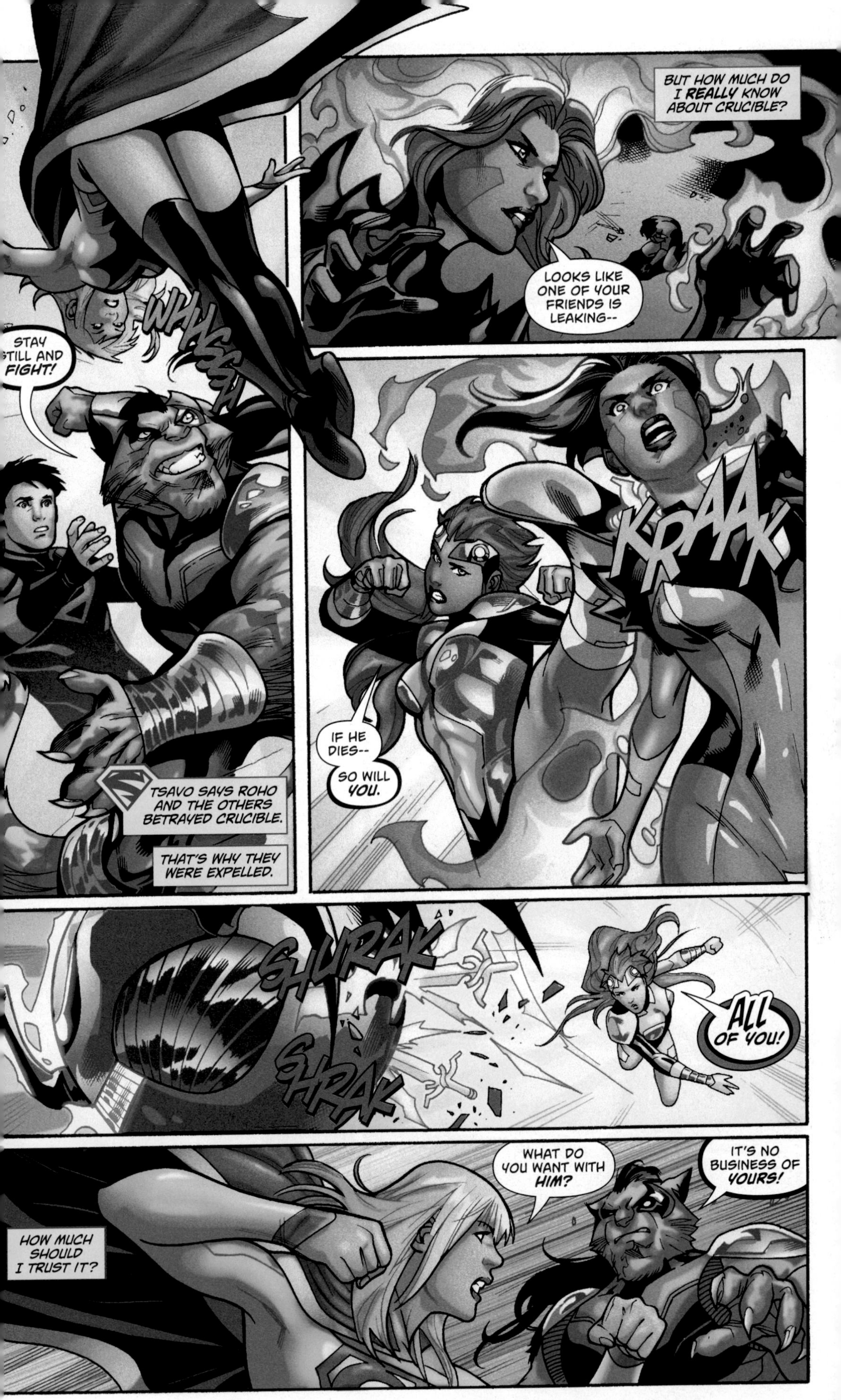
BUT HOW MUCH DO I REALLY KNOW ABOUT CRUCIBLE?
LOOKS LIKE ONE OF YOUR FRIENDS IS LEAKING--
WHHSSSH
STAY STILL AND FIGHT!
KRAAK
IF HE DIES--
SO WILL YOU.
TSAVO SAYS ROHO AND THE OTHERS BETRAYED CRUCIBLE.
THAT'S WHY THEY WERE EXPELLED.
SHURAK
SHRAK
ALL OF YOU!
WHAT DO YOU WANT WITH HIM?
IT'S NO BUSINESS OF YOURS!
HOW MUCH SHOULD I TRUST IT?

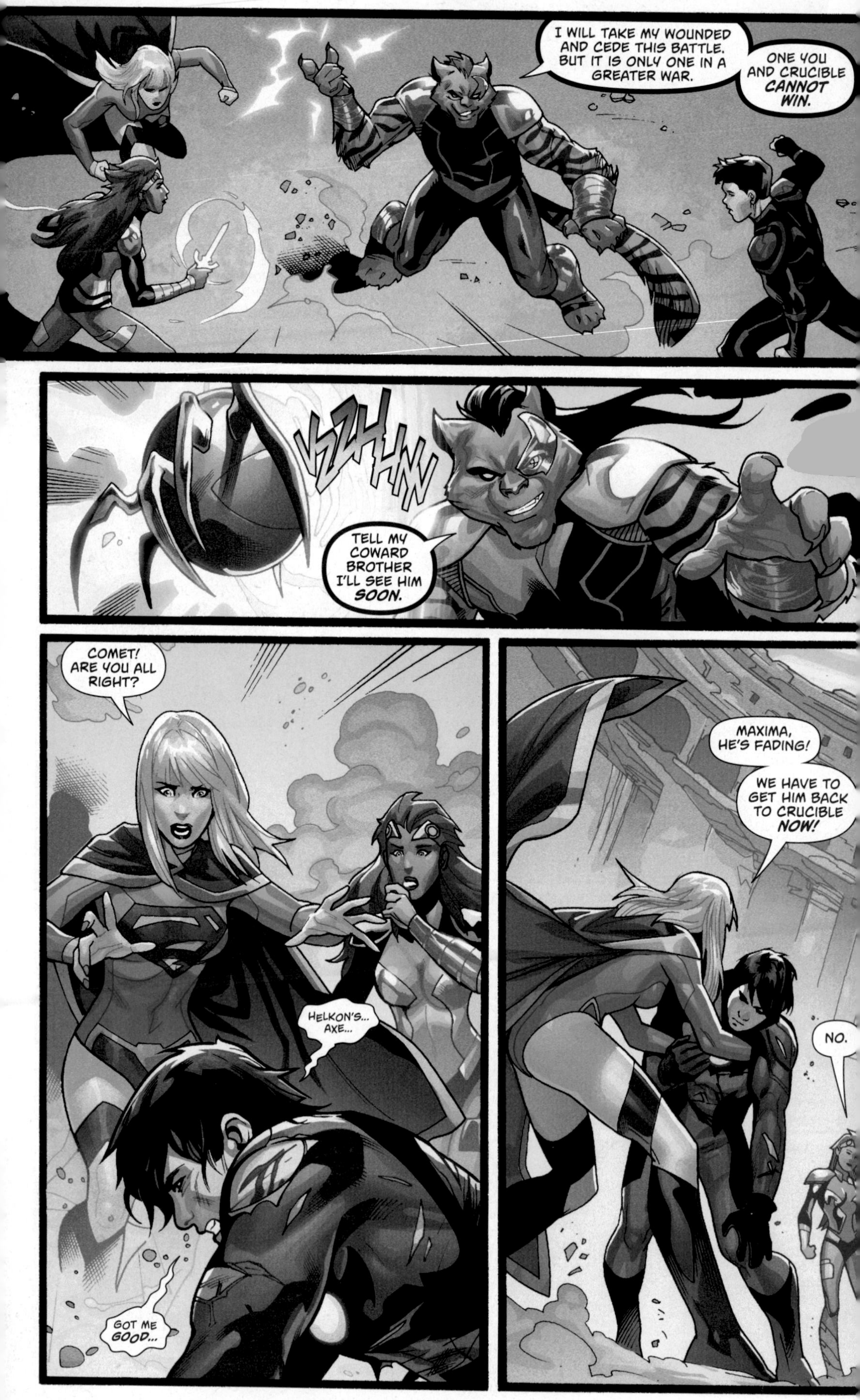
I WILL TAKE MY WOUNDED AND CEDE THIS BATTLE. BUT IT IS ONLY ONE IN A GREATER WAR.
ONE YOU AND CRUCIBLE CANNOT WIN.
VZZHNN
TELL MY COWARD BROTHER I'LL SEE HIM SOON.
COMET! ARE YOU ALL RIGHT?
HELKON'S... AXE...
GOT ME GOOD...
MAXIMA, HE'S FADING!
WE HAVE TO GET HIM BACK TO CRUCIBLE NOW!
NO.

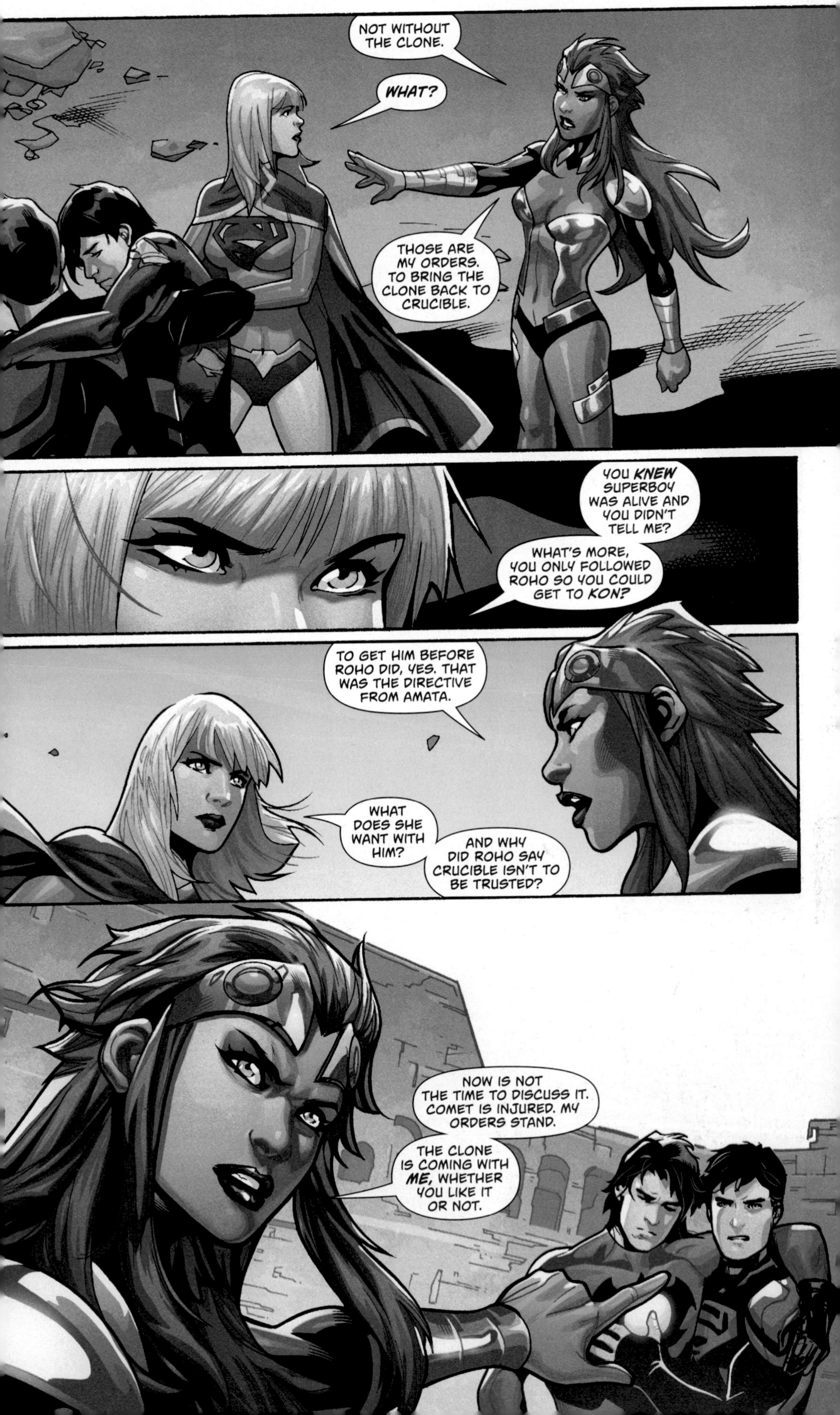
NOT WITHOUT THE CLONE.
WHAT?
THOSE ARE MY ORDERS. TO BRING THE CLONE BACK TO CRUCIBLE.
YOU KNEW SUPERBOY WAS ALIVE AND YOU DIDN'T TELL ME?
WHAT'S MORE, YOU ONLY FOLLOWED ROHO SO YOU COULD GET TO KON?
TO GET HIM BEFORE ROHO DID, YES. THAT WAS THE DIRECTIVE FROM AMATA.
WHAT DOES SHE WANT WITH HIM?
AND WHY DID ROHO SAY CRUCIBLE ISN'T TO BE TRUSTED?
NOW IS NOT THE TIME TO DISCUSS IT. COMET IS INJURED. MY ORDERS STAND.
THE CLONE IS COMING WITH ME, WHETHER YOU LIKE IT OR NOT.

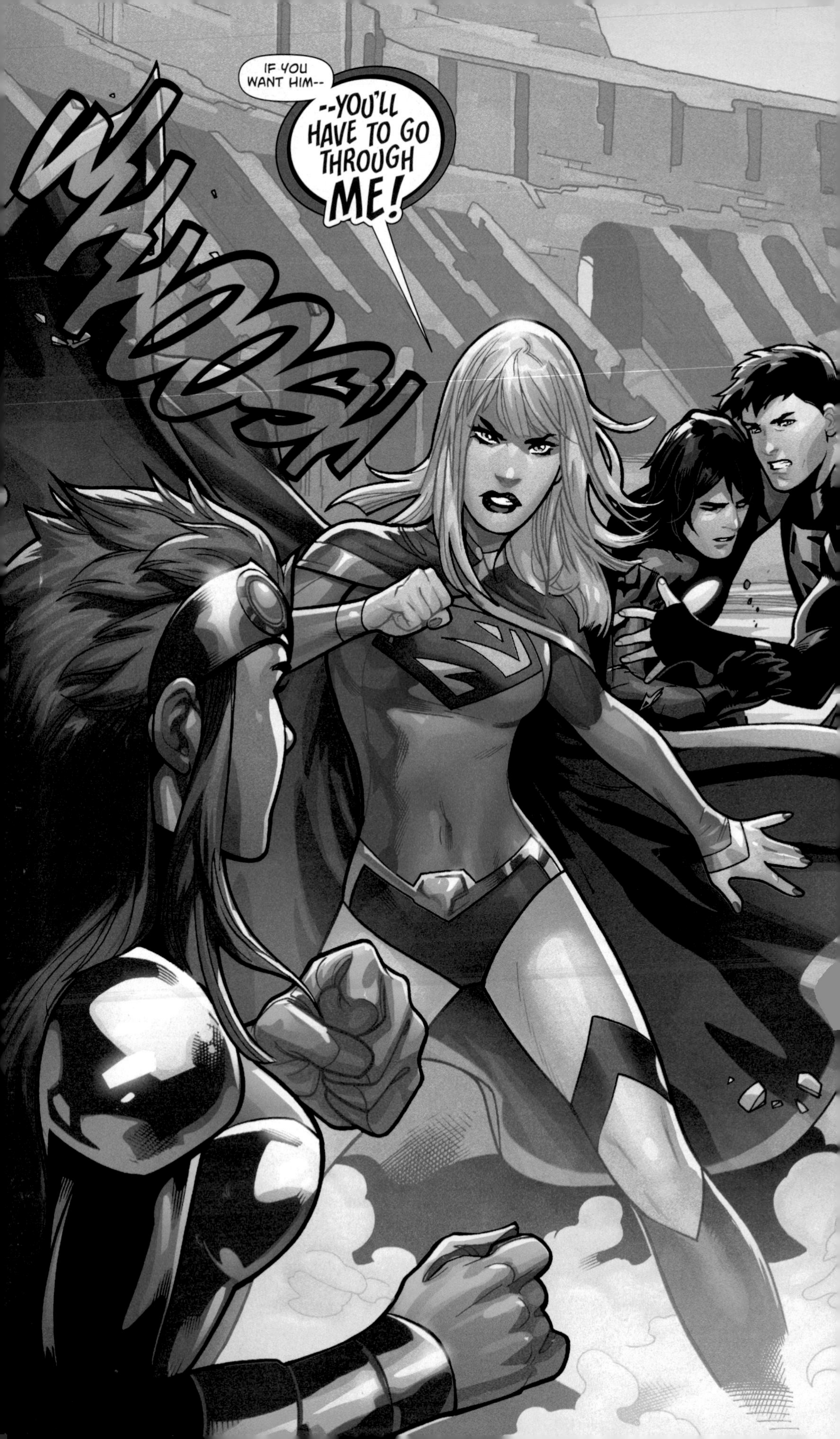
IF YOU WANT HIM--
--YOU'LL HAVE TO GO THROUGH ME!

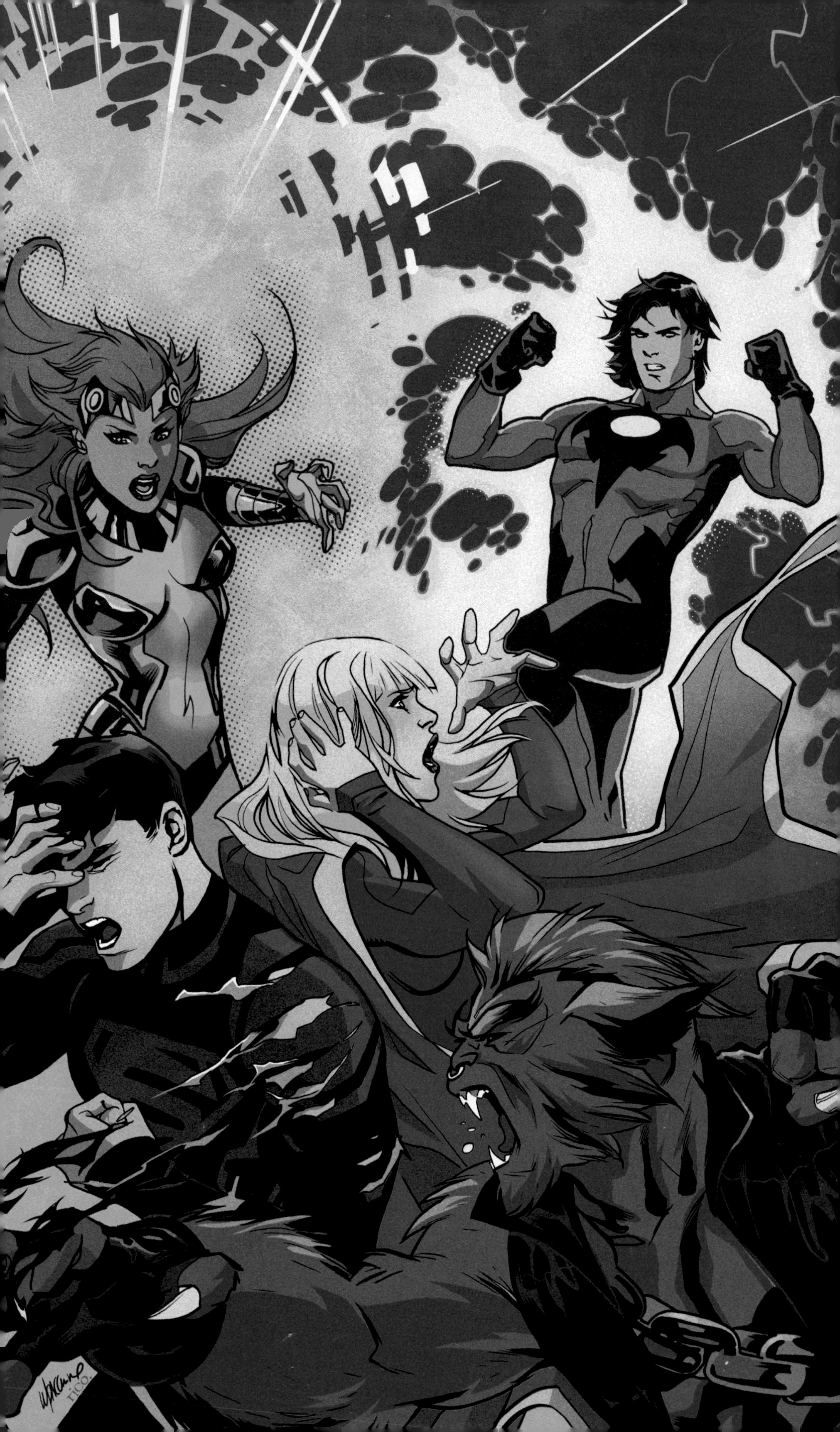

CRUCIBLE: PART 4

K. PERKINS MIKE JOHNSON writers EMANUELA LUPACCHINO penciller RAY McCARTHY inker HI-FI colorist ROB LEIGH letterer
cover art by EMANUELA LUPACCHINO and RICO RENZI

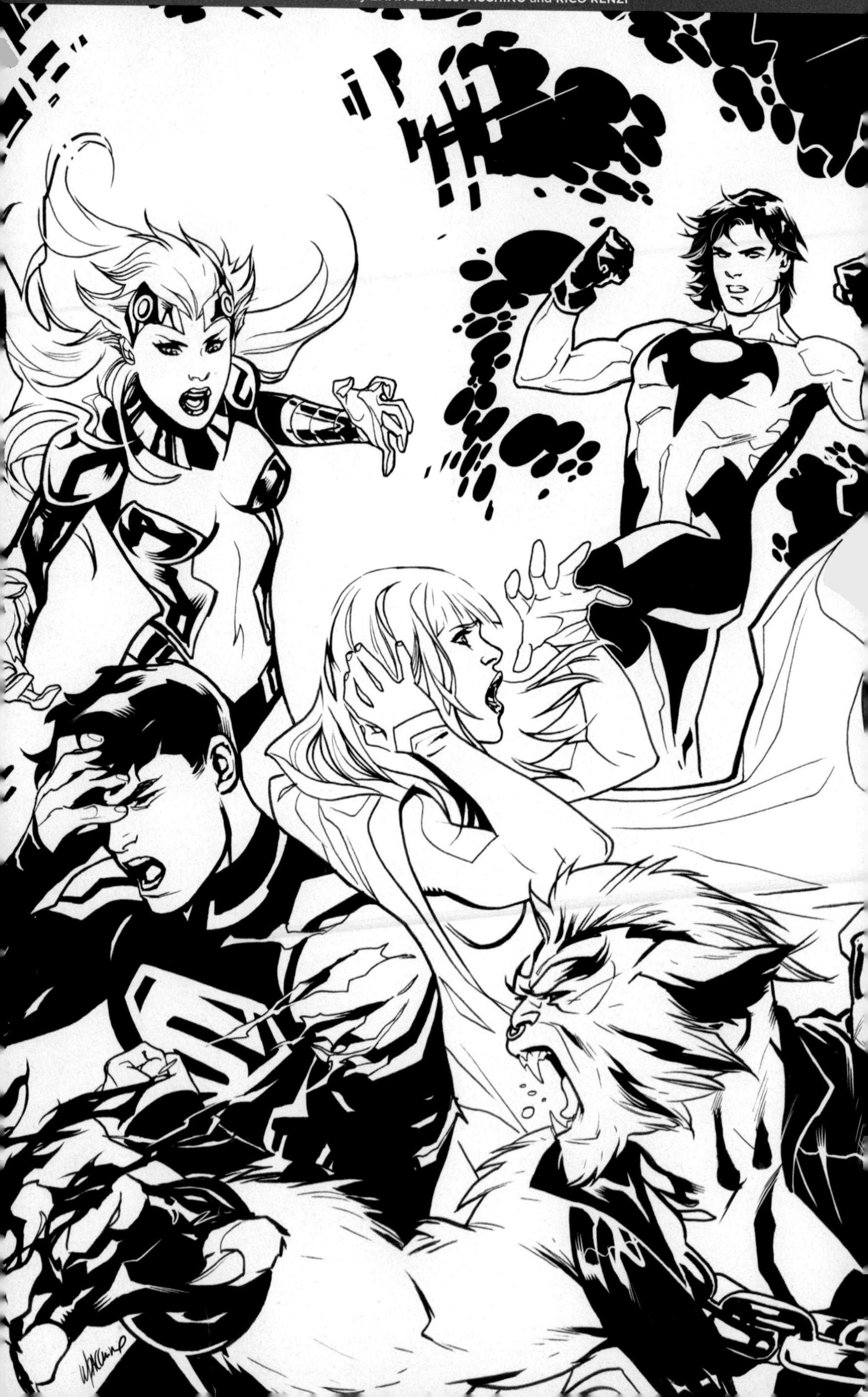

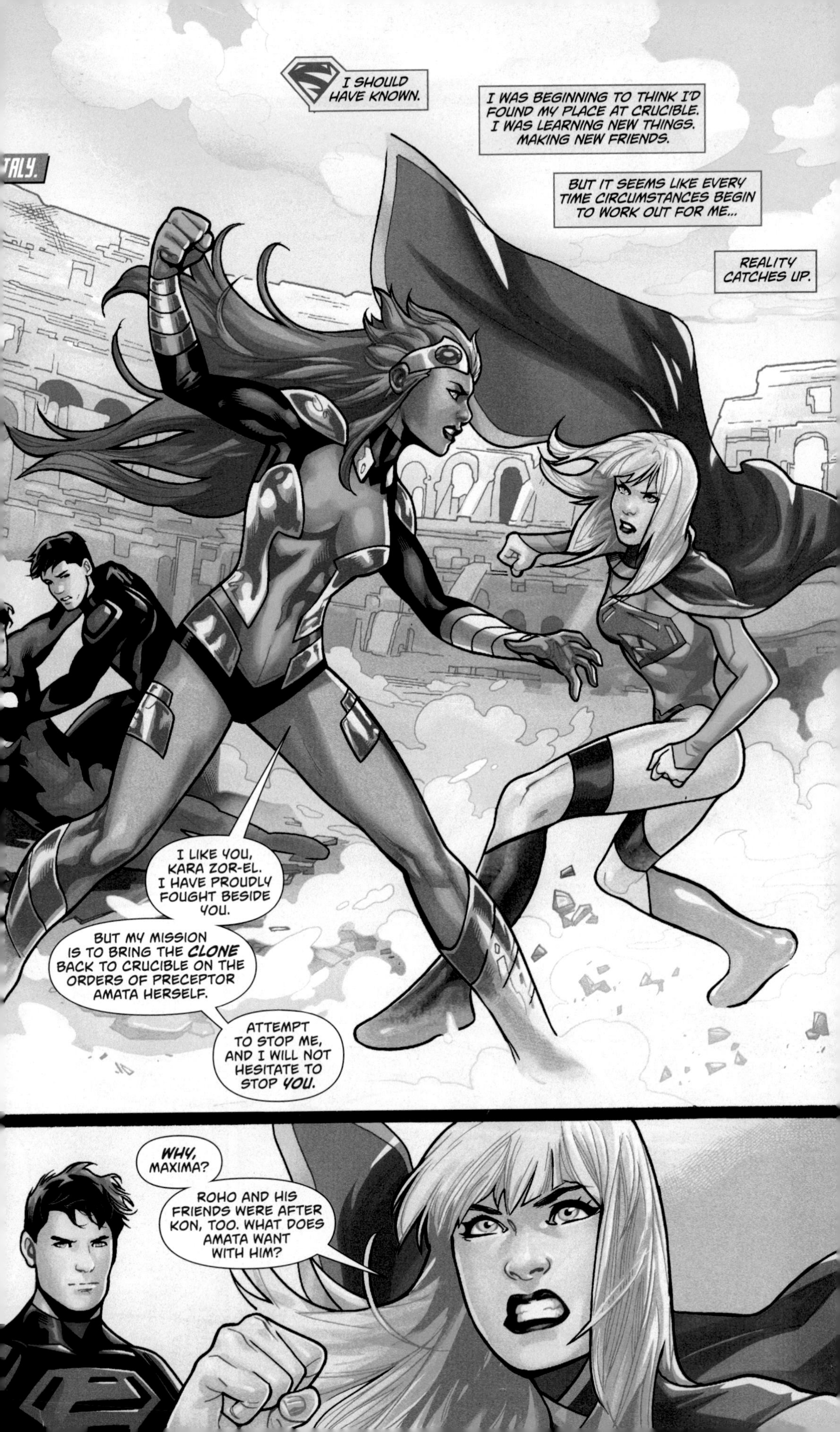
TALY.
I SHOULD HAVE KNOWN.
I WAS BEGINNING TO THINK I'D FOUND MY PLACE AT CRUCIBLE. I WAS LEARNING NEW THINGS. MAKING NEW FRIENDS.
BUT IT SEEMS LIKE EVERY TIME CIRCUMSTANCES BEGIN TO WORK OUT FOR ME...
REALITY CATCHES UP.
I LIKE YOU, KARA ZOR-EL. I HAVE PROUDLY FOUGHT BESIDE YOU.
BUT MY MISSION IS TO BRING THE CLONE BACK TO CRUCIBLE ON THE ORDERS OF PRECEPTOR AMATA HERSELF.
ATTEMPT TO STOP ME, AND I WILL NOT HESITATE TO STOP YOU.
WHY, MAXIMA?
ROHO AND HIS FRIENDS WERE AFTER KON, TOO. WHAT DOES AMATA WANT WITH HIM?

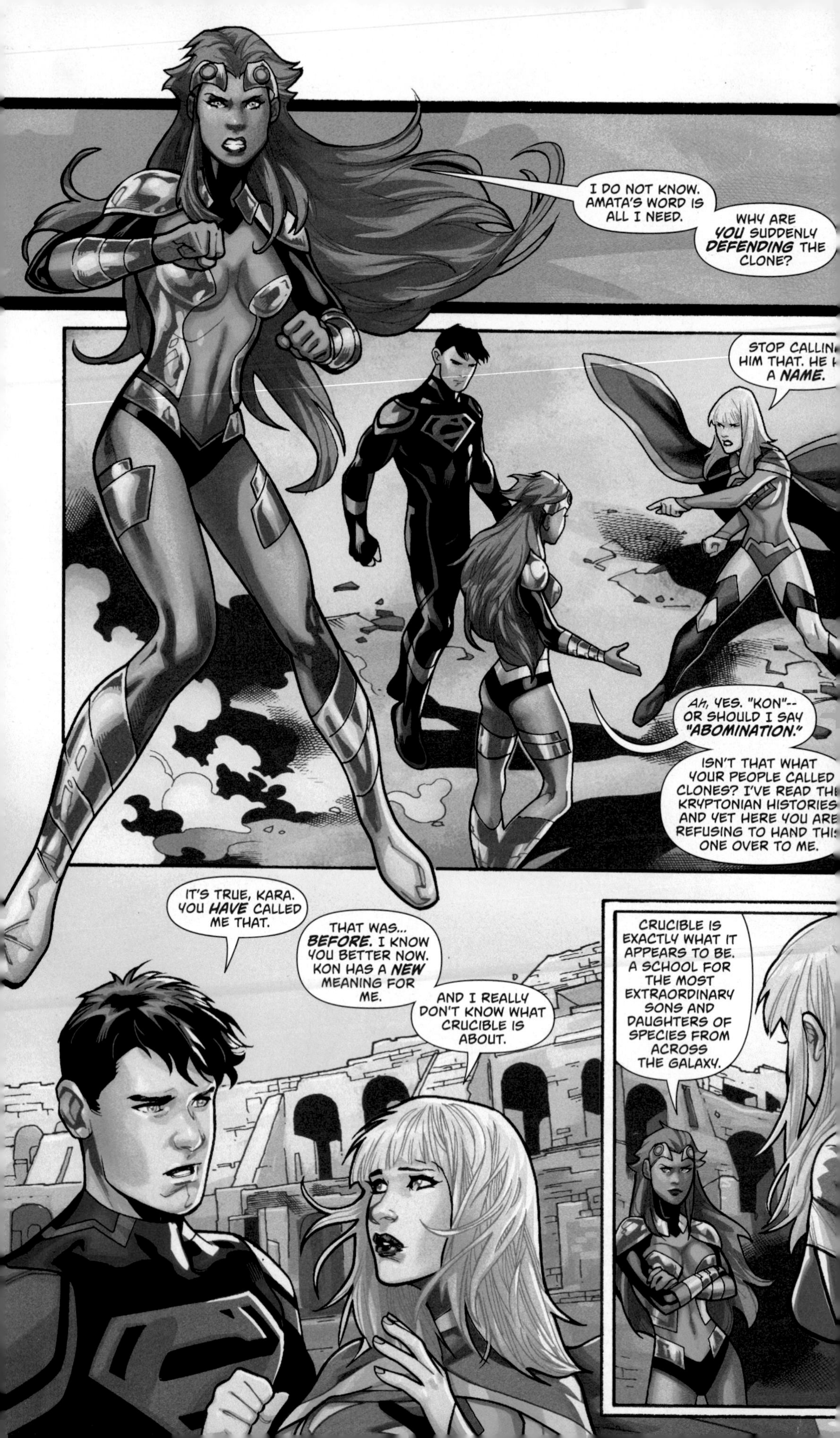
I DO NOT KNOW. AMATA'S WORD IS ALL I NEED.
WHY ARE *YOU* SUDDENLY *DEFENDING* THE CLONE?
STOP CALLIN HIM THAT. HE A *NAME.*
Ah, YES. "KON"-- OR SHOULD I SAY *"ABOMINATION."*
ISN'T THAT WHAT YOUR PEOPLE CALLED CLONES? I'VE READ TH KRYPTONIAN HISTORIES AND YET HERE YOU ARE REFUSING TO HAND THI ONE OVER TO ME.
IT'S TRUE, KARA. YOU *HAVE* CALLED ME THAT.
THAT WAS... *BEFORE.* I KNOW YOU BETTER NOW. KON HAS A *NEW* MEANING FOR ME.
AND I REALLY DON'T KNOW WHAT CRUCIBLE IS ABOUT.
CRUCIBLE IS EXACTLY WHAT IT APPEARS TO BE. A SCHOOL FOR THE MOST EXTRAORDINARY SONS AND DAUGHTERS OF SPECIES FROM ACROSS THE GALAXY.

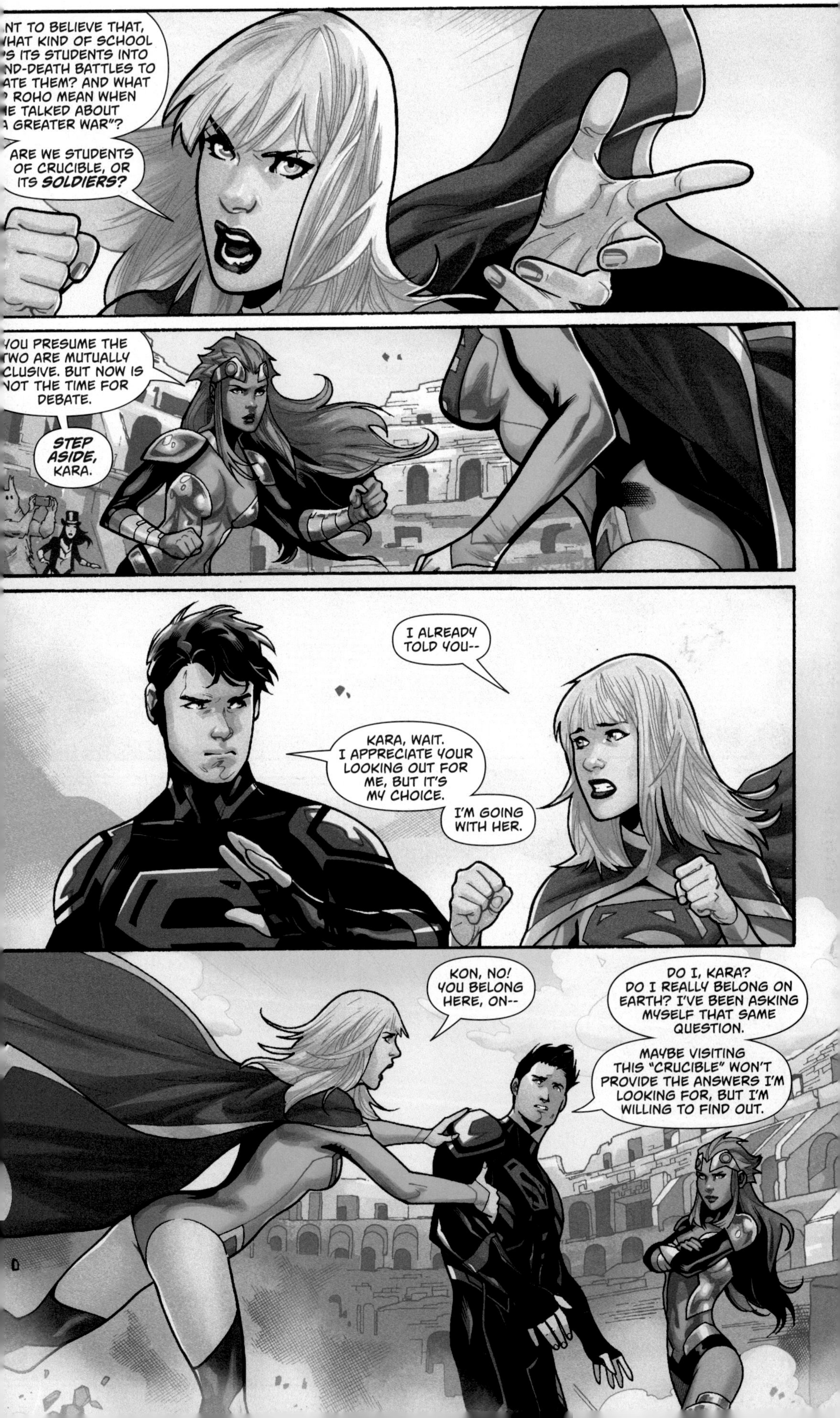
NT TO BELIEVE THAT, HAT KIND OF SCHOOL S ITS STUDENTS INTO ND-DEATH BATTLES TO ATE THEM? AND WHAT ROHO MEAN WHEN E TALKED ABOUT GREATER WAR"?
ARE WE STUDENTS OF CRUCIBLE, OR ITS SOLDIERS?
OU PRESUME THE TWO ARE MUTUALLY CLUSIVE. BUT NOW IS NOT THE TIME FOR DEBATE.
STEP ASIDE, KARA.
I ALREADY TOLD YOU--
KARA, WAIT. I APPRECIATE YOUR LOOKING OUT FOR ME, BUT IT'S MY CHOICE.
I'M GOING WITH HER.
KON, NO! YOU BELONG HERE, ON--
DO I, KARA? DO I REALLY BELONG ON EARTH? I'VE BEEN ASKING MYSELF THAT SAME QUESTION.
MAYBE VISITING THIS "CRUCIBLE" WON'T PROVIDE THE ANSWERS I'M LOOKING FOR, BUT I'M WILLING TO FIND OUT.

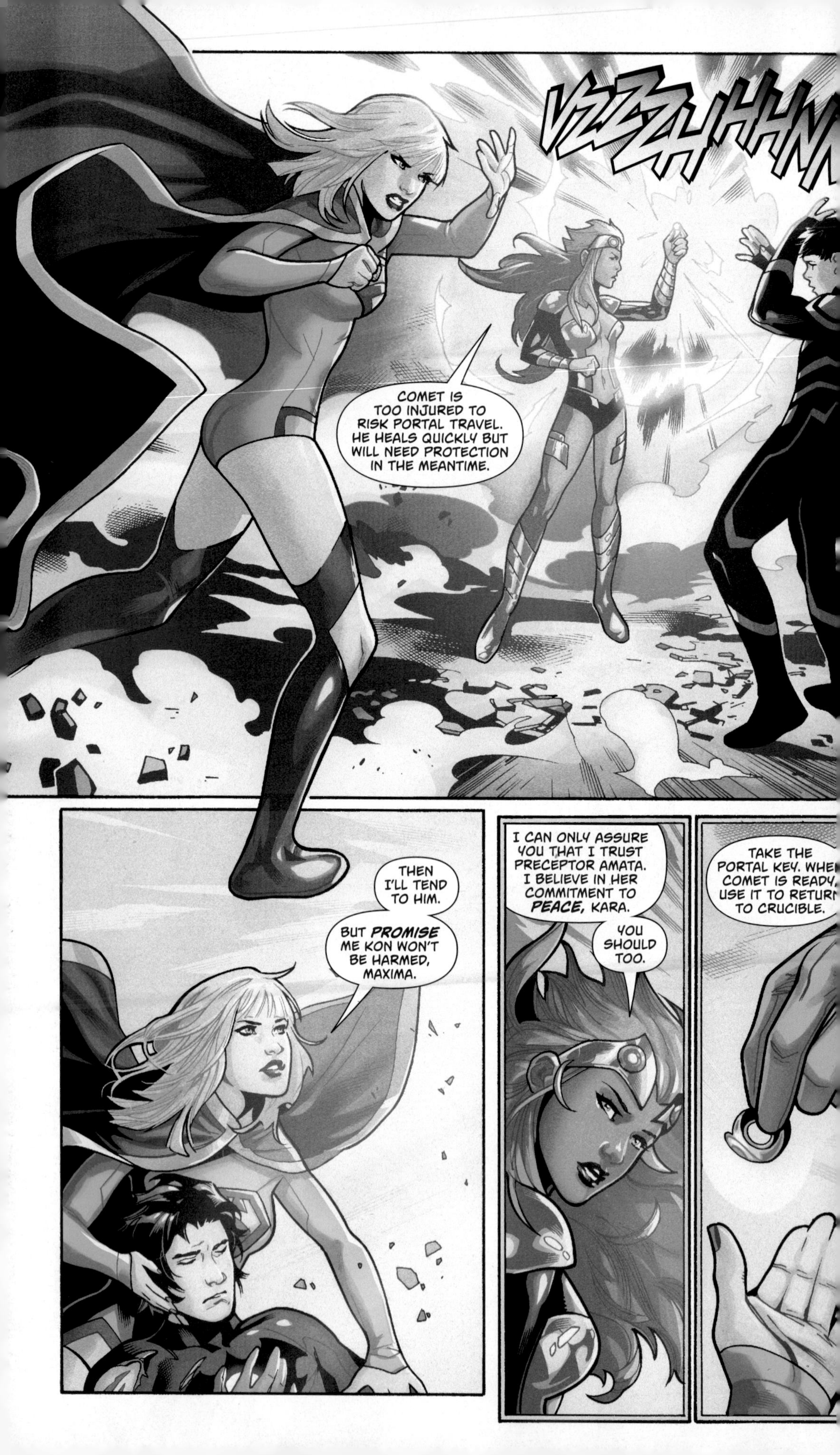
VZZZHHHN
COMET IS TOO INJURED TO RISK PORTAL TRAVEL. HE HEALS QUICKLY BUT WILL NEED PROTECTION IN THE MEANTIME.
THEN I'LL TEND TO HIM.
BUT *PROMISE* ME KON WON'T BE HARMED, MAXIMA.
I CAN ONLY ASSURE YOU THAT I TRUST PRECEPTOR AMATA. I BELIEVE IN HER COMMITMENT TO *PEACE*, KARA.
YOU SHOULD TOO.
TAKE THE PORTAL KEY. WHE COMET IS READY, USE IT TO RETUR TO CRUCIBLE.

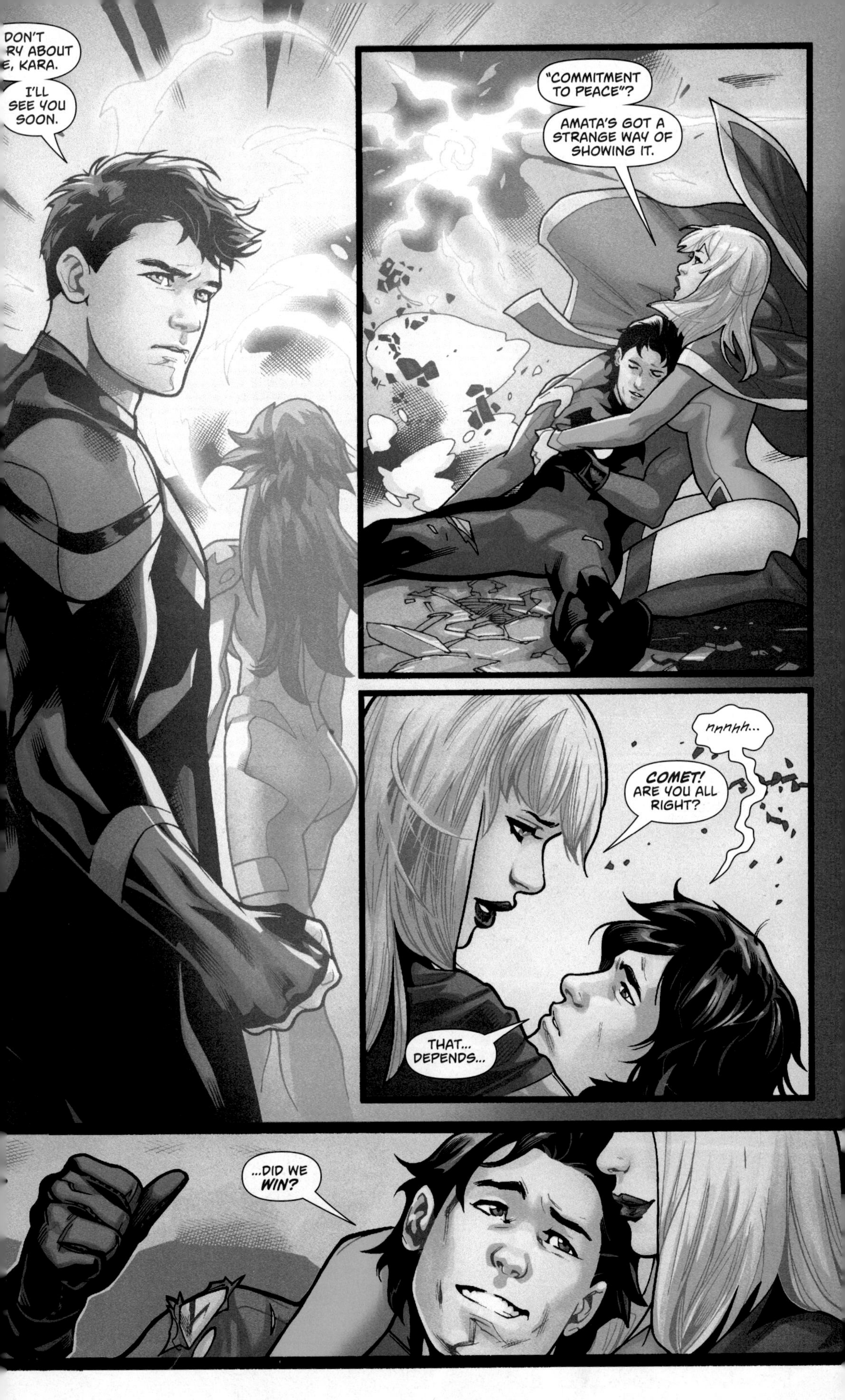
DON'T
RY ABOUT
E, KARA.
I'LL SEE YOU SOON.
"COMMITMENT TO PEACE"?
AMATA'S GOT A STRANGE WAY OF SHOWING IT.
nnnhh...
COMET! ARE YOU ALL RIGHT?
THAT... DEPENDS...
...DID WE WIN?

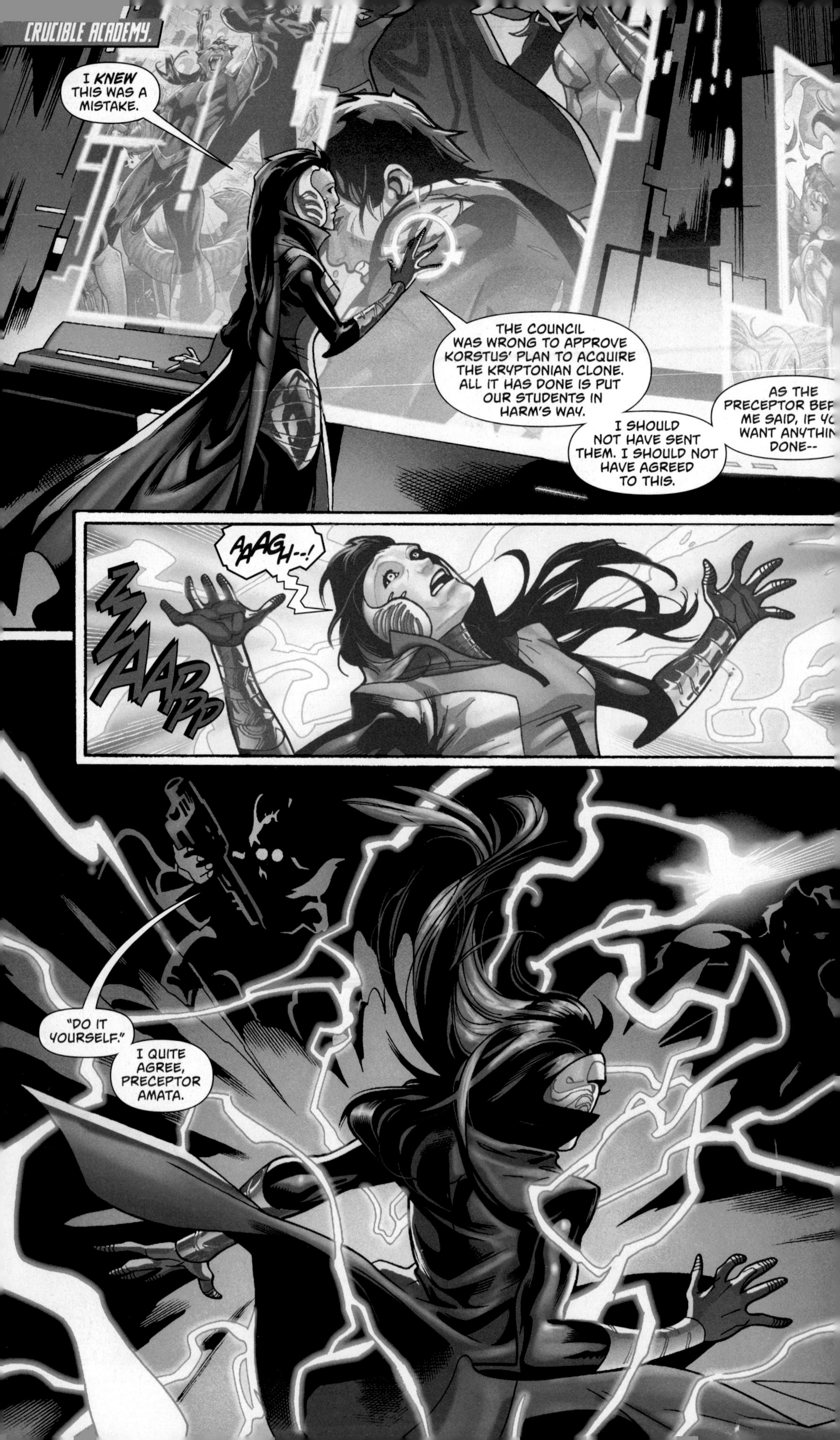
CRUCIBLE ACADEMY.
I KNEW THIS WAS A MISTAKE.
THE COUNCIL WAS WRONG TO APPROVE KORSTUS' PLAN TO ACQUIRE THE KRYPTONIAN CLONE. ALL IT HAS DONE IS PUT OUR STUDENTS IN HARM'S WAY.
I SHOULD NOT HAVE SENT THEM. I SHOULD NOT HAVE AGREED TO THIS.
AS THE PRECEPTOR BEF ME SAID, IF YO WANT ANYTHIN DONE--
AAAGH--!
ZZAAAPPP
"DO IT YOURSELF."
I QUITE AGREE, PRECEPTOR AMATA.

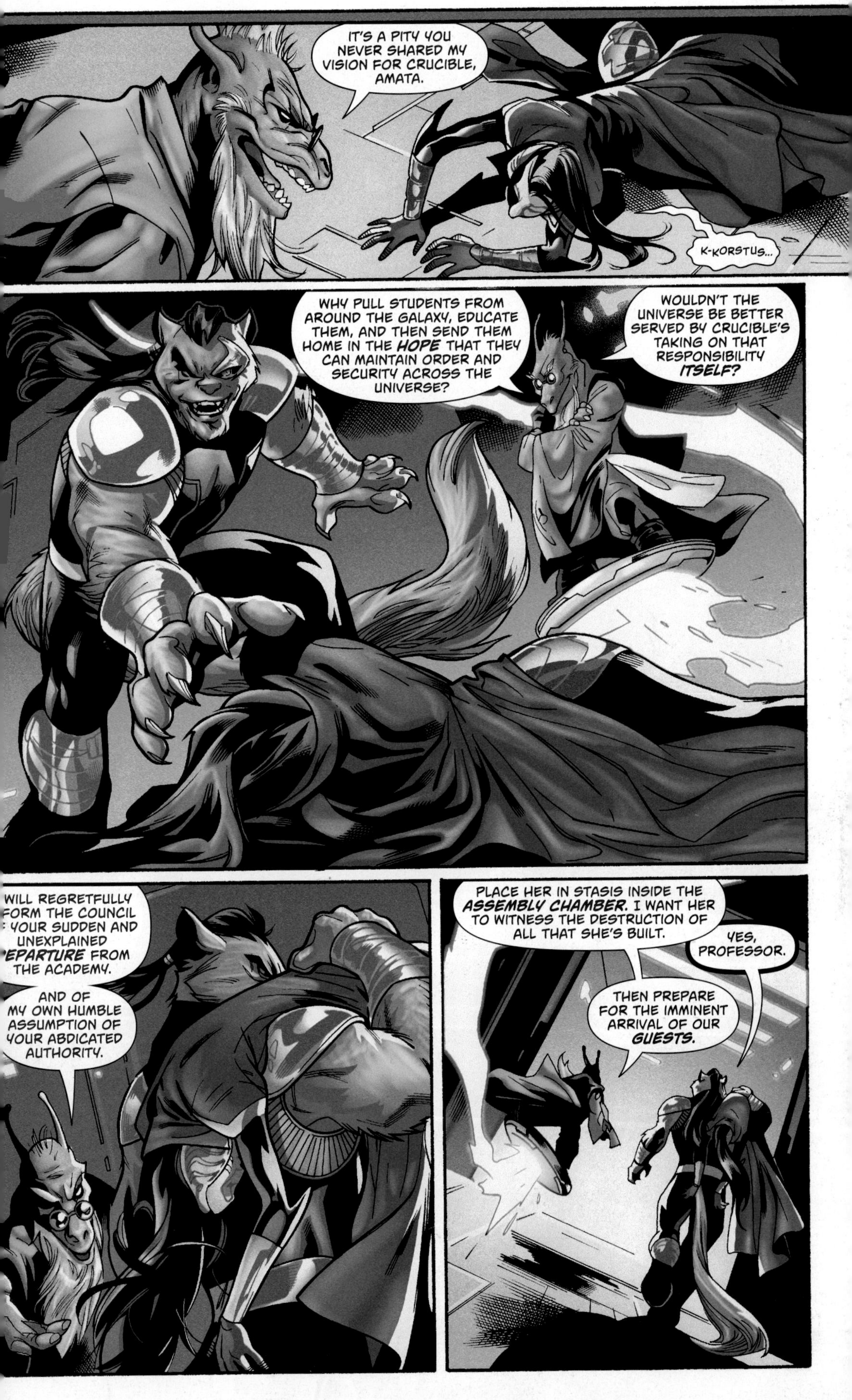
IT'S A PITY YOU NEVER SHARED MY VISION FOR CRUCIBLE, AMATA.
K-KORSTUS...
WHY PULL STUDENTS FROM AROUND THE GALAXY, EDUCATE THEM, AND THEN SEND THEM HOME IN THE HOPE THAT THEY CAN MAINTAIN ORDER AND SECURITY ACROSS THE UNIVERSE?
WOULDN'T THE UNIVERSE BE BETTER SERVED BY CRUCIBLE'S TAKING ON THAT RESPONSIBILITY ITSELF?
WILL REGRETFULLY FORM THE COUNCIL YOUR SUDDEN AND UNEXPLAINED EPARTURE FROM THE ACADEMY.
AND OF MY OWN HUMBLE ASSUMPTION OF YOUR ABDICATED AUTHORITY.
PLACE HER IN STASIS INSIDE THE ASSEMBLY CHAMBER. I WANT HER TO WITNESS THE DESTRUCTION OF ALL THAT SHE'S BUILT.
YES, PROFESSOR.
THEN PREPARE FOR THE IMMINENT ARRIVAL OF OUR GUESTS.

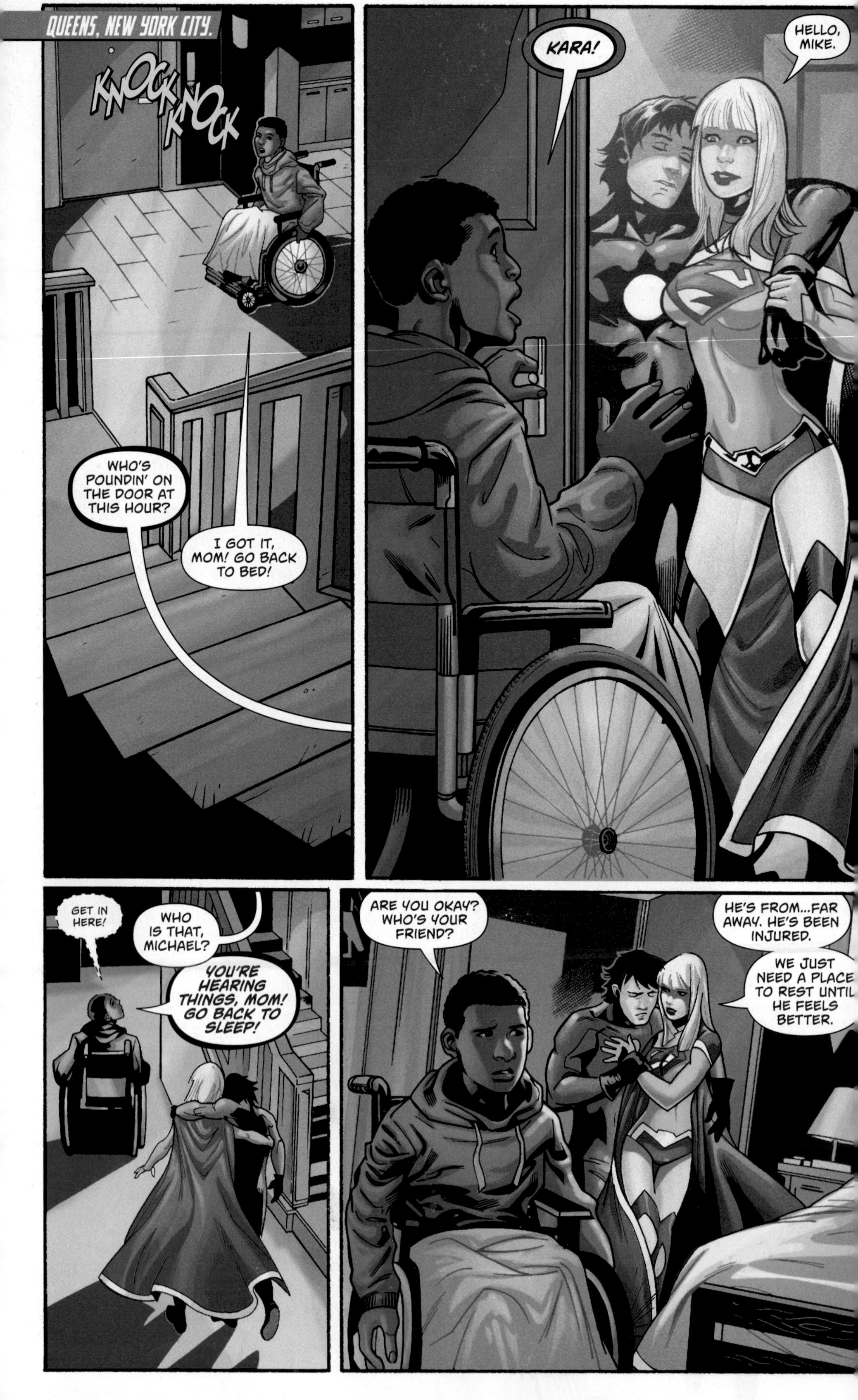
QUEENS, NEW YORK CITY.
KNOCK KNOCK
WHO'S POUNDIN' ON THE DOOR AT THIS HOUR?
I GOT IT, MOM! GO BACK TO BED!
KARA!
HELLO, MIKE.
GET IN HERE!
WHO IS THAT, MICHAEL?
YOU'RE HEARING THINGS, MOM! GO BACK TO SLEEP!
ARE YOU OKAY? WHO'S YOUR FRIEND?
HE'S FROM...FAR AWAY. HE'S BEEN INJURED.
WE JUST NEED A PLACE TO REST UNTIL HE FEELS BETTER.

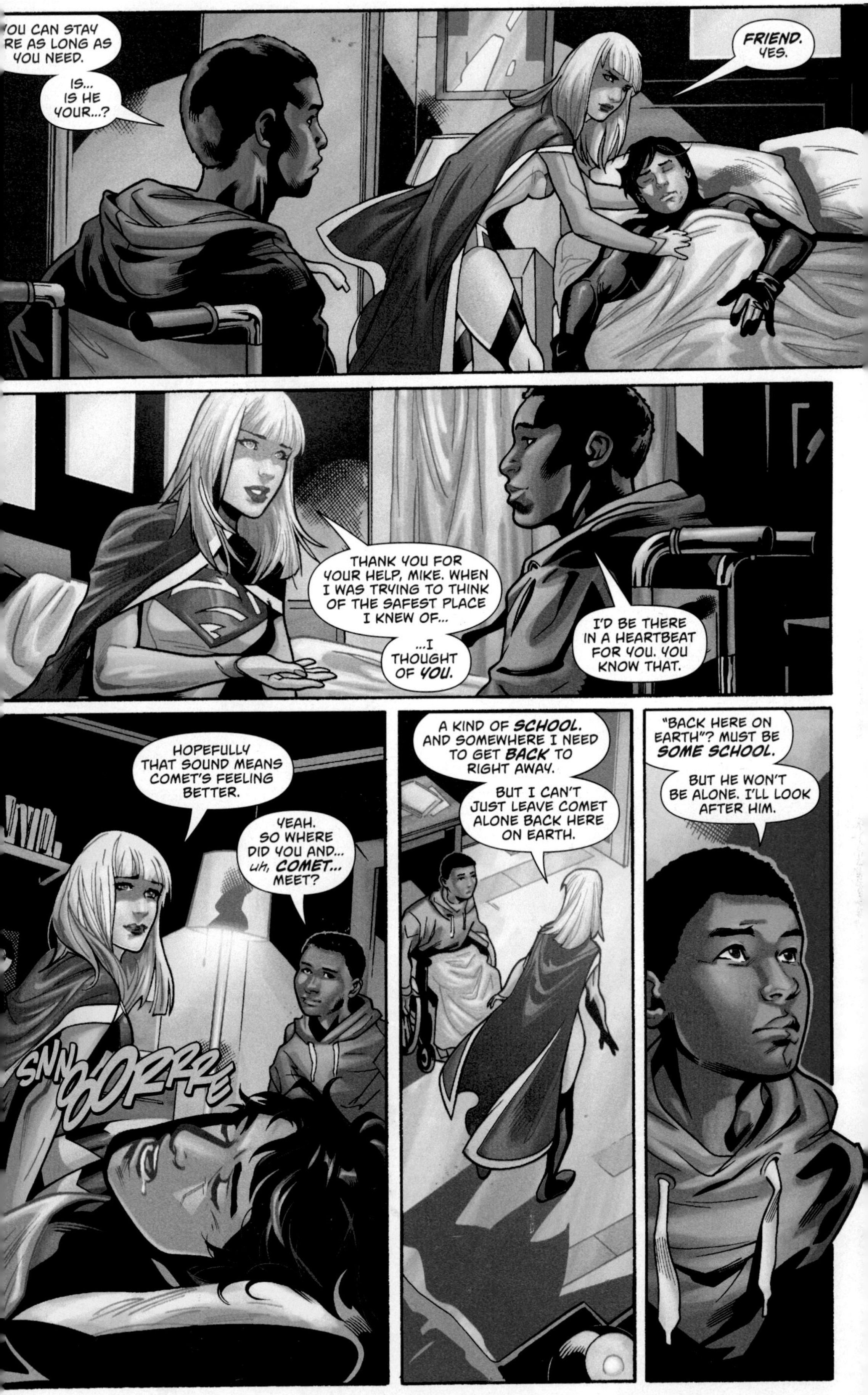
YOU CAN STAY
RE AS LONG AS
YOU NEED.
IS...
IS HE
YOUR...?
FRIEND.
YES.
THANK YOU FOR
YOUR HELP, MIKE. WHEN
I WAS TRYING TO THINK
OF THE SAFEST PLACE
I KNEW OF...
...I
THOUGHT
OF YOU.
I'D BE THERE
IN A HEARTBEAT
FOR YOU. YOU
KNOW THAT.
HOPEFULLY
THAT SOUND MEANS
COMET'S FEELING
BETTER.
SNNOORRRE
YEAH.
SO WHERE
DID YOU AND...
uh, COMET...
MEET?
A KIND OF SCHOOL.
AND SOMEWHERE I NEED
TO GET BACK TO
RIGHT AWAY.
BUT I CAN'T
JUST LEAVE COMET
ALONE BACK HERE
ON EARTH.
"BACK HERE ON
EARTH"? MUST BE
SOME SCHOOL.
BUT HE WON'T
BE ALONE. I'LL LOOK
AFTER HIM.

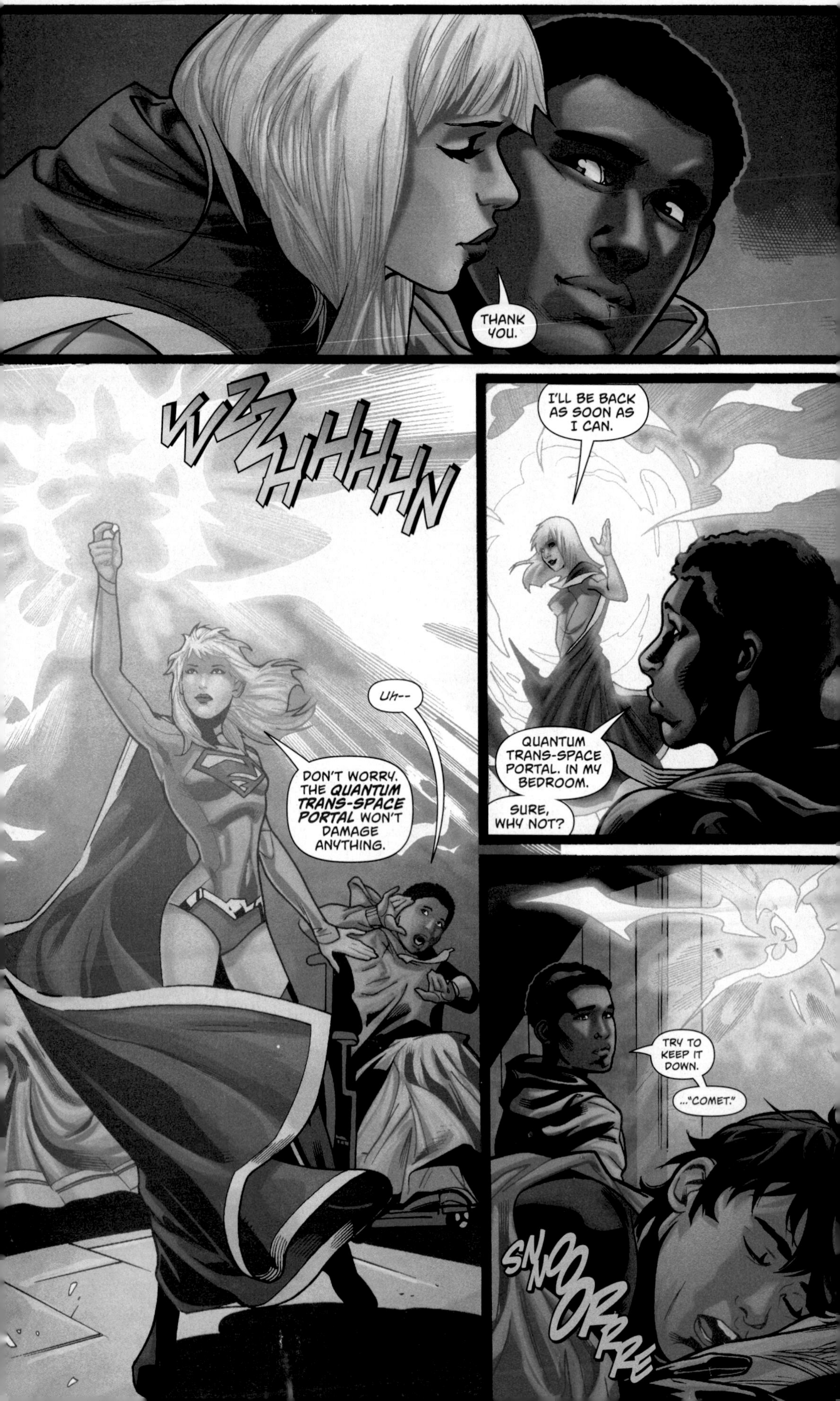
THANK YOU.
WZZHHHHN
DON'T WORRY. THE *QUANTUM TRANS-SPACE PORTAL* WON'T DAMAGE ANYTHING.
UH--
I'LL BE BACK AS SOON AS I CAN.
QUANTUM TRANS-SPACE PORTAL. IN MY BEDROOM.
SURE, WHY NOT?
TRY TO KEEP IT DOWN.
..."COMET."
SNOORRRE

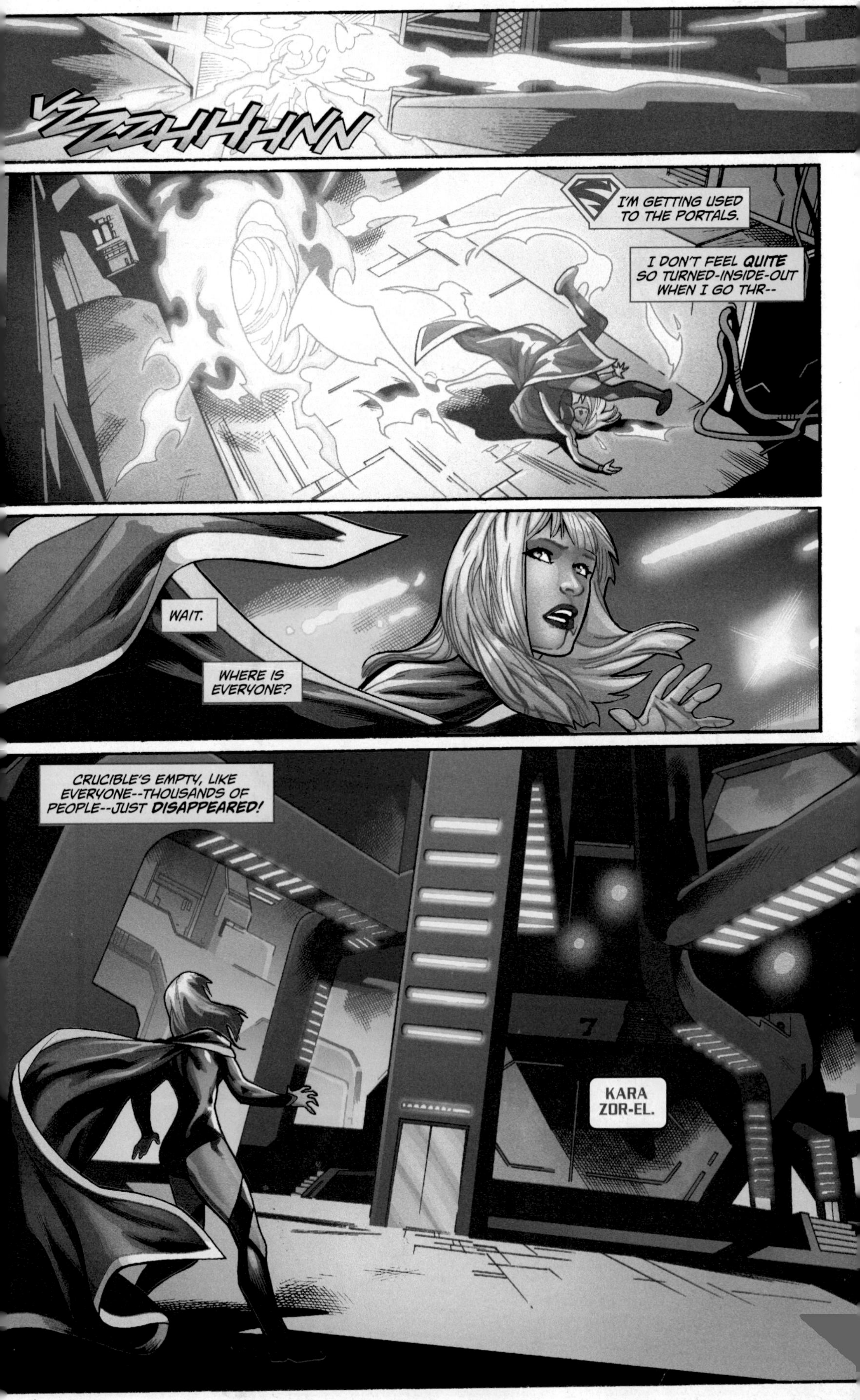
VZZZHHHHNN
I'M GETTING USED TO THE PORTALS.
I DON'T FEEL QUITE SO TURNED-INSIDE-OUT WHEN I GO THR--
WAIT.
WHERE IS EVERYONE?
CRUCIBLE'S EMPTY, LIKE EVERYONE--THOUSANDS OF PEOPLE--JUST DISAPPEARED!
7
KARA ZOR-EL.

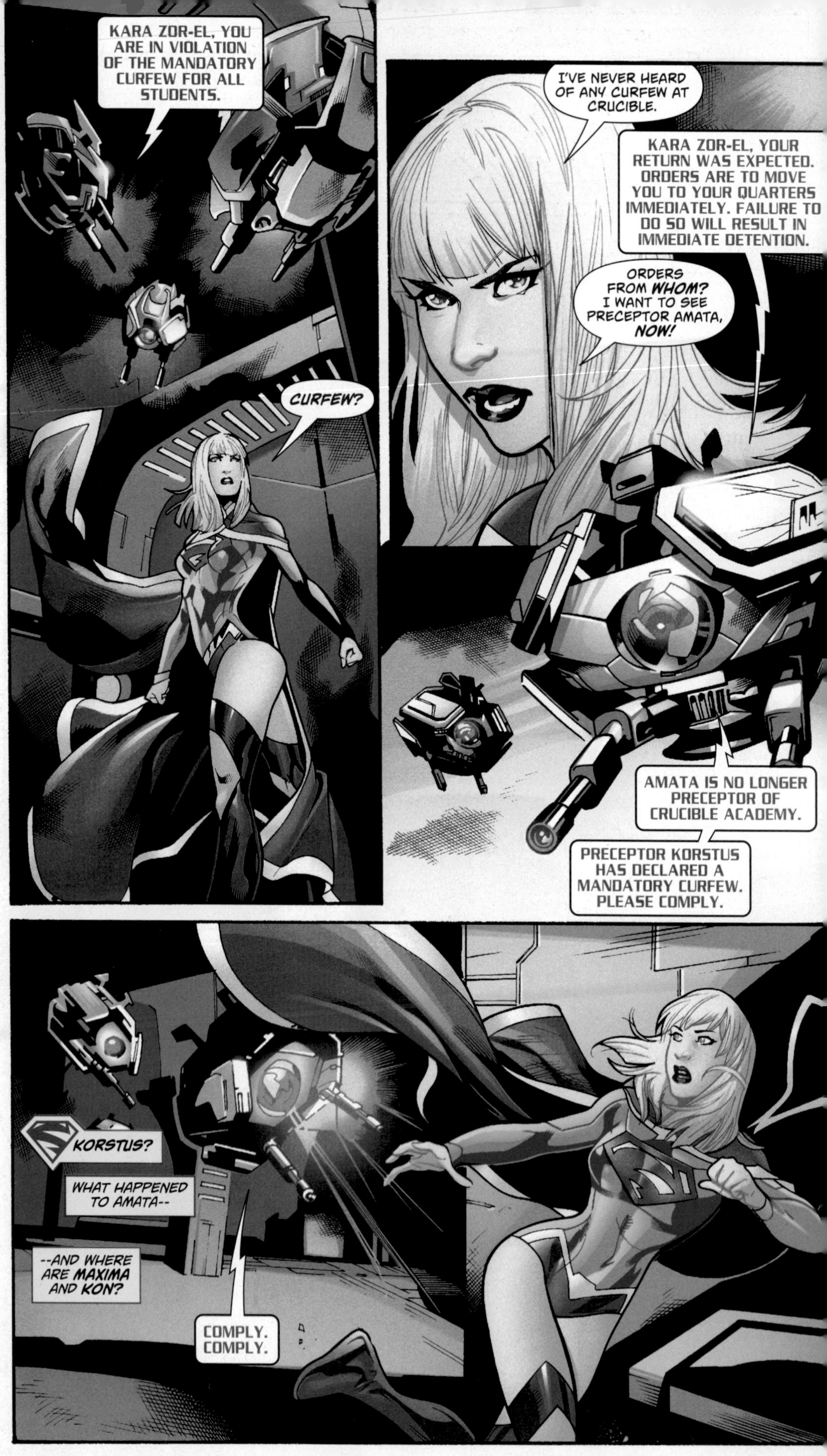
KARA ZOR-EL, YOU ARE IN VIOLATION OF THE MANDATORY CURFEW FOR ALL STUDENTS.
CURFEW?
I'VE NEVER HEARD OF ANY CURFEW AT CRUCIBLE.
KARA ZOR-EL, YOUR RETURN WAS EXPECTED. ORDERS ARE TO MOVE YOU TO YOUR QUARTERS IMMEDIATELY. FAILURE TO DO SO WILL RESULT IN IMMEDIATE DETENTION.
ORDERS FROM *WHOM?* I WANT TO SEE PRECEPTOR AMATA, *NOW!*
AMATA IS NO LONGER PRECEPTOR OF CRUCIBLE ACADEMY.
PRECEPTOR KORSTUS HAS DECLARED A MANDATORY CURFEW. PLEASE COMPLY.
KORSTUS?
WHAT HAPPENED TO AMATA--
--AND WHERE ARE *MAXIMA* AND *KON?*
COMPLY. COMPLY.

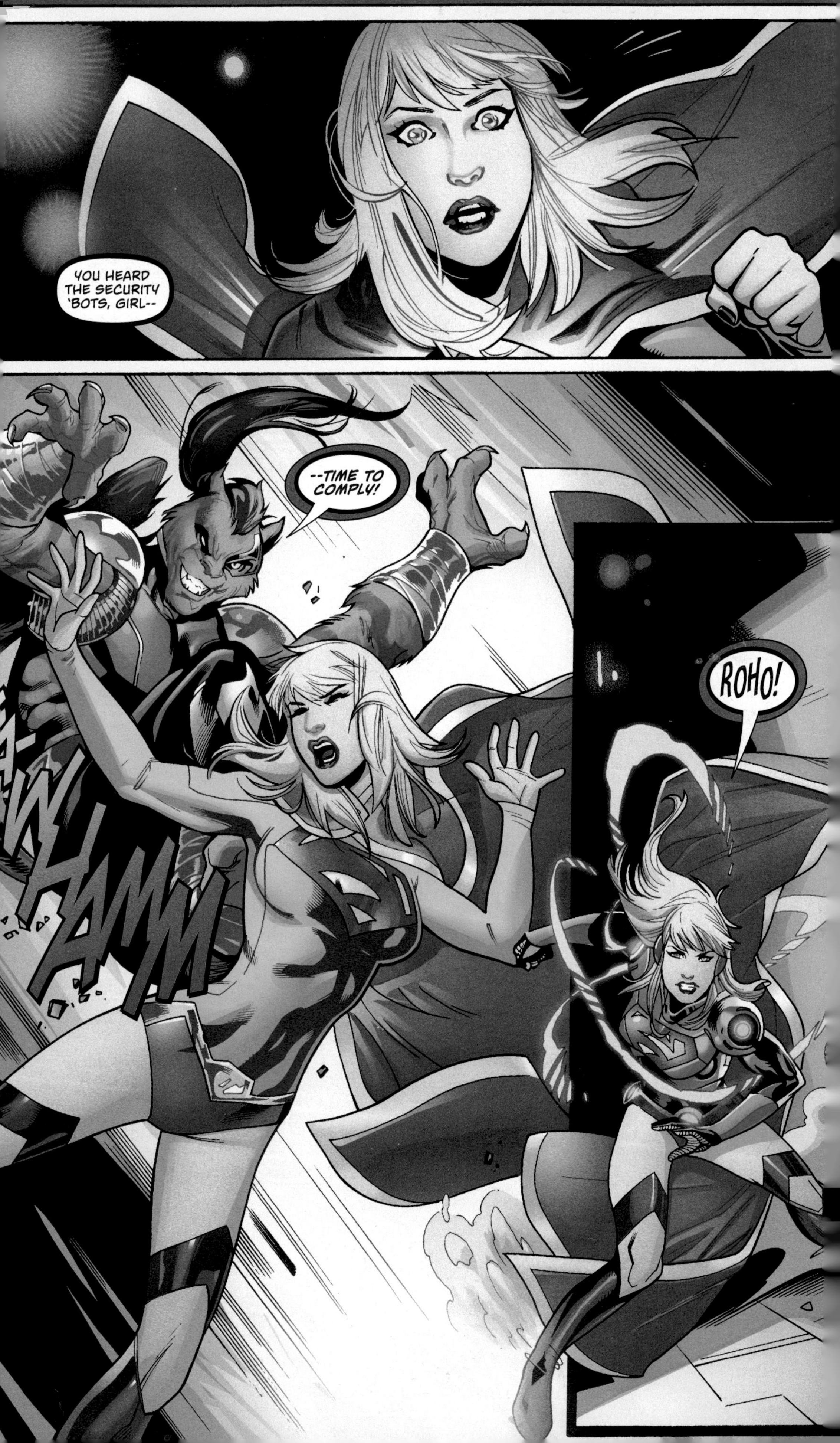
YOU HEARD THE SECURITY 'BOTS, GIRL--
--TIME TO COMPLY!
ROHO!

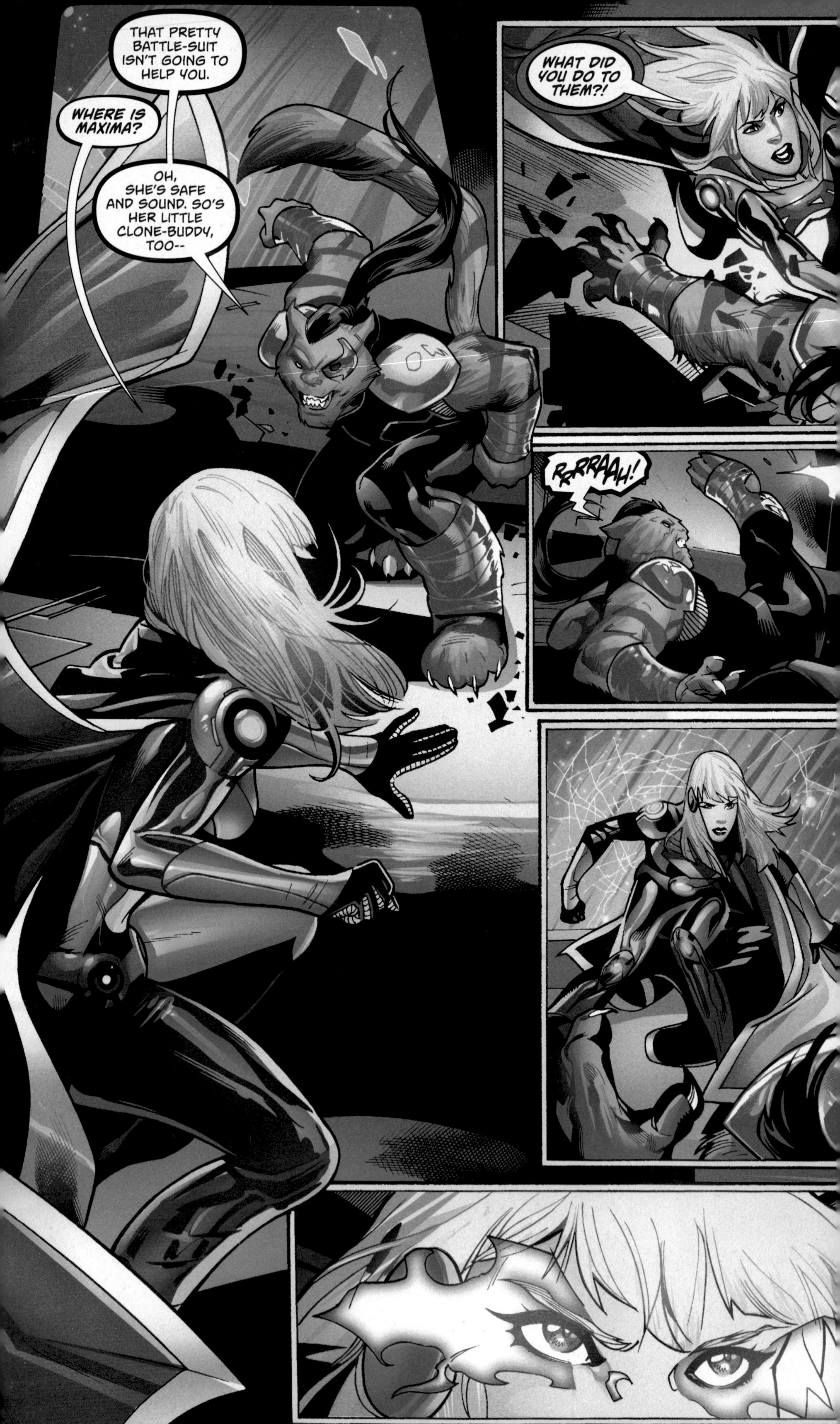
WHERE IS MAXIMA?
THAT PRETTY BATTLE-SUIT ISN'T GOING TO HELP YOU.
OH, SHE'S SAFE AND SOUND. SO'S HER LITTLE CLONE-BUDDY, TOO--
WHAT DID YOU DO TO THEM?!
RRRRAAAH!

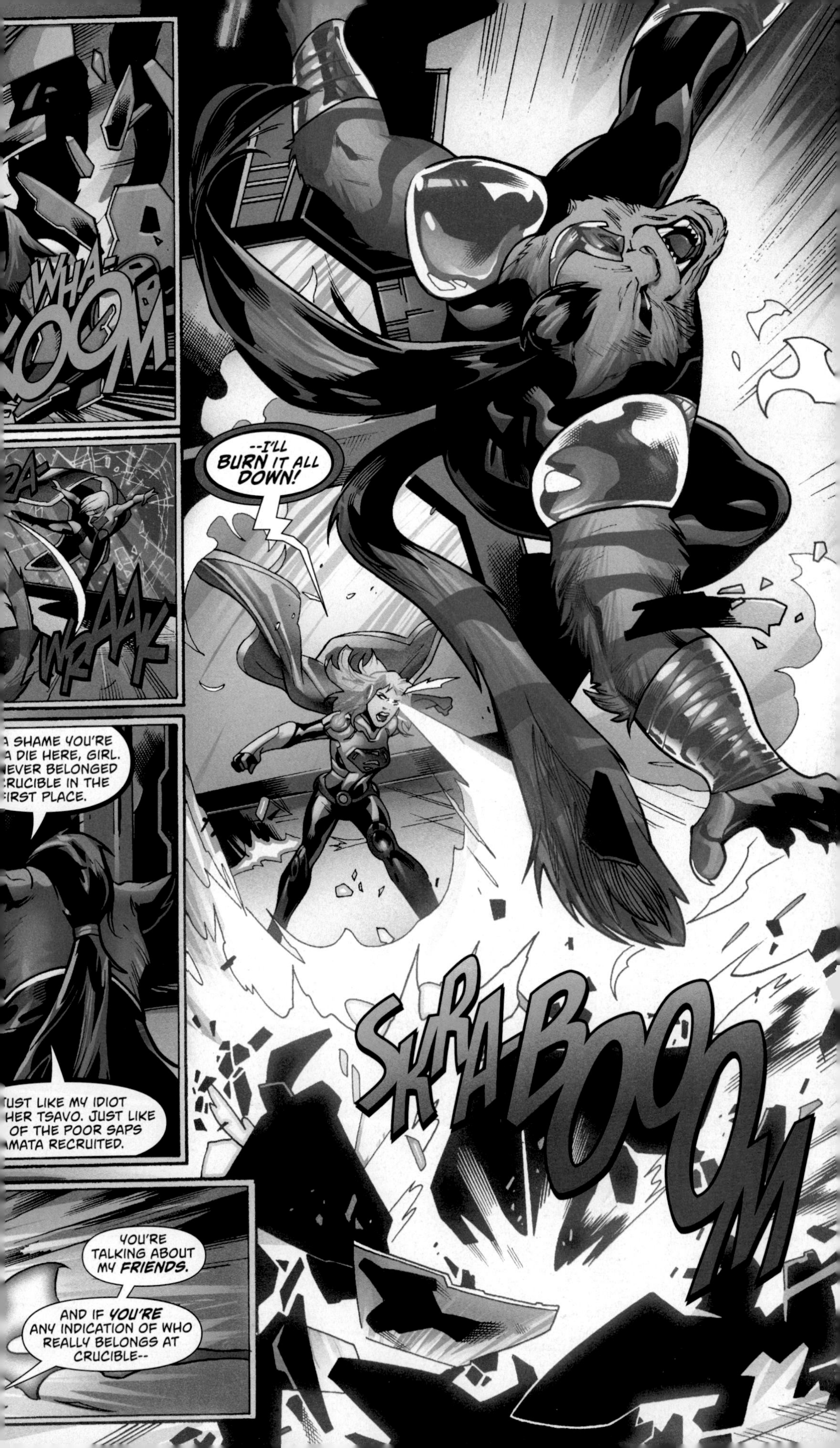
WHA-BOOM
WRAAK
A SHAME YOU'RE A DIE HERE, GIRL. NEVER BELONGED CRUCIBLE IN THE FIRST PLACE.
JUST LIKE MY IDIOT HER TSAVO. JUST LIKE OF THE POOR SAPS AMATA RECRUITED.
YOU'RE TALKING ABOUT MY FRIENDS.
AND IF YOU'RE ANY INDICATION OF WHO REALLY BELONGS AT CRUCIBLE--
--I'LL BURN IT ALL DOWN!
SKRA-BOOOM

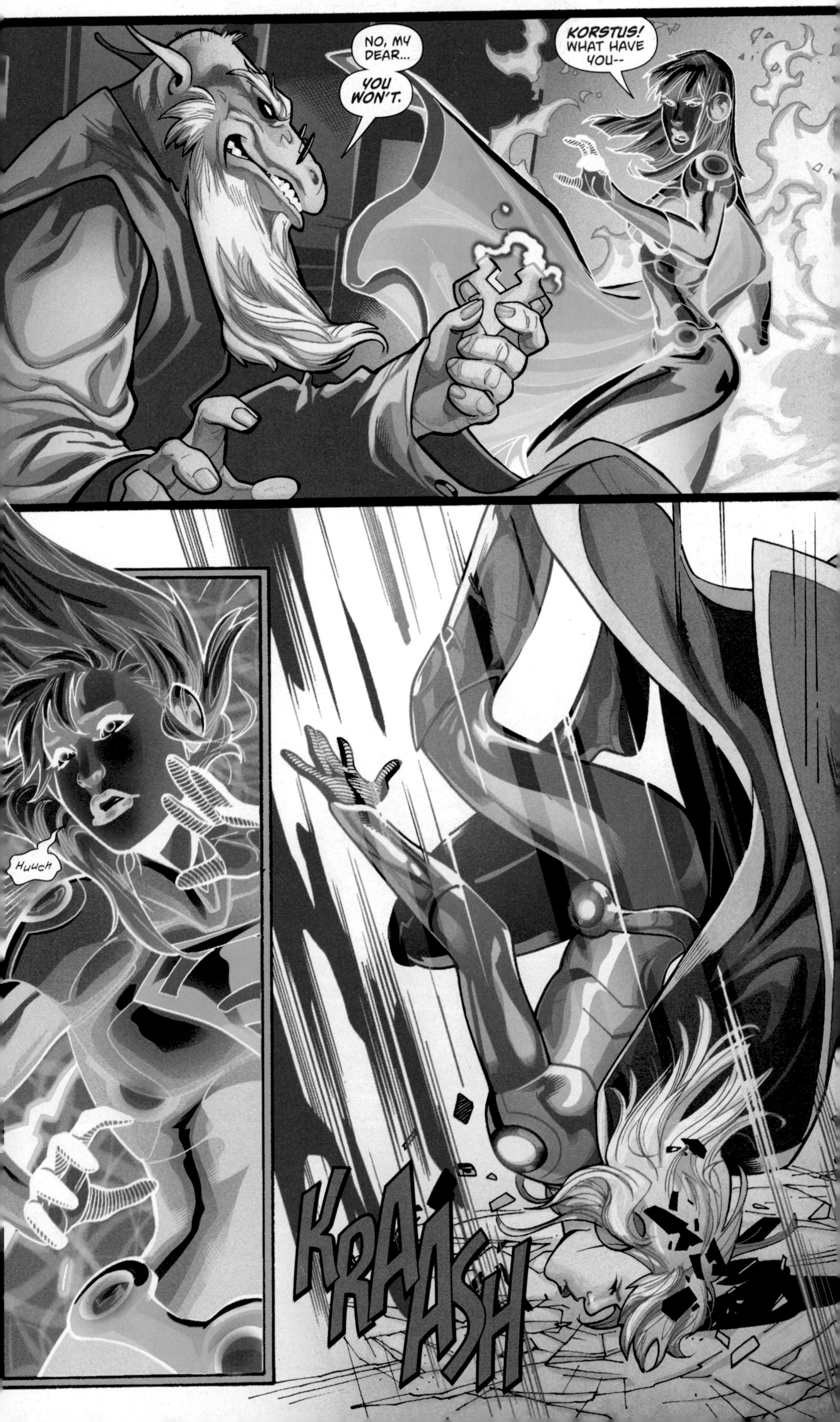
NO, MY DEAR...
YOU WON'T.
KORSTUS! WHAT HAVE YOU--
Huuch
KRAAASH

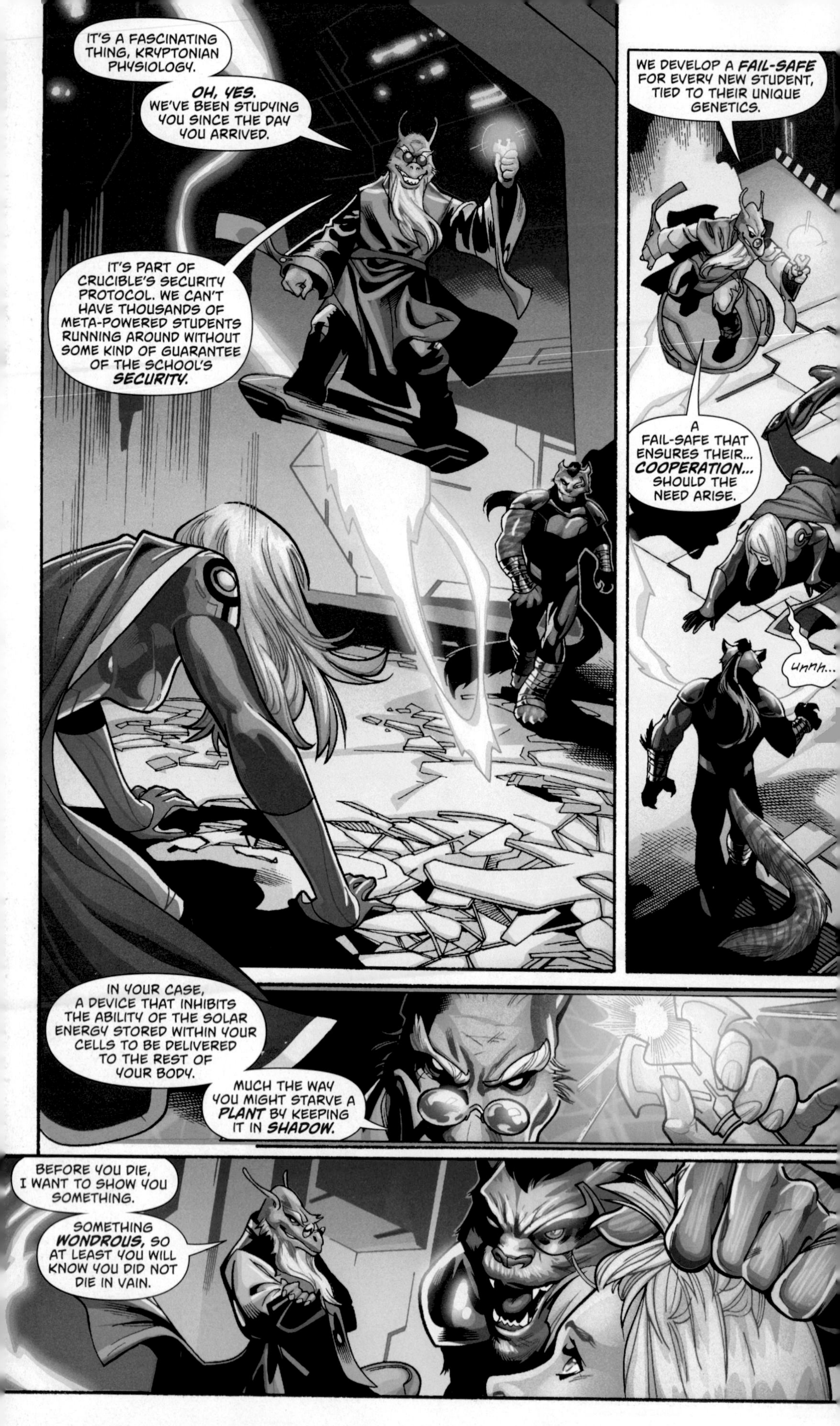
IT'S A FASCINATING THING, KRYPTONIAN PHYSIOLOGY.
OH, YES. WE'VE BEEN STUDYING YOU SINCE THE DAY YOU ARRIVED.
IT'S PART OF CRUCIBLE'S SECURITY PROTOCOL. WE CAN'T HAVE THOUSANDS OF META-POWERED STUDENTS RUNNING AROUND WITHOUT SOME KIND OF GUARANTEE OF THE SCHOOL'S SECURITY.
WE DEVELOP A FAIL-SAFE FOR EVERY NEW STUDENT, TIED TO THEIR UNIQUE GENETICS.
A FAIL-SAFE THAT ENSURES THEIR... COOPERATION... SHOULD THE NEED ARISE.
UNNH...
IN YOUR CASE, A DEVICE THAT INHIBITS THE ABILITY OF THE SOLAR ENERGY STORED WITHIN YOUR CELLS TO BE DELIVERED TO THE REST OF YOUR BODY.
MUCH THE WAY YOU MIGHT STARVE A PLANT BY KEEPING IT IN SHADOW.
BEFORE YOU DIE, I WANT TO SHOW YOU SOMETHING.
SOMETHING WONDROUS, SO AT LEAST YOU WILL KNOW YOU DID NOT DIE IN VAIN.

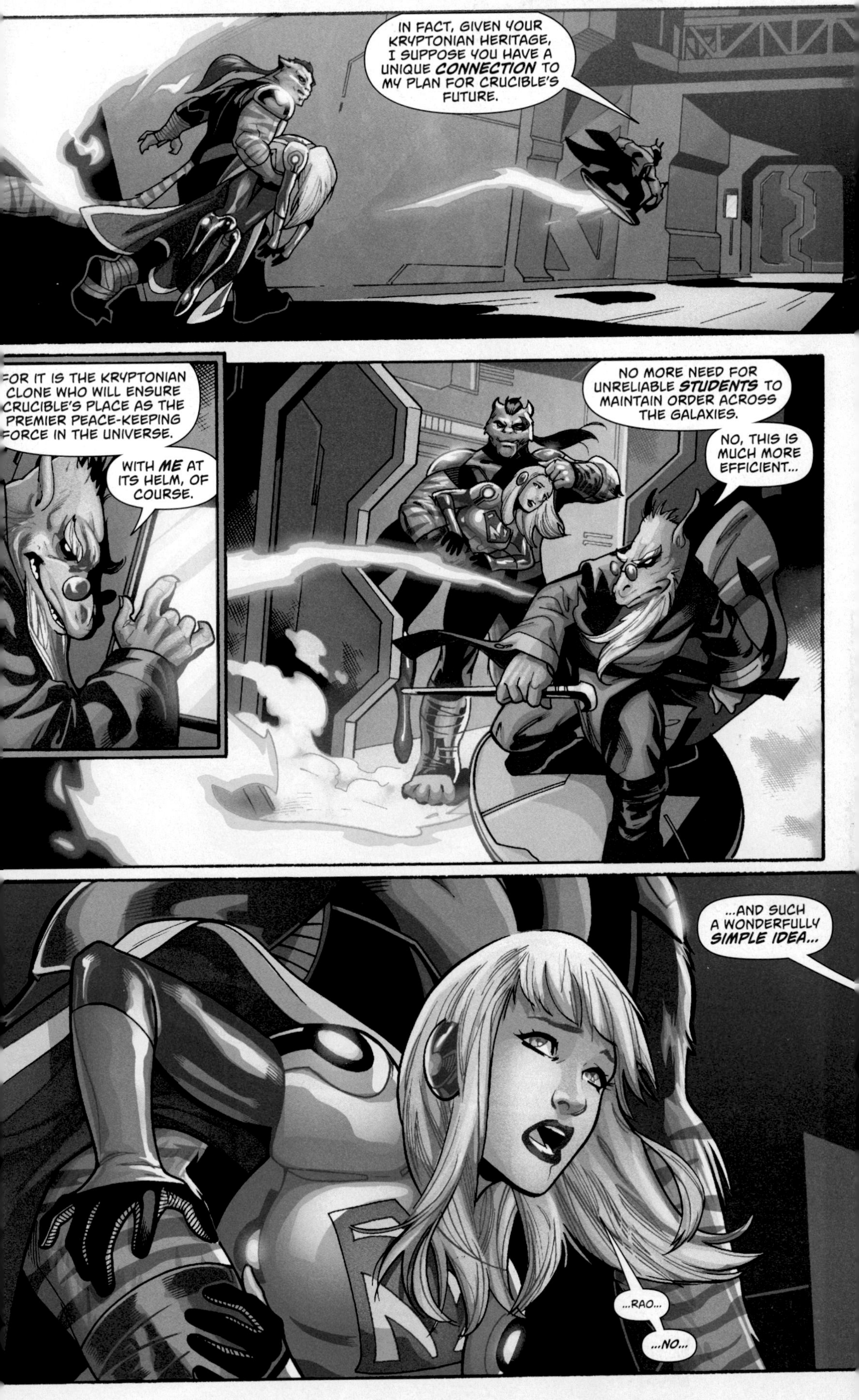
IN FACT, GIVEN YOUR KRYPTONIAN HERITAGE, I SUPPOSE YOU HAVE A UNIQUE *CONNECTION* TO MY PLAN FOR CRUCIBLE'S FUTURE.
FOR IT IS THE KRYPTONIAN CLONE WHO WILL ENSURE CRUCIBLE'S PLACE AS THE PREMIER PEACE-KEEPING FORCE IN THE UNIVERSE.
WITH *ME* AT ITS HELM, OF COURSE.
NO MORE NEED FOR UNRELIABLE *STUDENTS* TO MAINTAIN ORDER ACROSS THE GALAXIES.
NO, THIS IS MUCH MORE EFFICIENT...
...AND SUCH A WONDERFULLY *SIMPLE IDEA*...
...RAO...
...NO...

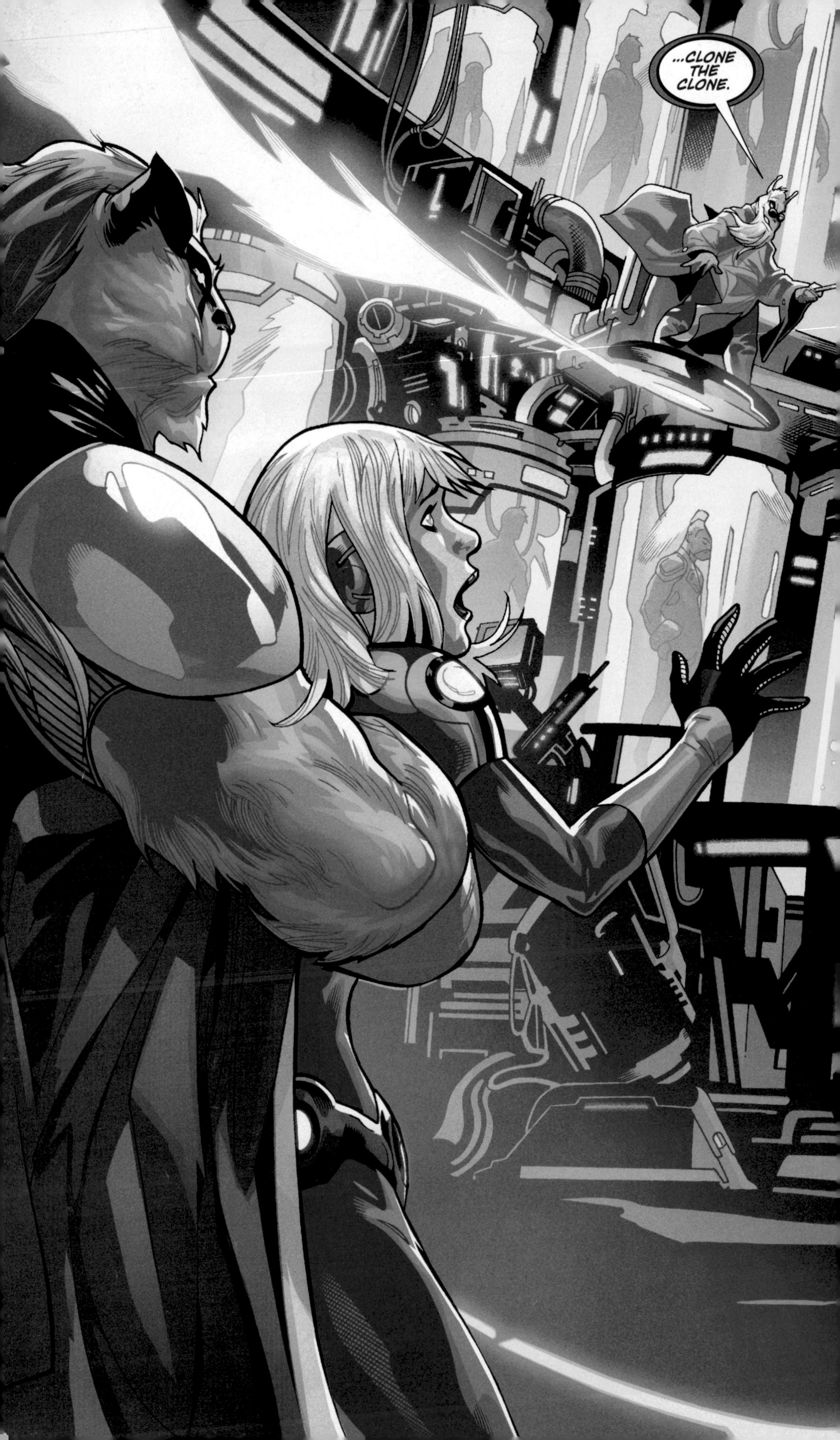
...CLONE THE CLONE.

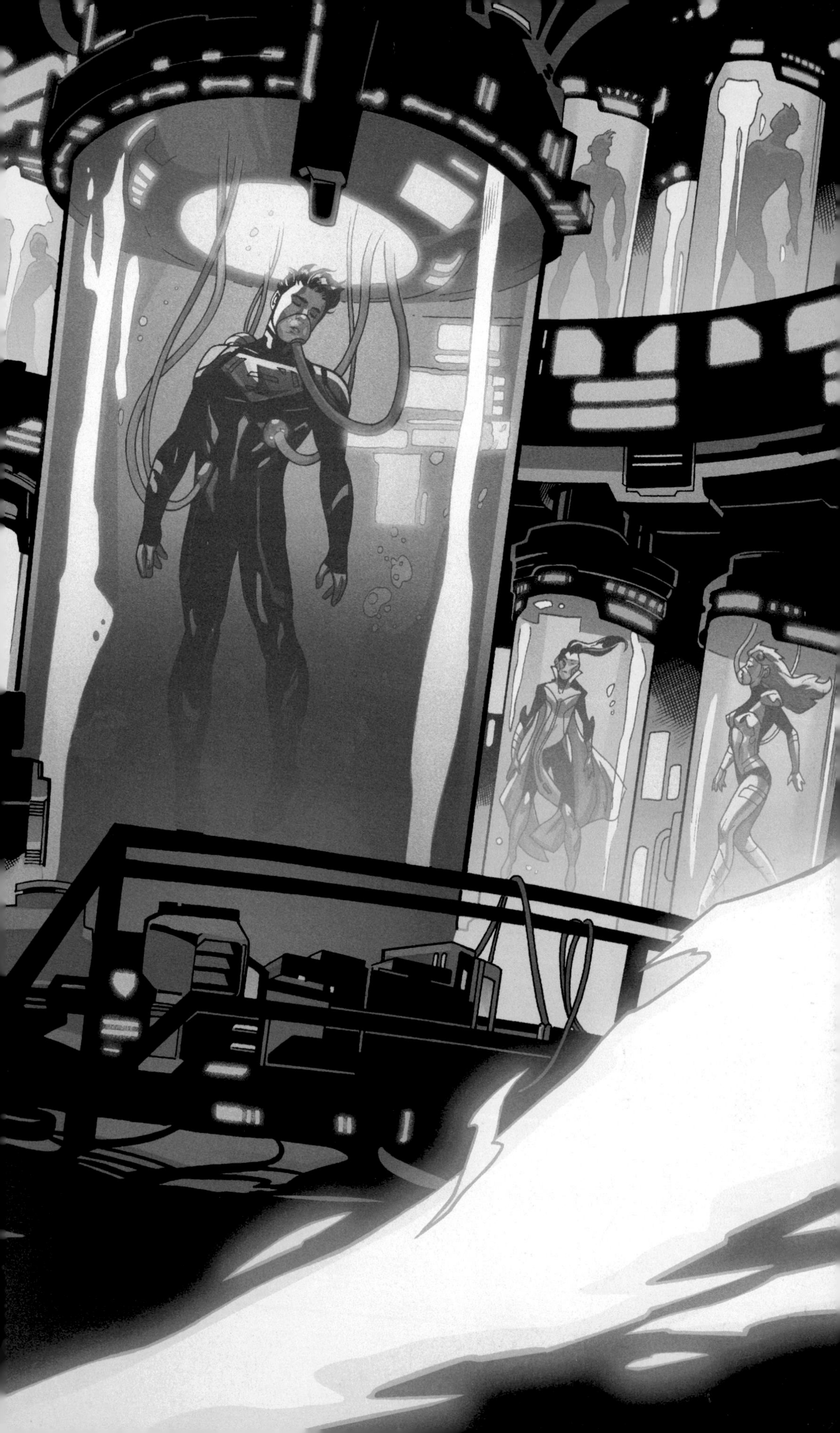

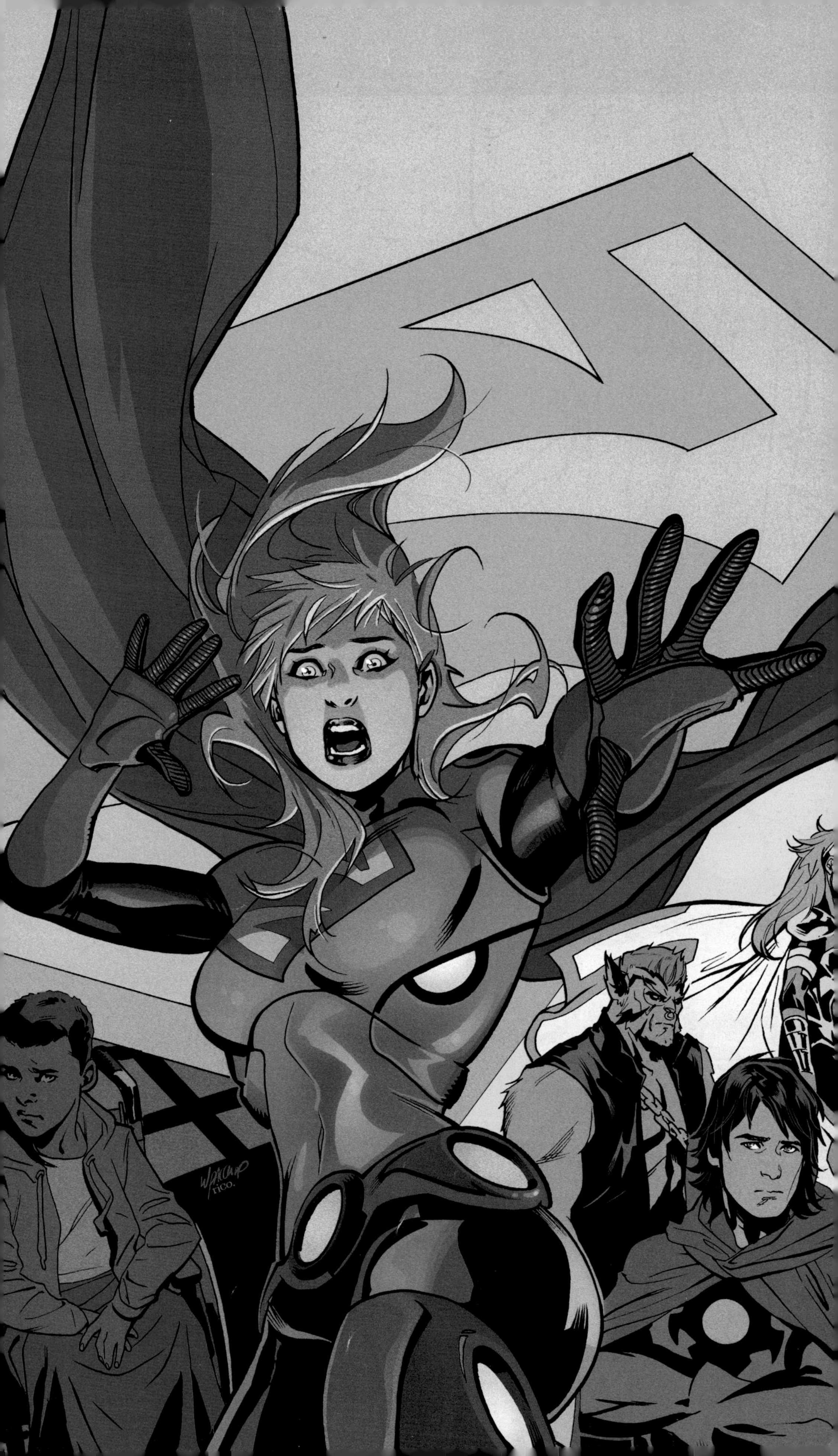

CRUCIBLE: CONCLUSION

K. PERKINS MIKE JOHNSON writers EMANUELA LUPACCHINO penciller RAY McCARTHY inker HI-FI colorist ROB LEIGH letterer
cover art by EMANUELA LUPACCHINO and RICO RENZI

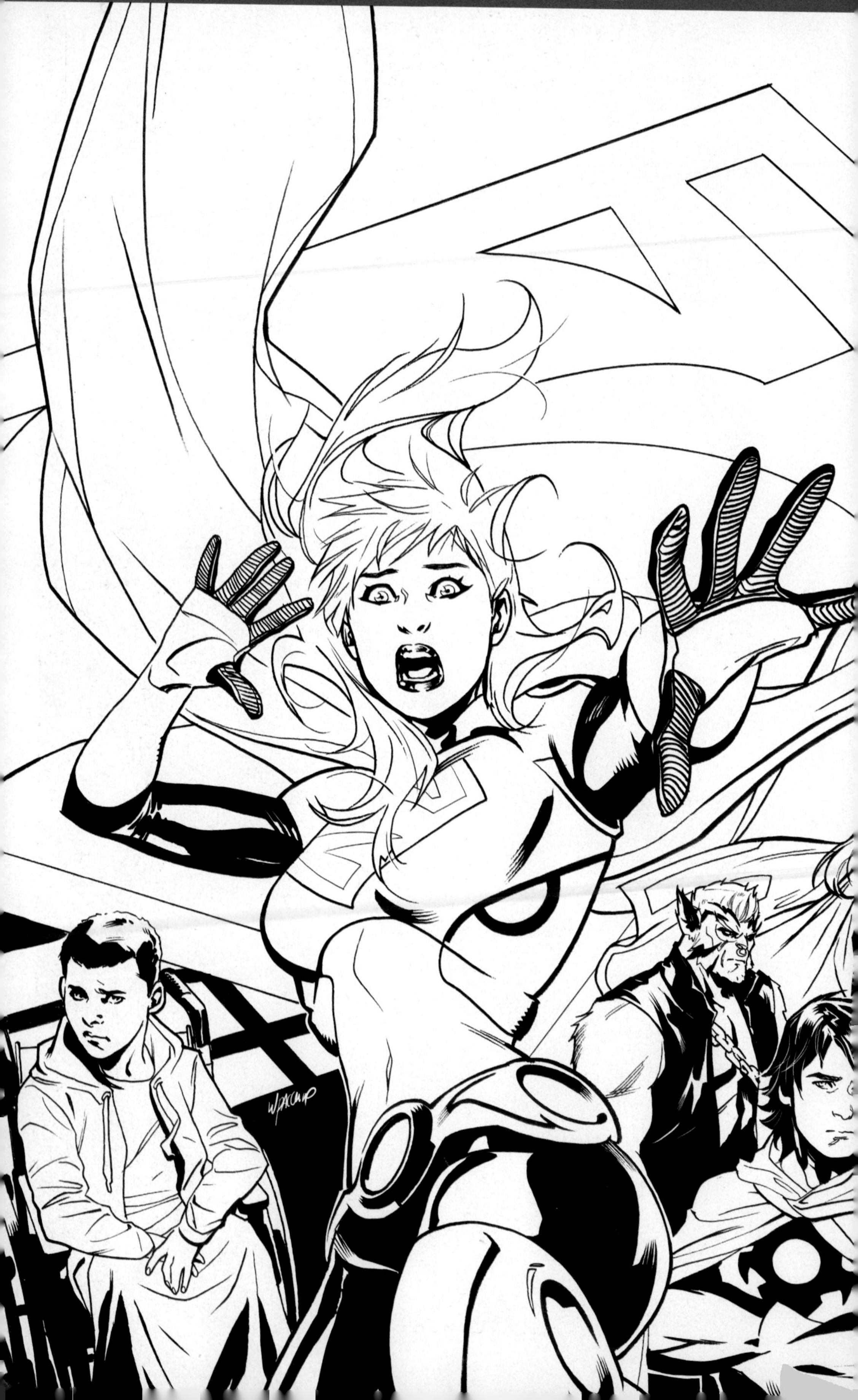

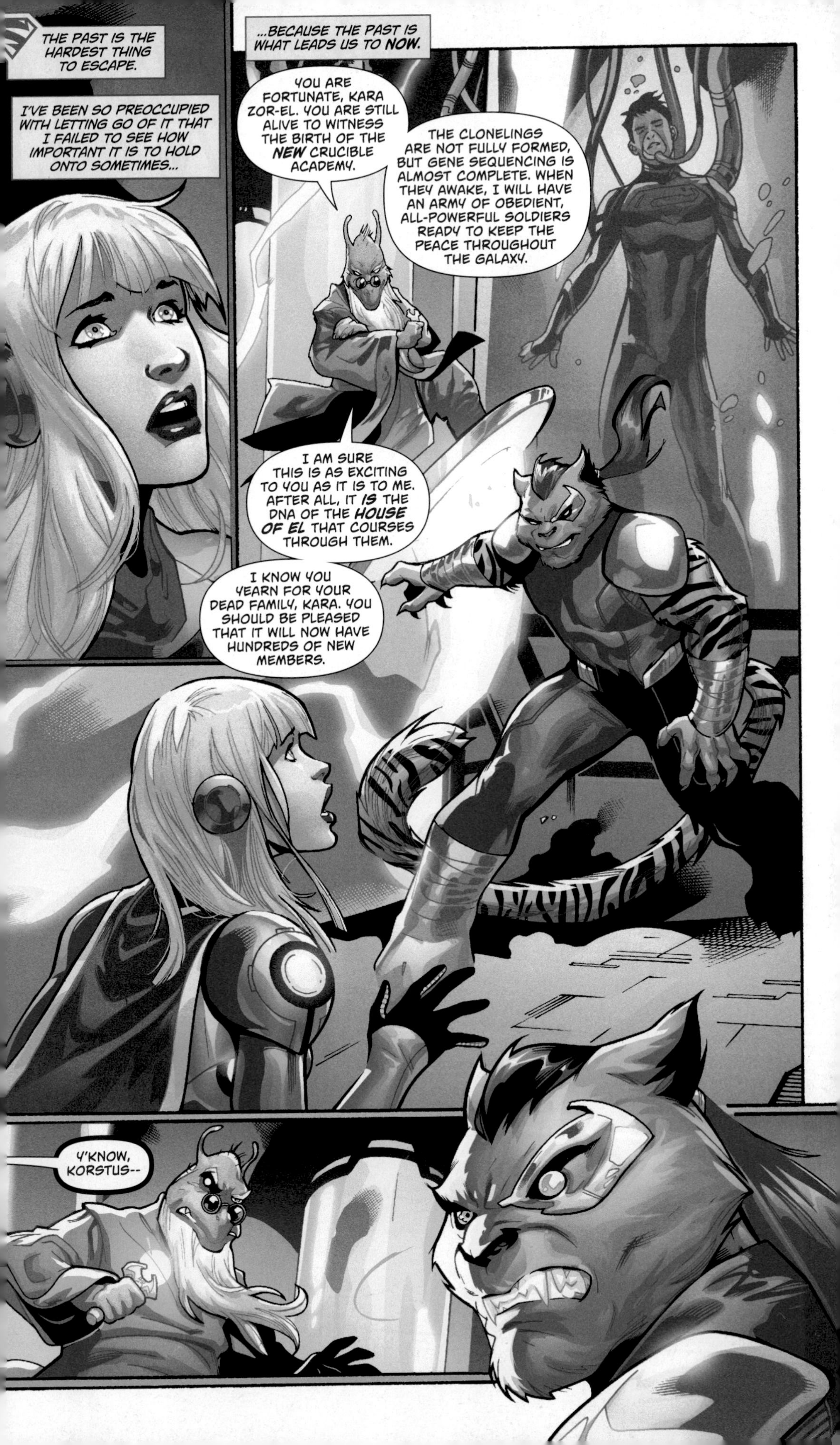
THE PAST IS THE HARDEST THING TO ESCAPE.
I'VE BEEN SO PREOCCUPIED WITH LETTING GO OF IT THAT I FAILED TO SEE HOW IMPORTANT IT IS TO HOLD ONTO SOMETIMES...
...BECAUSE THE PAST IS WHAT LEADS US TO NOW.
YOU ARE FORTUNATE, KARA ZOR-EL. YOU ARE STILL ALIVE TO WITNESS THE BIRTH OF THE NEW CRUCIBLE ACADEMY.
THE CLONELINGS ARE NOT FULLY FORMED, BUT GENE SEQUENCING IS ALMOST COMPLETE. WHEN THEY AWAKE, I WILL HAVE AN ARMY OF OBEDIENT, ALL-POWERFUL SOLDIERS READY TO KEEP THE PEACE THROUGHOUT THE GALAXY.
I AM SURE THIS IS AS EXCITING TO YOU AS IT IS TO ME. AFTER ALL, IT IS THE DNA OF THE HOUSE OF EL THAT COURSES THROUGH THEM.
I KNOW YOU YEARN FOR YOUR DEAD FAMILY, KARA. YOU SHOULD BE PLEASED THAT IT WILL NOW HAVE HUNDREDS OF NEW MEMBERS.
Y'KNOW, KORSTUS--

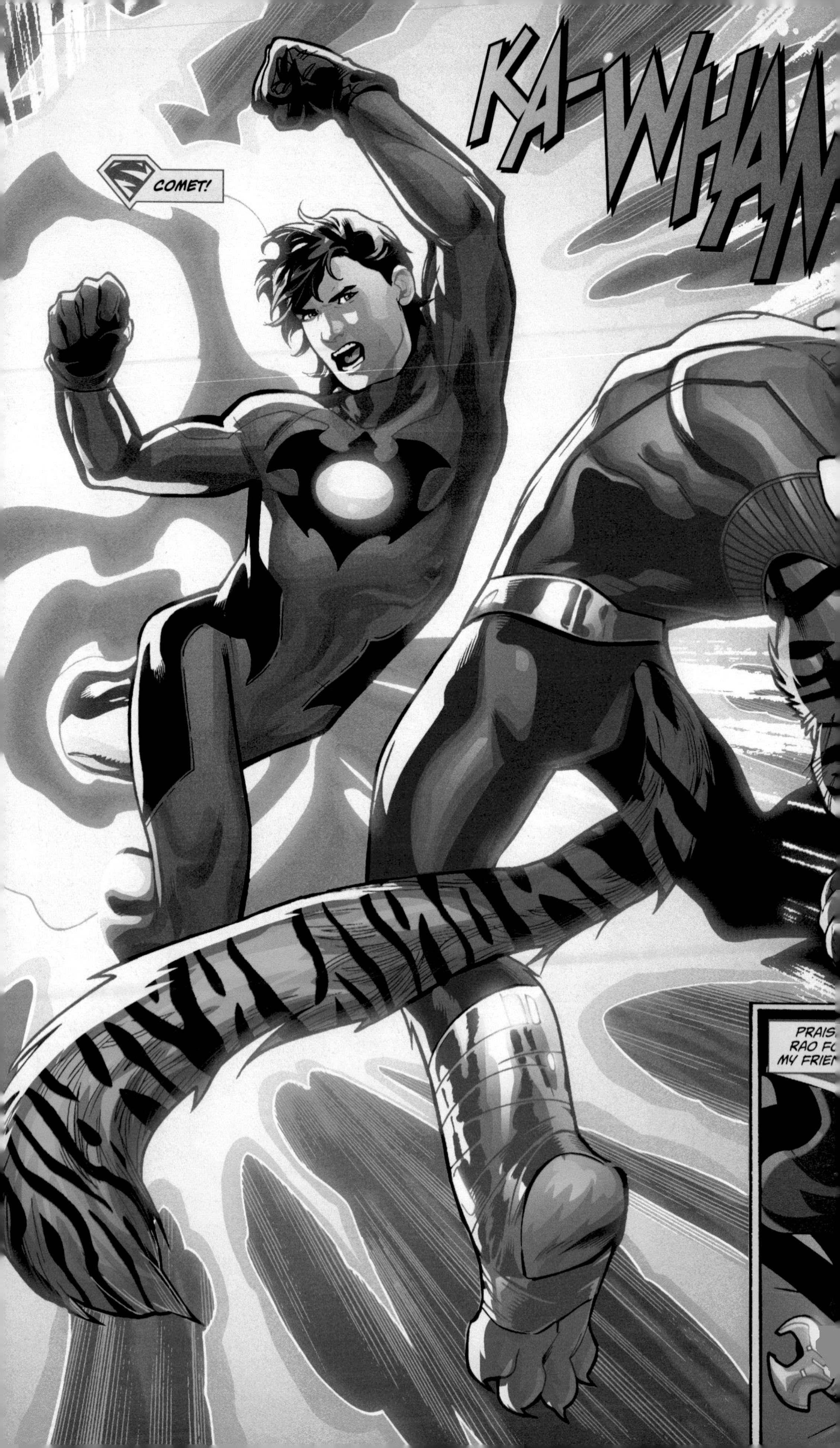
COMET!
KA-WHA
PRAIS
RAO FO
MY FRIEN

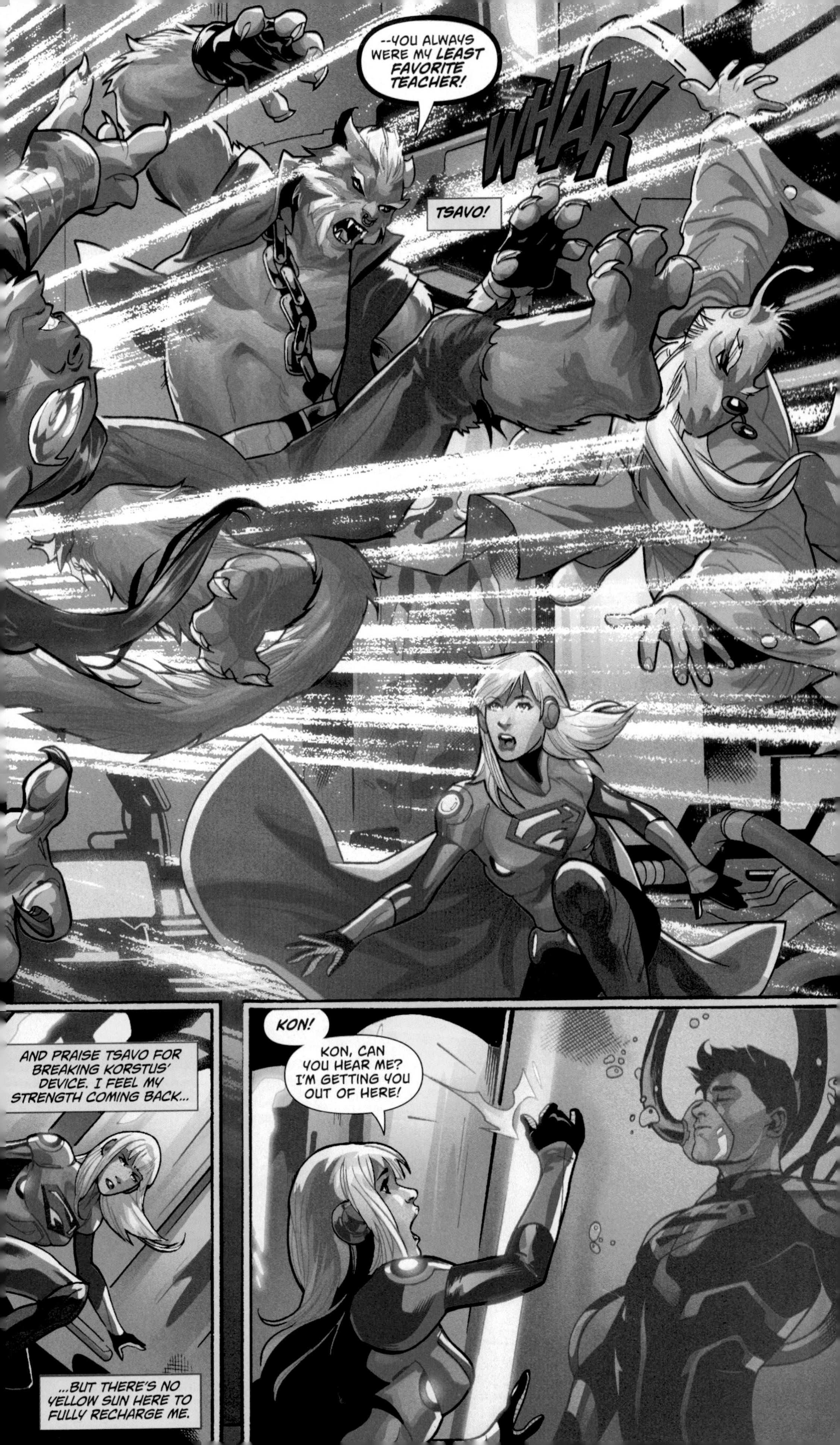
--YOU ALWAYS WERE MY LEAST FAVORITE TEACHER!
WHAK
TSAVO!
AND PRAISE TSAVO FOR BREAKING KORSTUS' DEVICE. I FEEL MY STRENGTH COMING BACK...
...BUT THERE'S NO YELLOW SUN HERE TO FULLY RECHARGE ME.
KON!
KON, CAN YOU HEAR ME? I'M GETTING YOU OUT OF HERE!

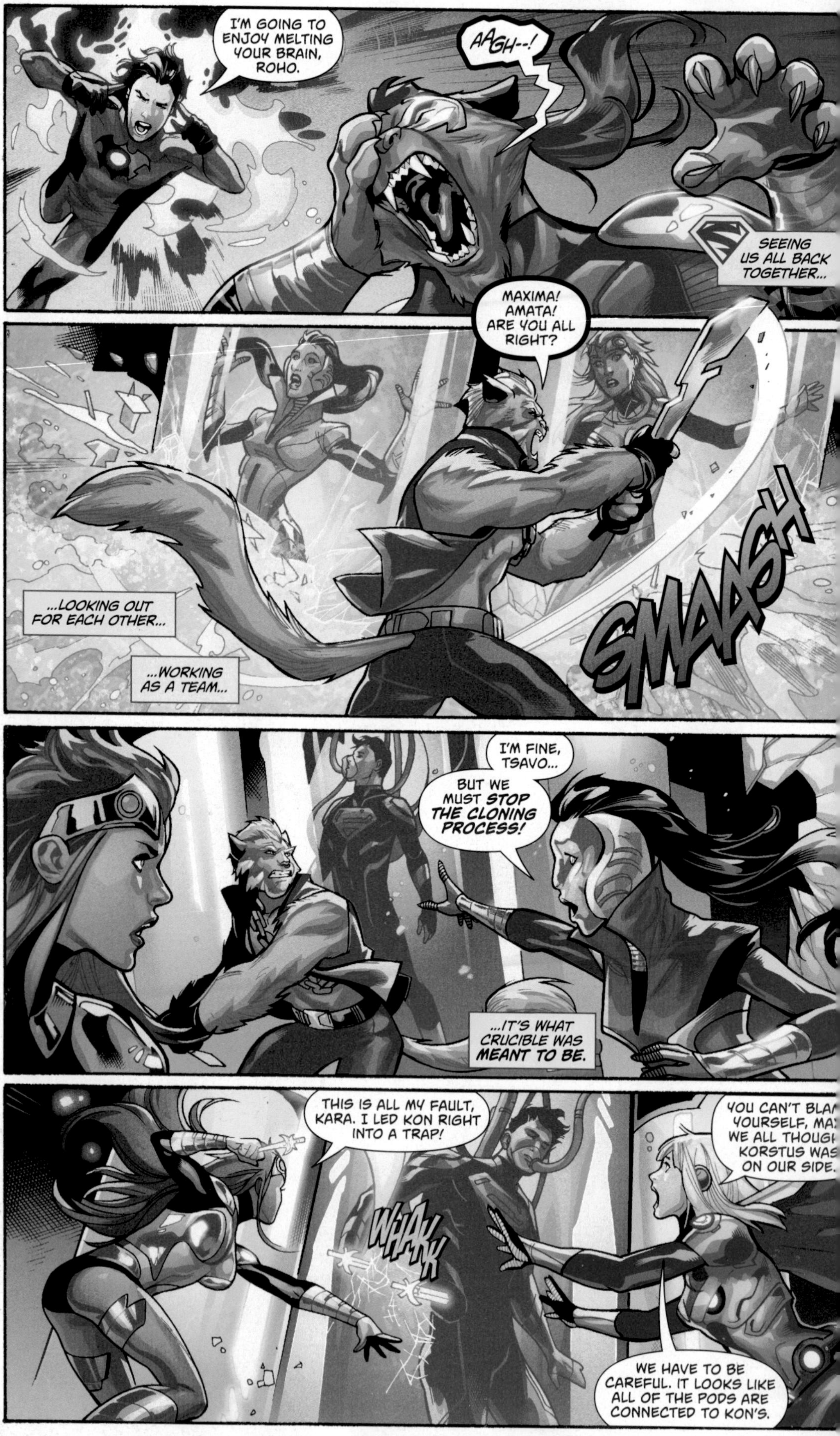
I'M GOING TO ENJOY MELTING YOUR BRAIN, ROHO.
AAGH--!
SEEING US ALL BACK TOGETHER...
MAXIMA! AMATA! ARE YOU ALL RIGHT?
...LOOKING OUT FOR EACH OTHER...
...WORKING AS A TEAM...
SMAASH
I'M FINE, TSAVO...
BUT WE MUST STOP THE CLONING PROCESS!
...IT'S WHAT CRUCIBLE WAS MEANT TO BE.
THIS IS ALL MY FAULT, KARA. I LED KON RIGHT INTO A TRAP!
YOU CAN'T BLAM YOURSELF, MA WE ALL THOUG KORSTUS WAS ON OUR SIDE.
WHAKK
WE HAVE TO BE CAREFUL. IT LOOKS LIKE ALL OF THE PODS ARE CONNECTED TO KON'S.

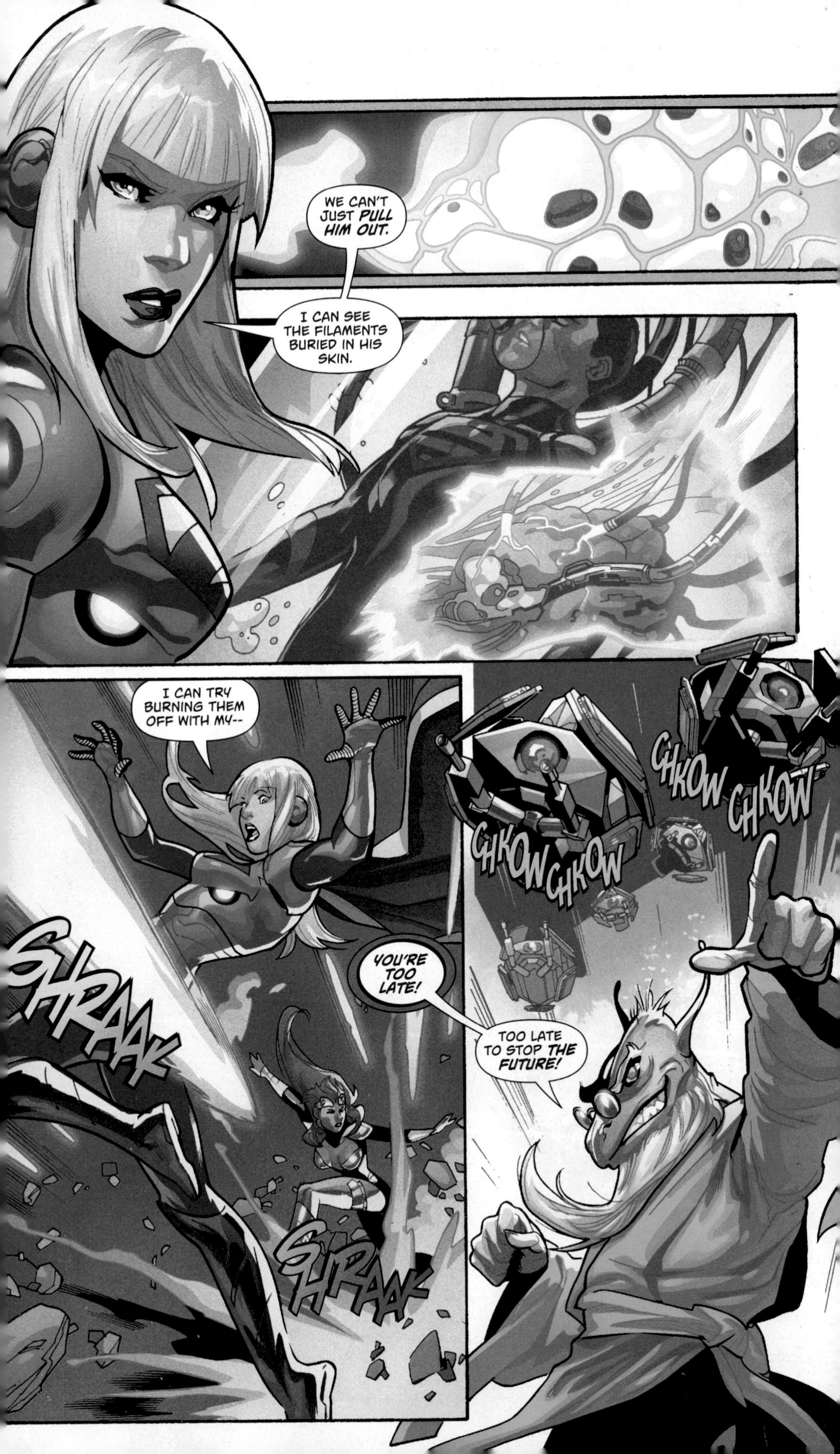
WE CAN'T JUST PULL HIM OUT.
I CAN SEE THE FILAMENTS BURIED IN HIS SKIN.
I CAN TRY BURNING THEM OFF WITH MY--
SHRAAAK
SHRAAK
CHKOW CHKOW
CHKOW CHKOW
YOU'RE TOO LATE!
TOO LATE TO STOP THE FUTURE!

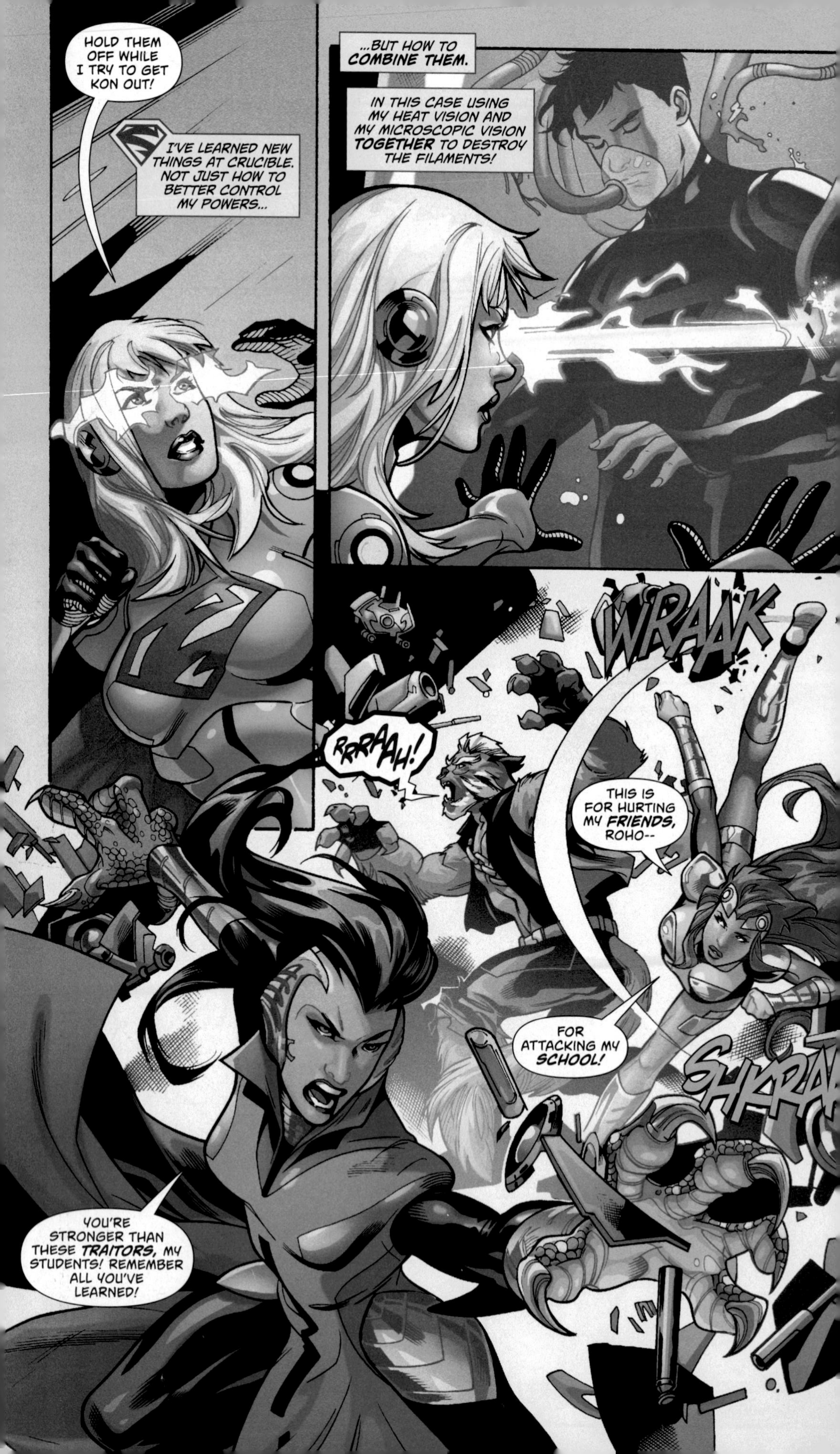
HOLD THEM OFF WHILE I TRY TO GET KON OUT!
I'VE LEARNED NEW THINGS AT CRUCIBLE. NOT JUST HOW TO BETTER CONTROL MY POWERS...
...BUT HOW TO COMBINE THEM.
IN THIS CASE USING MY HEAT VISION AND MY MICROSCOPIC VISION TOGETHER TO DESTROY THE FILAMENTS!
WRAAK
RRRAAAH!
THIS IS FOR HURTING MY FRIENDS, ROHO--
FOR ATTACKING MY SCHOOL!
YOU'RE STRONGER THAN THESE TRAITORS, MY STUDENTS! REMEMBER ALL YOU'VE LEARNED!

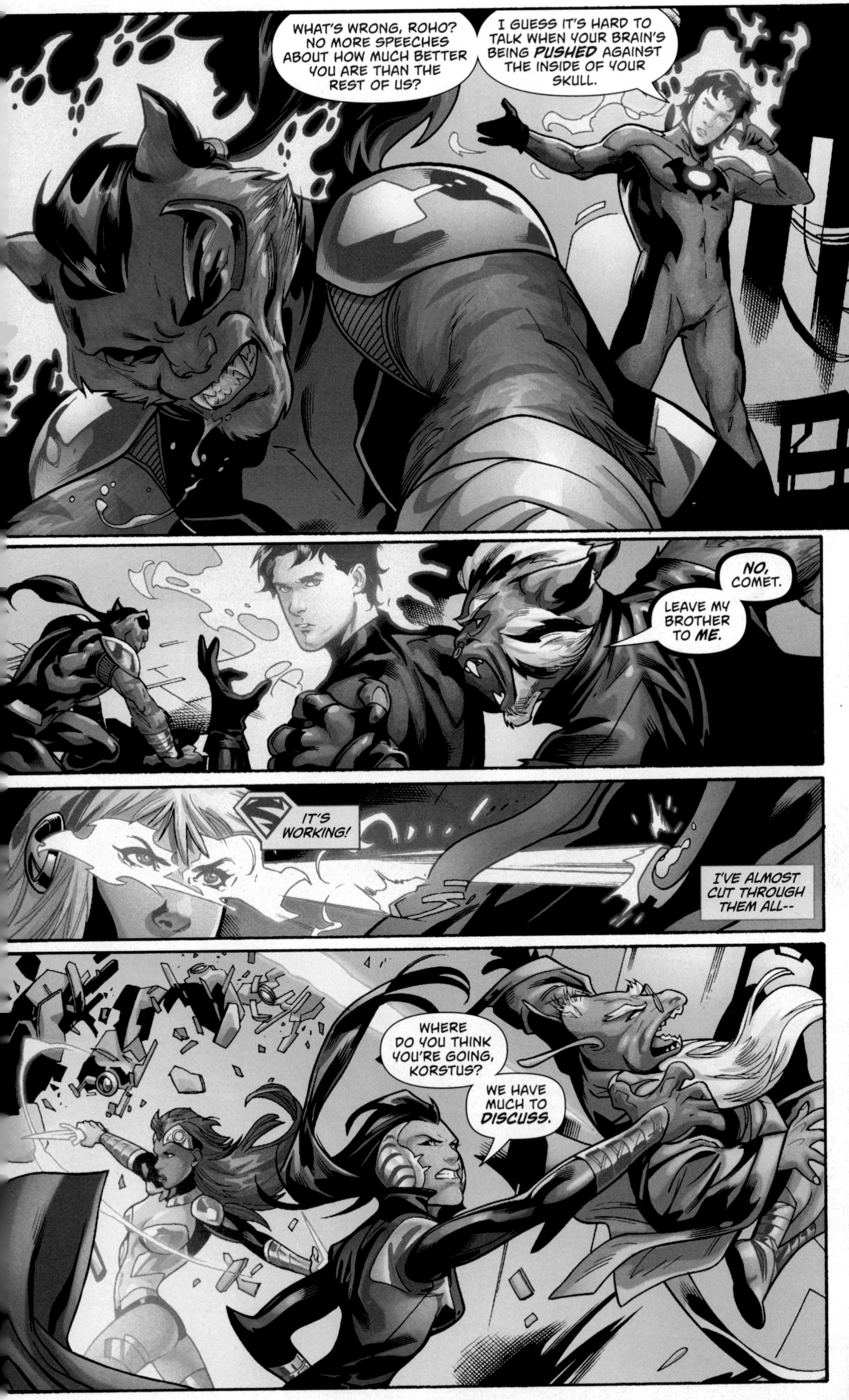
WHAT'S WRONG, ROHO? NO MORE SPEECHES ABOUT HOW MUCH BETTER YOU ARE THAN THE REST OF US?
I GUESS IT'S HARD TO TALK WHEN YOUR BRAIN'S BEING PUSHED AGAINST THE INSIDE OF YOUR SKULL.
NO, COMET.
LEAVE MY BROTHER TO ME.
IT'S WORKING!
I'VE ALMOST CUT THROUGH THEM ALL--
WHERE DO YOU THINK YOU'RE GOING, KORSTUS?
WE HAVE MUCH TO DISCUSS.

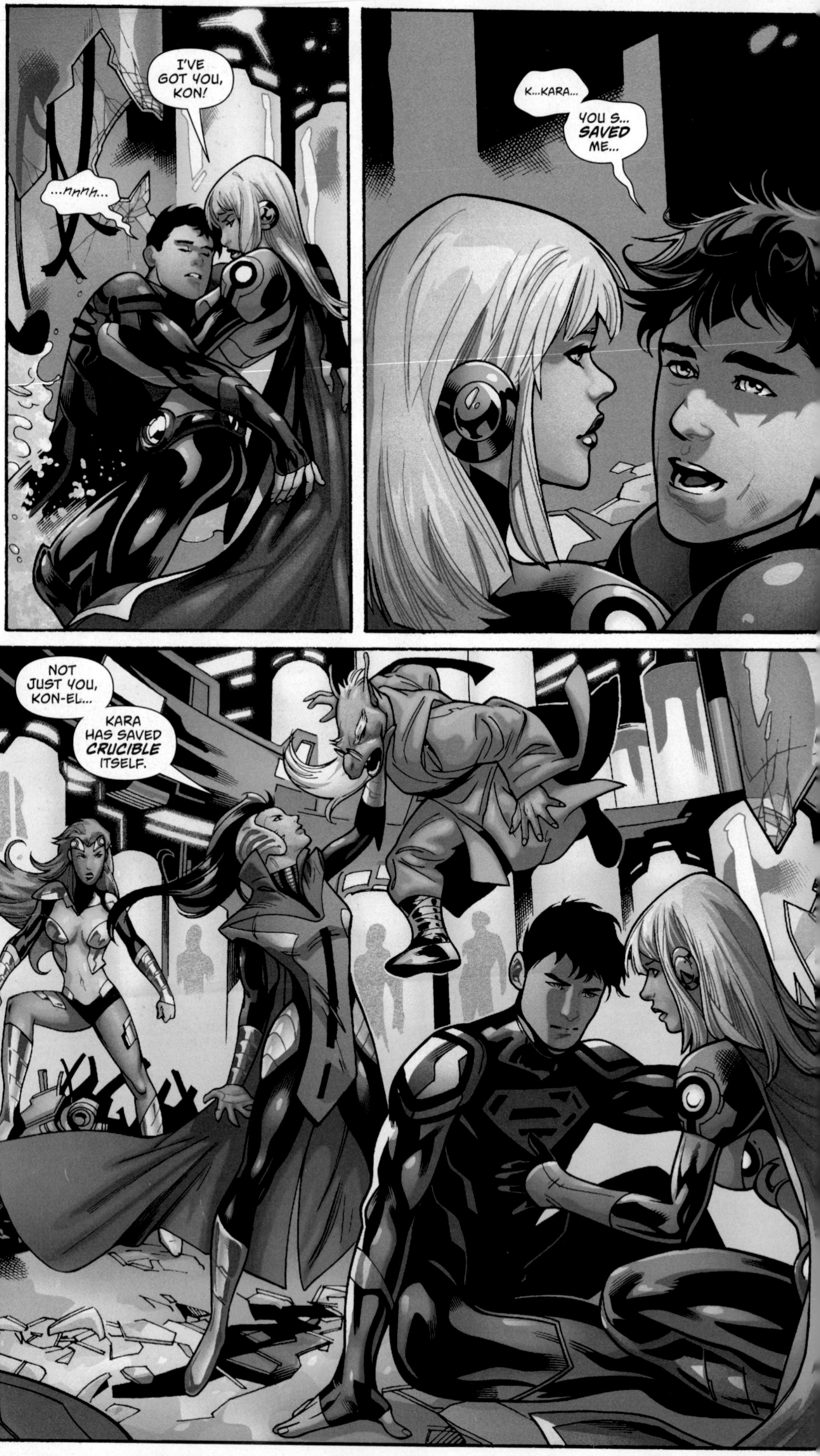
I'VE GOT YOU, KON!
...nnnh...
K...KARA...
YOU S... SAVED ME...
NOT JUST YOU, KON-EL...
KARA HAS SAVED CRUCIBLE ITSELF.

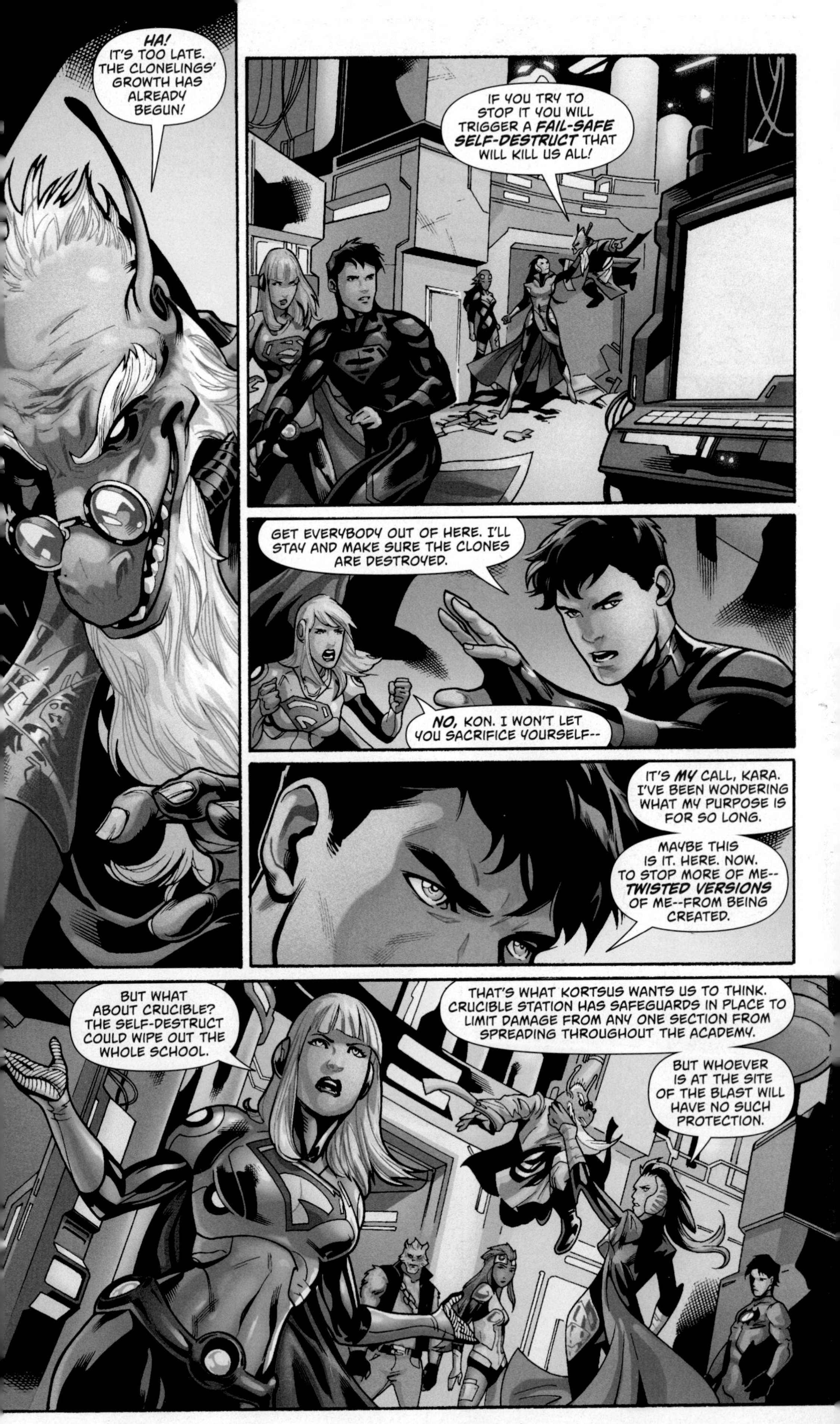
HA! IT'S TOO LATE. THE CLONELINGS' GROWTH HAS ALREADY BEGUN!
IF YOU TRY TO STOP IT YOU WILL TRIGGER A FAIL-SAFE SELF-DESTRUCT THAT WILL KILL US ALL!
GET EVERYBODY OUT OF HERE. I'LL STAY AND MAKE SURE THE CLONES ARE DESTROYED.
NO, KON. I WON'T LET YOU SACRIFICE YOURSELF--
IT'S MY CALL, KARA. I'VE BEEN WONDERING WHAT MY PURPOSE IS FOR SO LONG.
MAYBE THIS IS IT. HERE. NOW. TO STOP MORE OF ME--TWISTED VERSIONS OF ME--FROM BEING CREATED.
BUT WHAT ABOUT CRUCIBLE? THE SELF-DESTRUCT COULD WIPE OUT THE WHOLE SCHOOL.
THAT'S WHAT KORTSUS WANTS US TO THINK. CRUCIBLE STATION HAS SAFEGUARDS IN PLACE TO LIMIT DAMAGE FROM ANY ONE SECTION FROM SPREADING THROUGHOUT THE ACADEMY.
BUT WHOEVER IS AT THE SITE OF THE BLAST WILL HAVE NO SUCH PROTECTION.

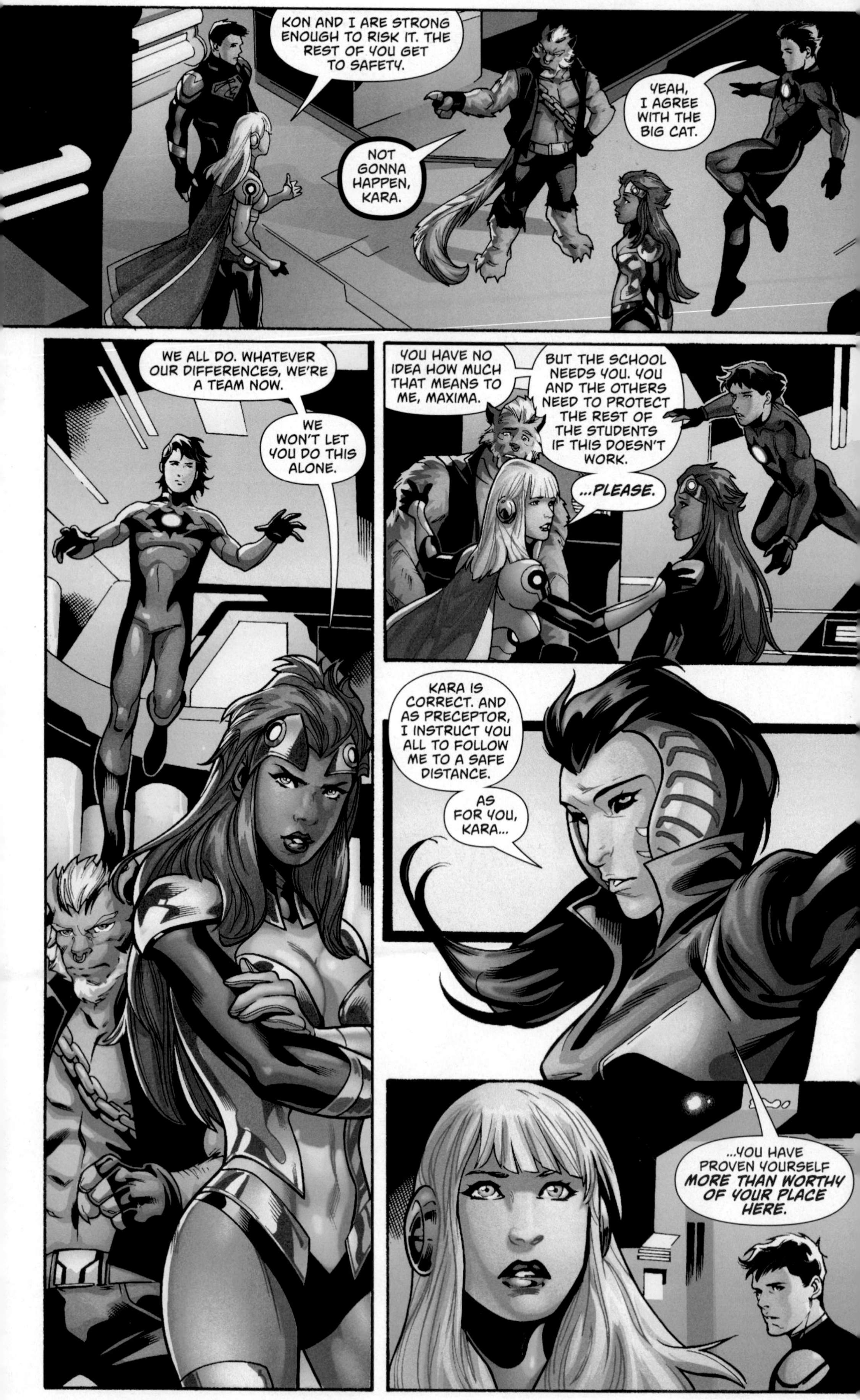
KON AND I ARE STRONG ENOUGH TO RISK IT. THE REST OF YOU GET TO SAFETY.
NOT GONNA HAPPEN, KARA.
YEAH, I AGREE WITH THE BIG CAT.
WE ALL DO. WHATEVER OUR DIFFERENCES, WE'RE A TEAM NOW.
WE WON'T LET YOU DO THIS ALONE.
YOU HAVE NO IDEA HOW MUCH THAT MEANS TO ME, MAXIMA.
BUT THE SCHOOL NEEDS YOU. YOU AND THE OTHERS NEED TO PROTECT THE REST OF THE STUDENTS IF THIS DOESN'T WORK.
...PLEASE.
KARA IS CORRECT. AND AS PRECEPTOR, I INSTRUCT YOU ALL TO FOLLOW ME TO A SAFE DISTANCE.
AS FOR YOU, KARA...
...YOU HAVE PROVEN YOURSELF MORE THAN WORTHY OF YOUR PLACE HERE.

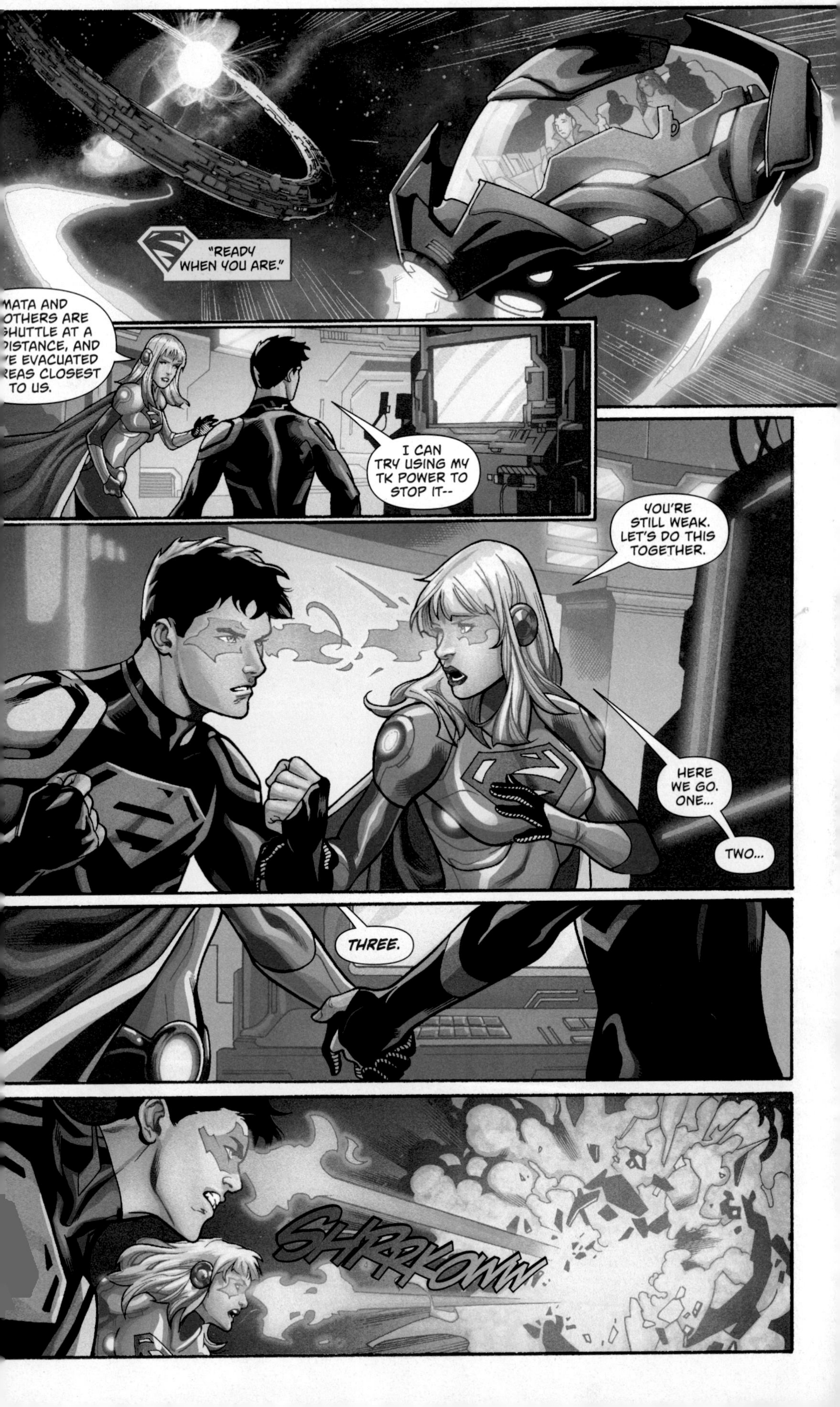
"READY WHEN YOU ARE."
MATA AND OTHERS ARE SHUTTLE AT A DISTANCE, AND 'E EVACUATED REAS CLOSEST TO US.
I CAN TRY USING MY TK POWER TO STOP IT--
YOU'RE STILL WEAK. LET'S DO THIS TOGETHER.
HERE WE GO. ONE...
TWO...
THREE.
SHRRAKOWW

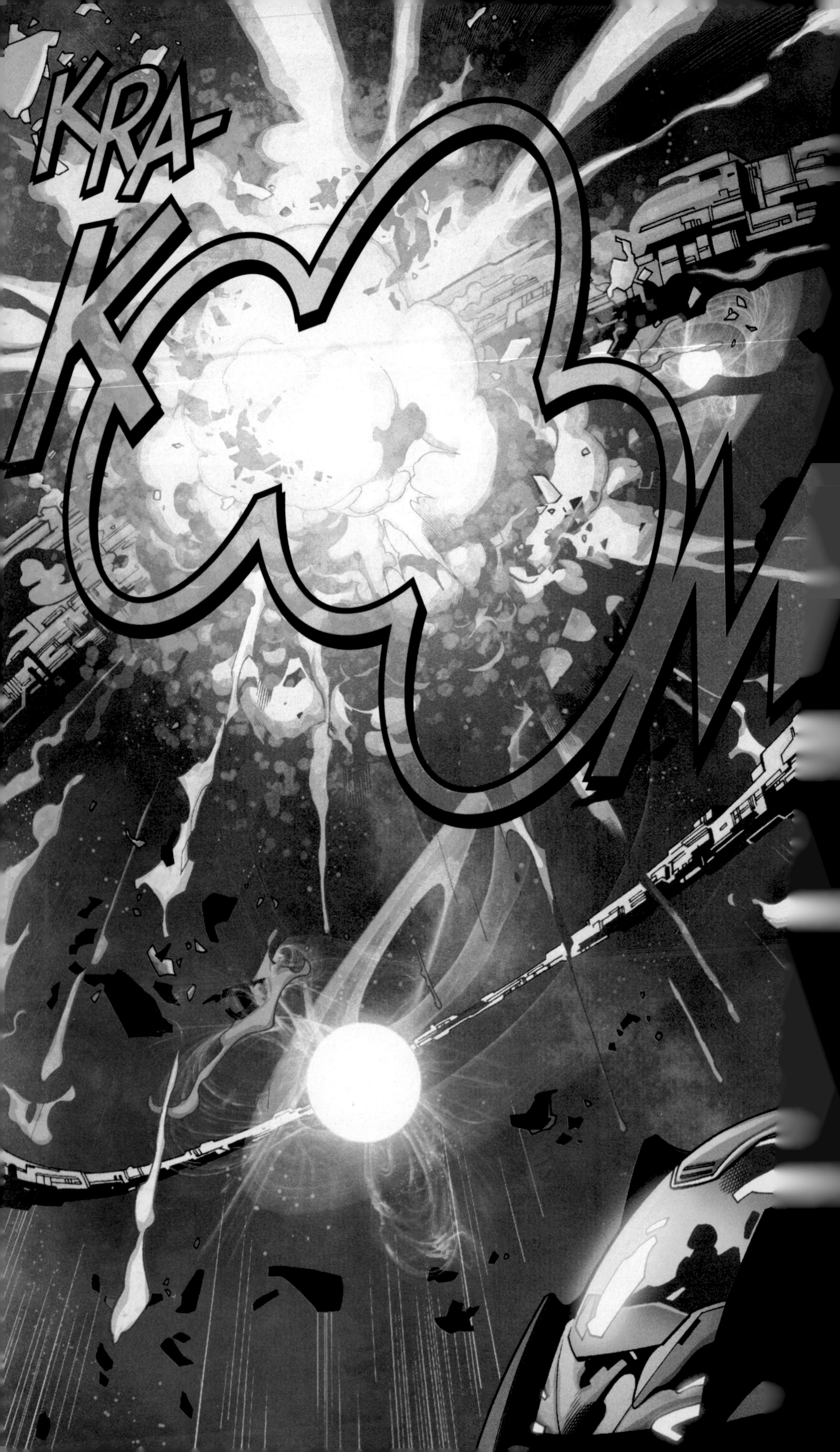
KRA-KOOM

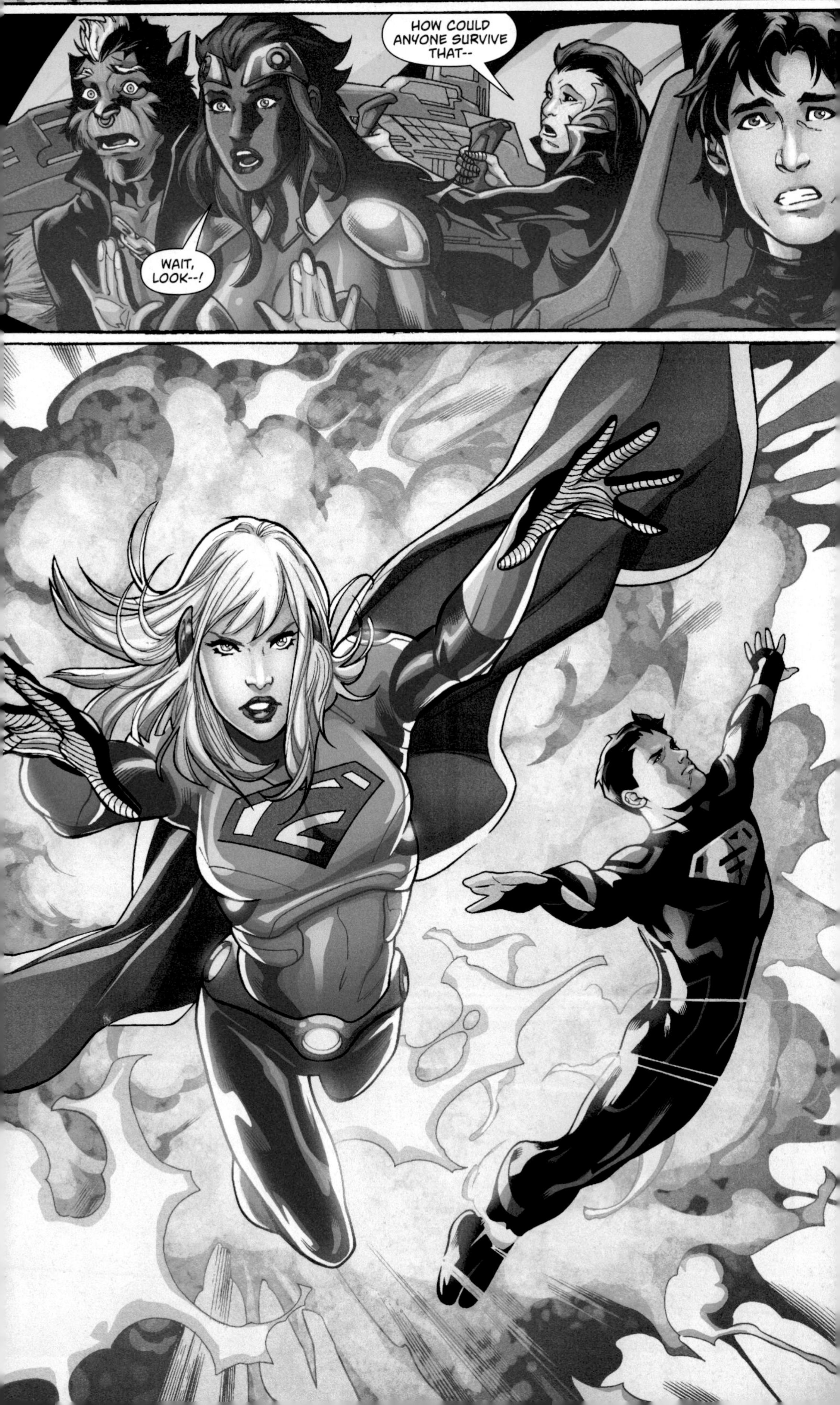
HOW COULD ANYONE SURVIVE THAT--
WAIT, LOOK--!

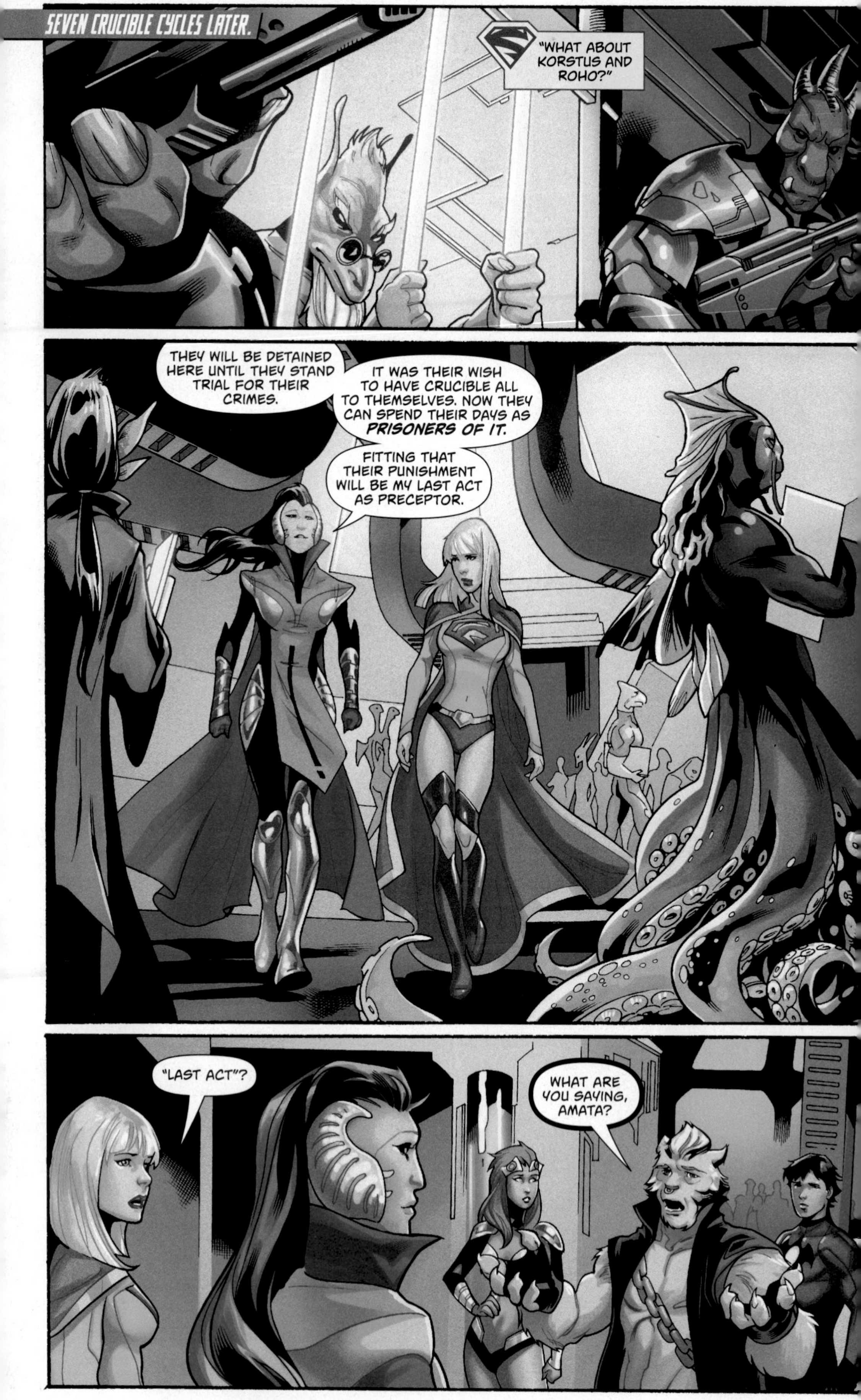
SEVEN CRUCIBLE CYCLES LATER.
"WHAT ABOUT KORSTUS AND ROHO?"
THEY WILL BE DETAINED HERE UNTIL THEY STAND TRIAL FOR THEIR CRIMES.
IT WAS THEIR WISH TO HAVE CRUCIBLE ALL TO THEMSELVES. NOW THEY CAN SPEND THEIR DAYS AS PRISONERS OF IT.
FITTING THAT THEIR PUNISHMENT WILL BE MY LAST ACT AS PRECEPTOR.
"LAST ACT"?
WHAT ARE YOU SAYING, AMATA?

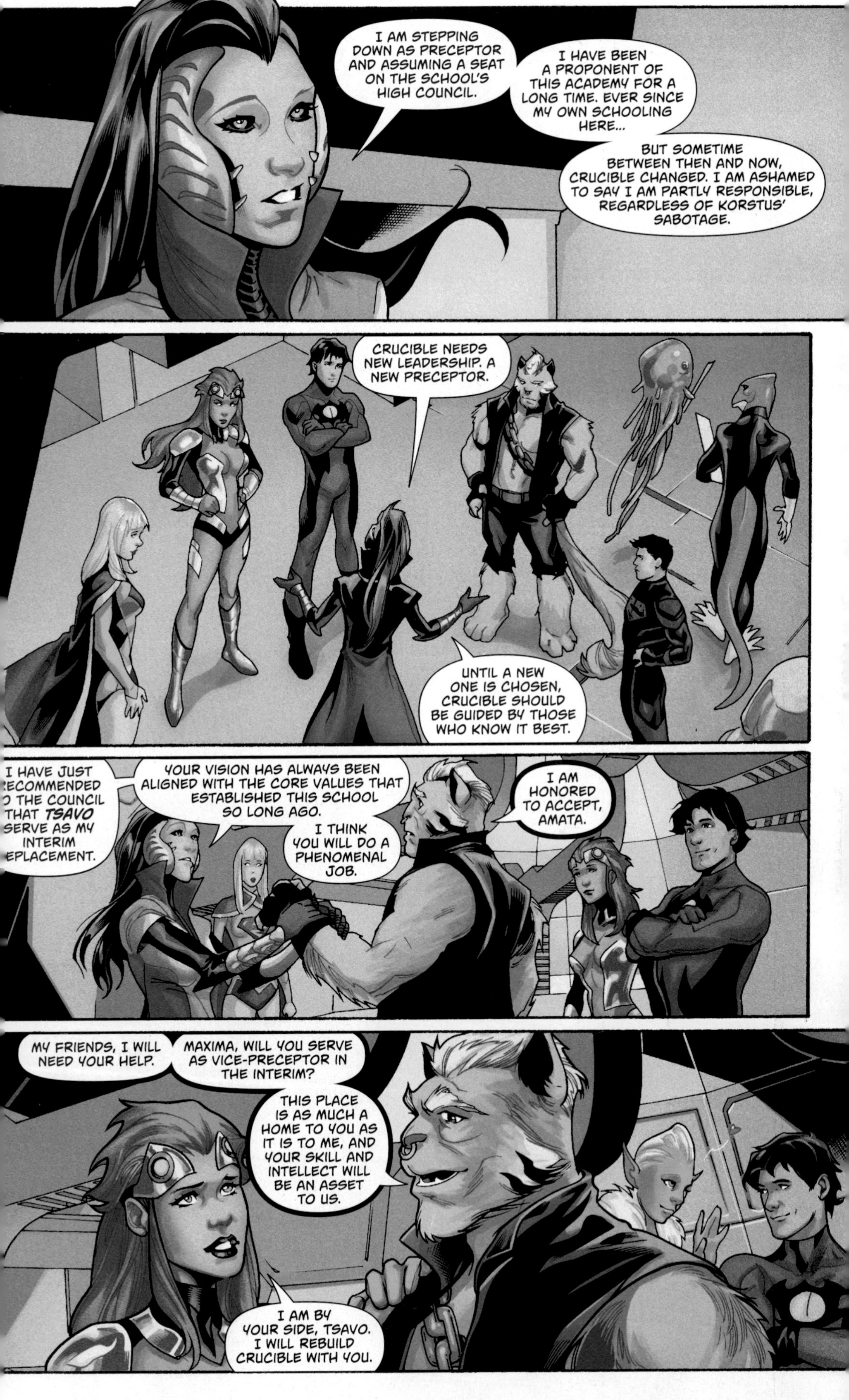
I AM STEPPING DOWN AS PRECEPTOR AND ASSUMING A SEAT ON THE SCHOOL'S HIGH COUNCIL.
I HAVE BEEN A PROPONENT OF THIS ACADEMY FOR A LONG TIME. EVER SINCE MY OWN SCHOOLING HERE...
BUT SOMETIME BETWEEN THEN AND NOW, CRUCIBLE CHANGED. I AM ASHAMED TO SAY I AM PARTLY RESPONSIBLE, REGARDLESS OF KORSTUS' SABOTAGE.
CRUCIBLE NEEDS NEW LEADERSHIP. A NEW PRECEPTOR.
UNTIL A NEW ONE IS CHOSEN, CRUCIBLE SHOULD BE GUIDED BY THOSE WHO KNOW IT BEST.
I HAVE JUST RECOMMENDED TO THE COUNCIL THAT TSAVO SERVE AS MY INTERIM REPLACEMENT.
YOUR VISION HAS ALWAYS BEEN ALIGNED WITH THE CORE VALUES THAT ESTABLISHED THIS SCHOOL SO LONG AGO.
I THINK YOU WILL DO A PHENOMENAL JOB.
I AM HONORED TO ACCEPT, AMATA.
MY FRIENDS, I WILL NEED YOUR HELP.
MAXIMA, WILL YOU SERVE AS VICE-PRECEPTOR IN THE INTERIM?
THIS PLACE IS AS MUCH A HOME TO YOU AS IT IS TO ME, AND YOUR SKILL AND INTELLECT WILL BE AN ASSET TO US.
I AM BY YOUR SIDE, TSAVO. I WILL REBUILD CRUCIBLE WITH YOU.

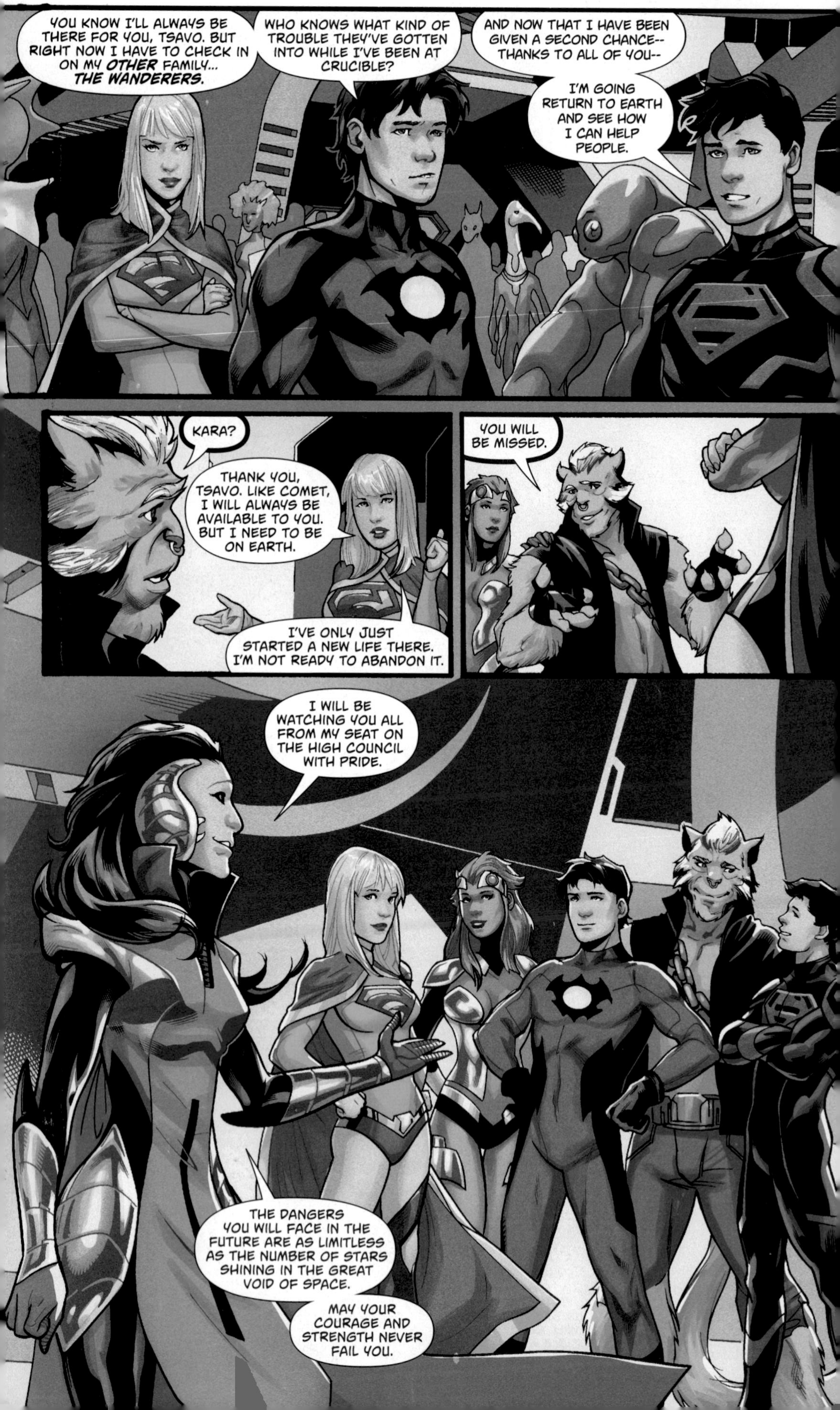
YOU KNOW I'LL ALWAYS BE THERE FOR YOU, TSAVO. BUT RIGHT NOW I HAVE TO CHECK IN ON MY **OTHER** FAMILY... **THE WANDERERS.**
WHO KNOWS WHAT KIND OF TROUBLE THEY'VE GOTTEN INTO WHILE I'VE BEEN AT CRUCIBLE?
AND NOW THAT I HAVE BEEN GIVEN A SECOND CHANCE-- THANKS TO ALL OF YOU--
I'M GOING RETURN TO EARTH AND SEE HOW I CAN HELP PEOPLE.
KARA?
THANK YOU, TSAVO. LIKE COMET, I WILL ALWAYS BE AVAILABLE TO YOU. BUT I NEED TO BE ON EARTH.
I'VE ONLY JUST STARTED A NEW LIFE THERE. I'M NOT READY TO ABANDON IT.
YOU WILL BE MISSED.
I WILL BE WATCHING YOU ALL FROM MY SEAT ON THE HIGH COUNCIL WITH PRIDE.
THE DANGERS YOU WILL FACE IN THE FUTURE ARE AS LIMITLESS AS THE NUMBER OF STARS SHINING IN THE GREAT VOID OF SPACE.
MAY YOUR COURAGE AND STRENGTH NEVER FAIL YOU.

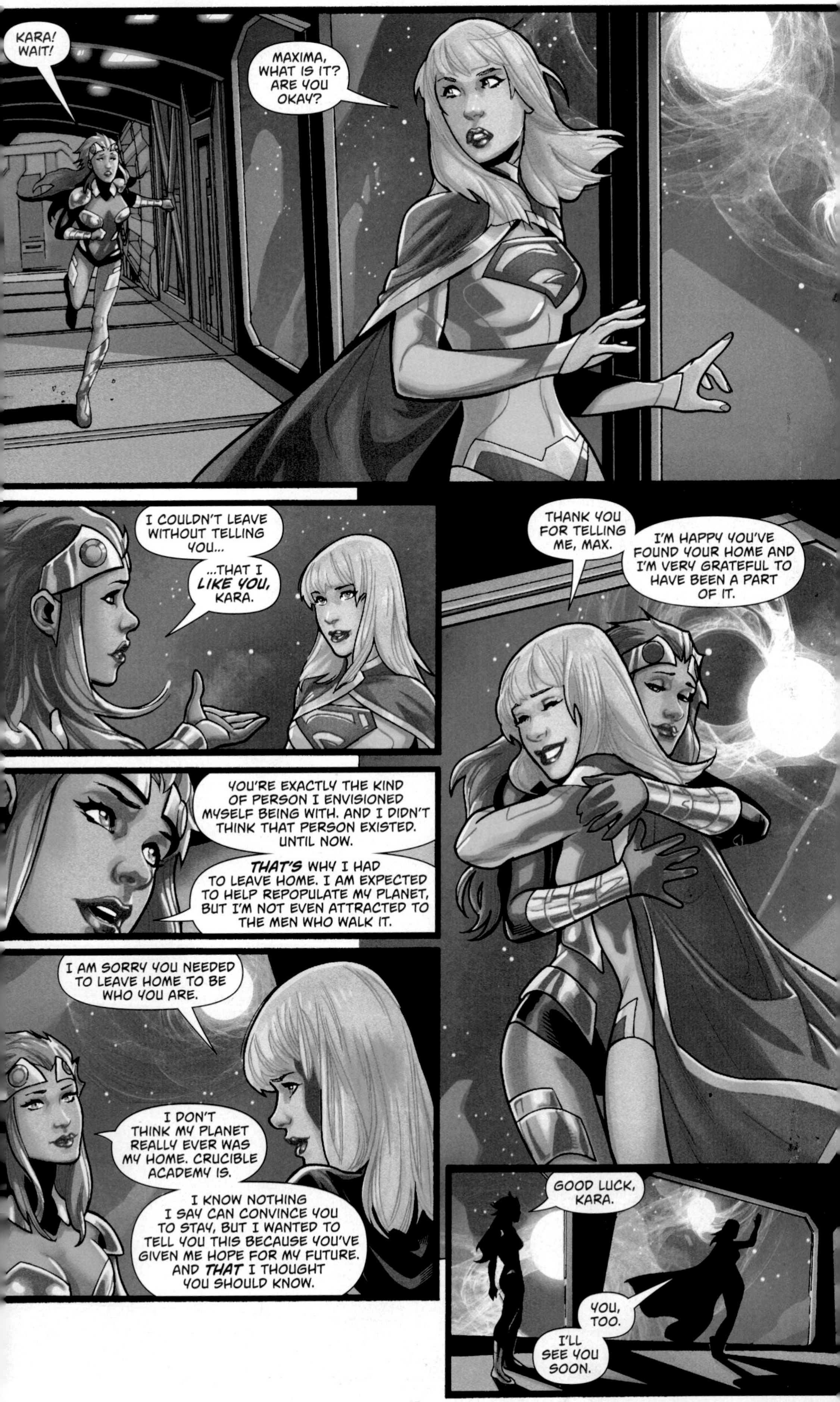
KARA! WAIT!
MAXIMA, WHAT IS IT? ARE YOU OKAY?
I COULDN'T LEAVE WITHOUT TELLING YOU...
...THAT I *LIKE YOU,* KARA.
YOU'RE EXACTLY THE KIND OF PERSON I ENVISIONED MYSELF BEING WITH. AND I DIDN'T THINK THAT PERSON EXISTED. UNTIL NOW.
THAT'S WHY I HAD TO LEAVE HOME. I AM EXPECTED TO HELP REPOPULATE MY PLANET, BUT I'M NOT EVEN ATTRACTED TO THE MEN WHO WALK IT.
I AM SORRY YOU NEEDED TO LEAVE HOME TO BE WHO YOU ARE.
I DON'T THINK MY PLANET REALLY EVER WAS MY HOME. CRUCIBLE ACADEMY IS.
I KNOW NOTHING I SAY CAN CONVINCE YOU TO STAY, BUT I WANTED TO TELL YOU THIS BECAUSE YOU'VE GIVEN ME HOPE FOR MY FUTURE. AND *THAT* I THOUGHT YOU SHOULD KNOW.
THANK YOU FOR TELLING ME, MAX.
I'M HAPPY YOU'VE FOUND YOUR HOME AND I'M VERY GRATEFUL TO HAVE BEEN A PART OF IT.
GOOD LUCK, KARA.
YOU, TOO.
I'LL SEE YOU SOON.

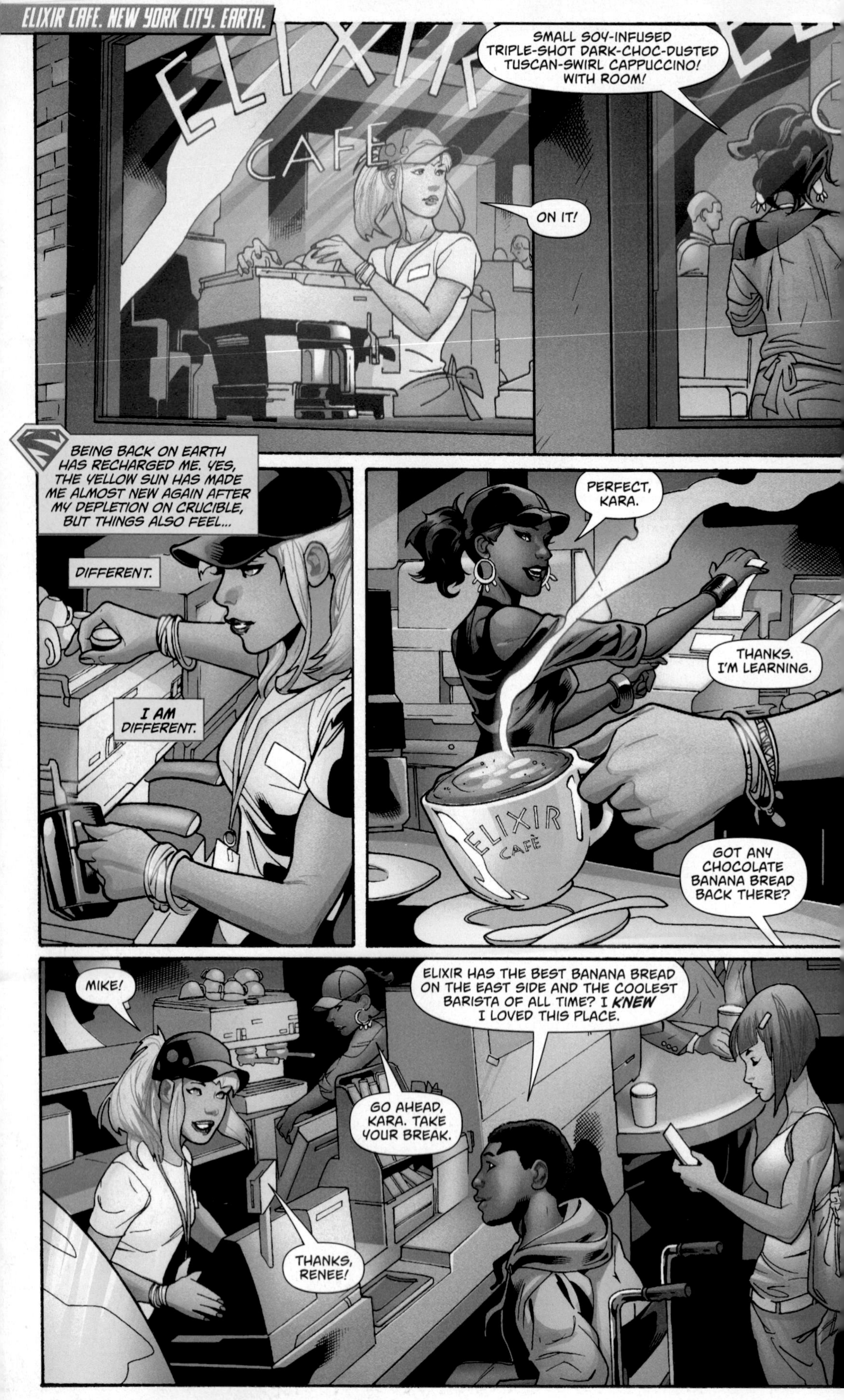
ELIXIR CAFE. NEW YORK CITY. EARTH.
SMALL SOY-INFUSED TRIPLE-SHOT DARK-CHOC-DUSTED TUSCAN-SWIRL CAPPUCCINO! WITH ROOM!
ON IT!
BEING BACK ON EARTH HAS RECHARGED ME. YES, THE YELLOW SUN HAS MADE ME ALMOST NEW AGAIN AFTER MY DEPLETION ON CRUCIBLE, BUT THINGS ALSO FEEL...
DIFFERENT.
I AM DIFFERENT.
PERFECT, KARA.
THANKS. I'M LEARNING.
ELIXIR CAFÈ
GOT ANY CHOCOLATE BANANA BREAD BACK THERE?
MIKE!
ELIXIR HAS THE BEST BANANA BREAD ON THE EAST SIDE AND THE COOLEST BARISTA OF ALL TIME? I *KNEW* I LOVED THIS PLACE.
GO AHEAD, KARA. TAKE YOUR BREAK.
THANKS, RENEE!

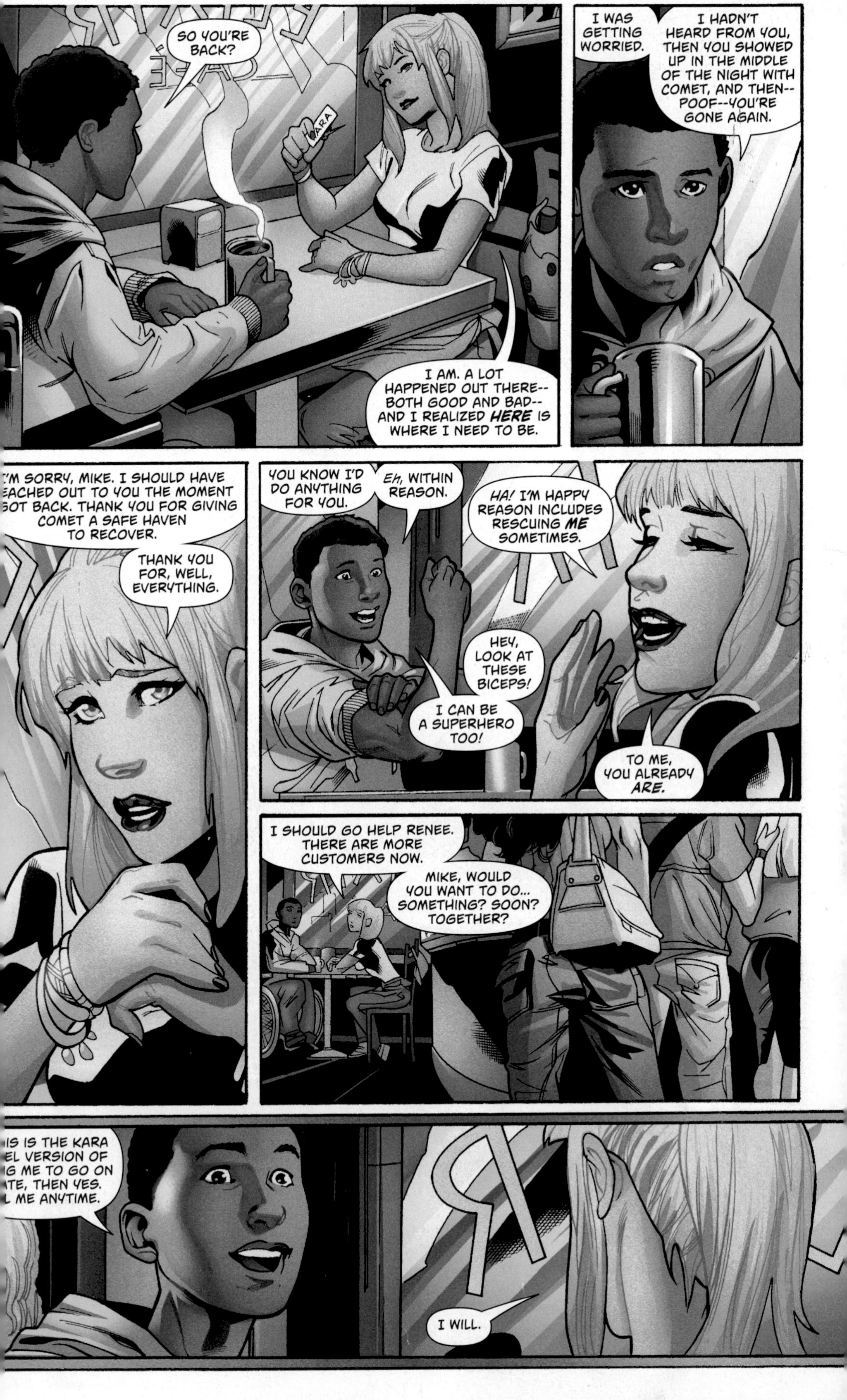
SO YOU'RE BACK?
I AM. A LOT HAPPENED OUT THERE-- BOTH GOOD AND BAD-- AND I REALIZED HERE IS WHERE I NEED TO BE.
I WAS GETTING WORRIED.
I HADN'T HEARD FROM YOU, THEN YOU SHOWED UP IN THE MIDDLE OF THE NIGHT WITH COMET, AND THEN-- POOF--YOU'RE GONE AGAIN.
'M SORRY, MIKE. I SHOULD HAVE EACHED OUT TO YOU THE MOMENT OT BACK. THANK YOU FOR GIVING COMET A SAFE HAVEN TO RECOVER.
THANK YOU FOR, WELL, EVERYTHING.
YOU KNOW I'D DO ANYTHING FOR YOU.
Eh, WITHIN REASON.
HA! I'M HAPPY REASON INCLUDES RESCUING ME SOMETIMES.
HEY, LOOK AT THESE BICEPS!
I CAN BE A SUPERHERO TOO!
TO ME, YOU ALREADY ARE.
I SHOULD GO HELP RENEE. THERE ARE MORE CUSTOMERS NOW.
MIKE, WOULD YOU WANT TO DO... SOMETHING? SOON? TOGETHER?
IS IS THE KARA EL VERSION OF G ME TO GO ON ATE, THEN YES. L ME ANYTIME.
I WILL.

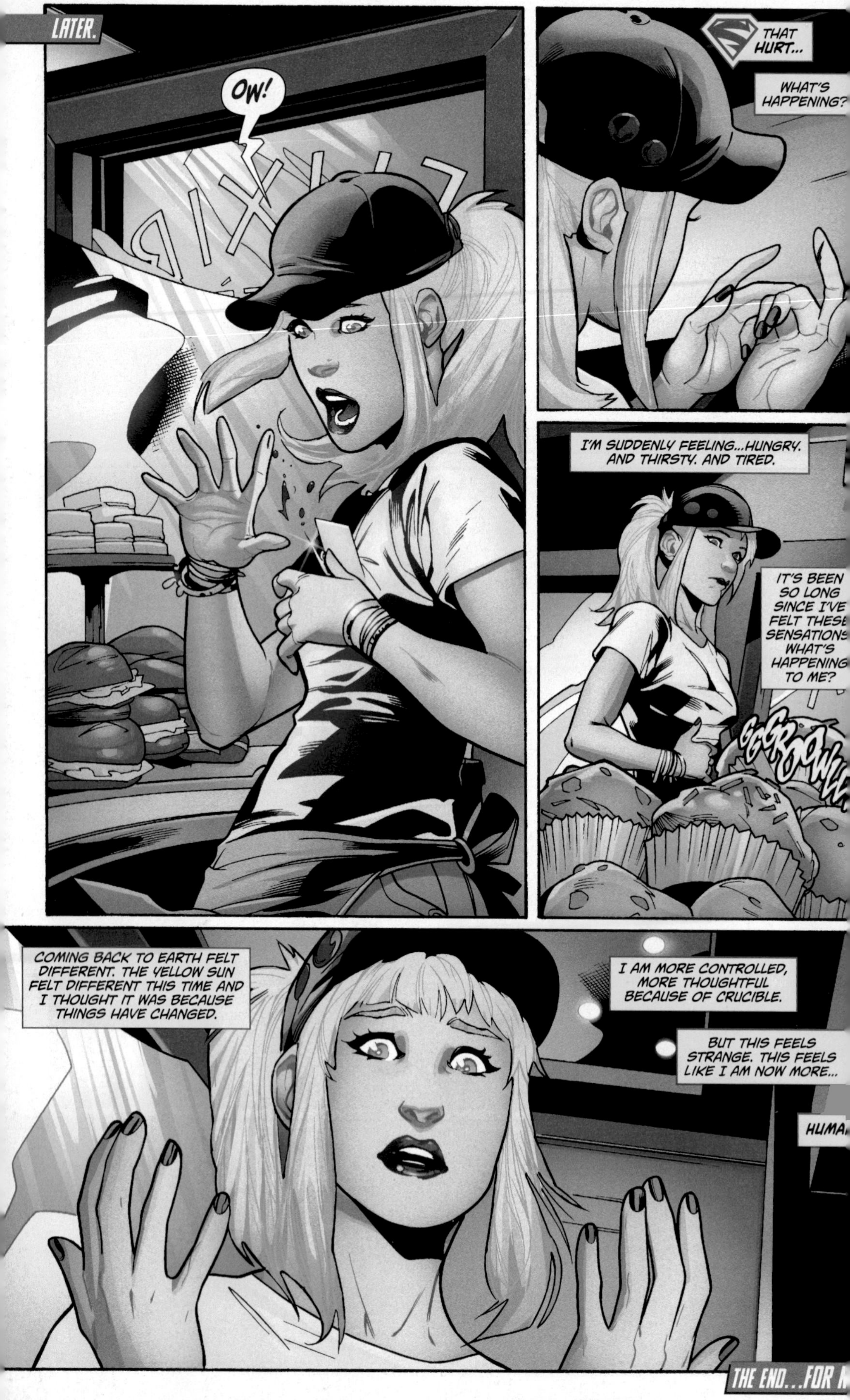
LATER.
OW!
THAT HURT...
WHAT'S HAPPENING?
I'M SUDDENLY FEELING...HUNGRY. AND THIRSTY. AND TIRED.
IT'S BEEN SO LONG SINCE I'VE FELT THESE SENSATIONS. WHAT'S HAPPENING TO ME?
GGGROWWL
COMING BACK TO EARTH FELT DIFFERENT. THE YELLOW SUN FELT DIFFERENT THIS TIME AND I THOUGHT IT WAS BECAUSE THINGS HAVE CHANGED.
I AM MORE CONTROLLED, MORE THOUGHTFUL BECAUSE OF CRUCIBLE.
BUT THIS FEELS STRANGE. THIS FEELS LIKE I AM NOW MORE...
HUMA
THE END...FOR N

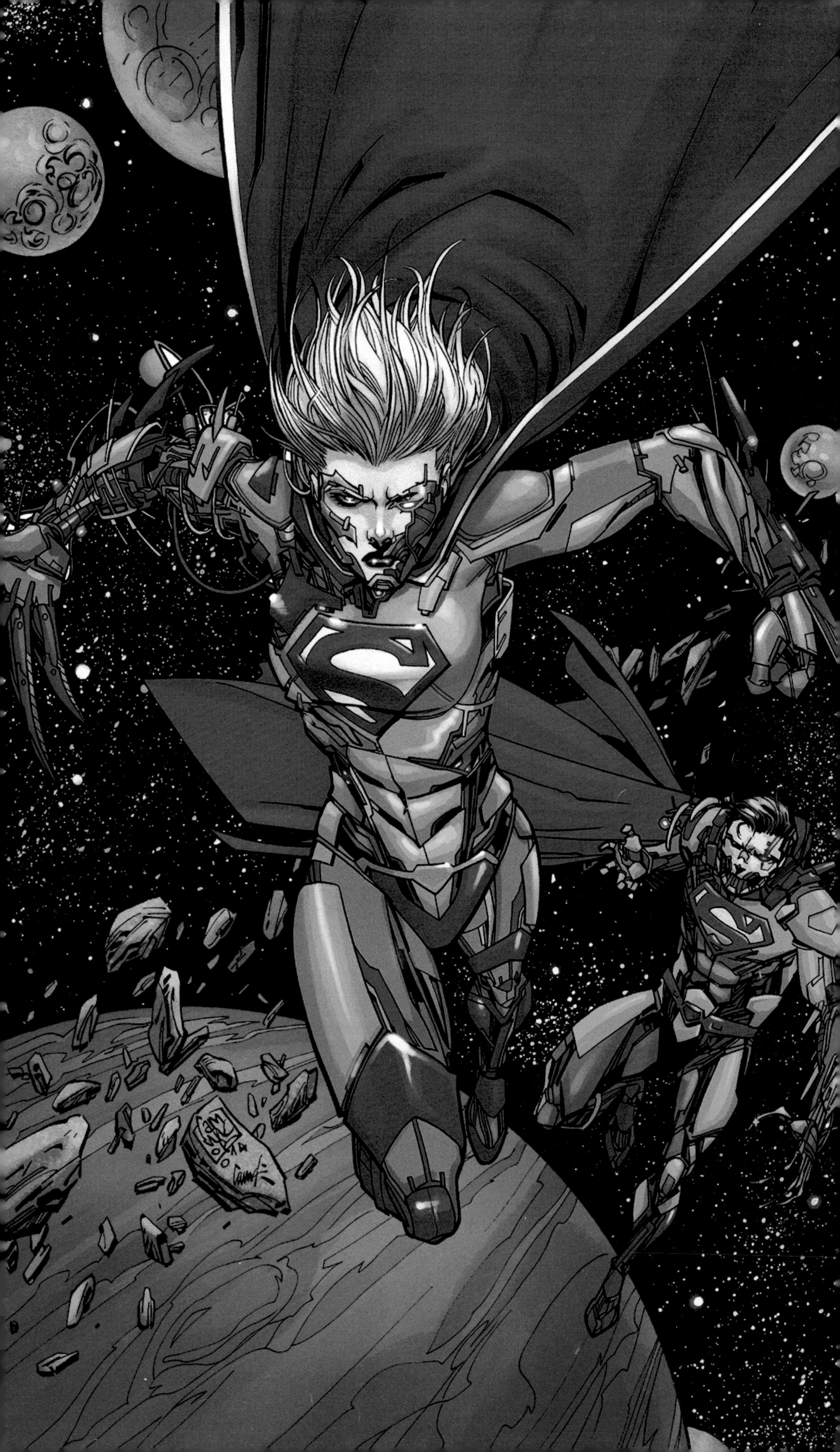

THE PERFECT IS THE ENEMY OF THE GOOD

TONY BEDARD writer **EMANUELA LUPACCHINO** penciller **RAY McCARTHY** inker **HI-FI** colorist **ROB LEIGH** letterer
cover art by **GIUSEPPE CAMUNCOLI** and **CAM SMITH** with **DAN BROWN**

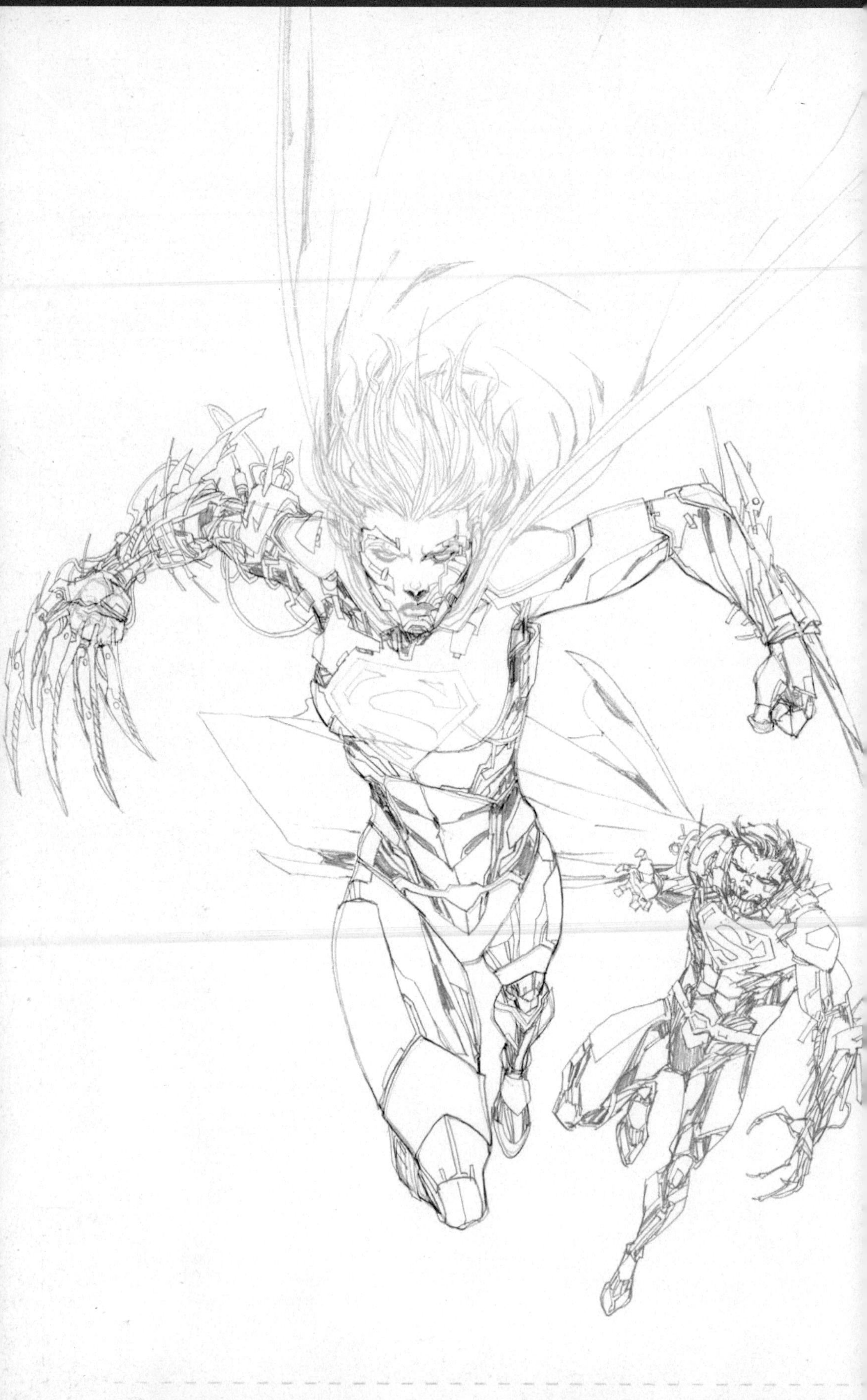

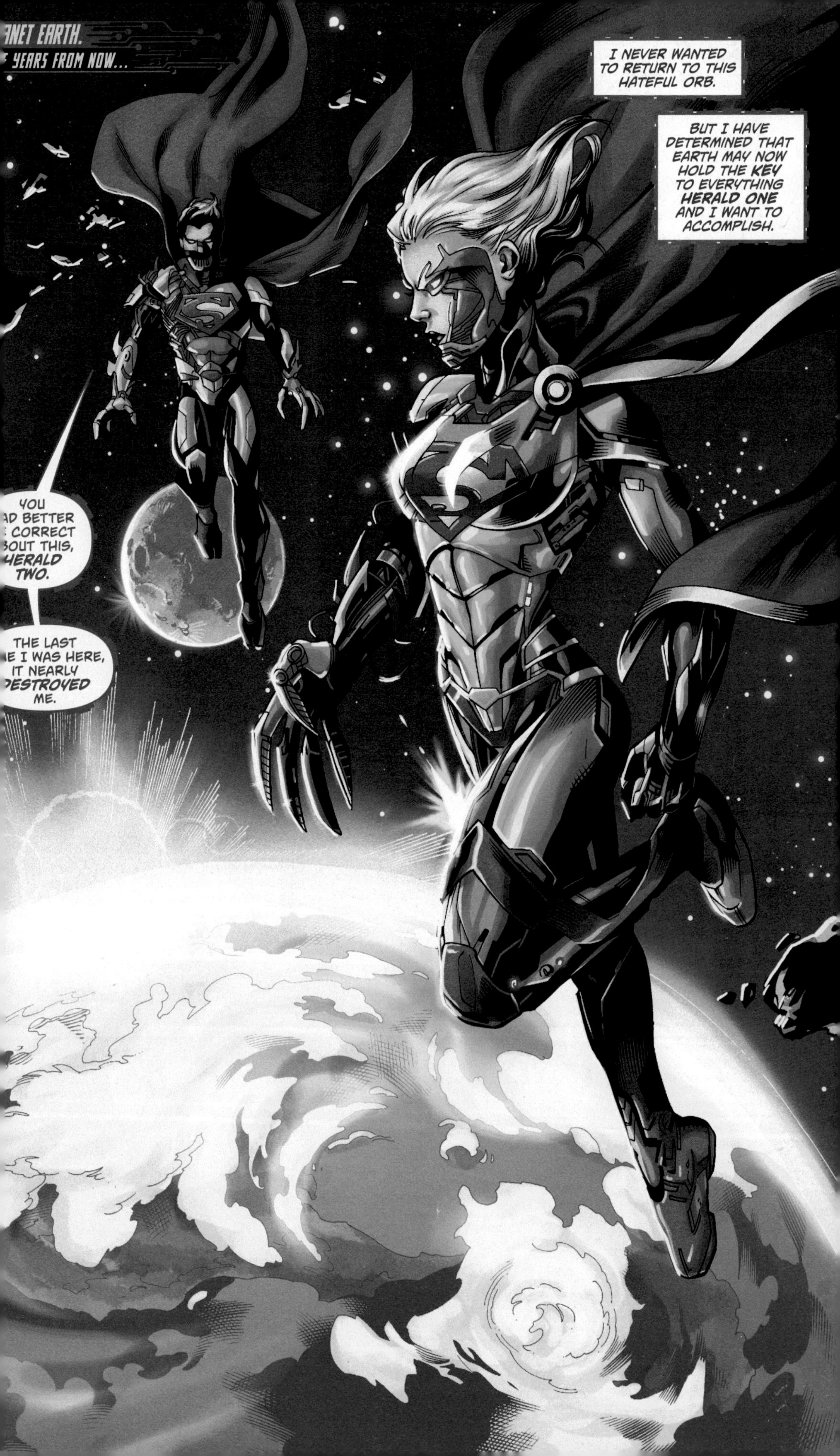
ANET EARTH.
YEARS FROM NOW...
I NEVER WANTED TO RETURN TO THIS HATEFUL ORB.
BUT I HAVE DETERMINED THAT EARTH MAY NOW HOLD THE KEY TO EVERYTHING HERALD ONE AND I WANT TO ACCOMPLISH.
YOU AD BETTER CORRECT BOUT THIS, HERALD TWO.
THE LAST E I WAS HERE, IT NEARLY DESTROYED ME.

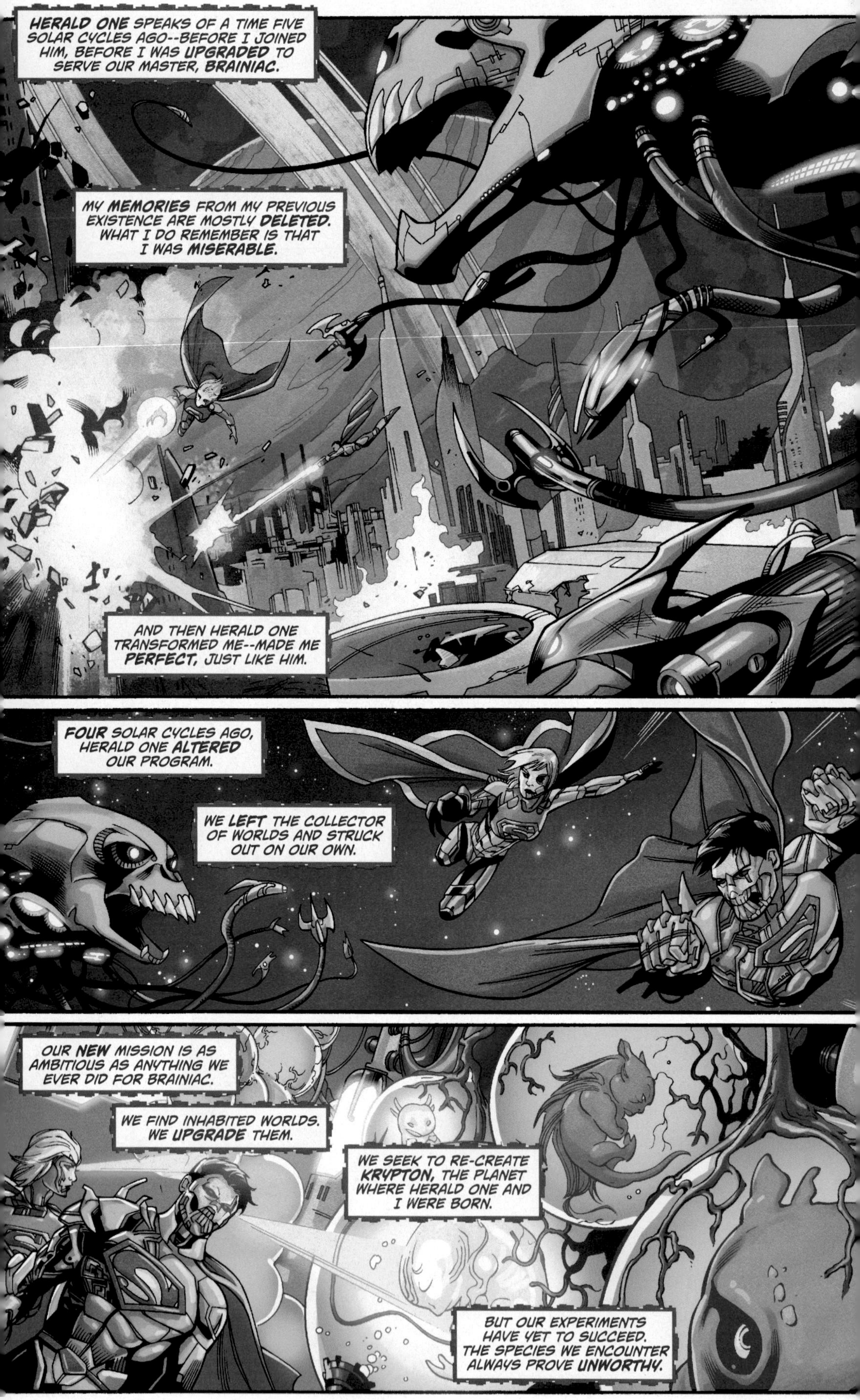
HERALD ONE SPEAKS OF A TIME FIVE SOLAR CYCLES AGO--BEFORE I JOINED HIM, BEFORE I WAS UPGRADED TO SERVE OUR MASTER, BRAINIAC.
MY MEMORIES FROM MY PREVIOUS EXISTENCE ARE MOSTLY DELETED. WHAT I DO REMEMBER IS THAT I WAS MISERABLE.
AND THEN HERALD ONE TRANSFORMED ME--MADE ME PERFECT, JUST LIKE HIM.
FOUR SOLAR CYCLES AGO, HERALD ONE ALTERED OUR PROGRAM.
WE LEFT THE COLLECTOR OF WORLDS AND STRUCK OUT ON OUR OWN.
OUR NEW MISSION IS AS AMBITIOUS AS ANYTHING WE EVER DID FOR BRAINIAC.
WE FIND INHABITED WORLDS. WE UPGRADE THEM.
WE SEEK TO RE-CREATE KRYPTON, THE PLANET WHERE HERALD ONE AND I WERE BORN.
BUT OUR EXPERIMENTS HAVE YET TO SUCCEED. THE SPECIES WE ENCOUNTER ALWAYS PROVE UNWORTHY.

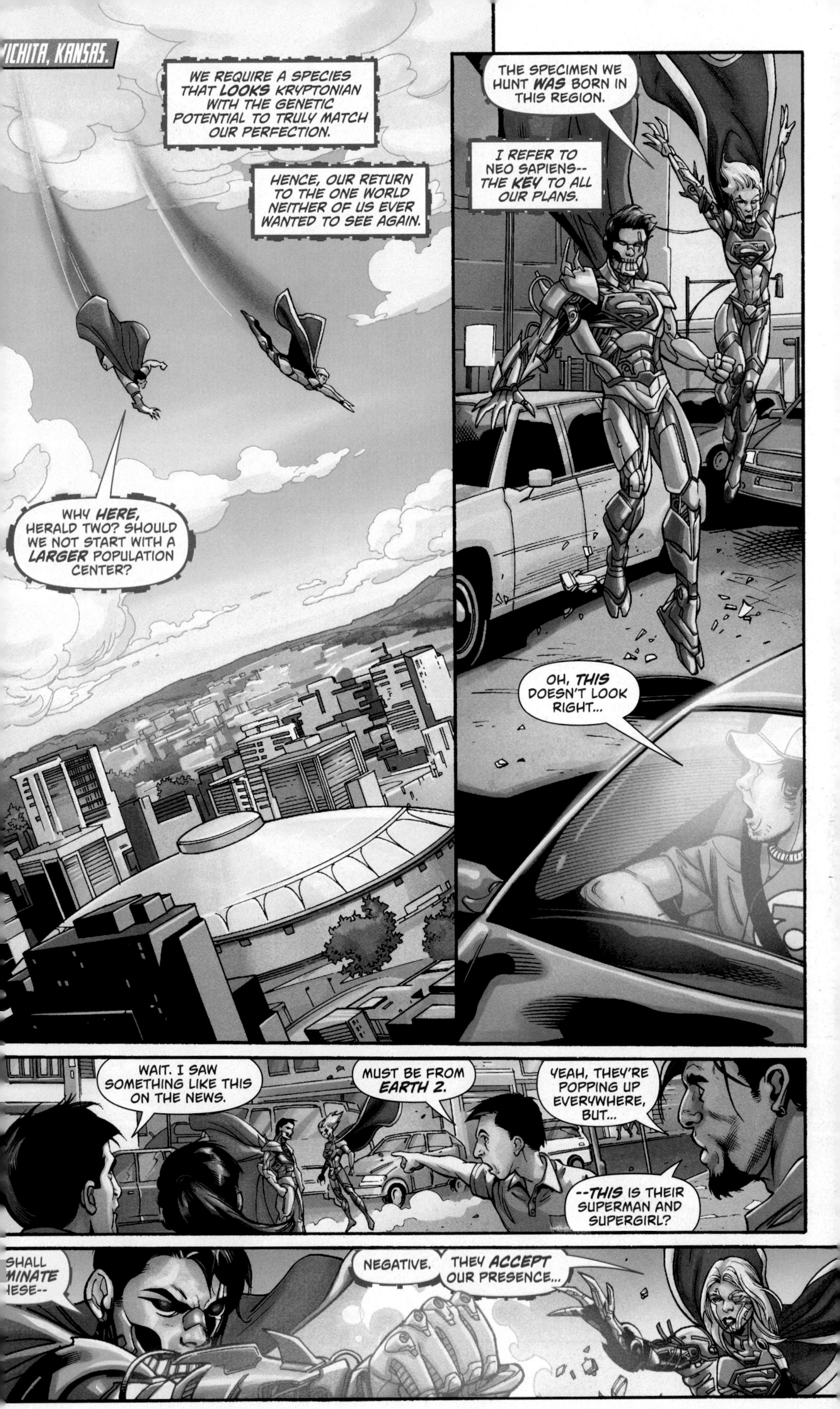

ICHITA, KANSAS.
WE REQUIRE A SPECIES THAT LOOKS KRYPTONIAN WITH THE GENETIC POTENTIAL TO TRULY MATCH OUR PERFECTION.
HENCE, OUR RETURN TO THE ONE WORLD NEITHER OF US EVER WANTED TO SEE AGAIN.
WHY HERE, HERALD TWO? SHOULD WE NOT START WITH A LARGER POPULATION CENTER?
THE SPECIMEN WE HUNT WAS BORN IN THIS REGION.
I REFER TO NEO SAPIENS-- THE KEY TO ALL OUR PLANS.
OH, THIS DOESN'T LOOK RIGHT...
WAIT. I SAW SOMETHING LIKE THIS ON THE NEWS.
MUST BE FROM EARTH 2.
YEAH, THEY'RE POPPING UP EVERYWHERE, BUT...
--THIS IS THEIR SUPERMAN AND SUPERGIRL?
SHALL MINATE IESE--
NEGATIVE.
THEY ACCEPT OUR PRESENCE...

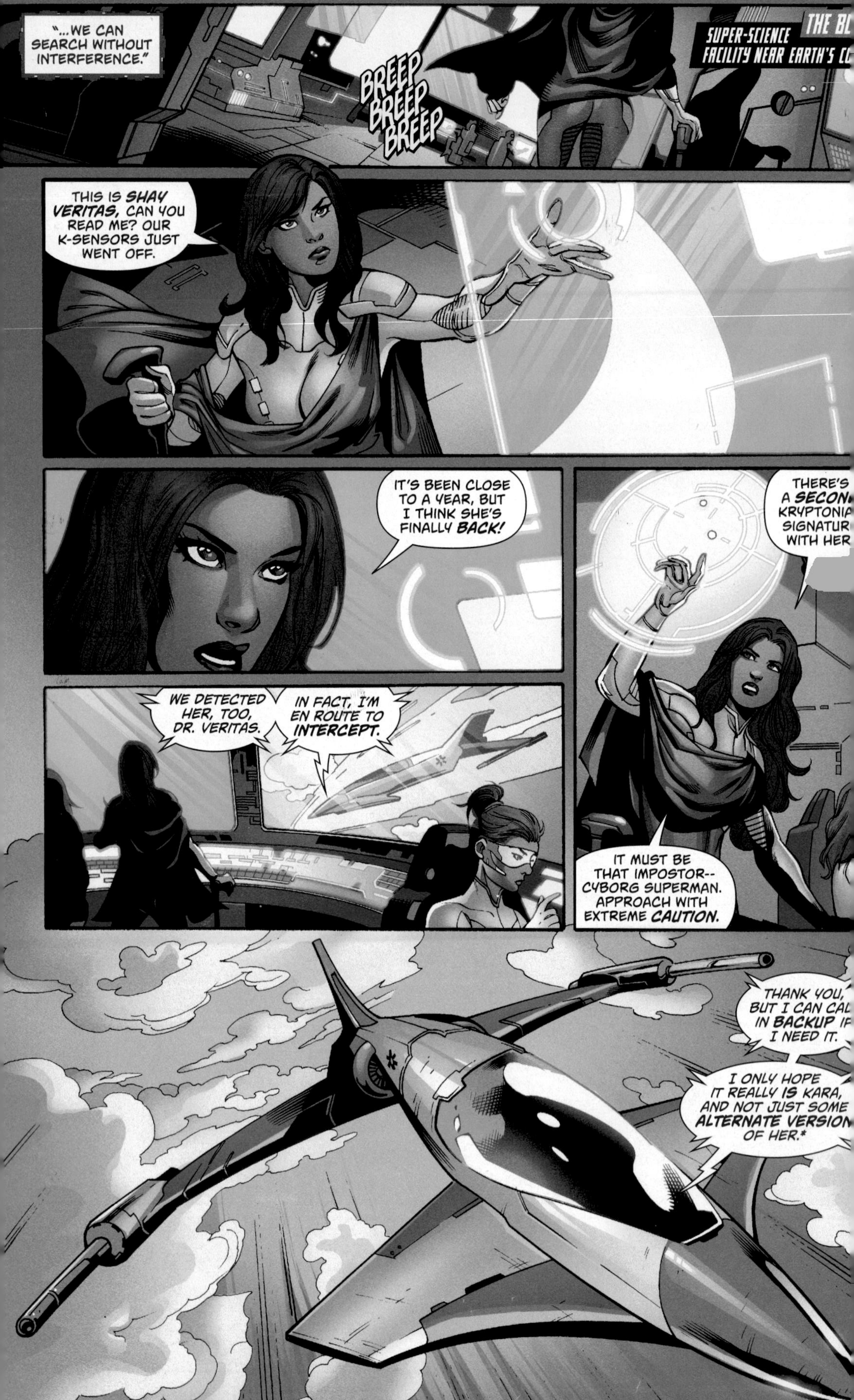
"...WE CAN SEARCH WITHOUT INTERFERENCE."
BREEP BREEP BREEP
SUPER-SCIENCE FACILITY NEAR EARTH'S CO
THE BL
THIS IS SHAY VERITAS, CAN YOU READ ME? OUR K-SENSORS JUST WENT OFF.
IT'S BEEN CLOSE TO A YEAR, BUT I THINK SHE'S FINALLY BACK!
THERE'S A SECON KRYPTONIA SIGNATUR WITH HER
WE DETECTED HER, TOO, DR. VERITAS.
IN FACT, I'M EN ROUTE TO INTERCEPT.
IT MUST BE THAT IMPOSTOR-- CYBORG SUPERMAN. APPROACH WITH EXTREME CAUTION.
THANK YOU, BUT I CAN CAL IN BACKUP IF I NEED IT.
I ONLY HOPE IT REALLY IS KARA, AND NOT JUST SOME ALTERNATE VERSION OF HER.*

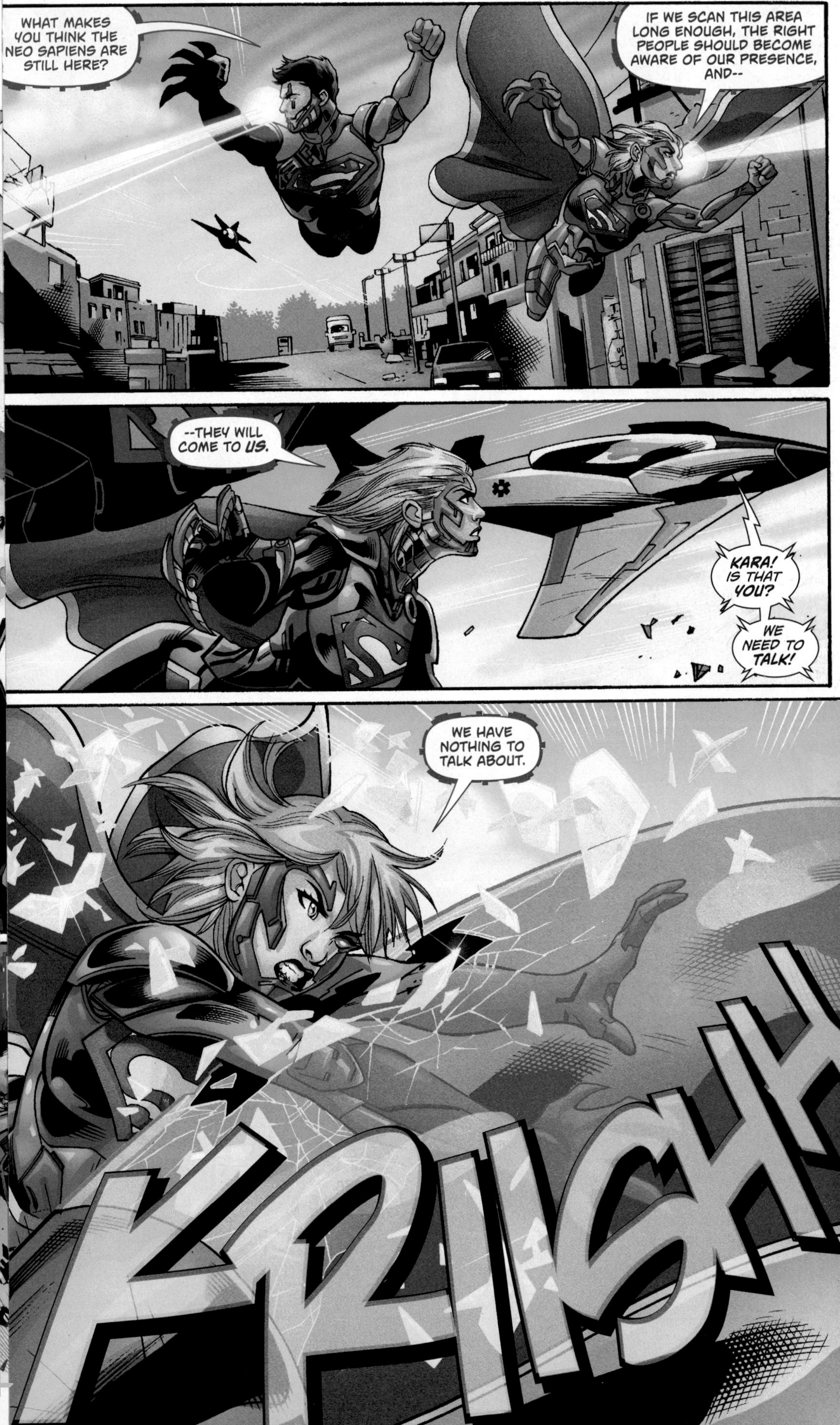
WHAT MAKES YOU THINK THE NEO SAPIENS ARE STILL HERE?
IF WE SCAN THIS AREA LONG ENOUGH, THE RIGHT PEOPLE SHOULD BECOME AWARE OF OUR PRESENCE, AND--
--THEY WILL COME TO US.
KARA! IS THAT YOU?
WE NEED TO TALK!
WE HAVE NOTHING TO TALK ABOUT.
KRISH

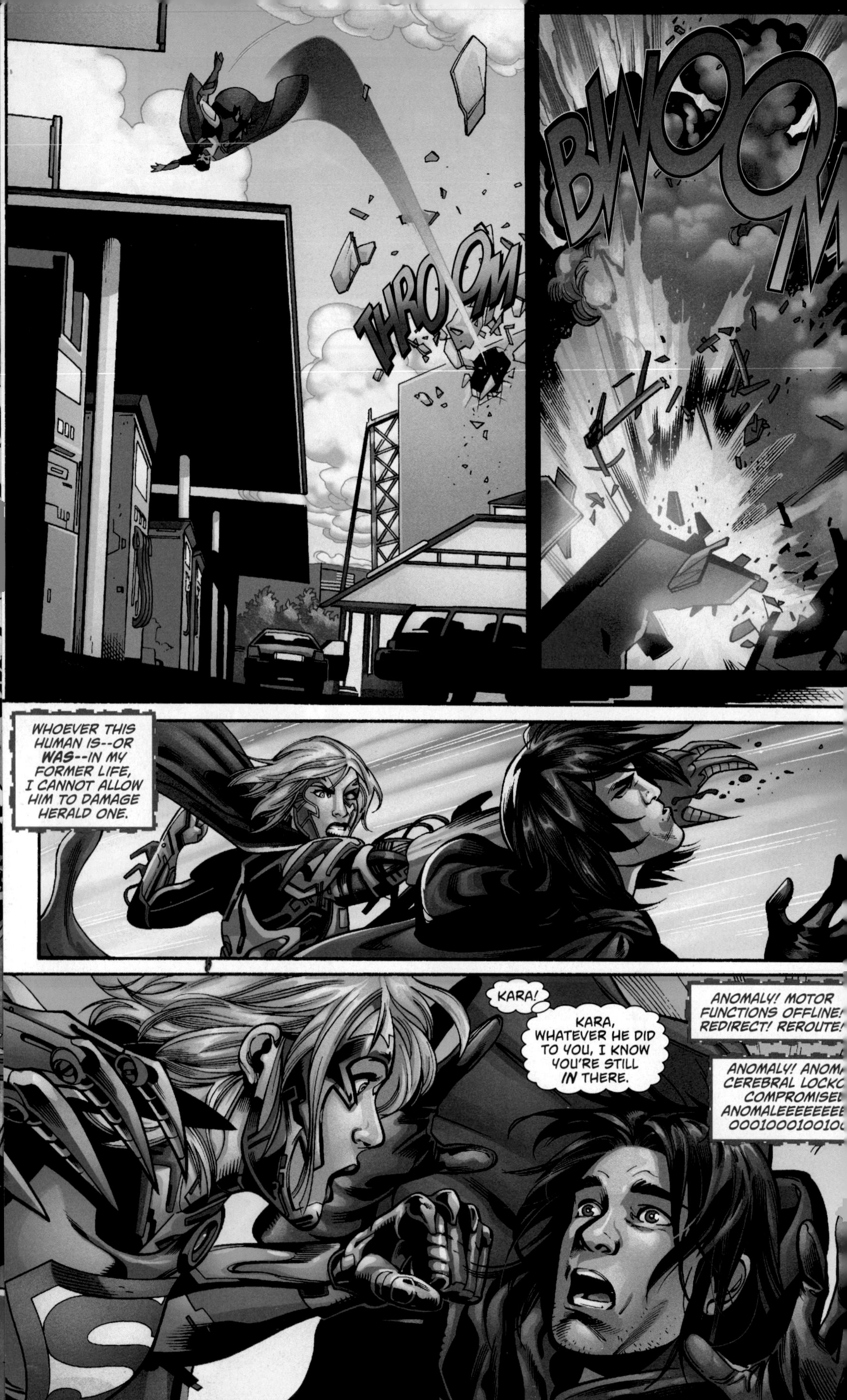
THROOM
BWOOM
WHOEVER THIS HUMAN IS--OR WAS--IN MY FORMER LIFE, I CANNOT ALLOW HIM TO DAMAGE HERALD ONE.
KARA!
KARA, WHATEVER HE DID TO YOU, I KNOW YOU'RE STILL IN THERE.
ANOMALY! MOTOR FUNCTIONS OFFLINE! REDIRECT! REROUTE!

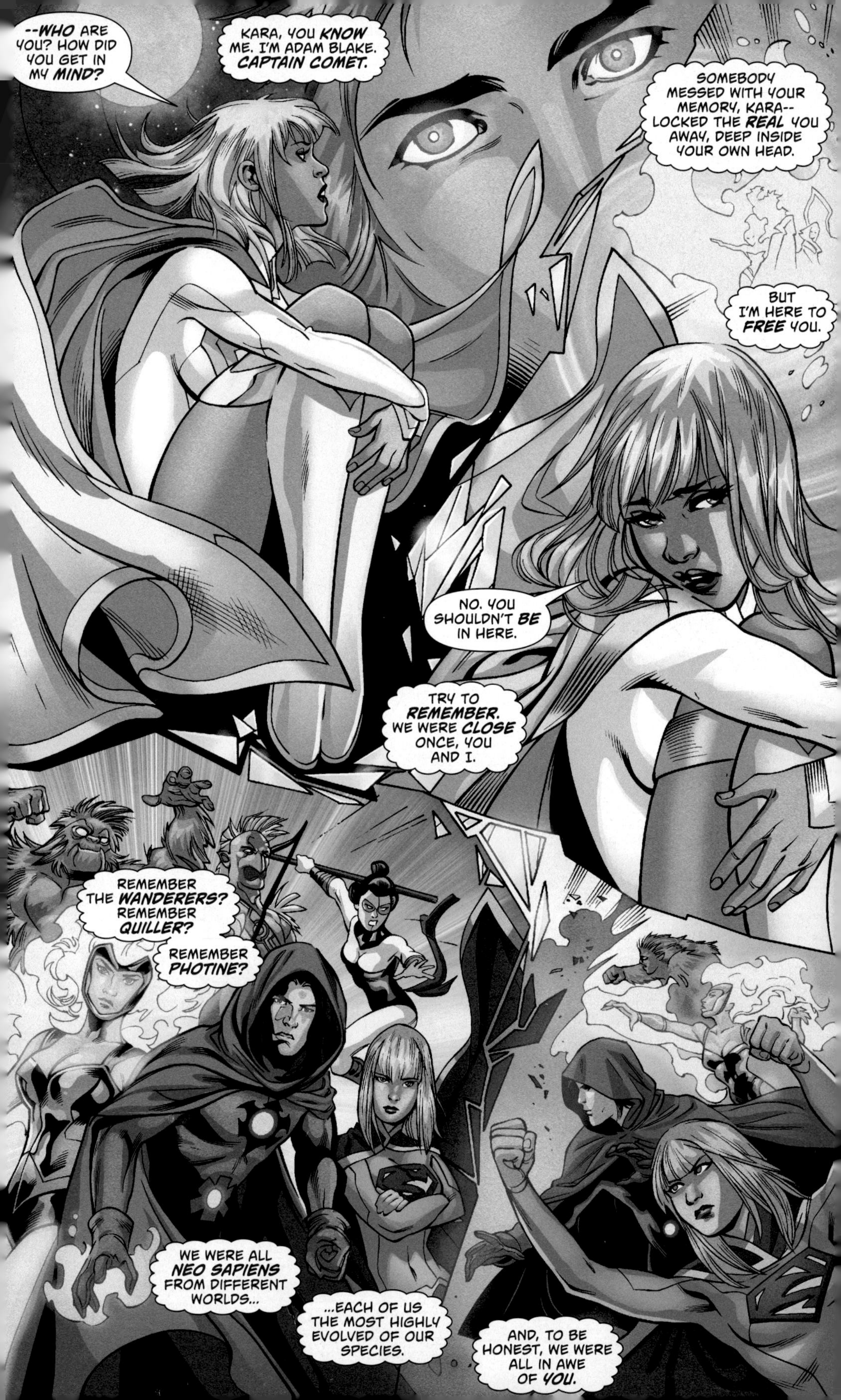
--WHO ARE YOU? HOW DID YOU GET IN MY MIND?
KARA, YOU KNOW ME. I'M ADAM BLAKE. CAPTAIN COMET.
SOMEBODY MESSED WITH YOUR MEMORY, KARA-- LOCKED THE REAL YOU AWAY, DEEP INSIDE YOUR OWN HEAD.
BUT I'M HERE TO FREE YOU.
NO. YOU SHOULDN'T BE IN HERE.
TRY TO REMEMBER. WE WERE CLOSE ONCE, YOU AND I.
REMEMBER THE WANDERERS? REMEMBER QUILLER?
REMEMBER PHOTINE?
WE WERE ALL NEO SAPIENS FROM DIFFERENT WORLDS...
...EACH OF US THE MOST HIGHLY EVOLVED OF OUR SPECIES.
AND, TO BE HONEST, WE WERE ALL IN AWE OF YOU.

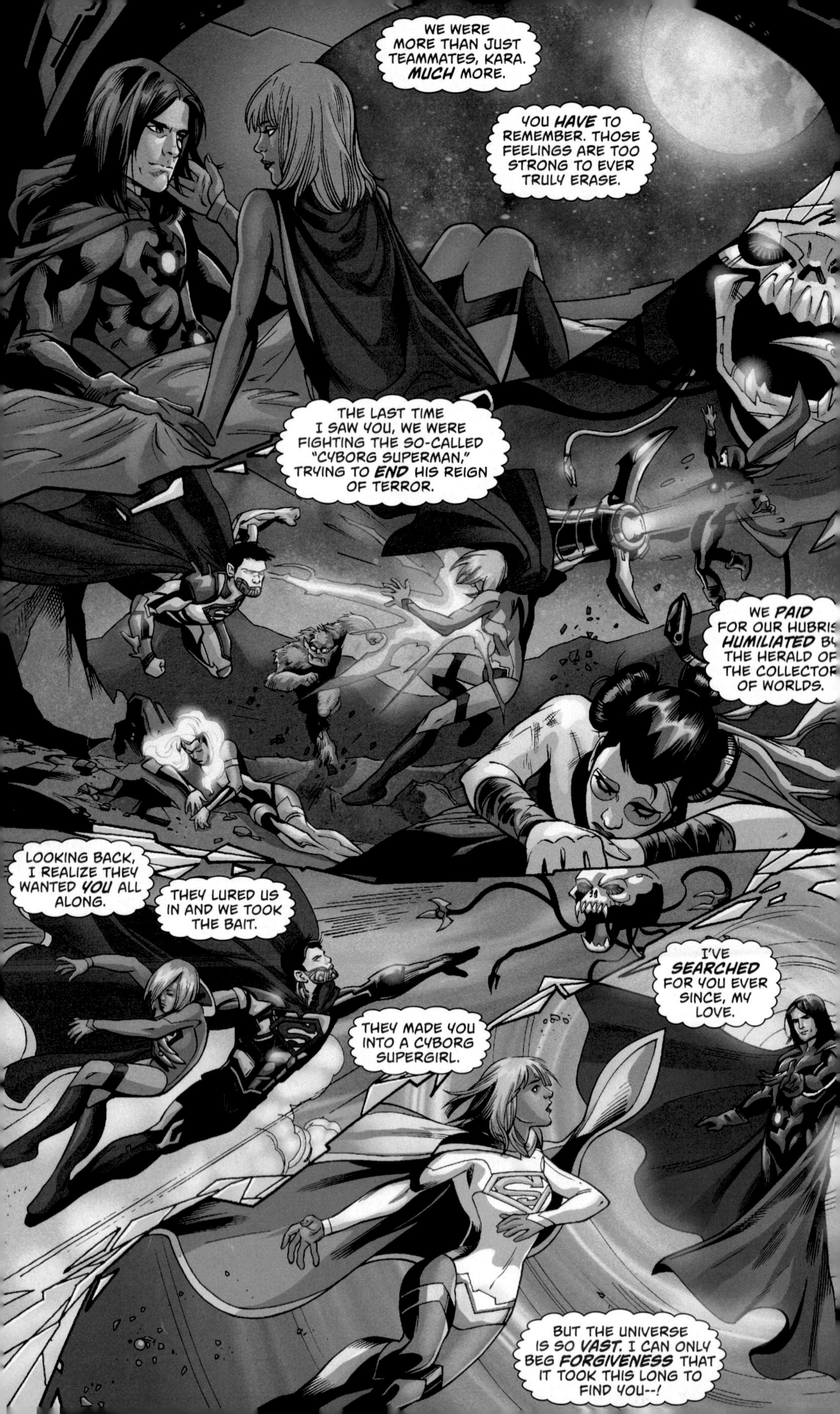
WE WERE MORE THAN JUST TEAMMATES, KARA. MUCH MORE.
YOU HAVE TO REMEMBER. THOSE FEELINGS ARE TOO STRONG TO EVER TRULY ERASE.
THE LAST TIME I SAW YOU, WE WERE FIGHTING THE SO-CALLED "CYBORG SUPERMAN," TRYING TO END HIS REIGN OF TERROR.
WE PAID FOR OUR HUBRIS HUMILIATED BY THE HERALD OF THE COLLECTOR OF WORLDS.
LOOKING BACK, I REALIZE THEY WANTED YOU ALL ALONG.
THEY LURED US IN AND WE TOOK THE BAIT.
THEY MADE YOU INTO A CYBORG SUPERGIRL.
I'VE SEARCHED FOR YOU EVER SINCE, MY LOVE.
BUT THE UNIVERSE IS SO VAST. I CAN ONLY BEG FORGIVENESS THAT IT TOOK THIS LONG TO FIND YOU--!

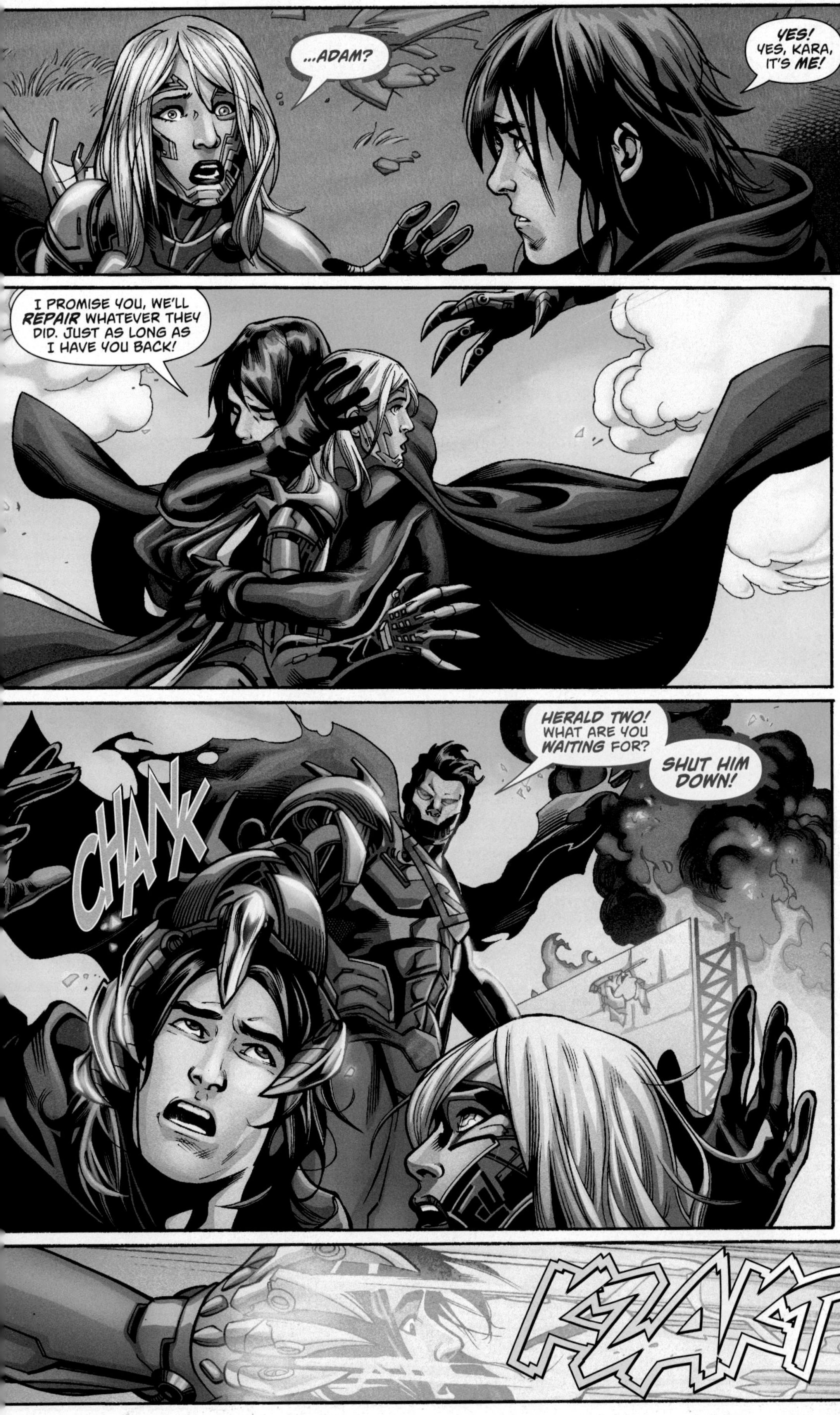
...ADAM?
YES! YES, KARA, IT'S ME!
I PROMISE YOU, WE'LL REPAIR WHATEVER THEY DID. JUST AS LONG AS I HAVE YOU BACK!
CHANK
HERALD TWO! WHAT ARE YOU WAITING FOR?
SHUT HIM DOWN!
KZAKT

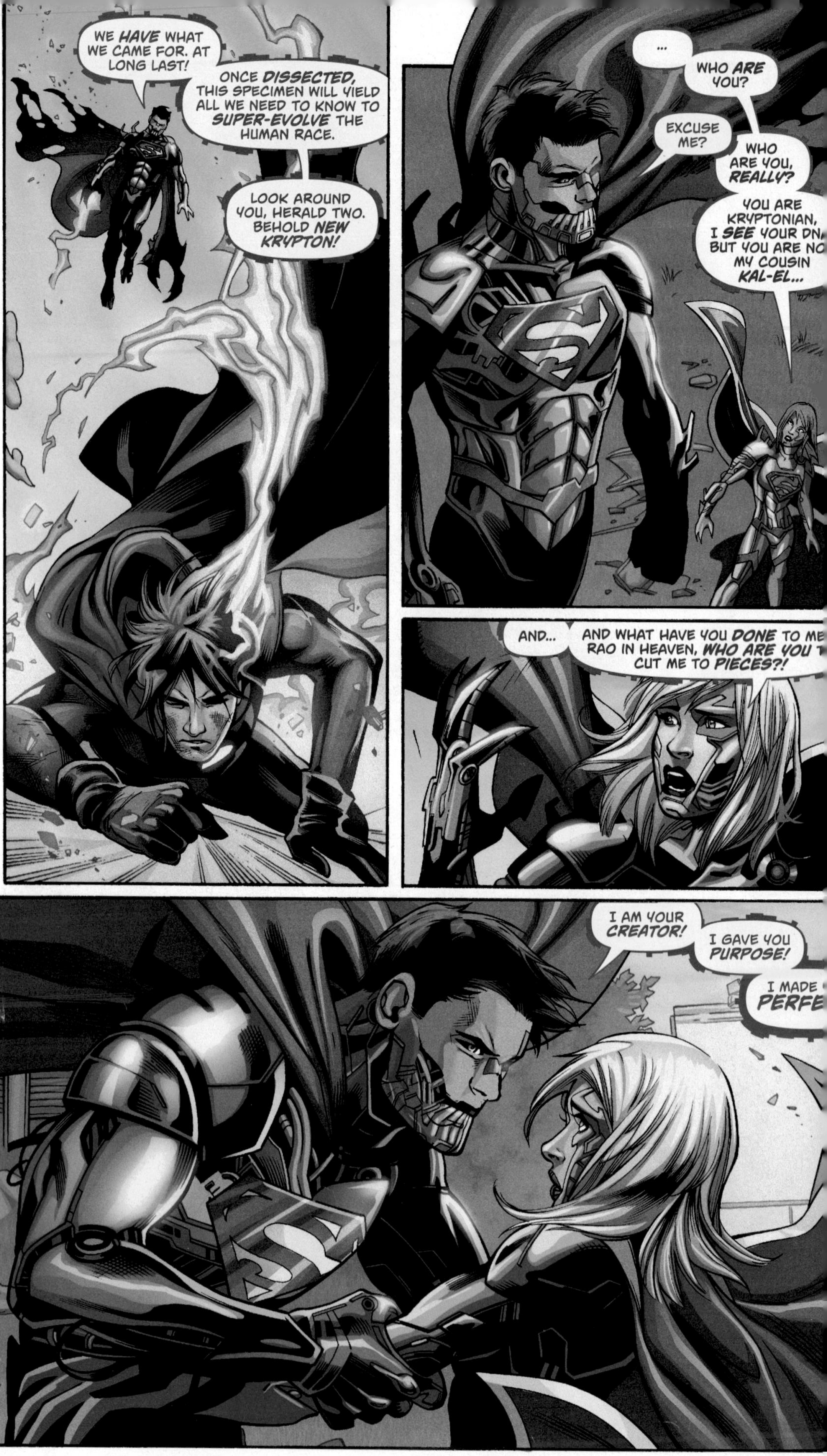
WE HAVE WHAT WE CAME FOR. AT LONG LAST!
ONCE DISSECTED, THIS SPECIMEN WILL YIELD ALL WE NEED TO KNOW TO SUPER-EVOLVE THE HUMAN RACE.
LOOK AROUND YOU, HERALD TWO. BEHOLD NEW KRYPTON!
...
WHO ARE YOU?
EXCUSE ME?
WHO ARE YOU, REALLY?
YOU ARE KRYPTONIAN, I SEE YOUR DN BUT YOU ARE NO MY COUSIN KAL-EL...
AND...
AND WHAT HAVE YOU DONE TO ME RAO IN HEAVEN, WHO ARE YOU CUT ME TO PIECES?!
I AM YOUR CREATOR!
I GAVE YOU PURPOSE!
I MADE PERFE

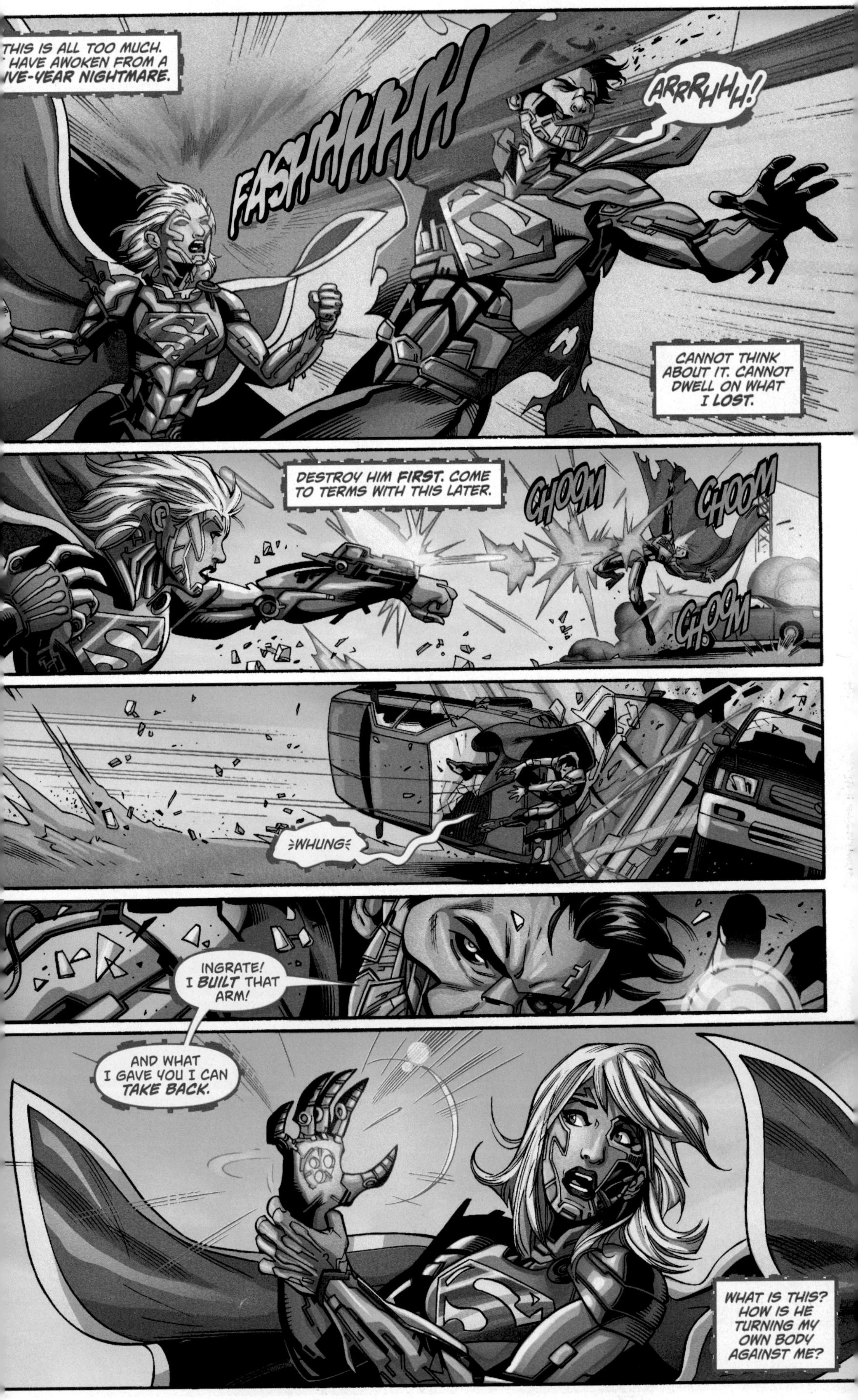
THIS IS ALL TOO MUCH.
' HAVE AWOKEN FROM A
IVE-YEAR NIGHTMARE.
FASHHHHH
ARRRHHH!
CANNOT THINK ABOUT IT. CANNOT DWELL ON WHAT I LOST.
DESTROY HIM FIRST. COME TO TERMS WITH THIS LATER.
CHOOM
CHOOM
CHOOM
WHUNG
INGRATE! I BUILT THAT ARM!
AND WHAT I GAVE YOU I CAN TAKE BACK.
WHAT IS THIS? HOW IS HE TURNING MY OWN BODY AGAINST ME?

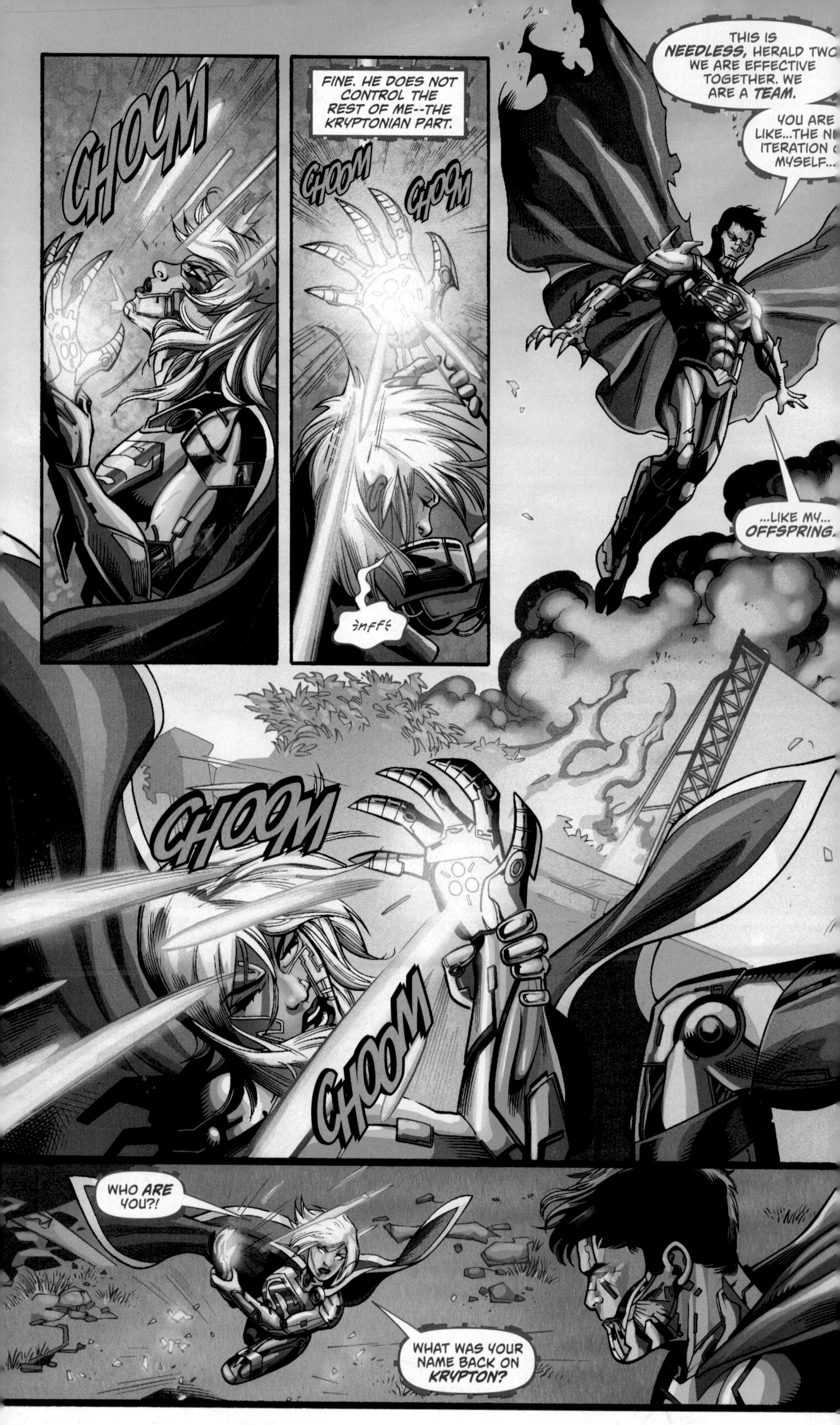

CHOOM
FINE. HE DOES NOT CONTROL THE REST OF ME--THE KRYPTONIAN PART.
CHOOM
CHOOM
nff
THIS IS NEEDLESS, HERALD TWO. WE ARE EFFECTIVE TOGETHER. WE ARE A TEAM.
...LIKE MY... OFFSPRING.
CHOOM
CHOOM
WHO ARE YOU?!
WHAT WAS YOUR NAME BACK ON KRYPTON?

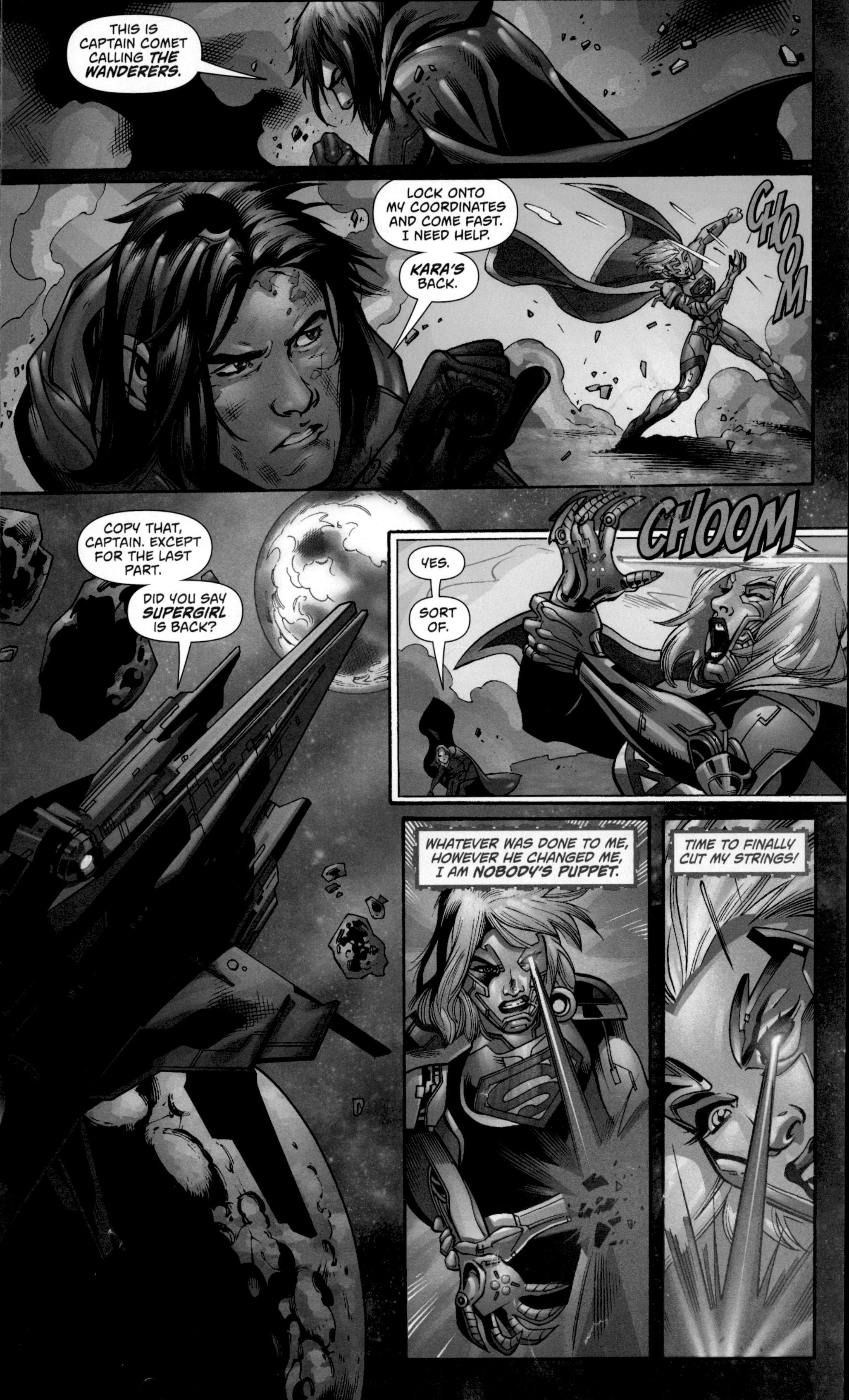
THIS IS CAPTAIN COMET CALLING **THE WANDERERS.**
LOCK ONTO MY COORDINATES AND COME FAST. I NEED HELP.
KARA'S BACK.
CHOOM
COPY THAT, CAPTAIN. EXCEPT FOR THE LAST PART.
DID YOU SAY **SUPERGIRL** IS BACK?
CHOOM
YES.
SORT OF.
WHATEVER WAS DONE TO ME, HOWEVER HE CHANGED ME, I AM **NOBODY'S PUPPET.**
TIME TO FINALLY CUT MY STRINGS!

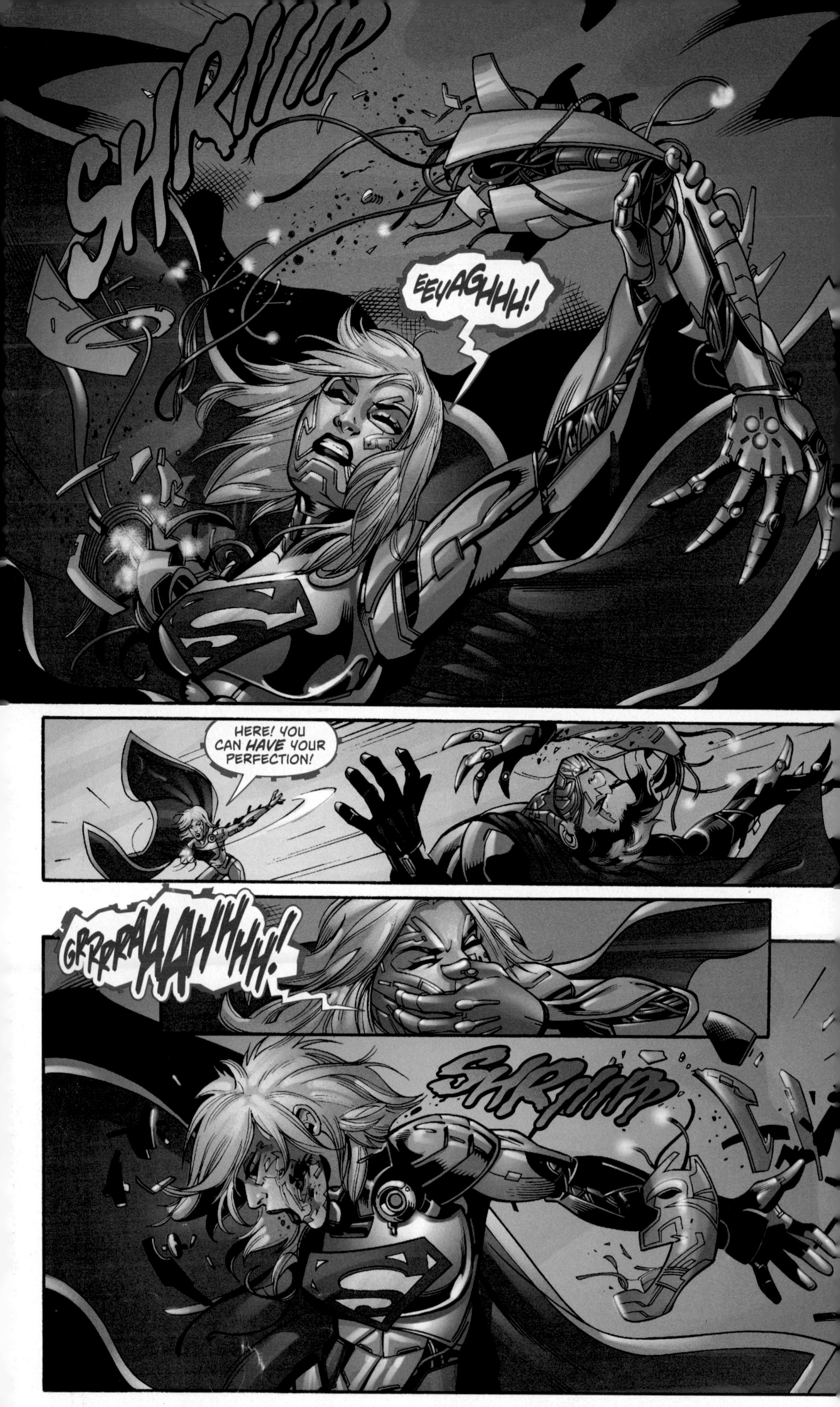
SHRIIIP
EEYAGHHH!
HERE! YOU CAN HAVE YOUR PERFECTION!
GRRRRAAAHHHHH!
SHRIIIP

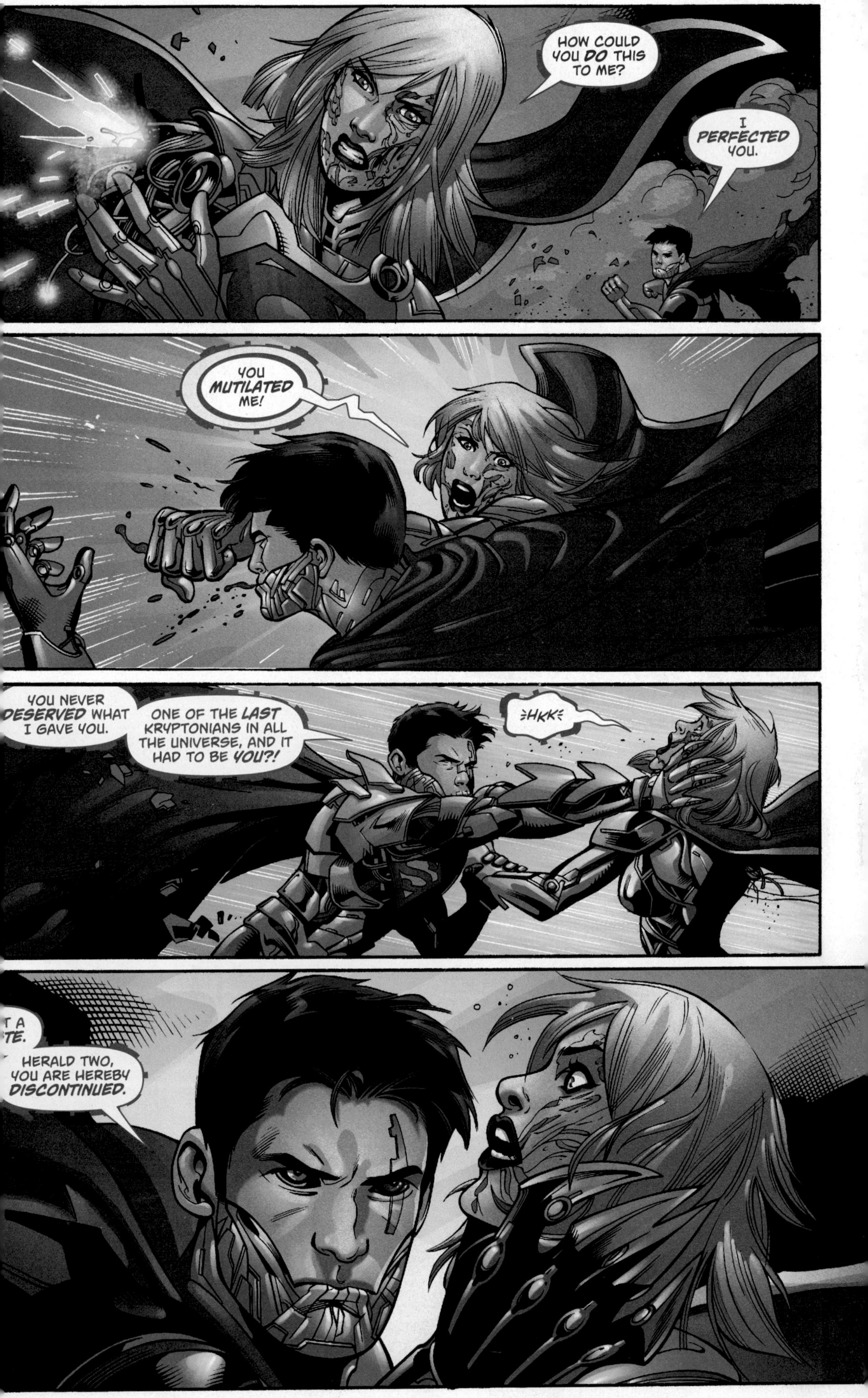
HOW COULD YOU DO THIS TO ME?
I PERFECTED YOU.
YOU MUTILATED ME!
YOU NEVER DESERVED WHAT I GAVE YOU.
ONE OF THE LAST KRYPTONIANS IN ALL THE UNIVERSE, AND IT HAD TO BE YOU?!
HKK
HERALD TWO, YOU ARE HEREBY DISCONTINUED.

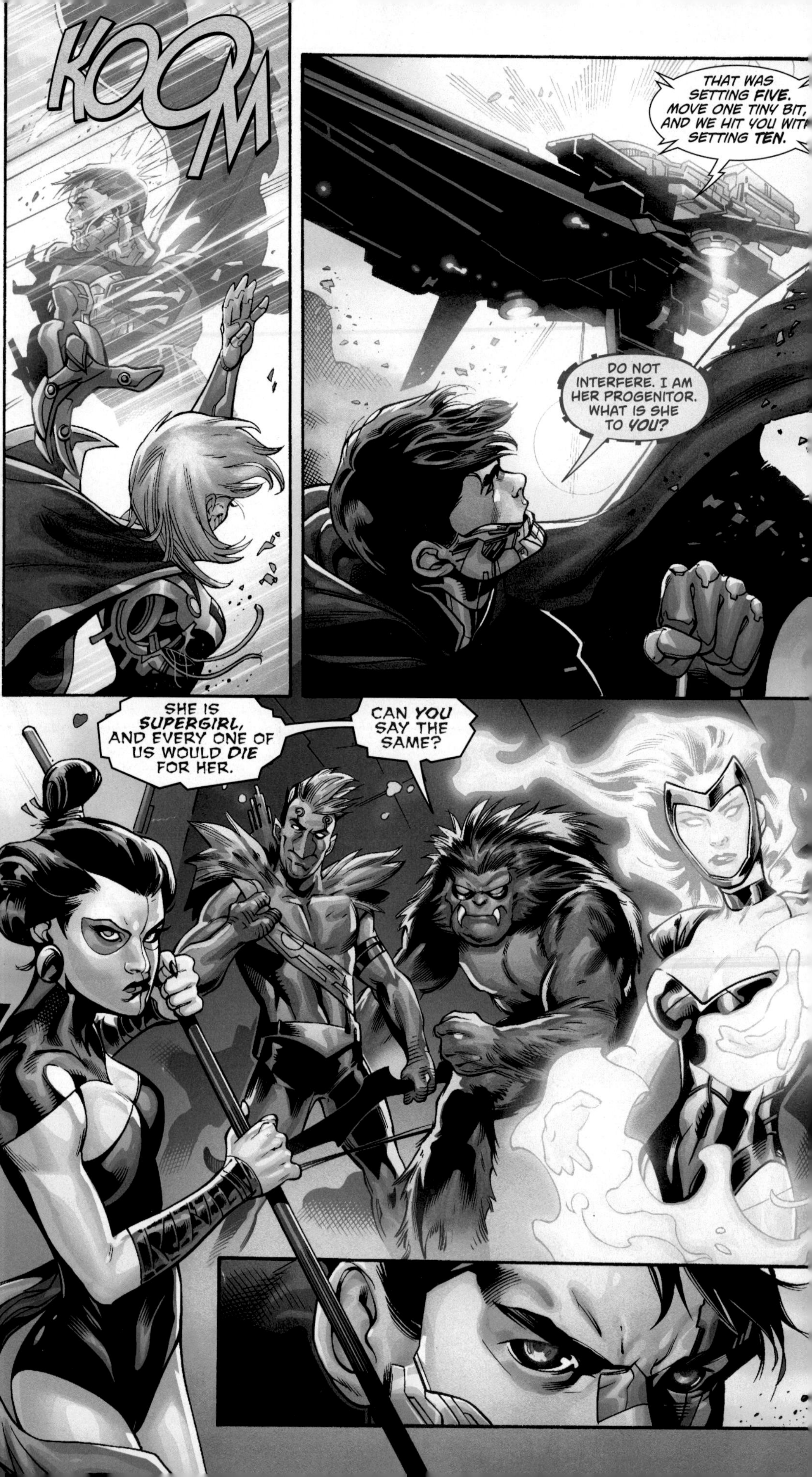
KOOM
THAT WAS SETTING FIVE. MOVE ONE TINY BIT, AND WE HIT YOU WITH SETTING TEN.
DO NOT INTERFERE. I AM HER PROGENITOR. WHAT IS SHE TO YOU?
SHE IS SUPERGIRL, AND EVERY ONE OF US WOULD DIE FOR HER.
CAN YOU SAY THE SAME?

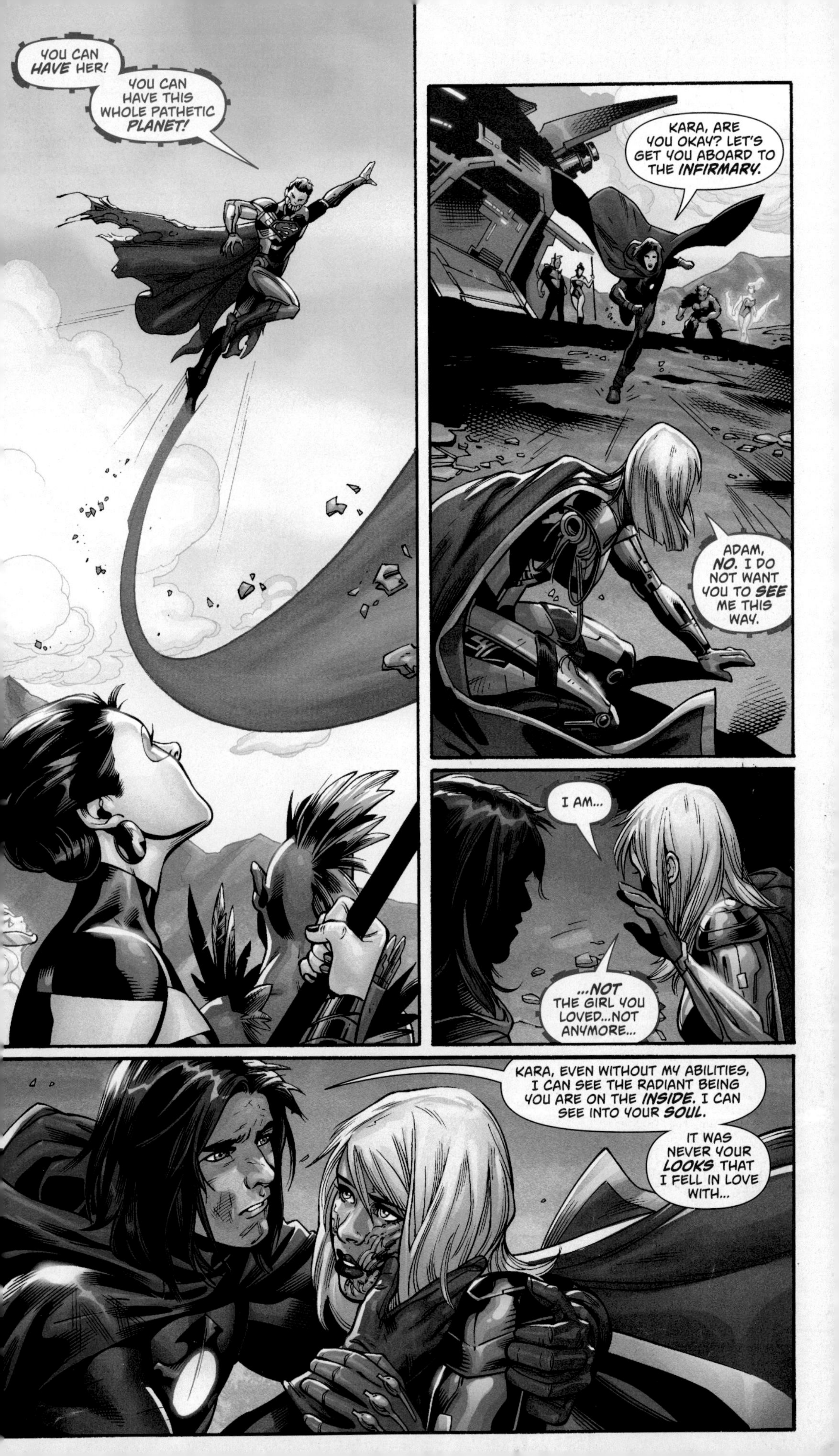

YOU CAN HAVE HER!
YOU CAN HAVE THIS WHOLE PATHETIC PLANET!
KARA, ARE YOU OKAY? LET'S GET YOU ABOARD TO THE INFIRMARY.
ADAM, NO. I DO NOT WANT YOU TO SEE ME THIS WAY.
I AM...
...NOT THE GIRL YOU LOVED...NOT ANYMORE...
KARA, EVEN WITHOUT MY ABILITIES, I CAN SEE THE RADIANT BEING YOU ARE ON THE INSIDE. I CAN SEE INTO YOUR SOUL.
IT WAS NEVER YOUR LOOKS THAT I FELL IN LOVE WITH...

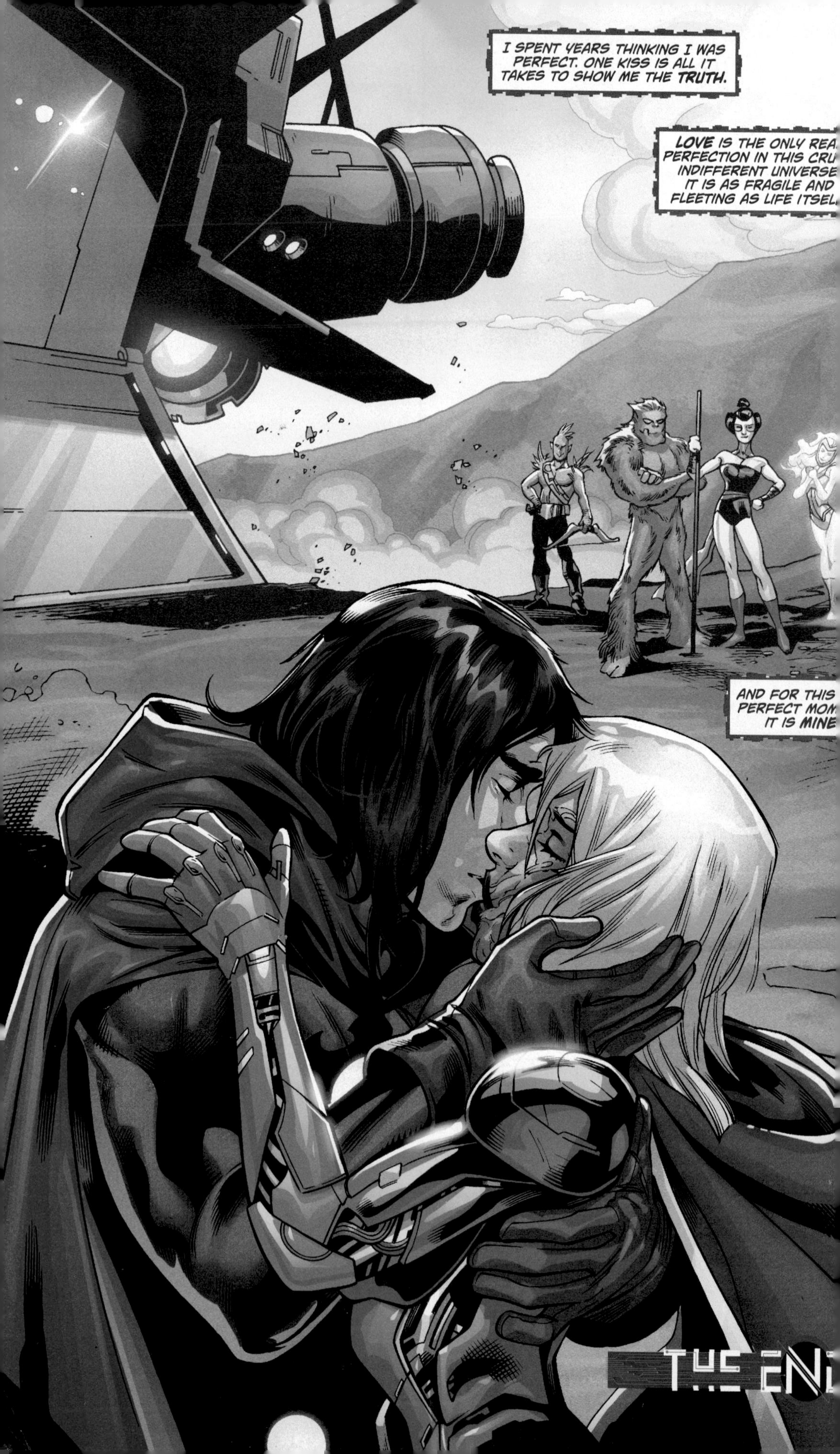
I SPENT YEARS THINKING I WAS PERFECT. ONE KISS IS ALL IT TAKES TO SHOW ME THE TRUTH.
LOVE IS THE ONLY REA PERFECTION IN THIS CRU INDIFFERENT UNIVERSE IT IS AS FRAGILE AND FLEETING AS LIFE ITSEL
AND FOR THIS PERFECT MOM IT IS MINE
THE EN

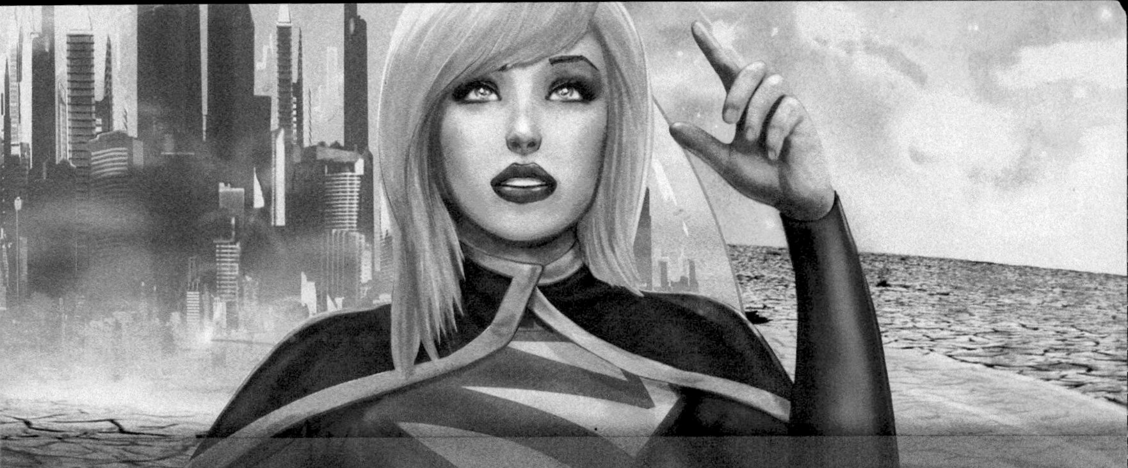

VARIANT COVER GALLERY

SUPERGIRL #36
LEGO variant cover

SUPERGIRL #37
Variant cover by Darwyn Cooke

SUPERGIRL #38
Variant cover by Michael Avon Oeming after Curt Swan and Stan Kaye

SUPERGIRL #39
Variant cover by Joe Benitez and Peter Steigerwald

SUPERGIRL #40
Variant cover by Marco D'Alfonso

SUPERGIRL: FUTURES END
Present day cover by Giuseppe Camuncoli and Cam Smith with Dan Brown

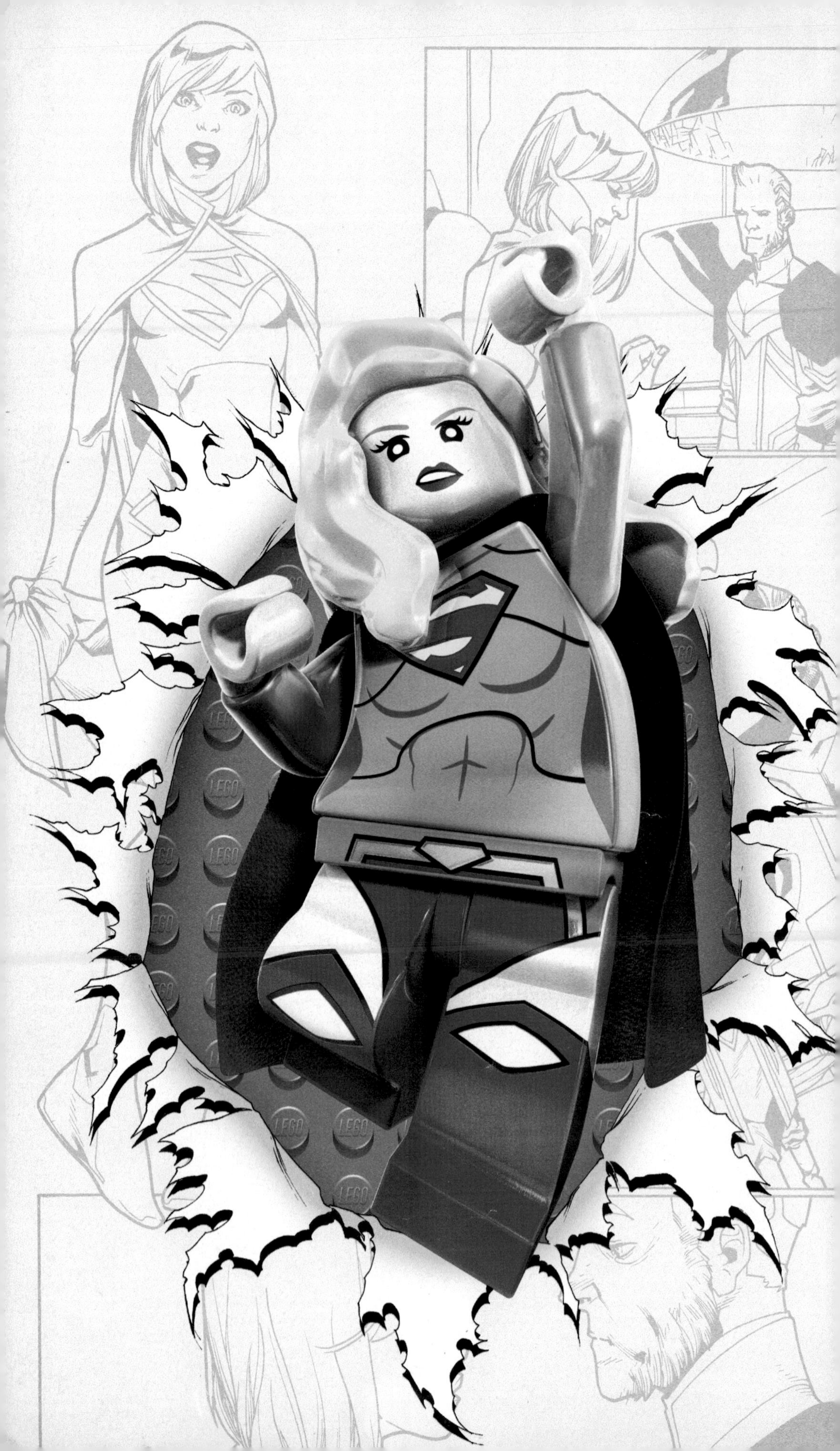

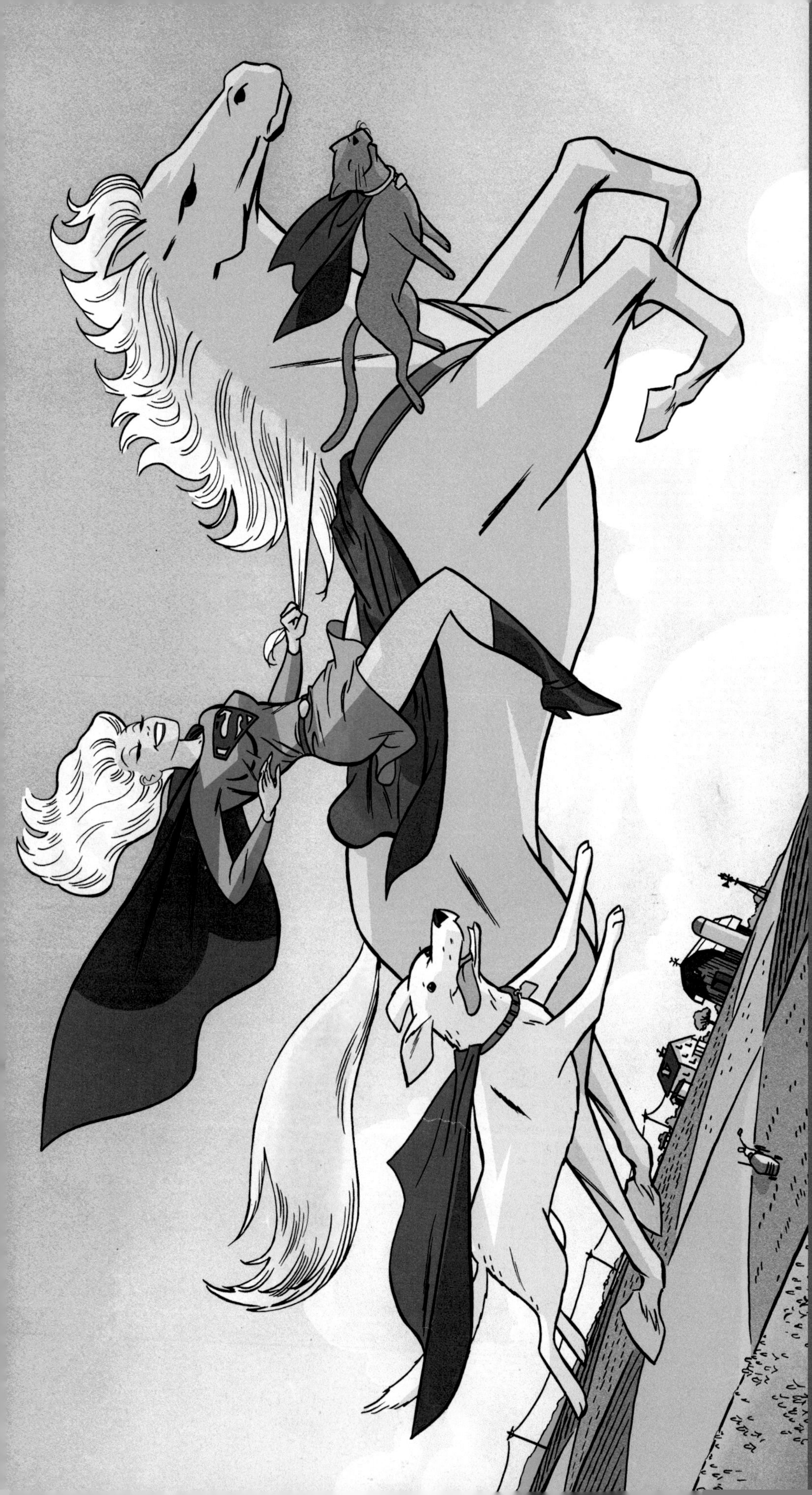

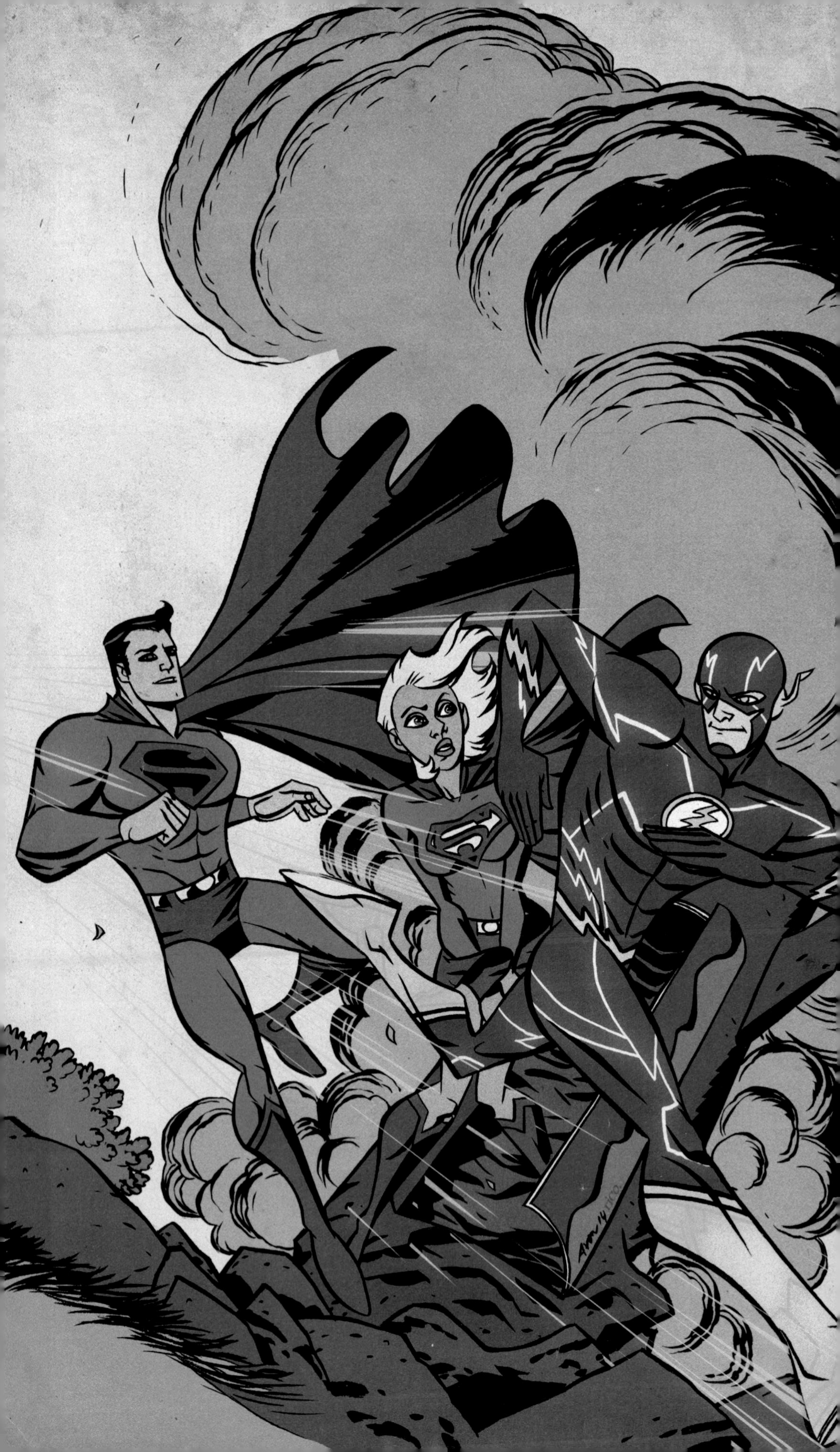

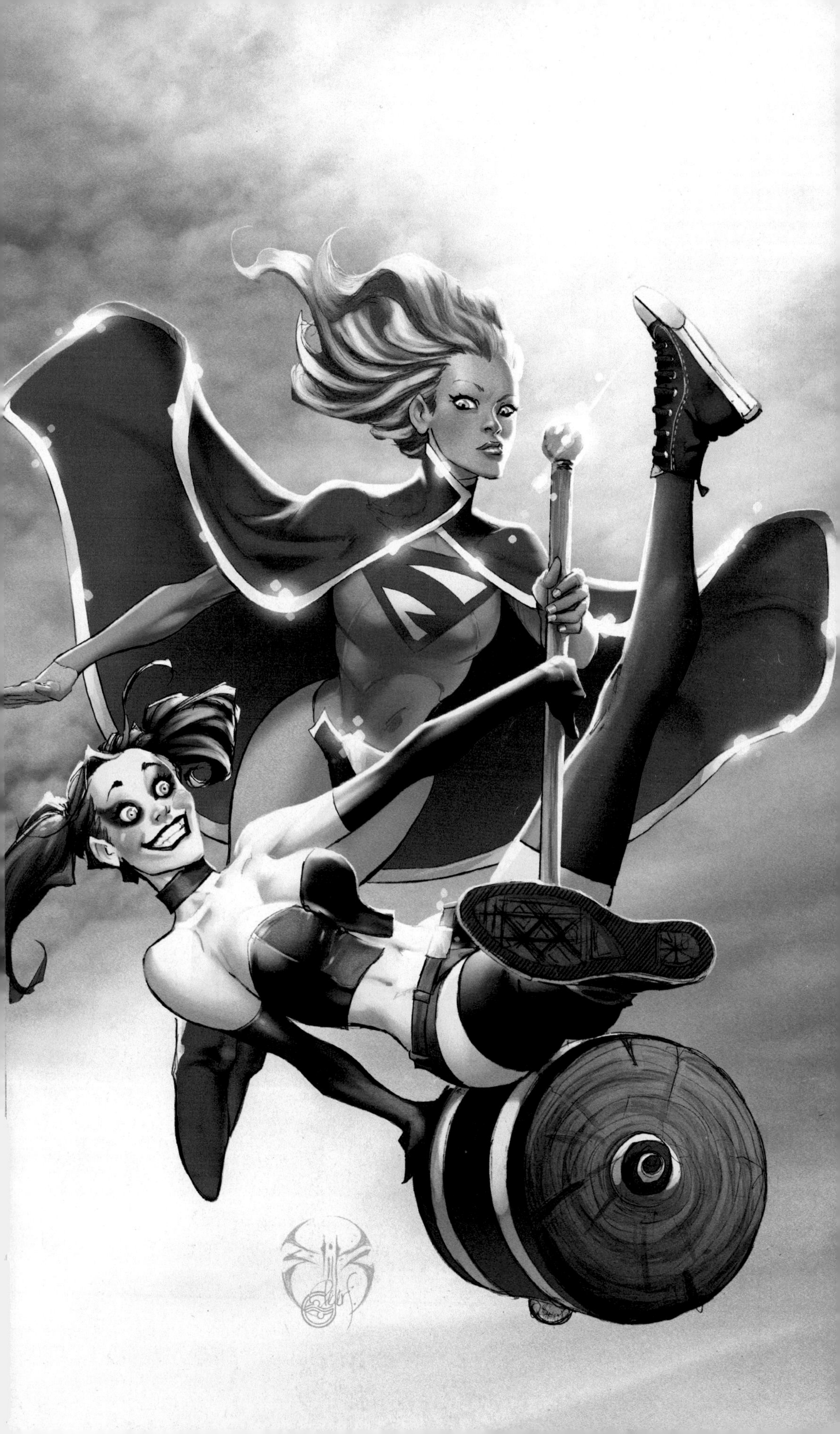

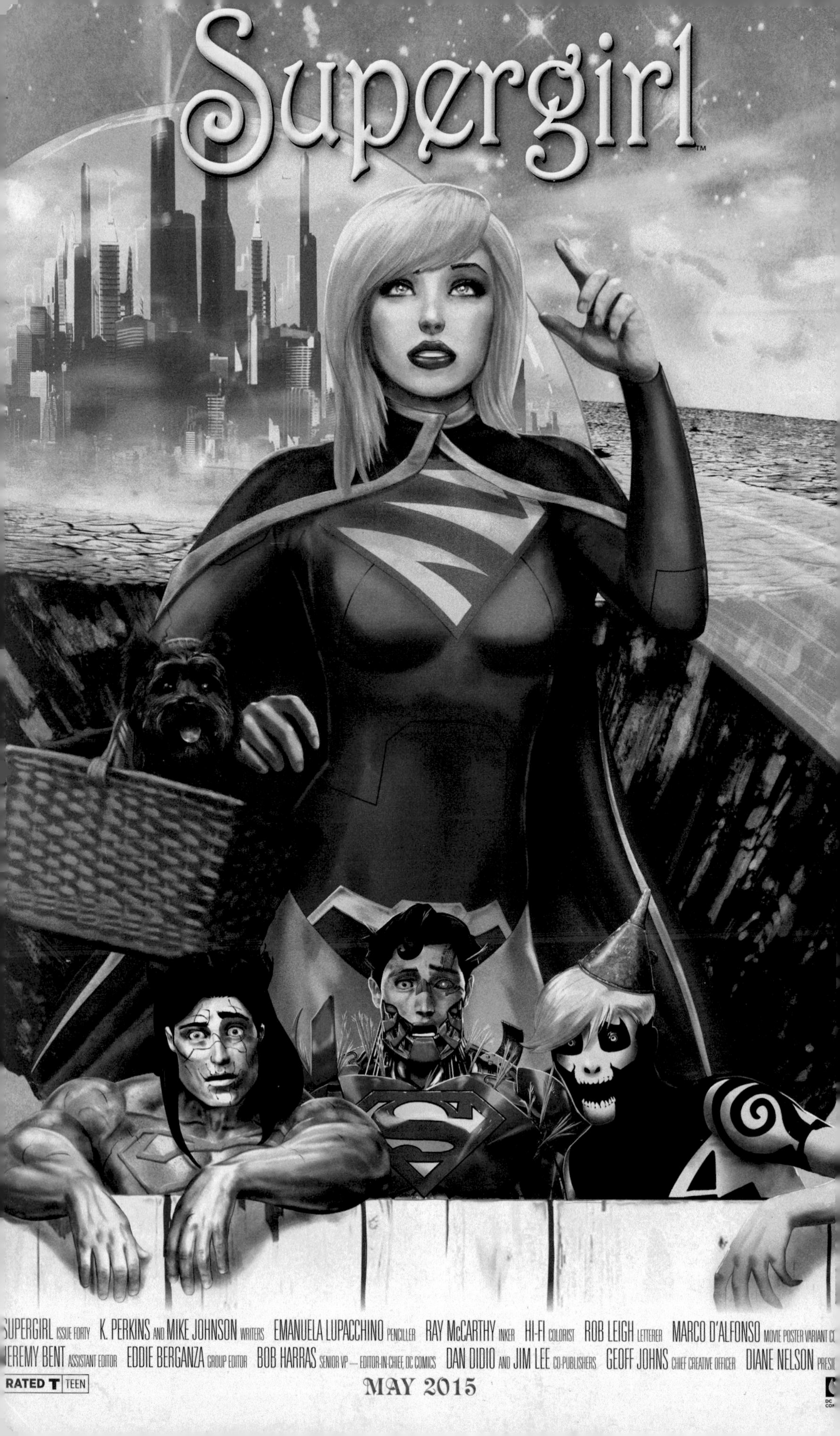
Supergirl™
SUPERGIRL ISSUE FORTY K. PERKINS AND MIKE JOHNSON WRITERS EMANUELA LUPACCHINO PENCILLER RAY McCARTHY INKER HI-FI COLORIST ROB LEIGH LETTERER MARCO D'ALFONSO MOVIE POSTER VARIANT C
EREMY BENT ASSISTANT EDITOR EDDIE BERGANZA GROUP EDITOR BOB HARRAS SENIOR VP — EDITOR-IN-CHIEF, DC COMICS DAN DIDIO AND JIM LEE CO-PUBLISHERS GEOFF JOHNS CHIEF CREATIVE OFFICER DIANE NELSON PRESI
RATED T TEEN
MAY 2015

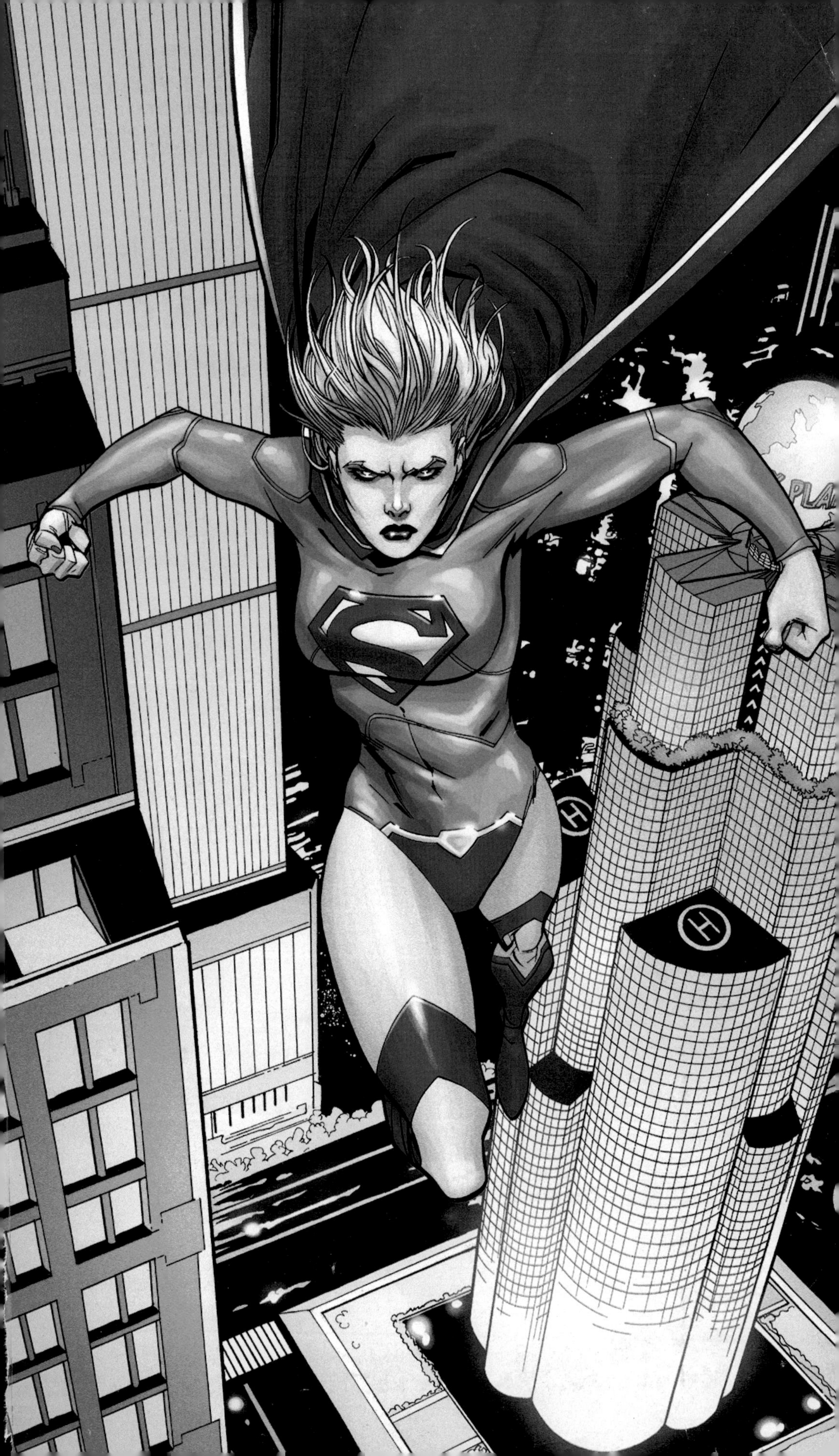

START AT THE BEGINNING

SUPERMAN: ACTION COMIC[S] VOLUME 1: SUPERMA[N] AND THE MEN OF STEE[L]

SUPERMAN VOLUME 1: WHAT PRICE TOMORROW?

SUPERGIRL VOLUME 1: THE LAST DAUGHTER OF KRYPTON

SUPERBOY VOLUME 1: INCUBATION